Singing Jeremiah

MUSIC AND THE EARLY MODERN IMAGINATION
Massimo Ossi, *editor*

Singing Jeremiah

Music and Meaning in Holy Week

Robert L. Kendrick

INDIANA UNIVERSITY PRESS

Bloomington and Indianapolis

This book is a publication of

Indiana University Press
Office of Scholarly Publishing
Herman B Wells Library 350
1320 East 10th Street
Bloomington, Indiana 47405 USA

iupress.indiana.edu

Telephone orders 800-842-6796
Fax orders 812-855-7931

Manufactured in the United States of America

Library of Congress Cataloging-in-
Publication Data

Kendrick, Robert L., author.
  Singing Jeremiah : music and meaning in
Holy Week / Robert L. Kendrick.
    pages cm — (Music and the early modern
imagination)
  Includes bibliographical references and
index.
  ISBN 978-0-253-01156-5 (cloth : alkaline
paper) — ISBN 978-0-253-01162-6 (ebook)
  1. Holy Week music—Europe—History and
criticism. I. Title. II. Series: Music and the
early modern imagination.
  ML3020.2.K46 2014
  781.72'6—dc23

                                  2013037077

1 2 3 4 5 18 17 16 15 14

Contents

Acknowledgments

My first debt is to the Franke Institute at the University of Chicago, Rich and Barbara Franke, its director Jim Chandler, and the other Fellows in the 2011–12 year for their encouragement during the writing of the book. To my Chicago colleagues Fred de Armas, Martha Feldman, Anne Robertson, and Jim Robertson I owe gratitude for advice on various topics. Several students past and present gave invaluable aid, including Kasia Grochowska, Nick Betson, Cesar Favila, Kirsten Paige, Erika Honisch, and Andrew Cashner, who performed incredible feats in making the music examples concise and legible. Craig Monson furnished unstinting support and a number of archival documents. My thanks to my colleagues in Renaissance/ early modern studies: Sabine Arend, Jane Bernstein, Franz Bosbach, John Butt, Alessandro Catalano, David Cranmer, Drew Davies, Simon Ditchfield, Lucero Enríquez Rubio, Ferran Escrivà Llorca, Martin Eybl, Myriam Fragoso Bravo, María Gembero Ustárroz, Jonathan Glixon, Manuel Gómez del Sol, Kenneth Gouwens, Rosa Isusi, Javier Jiménez Belmonte, Herbert Kellman, Gottfried Kreuz, Jeffrey Kurtzman, Franca Leverotti, Ignazio Macchiarella, Arnaldo Morelli, Elisa Novi Chavarria, Greta Olson, Edward Olszewski, Noel O'Regan, John S. Powell, Patrizia Radicchi, Colleen Reardon, Luis Robledo, Emilio Ros-Fábregas, Steven Saunders, Louise Stein, Kevin Stevens, Álvaro Torrente, and Gabriella Zarri. Some of the archivists, librarians, and others who made research possible include Giulio Battelli; Frs. Roberto Primavera and Joel Warden, C.O.; don Francisco Delgado; padre Miguel Navarro Sorní; don Giovanni Spinelli and don Mariano Colletta, O.S.B.; don Maurizio Brioli, C.R.S.; padre Adolfo García Durán, S.P.; dott. Andrea Cargiolli and dott. Domenico Rocciolo; Richard Schano; Profs. Marie-Agnes Dittrich and Sven Hansell; Martin Kahl and Prof. Hermann Max; the colleagues of the Fondazione Levi (Venice) and of Bratislava University Library; and especially Drs. Bonifacio Bartolomé in Segovia and Alfredo Vitolo in Bologna. Special thanks to the archivist of the ACSP, mons. Dario Rezza, and dott.

Vincenzo Piacquadio. At the last minute, my colleague Thomas Christensen tracked down an important source in Berlin. My Italian family—Giorgio Marchi, Massimo and Maria Giuseppina Liber—was unwavering in their help scouring archives in Emilia-Romagna, Liguria, and Tuscany. In Piacenza, Lucia Rocchi and mons. Giuseppe Busani went to great pains to provide the dust-jacket illustration. For advice on performance issues I am grateful to Jean-Marc Aymes, Geoffrey Burgess, Bruce Dickey, and Candace Smith. Despite the serious issues that much of this music raises, the sheer beauty of some of it—such as Charpentier's Tenebrae output to which I was first introduced by my late teacher H. Wiley Hitchcock—has inspired me, even in difficult times. I am deeply thankful to Massimo Ossi for soliciting this book proposal, to Prof. Christine Getz and anonymous Press readers for improving it, and to Raina Polivka for making it happen. In sickness and in health, Lucia Marchi variously advised, read, consoled, and encouraged, and without her there would be no book. This volume is for my sister Carroll Kendrick Burns, a severe critic of church music performances, who has looked after my well-being for a long time now.

Terminology, Abbreviations, Texts

As explained in chapter 1, the book uses a shorthand for the liturgical place-ment of those Office texts that were anticipated to occur the afternoon before their "normal" days and times. Items designated for liturgical Holy Thursday ("Feria V in Coena Domini") were thus normally sung on the afternoon of Holy Wednesday. In order to avoid confusion, I call the services by liturgical order; hence liturgical Thursday, with its Matins and Lauds sung on Wednes-day, is abbreviated as "F5," and similarly for Good Friday (= "Feria VI in Parasceve" or my "F6") and Holy Saturday ("Sabbato Sancto," my "SS"). I have designated the nine psalms, Lessons, and Responsories of Matins by consecutive number inside the Hour as a whole (L1, R7), and two items of Lauds in shorthand: the canticle *Benedictus Dominus Deus Israel* as "Bene-dictus" and the "expanding" antiphon *Christus factus est* as "CFE." Com-bining these systems allows e.g., "F6/L2" to be read as "the second Lesson of Matins for liturgical Good Friday, sung on Thursday afternoon," or "F5/R7" as "the seventh Responsory of Matins for liturgical Holy Thursday, sung on Wednesday afternoon" (I thus use the Nocturne system of Matins only spar-ingly, often to refer to those Lessons not normally set to music until about 1700, L4–9).

Normally, Lessons 1–3 at these Matins were taken from the biblical book of Lamentations. Citations from Lamentations are given as chapter:verse; verses chosen for a given Lesson are given inside curled brackets (e.g., F6/L2={2:12–15}), and the individual sub-sections (here called "sub-verses") of every verse are designated as letters with verse numbers or inside square brackets (e.g., 1:11a for the first section of chapter 1, verse 11). Collections of Holy Week Office texts or music, normally called *Officium hebdomadae sanctae,* are here abbreviated as "OHS." Those musical manuscripts that have *Census-Catalogue of Renaissance Music Manuscripts 1400–1550* sigla are so abbreviated; otherwise, I use standard RISM sigla for libraries and manuscripts. Actual pitches are given in scientific pitch notation (middle C=C$_4$; pitch-classes in general are given as capital letters; and pitches that come from chant models or chant finals in lowercase italics. Clef combinations for polyphony are given in the normal combination (e.g., C1/C3/C4/F4 for standard mixed-voice scoring). General abbreviations are in the bibliography.

Singing Jeremiah

Chapter 1

Symbolic Meanings, Sonic Penance

In the ritual year of early modern Catholics, the days before Easter represented the longest single commemoration, collective and personal, of the central events of salvation. Despite the survival or re-invention of historical Holy Week traditions today, it is still hard to imagine how much prayer and penitence were packed into the seventy-odd hours between the afternoons of Wednesday and Saturday. The three central days—the Triduum—recalling the Passion included the chanted words, participatory rites, and sonic behavior of liturgical Maundy Thursday ("Feria V in Coena Domini," hereafter F5), Good Friday ("Feria VI in Parasceve," hereafter F6), and Holy Saturday ("Sabbato Sancto," hereafter SS). Beyond the structures of the Divine Office and Mass, there were community actions: processions, "entombments of Christ," depositions from the Cross, ceremonies of mourning and weeping, and, less appealingly, group violence. The social re-enactment of Christ's atonement went hand in hand with individual purging of sin via penance and often Confession. This dialectic between the audible expression of mourning and the internalization of remorse was vital for the Week's meaning.

Sounds simple and complex projected the listing of human guilt, the recollection of the Passion in narration and allegory, and the meanings of liturgical action. In order to focus on allegory and narrative voice, this study considers largely the most renowned music of these days, the polyphony and chant for the Canonical Hours of Matins followed by Lauds, in the two centuries after 1550. These were combined as a single service in Catholic continental Europe and its outposts.[1] The Hours also drew lay participation, beyond the monks, nuns, or cathedral clergy who would have sung the texts.

From some point in the later Middle Ages onward, evidently first at the Papal court and then increasingly elsewhere, these services were in most places anticipated to occur in the late afternoon of the day preceding their liturgical assignment. Thus the texts of liturgical Thursday were read or sung on late

Wednesday afternoon, and similarly Friday's Hours on Thursday and Saturday's on Friday, each day as the natural light in churches waned. This ambient darkening was echoed and enhanced by the extinguishing of church lights as the service went on.[2] Because of this interaction, the Hours were known as the Office of Tenebrae: darkness/shadows.

Although the action and texts of the services were highly determined, they conveyed not only emotion but social meaning. To consider simply the written musical documents leaves out essential if irrecoverable elements: vocal/musical execution; the prescribed gestures and movement; and the behavior of participants. Before reducing sound to breviary prescriptions or written scores—in the case of Lauds' music, the level of improvised ornamentation suggests that much more was involved—we might take to heart Ernesto De Martino's critique of text-centered approaches to personal and collective threnodies for deceased family members in modern southern Italy.[3] For De Martino, neglecting performance meant missing major aspects of the rituals of lamenting.

FORMS AND PRACTICE

The overall structure of Matins and Lauds was roughly similar across the wide variety of late medieval practice, but the actual texts could differ locally until about 1580. From roughly 1500 onward, the items of the Week's Office were sometimes gathered into a single *Officium Hebdomadae Sanctae* in manuscript or print, whose precise selections varied by time and place. Starting around 1560, printed editions of the music, often with the Gospel Passions for Mass included, were issued under this title as well (unless specified as text-only, such music editions are henceforth called "OHS").

One idealized account of the service when presided over by a bishop can be found in the 1600 *Caeremoniale episcoporum,* which also furnished an equally stereotypical image (fig. 1.1) in its attempt to standardize practice.[4] Before Matins began, a triangular candelabrum, or "hearse," was set out with from nine up to seventy-two candles of common wax (depending on local tradition, although fifteen were typical even before 1600). Lights were lit on the stripped altar, only partially denuded on Wednesday, completely so the other days. As church bells were silenced during the Triduum until Vespers of Holy Saturday, the start of the Office was announced by the beating of wooden sticks. If a bishop were present, he would proceed to his throne, and all would then stand for the silent Pater Noster, Ave Maria, and Credo. In the *Caeremoniale*'s engraving, the hearse with fifteen candles is shown on the altar; the singers—choirboys and adult men—are clearly visible in the right foreground, and the perspective is from just behind them, rather as if the music were drawing the viewer into the ritual.

FIGURE 1.1. Tenebrae as in *Caerimoniale episcoporum* (Rome, 1600), p. 224 (Courtesy Special Collections Research Center, University of Chicago Library).

The texts sung at Matins consisted of three formally identical sections called Nocturnes, and each Nocturne started with three psalms (hereafter abbreviated as "P" plus consecutive number) with antiphons before and after each. This psalmodic group was followed by three readings or Lessons (Latin *lectiones*, here "L" plus consecutive number). The end of the opening three-psalm section was separated from the first reading by a versicle and another silent Pater Noster. The readings in the First Nocturne were verses from one or another of the five chapters of the Lamentations of Jeremiah (or *Threni*), normally sung to a repeating chant tone or recitation formula, which also often varied locally as late as 1600 (and beyond). Every Lamentations Lesson ended with a non-Scriptural refrain "Jersualem, convertere ad Dominum Deum tuum/Jerusalem, return to the Lord your God." The opening reading of each day had a title (usually set to music): for F5, "Incipit lamentatio Jeremiae prophetae," and for the other two, "De lamentatione Jeremiae prophetae." In most but not all places until 1600, the last reading of Nocturne I (L3) for SS used verses from chapter 5 of Lamentations, Jeremiah's Prayer, the *Oratio Jeremiae Prophetae*. Every Lesson was followed immediately by a Responsory (here "R" plus number), nine in all over the three Nocturnes of each day and thus twenty-seven over the course of the Triduum. Because of the days' extreme mourning, the Lesser Doxology ("Gloria Patri et Filio," normally ending psalms and canticles) was also omitted from liturgical Thursday to liturgical Saturday, and this helps identify musical settings meant for the Triduum as opposed to other occasions.

The following two Nocturnes repeated the structure with other psalms and Responsories, along with Lessons from other sources. The readings in these later Nocturnes were often taken from Augustine's sermons on the Psalms, and Paul's Epistles (Second and Third Nocturnes, respectively), while the variable literary voice and tone of the Responsories continued throughout Matins. After Matins ended with another silent Our Father, Lauds followed immediately, starting with three psalms and a canticle, then Psalm 148, *Laudate Dominum de caelis*. Although the other items changed on each day, the first two, Psalm 50, *Miserere mei Deus,* and 148 were invariable. After this psalmody, there followed the Gospel canticle, Zacharias's outpouring of joy at the upcoming births of Christ and John the Baptist (Lk 1:68–79), *Benedictus Dominus Deus Israel* (henceforth Benedictus, not to be confused with the Mass's Sanctus), with its Proper antiphon. Unless set to polyphony, all psalms and canticles were chanted to a simple tone antiphonally, and their antiphons sung chorally.[5]

In the late afternoon, around the spring solstice, whatever natural light there was in any church was fading. Throughout the course of Matins and Lauds the hearse lights were extinguished with some kind of snuffer one by one, leaving only the top candle lit when the Benedictus was reached. In institutions with fifteen candles, each snuffing typically occurred at the repetitions of the antiphons after the fourteen psalms over the two Hours (in Spain, the snuffer was known as the "mano de Judas"). At v.7 of the canticle, "Ut sine timore," the altar candles and all other lights except for the last hearse candle were also put out, thus leaving the space with a minimum of artificial illumination.[6] Then (in most places, at the repeat of the antiphon) the remaining candle was taken away from the sanctuary. Before 1570, this moment was often followed by a dialogue litany with short tropes, the "Kyrie tenebrarum," for which some sixteenth-century music survives. But after the arrival of the new liturgical books, the closing section of Lauds began with the verse "Christus factus est" (henceforth CFE), expanded with an additional phrase each successive day. By this point the remaining candle was to be hidden behind another altar, removing the last artificial light in the ritual space.

At the end of Lauds, the Miserere was repeated, louder or softer than the first time depending on local custom, followed by the Collect (prayer) "Respice, quaesumus, Domine." Finally, all those present—not simply the clergy singing the Office—made a loud noise, the *strepitus,* for some time with sticks or beaters, thus echoing the call to Matins.[7] Lauds closed with the single remaining lit candle being returned to the hearse.

Given its various allegorical meanings—the earthquake while Christ was on the Cross, the dispersion of the Apostles, the flaying while at Pilate's palace—the *strepitus* had a key role in the symbolic dramaturgy of Holy Week.[8] Its abolition was the first gesture of the Reformation in the south-west German town of Giengen in 1534.[9] But in early modern Europe, it also provided an opportunity for the social expression of excess and violence. A host of prohibitions against its "disorder," issued by Italian diocesan synods from the early Cinquecento onward, testifies to frequent explosions of energy, as bishops attempted to regulate the duration of the banging and even the materials used therein.[10] This "unruliness" was not limited to Renaissance Italy: a 1712 guide to Holy Week for the Austrian Netherlands warned against letting children use the moment as the catalyst for a game of "beating out Lent" with their rattles and mallets.[11] One measure of the longevity of the *strepitus,* and its link to collective penance, in rural Catholic Europe is the practice of children smashing poles on the ground at the end of Tenebrae in the Val Tidone, southwest of Piacenza, with the pieces then used later to light the Easter candle, a tradition known as "beating sins" ("batt i pcä") recorded as late as the 1950s.[12] Even today in Calabria, the wooden instruments used in Holy Week processions are called the "strumenti delle tenebre."[13]

The injunctions against "overdoing" the moment attempted to limit congregational agency during Tenebrae, and they raise the wider question of how the laity could intervene in what was supposed to be a service for clergy or nuns. Over the entire sonic continuum, the *strepitus* represents the opposite of complex polyphony or chant heard early in Matins: unorganized, collective noise with no verbal content whatsoever, relieving the tension of the long and intense service, but also acting as a conduit for both social conflicts and devotional sentiment.

Since the ritual action was central to, but not directly emblematic of, community enactment of the Passion, a series of liturgical commentators provided both a narrative for the whole rite and meanings for its individual actions. Here Guglielmus Durandus's *Rationale divinorum officium,* the classic thirteenth-century interpretation of the texts and actions of the Office, proved long-lived; at least eleven Cinquecento printed editions survive. Still, his was not the only guide, as many copies of Johannes Beleth's medieval treatise of the same name have been preserved. Beleth's *Rationale* (or *Summa*) offered a more limited and sometimes more logical set of allegorical explanations for the Office as a whole, hence probably its popularity.[14]

Such explications, which had begun with Amalarius of Metz in the ninth century, continued in early modern times, for instance the third treatise of Michele Timoteo's question-and-answer tract *In divinum officium trecentum quaestiones* (Venice, 1581). Timoteo borrowed liberally from past authors, while giving allegorical explanations for the peculiarities of the Triduum Office.[15] A generation later, Bartolomeo Gavanti's *Thesaurus sacrum rituum* (1628) synthesized medieval comments on the liturgy in a relatively logical reading. As late as the mid-eighteenth century, liturgists at Pisa Cathedral would repeat and critique Durandus's symbolism of the Days—doing so as their chapelmaster Giovanni Maria Clari was composing modern-style Lessons for their Duomo.[16]

One interpretive tradition considered Tenebrae in particular as being the "funeral of Christ," thus connected to the long-standing *planctus* or mourning piece; another considered the texts, especially the Lamentations readings, as a catalogue of human sin that had rendered the Passion necessary for salvation; and a third took it as an essentially moral and penitential experience of *metanoia,* turning away from sin, most evident in the Miserere. Durandus's interpretation of the Triduum Office is found in Book VI of the *Rationale,* and draws heavily on previous allegorical explanations.[17] Like most writers before and after, he treated the Matins/Lauds of all three days as a single unit, before his accounts of other Triduum liturgy. Durandus considered the Hours to be an enactment of the Church celebrating the exequies of Christ, and the Office shadows not so much a symbol of the darkness during Christ's Crucifixion but rather the spiritual night in the faithful's hearts. His understanding of such "exequies" would last into modern times.[18]

The bishop explained the "Jerusalem, convertere" refrain of the First Nocturne's Lessons as a call to Christian penance. He equated the three Nocturnes to the three states of humans—virgins, the married, and the chaste—whom Christ descended to Hell to redeem. Similarly, the psalms related to action, the Lessons to contemplation, and Responsories to angelic song; this abstract characterization strongly influenced early modern understandings. Durandus's conception of Jeremiah's words as funereal lament also raises issues of textual hermeneutics discussed below.

After allegorical explanations of the extinguished candles, the bishop gave three meanings for the return of the last one: the faithful Virgin, Christ's Resurrection, or the rebirth of faith in the hearts of the Apostles and the Church. He also noted a congregational cry at the Benedictus, symbolizing those present at the arrest of Christ, and considered the loud performance of the canticle as joy after the Antichrist would be killed. The "Kyrie" dialogue of Lauds represented the tumult among Christ's persecutors, and the tropes of this section stood for the laments of the three Marys at the Sepulchre. Finally, he took the *strepitus* to represent the terror of those facing Christ's captors, or the fear at the earthquake during the Crucifixion. The sheer noisiness—"vociferatio," "clangor canentium," "sonitus"—of Durandus's description of Lauds, not Matins, is noteworthy. His is not a single allegorical narrative but a multiplicity of possible meanings.

In early modern practice, the concrete actions outside the projection of the texts seem to have been limited to the movement of the clerics coming forward to chant the lessons or saying prayers silently, the snuffing of the lights, the hiding and return of the final candle, and the *strepitus*. The visual object of Triduum devotion in churches was normally some kind of representation of Christ's Tomb, the *sepulcrum*. In an environment in which many visual stimuli had been turned off, the projection of the texts took on a totalizing cast. Audiences could not help but pay attention to the words and whatever music went with them. Whether or not set to complex music, the Office texts display remarkable sacrality and canonicity, and their prominence was underscored by the conditions of their recitation: the altars and statues in the church draped, the lengthening shadows of the late afternoon, and even the dispensability of an officiating priest in female monastic houses.

LIGHT AND MEANING

For observers and participants then and now, these services have had their fascination, due to their interplay of music and light.[19] Their anticipation to the preceding afternoon had transferred the idea of shadows to the growing gloaming around the services, which was reinforced by the extinguishing of the candles. Indeed, the *Caeremoniale episcoporum* directed that Lauds end late, as the sun went down ("ut officium perficiatur hora tarda, hoc est, sole occidente"). The ending of the Hours in darkness—underscored by the real dangers and cultural inversions of the early modern night—resonated with the last verse of the Benedictus, Zacharias's prophecy of his son's future role for sinful humanity: "Illuminare his, qui in tenebris et umbra mortis sedent"/"to illuminate those who sit in darkness and the shadow of death."[20] The dark-bright duality was part of a larger system, resuming the Christmas cycle after Presentation BVM (2 February), and culminating in the Easter Vigil with the Paschal candle. With its allegorical meanings ranging from the shadows of the Crucifixion to those of human sin, Tenebrae was a social extinguishing of light, the music of which was increasingly important.

On a symbolic level, the darkening has a complex relationship to sound. Although in most places the snuffing of the candles in the hearse was associated with the psalms or antiphons of Matins, the musically heightened moments tended instead to be the Lessons and Responsories. If the complex music was separated from the action in Matins, the situation was different at Lauds, as the extinguishing of the altar (not hearse) lights took place at a Benedictus verse (v. 7) often sung in polyphony, but in seeming contradiction to the affect of the moment: "Ut sine timore" / "So that we may serve Him without fear, liberated from the hand of our enemies."[21] Thus only at this moment did the two communicative systems, visual and aural, join into a single ritual moment, and this connection suggests a closer examination of the canticle, its antiphons, and their music.[22]

Although the later prominence of music for Psalm 50 has tended to overshadow the canticle, most sixteenth-century settings of the Benedictus are more complex than those of the Miserere. Two cases bear this out: the elaborate Florentine works of Francesco Corteccia (printed in 1570), and the three lengthy pieces of Lasso, preserved in a Munich court choirbook together with a single Miserere (see chapters 3 and 4).[23] Although the psalm text is almost twice as long as the canticle's (twenty vs. eleven verses), Lasso's Benedictus pieces are about two-thirds as long as his Miserere.[24] These works alternate their two choirs and combine them for a nine-voice conclusion in the last verse. The ritual action seems to have generated musical consequences, and perhaps surprisingly at first, it was the text of praise, not of penitence, that received the emphasis.

The shadows also had practical effects. Although singers were usually in the choir and thus relatively near the altar, the lights of which burned until the canticle, the diminishing illumination, internal and external, would have made reading from manuscript or printed music parts more difficult. The Benedictus and especially the Miserere would have had particular problems. Much surviving music for the psalm, well into the seventeenth century, is simple chordal recitation or *falsobordone,* and thus easily memorizable. This simplicity also favored the kind of improvised ornamentation for this text familiar from the various versions of Gregorio Allegri's Miserere in the Cappella Sistina manuscripts. Lauds thus retained traces of its oral and improvisatory musical practice, and thus provides an intersection between historical ritual and performance studies.

POLYPHONY AND AFFECT IN THE HOURS

At the beginning of our period, three very different accounts testify to the role of music and ritual in Tenebrae. The first is Benedetto Guidi's "memory" of a discussion in autumn 1564 with Abbot Andrea Pampuro, the president of his Cassinese Congregation of Benedictine monks. The next spring, Guidi retold the conversation in his printed dedication to Pampuro of a massive edition of Holy Week polyphony that had been composed by his much older fellow Cassinese Paolo of Ferrara:

Above all, I was persuaded to do this [publish Paolo's Holy Week music] by my memory of a talk which Your Most Reverend Lord had with me six months ago, when . . . you told me with what displeasure you had heard the Lamentations of Jeremiah during Holy Week in Perugia and Arezzo (while on your journey, to us seeming quite dangerous, from Rome to Venice), sung with so many ornaments and vocal cacophony, that they seemed a chaotic banging ["strepito," as at Lauds] and noise, rather than intelligible, pious, and devout music, such as is appropriate for those holy Days on which the Passion and death of Our Lord Jesus Christ are enacted. On this, I remember your precise words: "The enemy of the human race, knowing no other way during those holy days to rob the faithful of that devotion which those saddest words evoke—capable in themselves of softening and breaking a heart of marble—attempted, by means of such ill-matched and chopped-up vocal lines, to make them incomprehensible, something which should sadden every good and faithful Christian greatly."[25]

Just two weeks before Guidi's dedication, on 18 April 1565, the experience of Jesuits headed to India on board a Portuguese galleon off the coast of Africa was entirely different. Here the vessel was transformed via Tenebrae polyphony into the Ship of the Church, as Fernando de Alcaraz, S. J., would remember it even nine months later after his arrival in Kerala:

On the afternoon of Holy Wednesday, we ordered how Tenebrae were to be said. A candelabrum [the hearse] was made in which the candles were placed, as they do in Europe, and there was even the thing called the "hand of Judas" with which they are extinguished. Very good voices sang the Lamentations in polyphony, as if [the ship] were a cathedral. The devotion of the people [i.e. crew] was so great that all joined the Office, and, since they did not all fit (and also to see better), they went up on the ship's masts and rigging, as if they were ascending to heaven . . . and, since the night was very dark and the candlelight illuminated their faces, most of them young lads, they glowed with the light's reflection, so that we seemed almost as in [heavenly] glory, since the way in which painters depict it seemed there to be for real. We finished our Tenebrae [with a *strepitus*] in which there were many slaps, and while the Miserere was recited, they showed great devotion.[26]

Another account from a decade earlier, by an insider who had turned away from his confession, upended everything. As part of his systematic demolition of the symbolic world of the Roman Church, the Protestant polemicist and former Catholic bishop of Capodistria Pier Paolo Vergerio aimed directly at the practices of Holy Week in his savagely ironic *Operetta nuova . . . nella qual si dimostrono le vere ragioni, che hanno mosso i Romani Pontifici ad instituir le belle ceremonie della Settimana Santa* (Zurich, 1552). His targets ranged from Durandus's *Rationale* to the decisions of the ongoing Council of Trent. Having taken on Palm Sunday's rituals, Vergerio turned to the Triduum Office:

> Of the Three Matins sung on Wednesday, Thursday and Friday. . . . The same bishop [Durandus] says then that the Romans ordered nine psalms, nine Lessons, and nine Responsories in each of these Matins, in order to show that Christ, descending into Hell, freed three kinds of people: virgins, the married, and the chaste. For this reason I assure you that your tonsured and anointed ones will do this very badly, since they are neither virgins, nor married, nor chaste, and certainly Christ would not have descended anywhere in order to free *them* . . . Our *Rationale*'s author also says that his Roman Church introduced these three Matins in order to celebrate the exequies for Christ's death . . . are your priests not charitable, since they perform exequies for Christ in order to liberate him from Purgatory? Indeed, more charitable than the Apostles or His own mother ever were, for they never did that much, but rather only began to preach [the Gospel] . . . Finally, when all nine [*recte* 14] psalms are sung, and all the candles extinguished, only one is left, and, behold, the sacristan runs anxiously around the entire church and extinguishes all the [other] lights, even those burning in front of that thing [the Eucharist] that you keep locked up as if in prison [Vergerio here conflates Matins and Lauds, omitting Lessons and Responsories]. And look, even the one remaining candle is hidden by the sacristan, leaving the whole congregation in the dark. And then suddenly a loud tumult and dreadful noise are made by a group of children and others with beaters and sticks, until the sacristan brings back the candle, elevating it, and then hides it again, and then a third time, and the congregation makes noise a second time, and a third time, as loudly as possible. And then everyone is sent home with these "lovely" acts of devotion, which your carnal Popes have dreamed up. You might say that all this symbolizes the tumult and noise made by those Jewish scoundrels the night that they went to arrest Christ, and what is the harm in acting it out for the people to hear? I know that the Popes, who had nothing better to do, ordered this comedy, or tragedy, and our Friar *Rationale* [Durandus] explains it thus . . . As for the psalms, we praise them as the divine thing that they are, and we have good translations, whereas yours is horribly corrupt, even though the awful "Council" of Trent has preferred it above all others. And we have translated them into the

vernaculars, German, French, and English, and we often sing them, not only in churches but also in houses and in the streets, in order to rejoice in the glory of God. And we understand what we are singing, whereas your tonsured ones do not understand a thing, not even you who are listening to them. Would you perhaps understand the line sung in polyphony? Another one of the stupid practices of your refined deceivers is how the word of God, which should be preached clearly and understood, is kept buried and hidden among you, not only in those symbols and figures, as I have shown, not only because it is spoken in Latin, but also [buried] underneath the notes of your polyphony, and inside the pipes of your organs, and sometimes under the sounds of bagpipes, cornetti, and cornamuses all mixed together.[27]

As different as these accounts were, so were their aftermaths. Paolo's edition had some success, but its dedicatee and putative inspiration Pampuro was soon to be stripped of his office by Pius V's curia and disgraced for his alleged softness on residual heresy in the Congregation. The original environment of the music, the monastery of S. Benedetto Po at mid-century, had already become suspect for heterodoxy, and one of Guidi's other publishing projects concealed a condemned text linked to the house. Although Guidi himself somehow managed to avoid punishment in the Roman crackdown, within fifteen years a younger Cassinese in Brescia, Placido Falconio, would publish a quite different complete set of music for Holy Week.

The monk's account is rooted in Renaissance Catholic demonology, recalling the diabolic imitation of human communication by distorted singing, considered as the communicative means ("strigimagis") of devils by Silvestre Prierio (*De strigimagarum daemoniumque mirandis* of 1521). The Benedictine's perception of this sung distortion would have later expressions. Such demonic reworking of sacred formulae, called "anti-benedictions" or *ensalmi* in Manuel do Valle de Moura's (1564–1650) *De incantationibus seu ensalmis* (Évora, 1620), perverted the sacrality of Scriptural or liturgical words. For Moura, devils preferred to sing, rather than speak, their incantations.[28] The production of a commentary on Lamentations by the seventeenth-century Jesuit demonologist Martin del Río also suggests overlap between the correct projection of Jeremiah's words and the vanquishing of devilish agency.

Alcaraz's Tenebrae the following night was interrupted by a catastrophic storm, which almost sank his boat. In a wider sense, his account reflects both the special place of musical Tenebrae for voyaging Jesuits and their ignoring of their Society's Constitutions by using music in the Hours, at least on the South Asian missions. Indeed, the detailed mention of his experience may well have been intended to remind his colleagues in Europe of polyphony's power to induce transcendence, especially important for clergy under the difficult conditions outside Europe. Jesuits recorded the sung Office on their ships from 1555 to 1574, and, once arrived, the missionaries organized Tenebrae in Goa (1563), Mozambique (1571), Cochin (Kochi, 1574), Malacca (1580), and even in the small mission at the court of the Mughal emperor Akbar the Great in Lahore (1596, where Akbar's courtiers were noted as attending, although what they might have thought of the probably improvised polyphony is unclear).[29] Elsewhere, however, the Society relied on visual, not musical, stimuli, to produce the desired weeping among its publics during Holy Week, as in Bahia (Salvador) the same year of Alcaraz's voyage, when they were proud of attracting more people to their recreation of Christ's Tomb (the *sepolcro*) than came to hear polyphony in the cathedral. Similarly, Tenebrae on the Japanese missions seem to have been chanted or spoken, not sung.[30] But Triduum *canto de órgano* throughout the Indian Province was constant from 1558 to the end of the century.

Vergerio's account of musical noise in the Office probably reflects his experience in Istria as bishop, although his strictures against polyphony in principle might also have resulted from his time at the Imperial Court or in France. But the pace of Triduum polyphony actually picked up across Italy after 1560. Even in his old diocese of Capodistria, a 1568 note in the cathedral ordinances reads "la settimana santa si canta figurato"/ "in Holy Week polyphony is sung."[31] Beyond the confessional attacks, one might turn his account on its head, as conveying a sense of pre-Reformation Tenebrae as a community experience with laity who brought even their humblest instruments (bagpipes) in order to participate in these social exequies of Christ.

All the accounts share important features. First is their emphasis on Tenebrae in the common experience of Holy Week, not limited to the educated elite to which Guidi, Alcaraz, and Vergerio belonged. They described services that had real impact on the communities participating in the ritual. On Alcaraz's ship, there is no mention of professional musicians; i.e., *canto de órgano* was something that many people could do. Thus, far from purely aesthetic expressions, the texts, actions, and sounds of Tenebrae were crucial in the social re-enactment of the Passion. Vergerio's slighting reference to "comedy/tragedy" underscores the theatricality of the Hours.

Second, Tenebrae was a liminal moment, one whose performance was open to both devilish and divine intervention. The exequies of Christ rendered ritual participants susceptible to supernatural effects on their affects. Above all, the musical performance of the Office—"correct" settings replacing "diabolical" improvisation for Guidi, the songs as an earthly foretaste of Heaven for Alcaraz, or the "burial" of God's Word through polyphony for Vergerio—was crucial to the experience of the entire Week. In this, the prophetic words of Jeremiah—the longest selections from any prophet to be heard in the liturgy—seem to have held incantatory power, unleashed all the more readily when expressed in the pitch and rhythmic ratios of figured music.

Finally, all the accounts refer to the widespread experience of improvised and entirely unwritten polyphony for Lamentations and other parts of the Office, music that has not survived but which must have represented the overwhelming practice in Europe, India, and the Americas. This practice seems to have consisted of the familiar chant and an improvised line above or below: simple in the tradition of *cantus planus binatim* or more expressive—but also more chaotic—individual improvisation.[32] Indeed, the production of much sixteenth-century written repertory can be viewed as an effort to provide the Triduum Office with "fitting" polyphony. Still, Tenebrae began as practice and not formalized genres.

RITUAL TEXTS

Across local liturgical Uses, the exact choice of Lamentations verses for the First Nocturne's Lessons varied across late medieval Europe, in both breviaries and musical settings. Even in the standardizing 1570s, the Office texts seemingly newly fixed by Pius V's 1568 Breviary were abridged. In 1572, a text-only *Officium hebdomadae sanctae* was issued in Rome that claimed to be the first to incorporate the readings of both the new Office as well as the Missal of 1570 ("ad Missalis & Breviarij reformatum rationem Pii V Pont. Max. restitutum").[33] But in reality this edition changed the verse selection of every Triduum Lesson in the only four-year-old Pian breviary, reducing their number in eight of the nine (all but F5/L3).[34]

Although commonly attributed to Gregory XIII, the changes must have come through Cardinal Guglielmo Sirleto, the post-1568 head of liturgical reform. In a letter of 24 November 1572, he complained of the cost that the "Offitio" had brought him, evidently both in terms of work and finances, and so he must have labored over it even before Gregory's consecration on the previous 26 May.[35] His ties, through his associate Paolo Manuzio, to the "In Aedibus Populi Romani" press would have made a quick issue in the summer of 1572 possible. The new readings were picked up in the same year by the Giunta press of Venice and in another Venetian *Officium* of the next year.[36]

Of the two surviving copies of the 1572 Roman book, the Vatican exemplar comes from the sacristy of the Jesuit *Collegio Romano*, and thus the order must have adopted these readings promptly. One measure of their effect is the general agreement of almost all the Roman musical repertory with at least the opening verses of the 1572 readings (see appendix, table 1). Since the Spanish court and the Escorial switched to the Roman books in the mid-1570s, their selection must also have been standardized thus.

But elsewhere in Europe, textual choice continued on the basis of oral, local, or even invented tradition. Despite the Venetian books, the first real conformity between north Italian polyphonic Lamentations and the post-1572 liturgical editions begins only with G. M. Asola's three-volume OHS of 1583/84.[37] After 1600, the preserved music largely matches the breviaries: verses from chapter 1 for the F5 Lessons, from chapters 2–3 for the F6 readings, and chapters 3, 4, and 5 for the SS selections. The only Lessons clearly based on Pius V's 1568 breviary are several items by Johannes Matelart in Rome, and the two Lamentation cycles by Orlando de Lasso at the Munich court.

In chapters 1 through 4, the text of Lamentations is written as acrostic poetry generated by the twenty-two-letter Hebrew alphabet. The Vulgate, the breviaries, and most musical settings retained the initial letters untranslated, beginning each of the twenty-two verses in chapters 1, 2, and 4. Chapter 3 groups three verses together, each prefixed by the same acrostic letter, hence sixty-six in all, and chapter 5 keeps the twenty-two-verse structure but drops the acrostic.[38] Each verse of chapters 1, 2, 4, and 5 consists of multiple clauses or phrases. For early modern exegetes, these corresponded to a line of the Hebrew poetry: tripartite (chapters 1 and 2) or bipartite (4, 5). All these smaller textual units are here called "sub-verses" and denoted as a, b, and c respectively. For example, in verse 1:11 the division runs: [a] "Omnes populus eius gemens, et quaerens panem"/"All her [Jerusalem's] people are groaning, and seeking bread"—[b] "dederunt pretiosa eius pro cibo ad refocillandam animam"/"they have given all their precious things for food to restore their spirit"—[c] (in which Jerusalem herself speaks) "'Vide, Domine, et considera quoniam facta sum vilis'"/"'Look, o Lord, and see how I have become vile/ugly.'" In contrast, chapter 3's verses are a single sentence each, often two short phrases, also considered as equivalent to a poetic line. This sense of the verse units as equaling a lyric line lasted even in the eighteenth-century comments on the book by the bishop of Bisceglie, Pompeo Sarnelli, and the correspondence underscores the units' importance in the musical analysis of any given verse.

The Responsories following each of the nine Lessons were far more stable and of different character: some are formed from Gospel verses from the Passion accounts; others are selections from the Psalms or Prophets with only allegorical reference to Christ's suffering; and yet others employ a non-Scriptural narrative summary of one or another event of the Passion. Their text is set out in the standard structure: response/repetendum/verse/repetendum

(ABCB), and (widely before about 1600, universally thereafter) the final Responsory (3, 6, 9) of each Nocturne had a complete da capo (ABCBAB, or "doubling"). When not performed in polyphony, their chant was musically florid (normal for their genre), and they were sung chorally except for the first words and the verse, apportioned to a soloist; in polyphony, the verse was usually set for reduced forces, a sonic reminiscence of the solo chant. As discrete Scriptural units used on other occasions, the Benedictus and Miserere had standard texts based on bipartite verses.

In times and places when they were not sung in polyphony, the selections from Jeremiah, like all Lessons, were chanted by a single cleric or nun, using one of the formulaic tones; these varied in pitch content and complexity according to place, but often repeated from verse to verse in any Lesson. From one hundred to two hundred different ones were found in late medieval Europe.[39] In some cases, these formulae are simple and syllabic, and the one in Tone 6, based on *f* and reciting on *a,* that has made its way into modern chant books is the most familiar. The Triduum antiphoner written for the Cappella Sistina in 1535 by Galeazzo Ercolano (I-Rvat-sistina 2) clearly gives the formula in Tone 6 along with the text of 1:1 (only) as a model for F5/L1 (example 1.1). But other tones were more florid and not necessarily on the same pitch. Locally or regionally across Europe, the *Oratio* could have its own formula, sometimes in Tone 4.

The opening and repeated pitches of the Tone-6 version are the most easily identifiable. Quite audibly, the internal subdivisions of a verse are marked by different cadences for any given phrase: the *mediatio aperta,* on the third degree of the mode (*a*), used for the opening sub-verse, and the *mediatio clausa* ending on the *finalis f,* and often found in the [b] sub-verse of tripartite verses. The formula for the end of the whole verse, touching the *finalis,* rising and then returning, is fairly standard. All these terminations had resonance, even in quite complex music, up to the eighteenth century.[40] Wherever it was used, this tone, repeated over the fifty-seven Lamentations verses plus titles and "Jerusalem" refrains that comprised the normal post-1572 selection over the Triduum, was inevitable.

For all the seeming post-1600 universality of the Tone-6 formula, chants could remain stubbornly local. Their variety in early modern Poland included the use of non-Lamentations texts for the Lessons, with the Hebrew letters and the refrain retained.[41] Here, thanks to the printing of a customary in 1591, "national" tones remained in use for the post-1572 Roman Lessons into the twentieth century.[42] In sixteenth-century Spain, chant formulae in-

EXAMPLE I.I. Chant formula for F5/L1, from RomeCS 2 (1535).

cluded two large families (Toledo and Zaragoza). Hispanic tones often fell
into three prominent versions: one beginning *acd* and reciting on *d;* a related
but not identical one beginning *ega* and reciting on *a;* and one beginning *gc*
and reciting on *c.*[43] The second of these can be found in modern books as an
alter tonus for the *Oratio.* The Spanish tones have different phrases for the
sub-verses of the text, and the final phrase of the *acd* formula family rises in
pitch, beginning on *f* and reciting on *a,* like the beginning of the Tone-6 version, with the crucial difference that it has *b♮* and not *b♭.*

The posthumous chant Passionale by Juan Sánchez Azpeleta, his *Opus
harmonicum* (Zaragoza, 1612, ff. 58v–70; example 1.2), canonized this diversity in print by providing nine different, quite florid tones across the Triduum.
These are set out on *d, f* (a more florid version of the Tone-6 formula), *e, f,
e, g, g, d* and *d;* the edition was preserved throughout the former Crown of
Aragón.[44]

The basic sonic experience of Matins for many audiences was the tones.
They became iconic for Tenebrae, and their relative simplicity meant that
their presence in polyphony was audible: not only the sixth-tone formula's
opening scalar third *fga* for the verse text, or its retrograde *agfgf* for the Hebrew letters, but also the upward leap of a third or fourth that begins other
formulae. One way or another, complex music in the Triduum Office was
surrounded by chant. Few sources show the interpenetration of chant and
polyphony better than does US-NYhs 392/278.[45] This codex, written for the
Escorial between 1587 and 1616, contains three L1s, one for each Day, plus
items for Palm Sunday, along with Passions, CFEs, and Misereres. Its Lamentations (one anonymous, two by Martín de Villanueva) mix chant and
polyphony not only inside Lessons but even inside verses, as in F5/L1. For

EXAMPLE 1.2. Chant for F5/L1, J. Sánchez Azpeleta, *Opus harmonicum* (1612).

those many polyphonic Lessons that set fewer verses than any breviary, presumably the "missing" verses should have been sung in chant, as the New York manuscript indicates. If this is the case, presumably there must have been Lesson tones available in any mode in which such polyphonic settings are to be found.

Some generations later, Adriano Banchieri's guide to chant for his Olivetan congregation of monks, the *Direttorio monastico di canto fermo* (Bologna, 1615), supplies a series of formulae, some quite florid, used to set every syntactical possibility (e.g., half sentence, question, full stop) in Lamentations verses. Its title is "Metro alle Lamentationi di Ieremia Propheta, per cantarsi la armonia del primo Tuono autentico, all'uso della corte Romana," or "Formula for the Lamentations of Jeremiah the Prophet, to be sung with settings in the first authentic mode, as used at the court of Rome" (i.e., in Tone 1, on *d*).[46] It seems that multiple tones were known—and used—at the Cappella Sistina into the Seicento.

This also casts doubt on the claims of Giovanni Guidetti that his standardizing but private chant OHS of 1587, the *Cantus ecclesiasticus officii majoris hebdomadae*, reflected Sistine practice.[47] The dedication of the manuscript presentation copy mentions Lamentations as having been sung according to Guidetti's book in Sixtus V's presence in Holy Week 1586/87, but the edition's use of only the sixth-tone formula suggests a one-time event. That the volume used the Pian verse selection of 1568, and not the reduced ones of 1572, shows that its origin was much earlier than its printing. Guidetti included chants for the whole Office: psalm antiphons, psalm-tones, the Lamentations tone with complete texts, Responsories, and even three different polyphonic *falsobordoni* by Palestrina for the Benedictus. However, he never received Papal sanction for the use of his work, printed cheaply enough that the edition seems to have been targeted at relatively poor and perhaps unmusical collegiate or parish churches.

Guidetti's work was later revised by the chapelmaster of the Cappella Giulia, Francisco Soriano, as *Cantus ecclesiasticus officii maioris hebdomadae* (Rome, 1619). The Bavarian Jesuits in Ingolstadt immediately (1620) reprinted the Lessons and Passions from this edition as *Cantus ecclesiasticus . . . lamentationum et lectionum pro tribus matutinis tenebrarum.* The 1620 book was often reissued, circulating widely throughout Catholic central Europe.[48]

VENUES AND REPERTORIES

As anyone who has experienced a liturgical reconstruction of these services knows, a good deal of Tenebrae consists of singing the fifteen psalms and first Lauds canticle to a simple psalm-tone (or polyphonic *falsobordone*)— and it is striking that much of the political and cultural elite of early modern Catholicism spent so much time listening to them, and devoting part of its social surplus to funding their performance. The overwhelming amount of the surviving polyphony sets only certain texts: at Matins, (1) some or all of the Lamentations Lessons for each day, an overall total of nine; (2) some or all of the twenty-seven Responsories over the Triduum; and three possible items at Lauds: (3) the Benedictus, treated as a psalm, antiphonally or in *alternatim* practice; (4) the Miserere, evidently most often sung in polyphony at its repetition at the end of the Hour; and (5) starting about 1550, the CFE. In a few times and places (e.g., seventeenth-century France) some psalm settings were meant for Tenebrae.

The idea of providing a cycle of nine Lessons for the liturgical slots, later followed in cathedral manuscripts, marks a change from sources that can be seen as "repositories of Lamentations," containing neither neat cycles of nine Lessons nor assignments to each Day (e.g., Ottaviano Petrucci's two Lamentations editions of 1506, or manuscripts like FlorBN285 from 1559). Around 1550, a series of Northern European and Italian prints, along with a number of Italian manuscripts, testify to new engagement with Triduum genres and their cycles, the musical starting point for the present study.[49] The early Cinquecento repertory already contains one of the tensions found later in the century: on one hand, Lessons were "open" objects of liturgical use that could be shortened, reworked, rearranged, or even rewritten according to local need or preference. On the other, the reception and practice of Tenebrae polyphony display a tendency toward conservatism if not archaism, rather as if only music with some kind of historical lineage could be used on such important occasions, and these conflicting cultural desires intersected in musical practice.

The meaning of Lesson cycles present particular problems. They usually appear as complete units, and certainly some of the unusual text selections in sixteenth-century cycles invite a narrative reading of all the Lessons together; thus they can be considered as aesthetic objects, social statements, and products of specialized labor. In later works, with a standardized liturgical text, the musical procedures or gestures also suggest some kind of overarching unity. But their actual creation often was fragmented or separated in time, as the evidence of Palestrina's works in RomeSG 59 discussed later seems to indicate. Many institutions seemed to have performed only individual polyphonic Lessons, choosing among their available settings, in any given Week; thus their sonic projection did not necessarily line up with their written presentation.

The first mention of polyphonic Responsories stems from late fifteenth-century Florence, and the earliest surviving cycle by Bernardo Pisano at the city's Duomo dates to around 1520, followed by the first printed ones by Paolo de' Bivi (Aretino) in Arezzo (1544), and a cycle aimed at the Urbino/Pesaro court by G. B. Corvo (1556). Corteccia's set, composed probably in the 1550s for the Medici, appeared more than a decade later.[50] After 1560, Responsories became a better-defined genre, largely in north-central Italy and south Germany, spreading later to Portugal, Naples, and Rome. Although most Benedictus settings come from the sixteenth century, the canticle was also given new music in eighteenth-century Rome, Naples, Venice, and Dresden. The CFE's first surviving appearance in an Office context (it was also used at F5's Mass) is in Tuscan sources, while Tomás Luis de Victoria's famed 1585 *Officium Hebdomadae Sanctae* marks its presence in Rome. The first printed polyphonic OHS in one volume, containing Lessons, Responsories, Passions, canticles, and Misereres, was that of Giovanni Contino (*Threni Jeremiae cum reliquis ad Hebdomadae Sanctae Officium pertinentibus* [Venice: Scotto, 1561]), followed by Paolo Ferrarese's 1565 print with Guidi's dedication.

Although a good part of the musical repertory after 1530 outside Iberia is transmitted in cycles—nine Lessons, nine or eighteen or twenty-seven Responsories—it is clear that not all institutions always featured sung polyphony for each of these Matins items on any given Day. In sixteenth-century Toledo cathedral, only the first Lesson was mandated to be sung in polyphony, and the 1520 customary of Granada suggests the same procedure.[51] The survival of L1s only in the Mexico City choirbooks—echoed by the surviving sources from Valencia into the seventeenth century—suggests that this was more the rule than the exception for pre-1700 Spain and New Spain.[52] The first Iberian manuscripts to transmit a complete cycle of nine Lessons are a copy of Pedro Rimonte's 1607 print in Albarracín, and the Catalan source BarcOC11altre, the latter largely taken from Palestrina's 1588 print with added Lessons by Joan Pujol.[53] Even E-Bbc M.1623, an early seventeenth-century collection of Pujol's Lessons for Barcelona Cathedral, originally contained only L1/3s, with the L2s and even the Prayer added later. Still, an opening polyphonic Lesson conveyed clear sonic messages about the affect of Matins, the aesthetic preferences of a given community, and the abilities of its composer.

By 1580, Triduum polyphony can be documented in much of Italy, the courts of Austria, France, Spain, and Poland, many Iberian cathedrals (and some monasteries), the missions in India, and in the major cathedrals of colonial America. Outside ecclesiastical institutions, dynastic Triduum music highlighted the role of the prince (or princess) as chief penitent in all the Holy Week rites, but also as a musically sophisticated patron/listener. Some of the most unusual Lamentations, in their texts and music, come from various courts over the whole period. The presence of a noble audience for Tenebrae also involved precedence and politics, as Celliero Bonatti, the Mantuan ambassador to Spain, found out the hard way on Holy Wednesday 1604 in Valladolid. While attending the Office in the church of the female Discalced Carmelites, he was physically muscled out of his privileged place behind the Venetian ambassador by the more important Savoyard envoy. Presumably Bonatti was listening to Mateo Romero leading the *Capilla Flamenca* in polyphonic Lessons; the account of the French traveler Barthélemy Joly the same year, but for a different Day, mentions "ravishing" music in the chapel of Valladolid's Royal Palace at Tenebrae.[54]

POLITICS AND IDENTITY

The words of Lamentations had social connotations at such times and places as the Sack of Rome in 1527, or the mutual pillage by Spanish and Dutch forces in the Low Countries after 1565. In the confessionalized world of sixteenth-century Europe, such verses (1:10–11) often set to music as: "The enemy has put his hand to all her desirable things, for he saw those people entering her sanctuary whom You ordered not to enter Your church" would have obvious relevance to the disorder of heresy, the effect of sin, and the destruction of cities.

Jeremiah's book lists the guilt and punishments of Jerusalem's inhabitants. Some exegetes took this as meaning not only those of the historical Jews of the prophet's time or as allegorical prefigurations of the Scribes and Pharisees who handed Christ to Pilate, but rather as all human misdeeds since the Fall. The unchanging "Jerusalem, convertere" refrain meant a penitential call to all Christian inhabitants of the city of God, real or imagined. But especially in the context of Holy Week, the injunction could also be directed to the single religious group physically present in early modern Catholic Europe, identified with the biblical Jerusalem, and subject to well-known conversion attempts during Holy Week and throughout the year: Jewish communities. Such issues revolve largely around the Lamentations, and some Responsories. The projection of the non-Scriptural reproaches of Christ, the *Improperia,* sung during the Friday Adoration of the Cross/Eucharist and set to polyphony a few times, had obvious meaning. The Office repertory should be considered in the whole continuum of Catholic behavior toward Jews in Holy Week, ranging from the largely unsuccessful pacific preaching at them to the actual outbreaks of anti-Jewish ritual violence.[55]

The Jewish convert to Catholicism Giovanni Paolo Eustachio (c. 1530–1602) underscored his former people's "ignoring" of Lamentations in his *Salutari discorsi* of 1582, interpreting the book in a Christological manner. In his manuscript "Discorso sopra le Lamentationi di Geremia," probably intended for his Milanese patron Federigo Borromeo, Eustachio attacked the Jewish view of Jeremiah's text as simply history and not a prophecy of Christ's suffering.[56] He also sought to explain the use of the Hebrew letters as enunciated in the Office Lessons.[57]

In many places, the first polyphony for F6's Tenebrae was the opening verse of L1, "Heth. Cogitavit Dominus dissipare murum filiae Sion," and thus the question of what it might have meant to sing, "The Lord has decided to tear down the wall of the daughter of Zion" at this moment is sharply posed. At least in the late Middle Ages, its resonances were evident from the amount of Christian outbreaks during Holy Week directed quite literally at the walls of ghettos. Some of the early medieval centos that are the Responsories could also suggest Jewish "responsibility." Certainly the worst of them is F6/R5, *Tenebrae factae sunt,* the only Responsory to mention the Crucifixion directly. Its opening goes well beyond the Gospel source (Mt 27:45) by saying that the Jews actually crucified Christ ("Tenebrae factae sunt, dum crucifixissent Jesum Judaei"). Surrounded as it was by R4 and 6 (*Vinea mea electa* and *Animam meam dilectam*), easily interpreted in an anti-Jewish sense, and by Second Nocturne Lessons that point directly at "guilt," the projection of this slur in the Office on Holy Thursday afternoon anticipated the more explicit anti-Judaism of texts in the Cross ceremonies on Friday.

However, other Catholic exegesis and vernacular guides to the Week eschew blaming Jewish agency for the Passion, and hence not every Tenebrae would have carried such meaning. None of the dedications or prefaces to printed Triduum music refers to Jews. In addition, the Lamentations verses after 1600 were largely standardized, and hence the issue of polemical text selection in this repertory was not a matter of choice.[58] Indeed, there is no direct Italian evidence that participants in Tenebrae went forth specifically from the Office to commit anti-Jewish acts. To some degree, the curfew over Italian ghettos, variably from Wednesday night or Thursday afternoon until some point on Saturday, kept Jews out of harm's way for at least two out of the three Days. Rather, the projection of the texts reinforced anti-Jewish aspects of Christian ideology—and self-definition—in the consciousness of listeners.

Despite Vergerio's withering attacks on Tenebrae, Lutheran Lamentations were not inconceivable. The 1591 ordinal of the biconfessional (Lutheran/ Catholic) chapter of Halberstadt Cathedral retained the First Nocturne of Matins with the familiar Lessons, along with a selection of Responsories probably based on local tradition (all in Latin).[59] In the Upper Lusatian city of Zittau, reformed since the early 1520s, the *Lateinisches Gesang-Buch* (Zittau, 1729) preserves a remarkably traditional Tenebrae, mentioned as early as 1564. Matins and Lauds were anticipated and sung at 4 p.m., and, as in Halberstadt, reduced to the equivalent of a single Nocturne plus some Lauds items. F5 had three Lessons of {1: 1–3}; {4: 9, 10, 18}; and {2: 18, 20, 19}, each with their traditional Responsory; the Benedictus and its antiphon; the Kyrie dialogue/trope; a hymn; the CFE and Miserere; and a concluding prayer.[60] The Hours on the other Days employed a similar plan, except in the Lessons selections. The Latin texts probably did not receive polyphonic treatment, as a note from 1690 mandated that only the most senior students in the local Gymnasium would sing the Passions and Lamentations, without aid of others.[61] Although these young men would have been familiar with polyphony, the wording suggests reciting-tones. Zittau's practice stands in sharp contrast to most Lutheran liturgies, in which Triduum Matins/Lauds are not recorded.

THE SOCIAL PRODUCTION OF PASSION COMMEMORATION

The Hours had different cultural meanings according to social rank, time, and place. The preserved polyphonic music implies (in descending order of frequency) the following venues: cathedrals (or basilicas, less so collegiate churches); courts (including the Papal one, or even private households); and monastic foundations. From a professional point of view, in cities with multiple musically active churches or monastic houses, this Office represented one of the occasions for singers to perform and to be paid, one of the few advantageous moments for working musicians, and the frantic copying of sources plus the recruitment of singers just before the Days testify to the need for musical work.[62] The Office called on almost all available singers in any given place, a moment of maximum labor—and remuneration—for the musical workforce. Performers not on the roster of a permanent ensemble needed either to use their mobility to work at different services, or to find a well-paying institution, while more regularly employed musicians knew that special attention would be paid to their performances. The Lauds items suggest musicians' work as improvisation, a further "labor of penance" besides whatever had been sung before. The Week combined the enactment of collective salvation with an important part of musicians' livelihoods and maximum strain on the financial resources of sacred institutions, rather as if all the productive sonic labor of a community was in high demand during the Days.

Not only singers were involved. In many times and places, the musical timbre of the Office reflected the low pitch of the wooden objects used to announce it (in place of the bells) and to end it (the strepitus). Theoretically, instruments of any kind were forbidden during the Triduum. But even printed title pages of some late sixteenth-century Lamentations include the option of using instruments, and certainly the solo-voice repertory from the 1590s onward required some kind of support, to be provided by theorbos, harpsichords, harps, or other chordal instruments. Organs, however, were banned from Wednesday until Saturday. In northern Italy around 1600, a number of important foundations employed string instruments in Lessons, probably for doubling voices, but with the added effect of lowering timbre.[63] Soon thereafter, independent solo instruments were required in Lessons by the Italian monks Giovanni Francesco Capello and Antonio Burlini (1612/14), and the use of obbligato lines was already widespread at this point, certainly at north Italian cathedrals.[64] In the early seventeenth century, solo instruments are found in both Lessons and Responsories from Zaragoza and Seville.[65]

That much of the sixteenth-century repertory is cast in the equal-voice scoring known as *voci pari* and usually set out for lower voices, typically in a C3/C4/C4/F4 clef combination, was in some cases a practical necessity, as with the Lamentations of Waclaw z Szamotuł, written for a Polish court chapel that had no choirboys, only adult men in Lent 1552.[66] But given the ritual occasion, this kind of sonic marking by low timbre seems almost inescapable. The origin or destination of much music in monastic houses, or in the all-male environments of cathedral choirs, might underscore this sense of the repertory's projection by men only. The purely musical evidence for women—essentially nuns or their cloistered students—singing Tenebrae seems, at first glance, late and scattered, and not coincidentally in places where Roman authority was weak: Tuscany, Naples, France.[67]

But still, the fragmentary archival evidence suggests earlier and far more widespread practices in women's foundations. The vicar general of Bologna issued an order for all female houses on Holy Wednesday 1569 that no polyphony be sung in female houses except for the Benedictus and Miserere in *falsobordone*, and that only inside choir space.[68] There are similar curial restrictions or rulings from Naples, and probably other cities as well. Clerical unease with women singing polyphony during these Days clearly relates to the highly charged nature of Triduum Office music, an occasion for "diabolical" intervention to begin with, all the more so when projected by nuns. Besides a certain paucity of archival evidence for the practice, the powerful and dangerous associations of female monastic Tenebrae are also evident in the fact that the two later printed Lamentations editions that do mention nuns—Alessandro della Ciaia's *Lamentazioni* (Venice, 1650), and the "Avertissement" to François Couperin's famed *Leçons de ténèbres* of 1714—do not name the specific houses for which they were written.

The spread of Office polyphony for the Week is a testimony to the musical expression of Passion devotion across the Catholic world. Despite the loss of much repertory, it was extensive; a conservative count arrives at some seven hundred composers who wrote such works between 1430 and 1800, from those with a few surviving Office pieces all the way to those with massive output: Palestrina's three Lamentation sets transmitted as cycles (with a fourth stitched together by Raffaele Casimiri from the materials in RomeSG 59), or the five Holy Week publications of his north Italian contemporary G. M. Asola. Still, composed music was far from predominant, at least at first; the traditional and widespread use of improvised polyphony is underscored by the accounts of Guidi and Alcaraz. The mandating of "canto de órgano" for Lamentations and the Miserere at Lima Cathedral in 1612 may well refer to improvisation; the first surviving Lesson from the church is that of Tomás de Torrejón at the turn of the next century.[69] Many parish churches seemed to have used only chant, while the creation of new recitation tones for Lessons can be traced well into the eighteenth century in Italy.[70]

Some Triduum production was impressive: the thirty-two Lessons (plus preludes and separate settings of the Hebrew letters), nineteen Responsories, four Misereres, one Benedictus, and three Matins psalms composed over thirty years by Marc-Antoine Charpentier in late seventeenth-century Paris; Miguel de Irízar's roughly twenty Lessons for his cathedral of Segovia in the 1670s; or, at a time of changing devotional aesthetics, the sixty-four surviving Lessons (all but one with orchestra) that Francesco Corselli (François Courcelle) created for the Bourbon court in Madrid in the mid-eighteenth century.[71] The Neapolitan repertory includes Lessons and Responsories from around 1600 and through the following two centuries, as Lessons by Pietro Antonio Ziani, Cristoforo Caresana, and Gaetano Veneziano around 1680 were followed by numerous eighteenth-century settings. In the Settecento, Tuscany witnessed both new Lessons (Clari and Giovanni Gualberto Brunetti in Pisa, or the Puccini family in Lucca) and Responsories written by Carlo Antonio Campion, the latter for the Florence Habsburg court.

TIMES AND TIMINGS

In the largest sense, the beginning of the Triduum reenacted a fundamental transition in salvation history. Two late medieval German breviaries followed Beleth's interpretation with the rubric that "the end of Lent is [at the beginning of] Holy Thursday, [this is] the start of the Paschal observance, the conclusion of the Old Law, and the beginning of the New Testament."[72] Thus the first item chanted in F5's Matins, normally the antiphon "Zelus domus tuae comedit me"/"Zeal for Your house has consumed me, and the reproaches of those who reproached You have fallen on me" (Ps 68:10) was the first text heard under the New Law. Timoteo glossed this verse as meaning Christ's love for the Church ("domus"), which brought Him to death.[73] Hence the first Lesson that followed had to be understood as referring not only to Old Testament history but also to the new dispensation of the Gospel. Thus the famed beginning of F5/L1, "Incipit lamentatio Jeremiae prophetae. Aleph. Quomodo sedet sola civitas plena populo"/"Here begins the lamentation of the prophet Jeremiah. Aleph. How the city now sits alone, [once] full of people," would have been the first polyphony heard after this break in soteriological time.

The Triduum and its music could fall anywhere between late March and late April. For much of Europe, this meant around the time of preparing land and sowing seeds, and nutritionally the end of the long winter consumption of leftover staples. Lent was a season of abstinence from meat, and along with its Friday fasts, this meant that performers and audiences alike were engaged in the busy ritual activity while on minimal food consumption. Jerusalem's hungering for bread, and general famine, evoked in many verses of the Lamentations including the musically prominent one cited above ("Omnes populus eius gemens, et quaerens panem," 1:11), had a literal parallel in the bodies of the participants; such references reminded singers and audiences of their own fasting and late-winter lack of food.[74] In times of agricultural crisis, the reference was unavoidable. The physical stress of singing the music and participating in the rituals of the Week while fasting also suggests that many performances were on the edge.

The relative lack of complex music in Lent up to Palm Sunday, and thus a certain amount of free time for musicians, conditioned the times of composition of Office music, squeezed into the weeks or even days immediately before the Triduum. Some Lessons of Szamotuł bear specific dates. The print containing his F5/L1 reads "Kraków, 17 March 1552," four weeks before its presumptive first performance on Holy Wednesday that year.[75] Many dedications of Holy Week prints were signed during Lent, reflecting the increased amount of free time for musicians during the season, along with the sales incentive of having new music out for the Triduum—but also a sense that composing such music was itself a kind of penitential task.[76]

The anticipation of Matins/Lauds to the preceding Day had effects both on the overall ritual rhythm and on the coordination of the Office items, devotionally appropriate to each Day, with the events reenacted. In the overall liturgy of the Week, Monday and Tuesday seem to have featured little or no polyphony; rather, these were days used by singers, in the Papal court at least, to learn and to practice their music for Tenebrae, particularly the Lamentations.[77] The liturgy of Wednesday before the Office was short, with the major event the St. Luke Passion at Mass, rarely set to polyphony. Some Lamentations for the first Day can be quite long, reflecting the greater ritual time available for the music.

The lengthening of the Office gave it greater weight, but also led to practical problems, ranging from singers' reading music in dim churches to the Hours' ending in the alterity and danger of the early modern night. The *Caeremoniale* of 1600 mandated the start at the twenty-first hour after the previous sunset. Depending on the exact date of the Triduum, plus local latitude (and lack of time zones) in Europe, this could mean anywhere between 3:00 p.m. and 4:30 p.m. in modern terms, and there were about three hours to fit it all in before dark. If the service was done in chant only, the approximately three hundred psalm and canticle verses would have taken around an hour, the Lamentations and other Lessons around twenty minutes, and the Responsories another half hour. The Triduum liturgy of the Jesuit missions in Japan—the most experimental of their outposts—mandated a reduction in the number of psalm verses chanted so as to reduce tedium for native converts who would have had no idea what all the Latin meant.[78] Some Renaissance Lamentations take notably more time than chant for the same text, one extreme being Alonso Lobo's SS/L1 in Seville at about twenty minutes, taxing the singers who would have just performed all Friday afternoon during the Adoration of the Cross.

Polyphony often prolonged the projection of Lamentations, even after the sixteenth century. Some Lessons by Charpentier run to almost twenty-five minutes, while in the eighteenth century, each Lamentation of the remarkable cycle of nine, commissioned in 1746 for S. Giacomo degli Spagnoli in Rome to Nicolo Jommelli, Davide Perez, and Francesco Durante, comes in between twenty and twenty-five minutes, more than an hour of Lessons alone per Day. With three such settings, and/or polyphonic Responsories, the total timing would extend close to three hours, and complex music would comprise much of the experience. As the musical weight of the Hours increased, their actual timing could also change. Evidence from early Seicento Naples and late eighteenth-century Rome suggests that Tenebrae could be moved earlier or later so as to accommodate publics—and musicians—who needed to attend the same service at different churches. This arrangement obviously favored Matins, as singers and listeners could leave before Lauds, and go to another church to start the service again.[79] Beyond the actual duration, ritual time inside Tenebrae was marked only by the extinguishing of the candles, the recitation of texts, and the race to finish before nightfall.

Because of the anticipation of the Office, the texts sung often do not match the sequence of historical events on any given Day. The very first narrative reference to the Passion is found in F5's first Responsory, *In monte Oliveti oravi[t] ad Patrem,* sung on Wednesday but having to do with the Agony in the Garden, part of the recalled action of the night between Thursday and Friday, more than twenty-four hours after the text's recitation.[80] The tension between the allegorical/narrative references in the anticipated Office and the re-creation of the Passion became more complex on the two successive days. On Thursday, Tenebrae was crowded up against other music and ritual; in terms of narration, the collective and joyous *recollectio* of the Eucharist at Mass with its other ceremonies preceded the allegorical and narrative references to Good Friday in the Office. Thursday's actions also included the public processions outside the Mass and Office, the objects of much social disciplining.[81] Some of these seemed to have happened during the afternoon and some at night.

The web of action and meaning thickened on Good Friday, the actual moment of the Crucifixion. Besides the Adoration of the Cross with distribution of Communion, processions were almost ubiquitous in Europe and the Americas. Since the Cross ceremony also involved the St. John Passion, musicians would have had a lot to do even before Matins. Friday's Tenebrae began after the enormous emotional charge of previous enactments, and the first Office polyphony was often a Lamentation reading, which seems almost too optimistic for its devotional moment, the immediate aftermath of the Crucifixion: "Heth. Misericordiae Domini, quia non sumus consumpti, quia non deficerunt miserationes eius"/"[It is] the mercy of the Lord that we have not been destroyed, for His compassion has not failed [us]."

This moment of temporary relief in Jeremiah's narrative was followed by Friday's first Responsory, which carries clear reference to Christ the Lamb brought to slaughter: "Sicut ovis ad occisionem ductus est." Because of anticipation, the SS Tenebrae texts, originally chosen for the liminal meditation of Holy Saturday and thus separated from the Passion, were now jammed up against the immediate aftermath of the Crucifixion: the Deposition, the

Lamentation over Christ, and the Entombment, whose reenactments were often being performed in the streets after the end of Tenebrae (or even during it). The final Matins Responsory in most places, *Sepulto Domino,* thus sums up the events of Friday; in early modern understanding, it sealed the ritual "exequies of Christ." Clearly, the character of each Day influenced the tacit dialogue between Lessons and Responsories.

The actions and sounds of the Hours both presented the Passion for internalization (*commemoratio*) and enacted non-sacramental penance in the praxis of a given community. Of the pieces set to complex music, the Responsories had obvious direct application to the events enacted during Holy Week, and thus to personal and collective meditation. The Lamentations in particular, along with the celebratory Benedictus and the penitential Miserere, needed allegorical explanation so as to present the Passion for internal perception. The actions around these items underscore how they were at once social practices and textual/musical genres. Hence the ritual provided a penitential and Passion-related frame of minimal action for the words' projection. To get at contemporary meanings for the texts, it is necessary to engage their literary place and exegetical management.

Chapter 2

✤

Textual Understandings, Musical Expressions

Different voices were present in the Tenebrae texts. The psalms and their antiphons are largely first-person accounts of tribulations not linked to specific biblical events. Jeremiah tells of the destruction of Jerusalem and the sins of the city; the Responsories are written in a variety of grammatical persons and range from allegory to summations of Passion events; the Benedictus is a song of praise to God for having redeemed Israel through the upcoming births of Christ and the Baptist; and the Miserere is a personal recognition of sin and expression of penance with no reference to the Passion. The horrific destruction told in Lamentations verses suggests that such a narrative tone might evoke *compassio* (literally suffering the Passion together with Christ), a problem familiar from late medieval devotional literature.[1] Early modern understandings of all the texts discerned varying literary voice, allegorical complexity, and relevance to meditation or *metanoia*.

LEVELS AND GENRES

The musical procedures at work in Lamentations derive partly from the book's subject and the background of chant, but also from its literary character and narrative voices. In 1588, the Cremonese composer Marc'Antonio Ingegneri formulated such characteristics in the dedications to his two volumes of Lamentations and Responsories (these form an OHS). In the preface to his Lessons, addressed to Abbot Paolo Camillo Sfondrati (1560–1618; still in public grief for the death of his father, Baron Paolo Sfondrati in April 1587), the composer reacted to genre:

> And my lyre turned to mourning [cf. 5:15], and having taken up the
> threnodies and lamentations of Jeremiah, I have sung elegies, dirges,
> and sad songs, or better said, I have wept bitterly. And whenever I

wept, sorrow constricted me in mourning, so that I might weep with some spiritual fruit of my soul, and so, weeping and mourning, I would find some consolation in these very same tears and weeping.[2]

On the other hand, the inscription of his Responsories, signed five days earlier (27 March in mid-Lent), took its occasion from a previous discussion on the origin and use of Office items. Writing to his dedicatee Marc'Antonio Amidano Jr. (1530–98), Ingegneri explained the origins of his print:

I remember that you said this [past] year that . . . Ignatius [of Antioch], near the time of the apostles, ordered that, in praising God, responsories were to be sung by priests in churches in the same form in which the Church represents the celestial hierarchy and angelic melody. And so I, inspired by these discussions, immediately prepared in musical ratios [harmonic intervals] these Responsories, which the Church uses to lament the death of Christ our Lord. Thus I, together with my singers in our basilica [Cremona Cathedral] might be brought to weep, along with the angels who once bitterly mourned the death of Christ our Lord, and with the Church commemorating His terrible death with tears and mourning at its proper time, namely these sad and holy Days; in doing so, I could sing with the angels.[3]

Ingegneri's singers would have performed this music on the cathedral's *cantoria,* able to look out at the massive Passion fresco cycle in the nave (including a *Lamentation* and images of prophets) that Giovanni Antonio da Pordenone and others had painted two generations earlier.[4] Its *gravitas* sets it apart among early Cinquecento depictions of the Passion, as it demarcated the Church of the New Testament from the Synagogue of the Old, possibly also reflecting local conflicts with the Jewish community.[5]

Such perceived differences between Lamentations and Responsories resonate with Durandus and Guidi. Although both forms have to do with weeping, Lamentations were affective elegies or dirges, to have immediate emotional impact upon listeners, but also written in the highest literary register. They were in prophetic "tone" and thus lamented the past while foreshadowing the future: both the two later destructions of Jerusalem (70 and 135 CE) and allegorically the Passion. Insofar as Zacharias was viewed as prophesying, and David also was a prophet, the Benedictus and Miserere shared this "tone." On the other hand, Responsories were angelic melodies sung by the Church, in this case as a direct commemoration of the death of Christ. They were largely in collective tone, and, unlike the joy that they represented on most feasts, at Tenebrae they voiced angelic and corporate mourning.

Beyond the issue of ritual genre, exegetical traditions and innovations conditioned meaning. Early modern interpretations of Lamentations drew on a long medieval tradition, sometimes mentioning the ninth-century commentary of Pascasius Radbertus (first printed in 1503). Other early explications circulating in print include those of (pseudo-)Bonaventure, Aquinas, and Denys the Carthusian. Most, such as Denys's, alternated a literal guide with some kind of anagogic, spiritual, or mystical interpretation for the verses. Multiple allegorical levels continued into early modern times, suggesting that any given Lamentations verse could have had diverse meanings for singers, composers, and listeners. Musical settings would certainly have resonated with exegesis for learned musicians and publics: cathedral canons, prelates, monks, but also well-educated nuns.

One major source for understanding Jeremiah was the *Glossa ordinaria;* it was reprinted in Venice as late as 1603.[6] This collection of medieval commentaries and interlinear glosses was used by early modern Jesuits for their understanding of Scriptural images.[7] The definitive version of the *Glossa* on Lamentations is owed to Gilbert the Universal (twelfth century), and contains several aspects important for understanding later musical settings.[8] Gilbert synthesized Radbertus's ideas, but added important *loci* (topics) and rhetorical terms to his comments. In a Ciceronian vein, he also differentiated between verses of complaint (*conquestio*) and those of anger (*indignatio*).[9] Complaint raises pity in listeners, based on their own experience of misfortune; literally, in the case of Jerusalem and Jeremiah's disgrace, or tropologically in the piteous state of the human soul affected by sin. Anger denounces the misdeeds that led to such a condition; in Lamentations, the sins of Jerusalem and its (false) prophets, but also universal human evil seen allegorically. This distinction within Jeremiah's text seems to have had effect; three of Cristóbal de Morales's most widely circulated Lessons, for which no breviary or previous polyphonic source has been found, each begin with verses that Gilbert considered to embody *topoi,* two of anger and one of complaint.[10]

For all the medieval legacy, early modern interpretations were not long in arriving. A wave of new commentaries on Lamentations began about 1580 and circulated widely, including the Portuguese Jeronymite Heitor Pinto's *In Danielem, Lamentationes . . . Commentarii* (Venice, 1583); the Augustinian Pedro de Figueiro's *Commentarii in Lamentationes* (Paris, 1596); and the Theatine (living in Cremona from 1579 and hence probably known by Ingegneri) Antonio Agelli's (1532–1608) *In Lamentationes . . . Commentarium* (Rome, 1589). Figueiro's influence was clear in Francisco de Quevedo's unpublished paraphrase of Jeremiah's text, the poet's *Lágrimas de Hieremías Castellanas* (1609–12).[11] Given the polyphonic traditions at his monastery of Santa Cruz in Coimbra, the exegete would have heard polyphonic Lamentations and Responsories every year in settings by his fellow Augustinian Pedro de Cristo.[12] Another commentary, that of the Évora cathedral canon Sebastião da Costa de Andrade, specifically discussed the use of the book in the Tenebrae Office as well as the meaning of the Hebrew letters, using Durandus to explain the symbolism of Matins and the ways in which Jeremiah's text intersected with the ritual.[13] Andrade would have heard the choir of his cathedral, under Manuel Mendes or Manuel Rebello, singing Lamentations every Triduum (although no settings by either choirmaster survive), and he worked in the same place as Manuel do Valle de Moura.

Many seventeenth-century explications were owed to Jesuits: Martin del Río's *Commentarium litteralis in Threnos* (Lyon, 1608); Cristóbal de Castro's *Commentarii in Jeremiae Prophetias, Lamentationes . . .* (Paris, 1609); Gaspar Sánchez's *In Jeremiam Prophetam Commentarii . . . Paraphrasis item poëtica ad Threnos* (Lyon, 1617; this also contains a Latin paraphrase of the book), and the tome of the great synthesizing biblical exegete working first in the Low Countries and then at the Jesuit Collegio Romano (1616–37), Cornelius a Lapide's *Commentarius in Jeremiam Prophetam, Threnos . . .* (Antwerp, 1621, with many later editions). Lapide's works would continue to be the standard for European exegesis into the eighteenth century, known even by the opera and oratorio librettist Apostolo Zeno (1688–1750). The Jesuits' advocacy of Ciceronian rhetoric suggests that Lamentations' reliance on complaint and anger made it an ideal text for them. Their involvement with the book echoes the order's tendency to sing Lamentations outside of the Triduum Office; possibly the kinds of weeping evoked by Jeremiah resonated with the Society's emphasis on tears in penance.

Of all these books, clearly Lapide's had the widest diffusion; given the author's link to demonology, del Río's also should be considered, and in light of its possible link to Ingegneri's OHS, Agelli's stemmed from a place that was renewing its Triduum repertory. None of the commentaries mention chant or polyphony, nor do any of the Lamentations settings seem to be musical realizations of any single exegetic plan. But their articulation of the book's character, their identification of rhetorical tone, and their allegorical/moral meanings for any given verse, all help clarify the associations of the often obscure words.

The first chapter begins with the prophet's shock at the vision of the desolated city, destroyed for its sins; it features halfway through (1:11) Jerusalem's own voice of misery in a moment of first-person *conquestio*. Chapter 2, in third person, starts with God's preparation and execution of wrath at Jerusalem's sins, and then passes to the devastating effect on the city: the destroyed walls, the elderly and virgins groaning in sackcloth, and the death of children. At 2:13, Jerusalem herself reiterates her desolation ("posuit me desolatam"), and the chapter ends with another call to penance mixed with the city's destruction at the hands of the enemy.

The tone of chapter 3 contrasts sharply with the rest of the book; largely in first-person prophetic voice, it opens with Jeremiah's personal state ("Ego vir videns pauperitatem meam in virga indignationis eius"/"I am the man who sees my poverty in the rod of His indignation"). Through an obscure vocabulary taken as symbols of penance (the "wormwood and bile" of 3:19), the chapter turns to a moment of hope. Thus a middle section in first-person plural adumbrates Divine clemency ("Heth. Misericordiae Domini . . . "/"It is the mercy of the Lord that we have not been consumed," 3:22). But the chapter closes with a section again on His wrath ("You acted in furor," 3:43ff), followed by a prophetic final plea to take vengeance and to punish evildoers. In yet another shift, chapter 4 is an exhaustive and gruesome account, largely in third person, of all the city's ruin, leading up to its utter depravity; this chapter is the only one to mention a savior trapped by human sin (4:20, "Spiritus oris nostri, christus dominus, captus est in peccatis nostris"/"The breath of our mouth, our lord the Christ, has been taken in our sins"). Finally, the *Oratio,* entirely in first-person plural, is a summary of Jerusalem's misdeeds and ruin, with a final (but unanswered) plea for mercy.

Some of the thematic shifts in the text correspond to common (and universal, after 1600) openings of Lessons set to music (2:8, 2:13, 3:1, 3:22, 4:1). To take only typical selections, F5/L1 {1:1–5} starts with the city's desolation and ends with the enslavement of children; L2 {1:6–9} goes from the description of Jerusalem's despoiled beauty to a first-person plea to God; and L3 {1:10–14} starts with the enemy's depredations, changes to another first-person deprecation ("Vide, Domine"), and finishes with the utter captivity and powerlessness of the city. Others are more problematic: the standard version of SS/L1 {3:22–30}, the first text heard in polyphony after the Adoration of the Cross, starts with its moment of hope, then passes to a set of hortatory maxims ("Bonus est Dominus sperantibus in eum"/"The Lord is good to those who hope in Him"). Technically, these are an example of wisdom *paraenesis* (admonitory listing). The Lesson closes with three verses about individual suffering taken as referring to the Passion ("Sedebit solitarius et tacebit"/"He shall sit alone and be silent" . . . "dabit percutienti se maxillam, saturabitur opprobriis"/"he shall give his cheek to those who strike him, he shall be filled with reproaches"). The end of the Prayer (5:11), normally the last Lamentations verses heard in complex polyphony, had special weight in its reference to the sexual humiliation of Jerusalem's women. Most exegetes (except Lapide) gave it a brief but literal explication, a few referring to Jerome's symbolic interpretation of the verse as the "violation" of the sinning soul.[14] In any case, it marked a somber (and not clearly Passion-related) end to musical Lessons.

The shifts of voice and theme inside any Day's Lessons presented challenges and opportunities for musical settings, especially cycles. Each set involved both third-person description of the city's ruin—allegorically, the destruc-

tion wrought by sin on the human condition, necessitating the Passion—as
well as first-person complaint, the gruesome experience of Christ's, Jeremiah's,
or Jerusalem's suffering. The SS Lessons alone range from paraenetic advice (L1) to urban misery (L2) to collective humiliation (L3). If the misery
described represents sin from which *metanoia* turns away, the "Jerusalem"
refrain caps them by its call to alignment with God ("convertere," or *epis-
trefein*).

LAMENTATIONS: VOICE AND VERSE

One specifically early modern aspect of the new commentaries has to
do with the book's genre and its rhetorical structure.[15] From Pinto onward,
exegetes considered Lamentations as a *carmen* (ritual song), with the incantatory associations of the classical term, including its ancient meaning as
rhythmic prose and not exactly poetry; Jerome himself had referred to the
"quasi-Sapphic" meter of the first two chapters.[16] This idea of the imperceptible but essential metric construction of the book continued as late as the
Della perfetta poesia italiana (1706) of the modernizing Italian critic and liturgist Ludovico Muratori.[17] This has some important musical implications.
The compositional procedures involved are those suitable to verse, e.g., the
complex text/music interactions typical of the madrigal. And some settings
might be considered as attempts to recover the original meter, thus entail-
ing consideration of mensuration and large-scale phrasing in such Lessons.

A second point is the literary register. In his opening words, Lapide made
the widest claims for the book by citing Radbertus and by viewing Lamentations as the dialectical opposite of another important Old Testament volume.
Here Jeremiah's text pushed beyond the extremes of classical literature, as
the exegete viewed the prophet as possessed by tragic *furor:*

> Lamentations are the single part of all Scripture most laden with af-
> fect and pathos . . . Pascasius considers that this sad song [*carmen*] of
> Jeremiah could be called "The Lamentations of Lamentations," just
> as Solomon's joyous epithalamium is called "The Song of Songs";
> just as nothing more joyful can be found than the latter, so nothing
> sadder than the former [exists] in all Scripture and profane literature;
> compared with [Lamentations], the tragedies of Seneca and others
> seem like mere shadows, poetic games written with rhetorical art. For
> in [the book] there speaks and groans, not art but rather the Divine
> Spirit itself, which took over Jeremiah completely, so that he might
> bewail the destruction of his nation—the people of God—with un-
> speakable moaning.[18]

A third aspect is the singer. Del Río and Lapide continued the medieval identification of Jeremiah as a prefiguration of Christ: both were sanctified in the womb, preached, wept over Jerusalem (Lk 19:41), and were eventually put to death.[19] Thus the prophet's words were also the Savior's, which underscores the book's dual role as history and prophecy.

The high literary level of the text made it a showcase for Cinquecento composers displaying new compositional strategies. Versions presented as testing grounds include the five-voice Lessons of Nicola Vicentino (all lost except for the "Jerusalem, convertere" section given in his treatise *L'antica musica ridotta alla moderna prattica;* the scoring is unusually ample for Italy c. 1550) using the chromatic genus. Vincenzo Galilei's monodic setting of "sections" of the Lamentations and Responsories was probably performed in a domestic context in the 1580s. This must have been the same music with only one line sung (and the rest on instruments?), described by the composer in a Lenten letter to Guglielmo Gonzaga of Mantua as "not lacking that affect which the praying prophet Jeremiah attempted to induce in his listeners as he lamented." Galilei asked the musical prince to hear it in or out of Holy Week, another indication of non-liturgical Lamentations in court situations, and a further sign of their highly charged emotion (*musica reservata*).[20]

The multiple hidden meanings of the book, explicated in different ways by the medieval commentaries, are best summarized by the Jesuit exegetes, as del Río offered the clearest statement of four levels of textual meaning. For him, the literal sense was both historical (the Babylonian Captivity) and prophetic (the later destructions of Jerusalem); the allegorical level referred to the persecution and oppression of the Church over time; the tropological meaning outlined the state of the sinning soul, ravaged like the destroyed city; and anagogic understanding treated the future state of the damned as symbolized by Jeremiah's description of Jerusalem.[21]

The rhetorical structure of the individual verses might have been clear to any attentive reader, but again del Río, concerned as he was with poetic procedure, put it in the most systematic way. Commenting on 1:2 ("Beth. Plorans plorabit in nocte, et lachrymae eius in maxillis eius; non est qui consoletur eam ex omnibus caris ejus; omnes amici eius spreverunt eam, et facti sunt ei inimici"/"Weeping, she [Jerusalem] cried in the night, with her tears on her cheeks; there is no one from among her lovers to console her; all her friends scorned her and have become her enemies"), the Jesuit noted that the passage from bad to worst in this and other verses was a tripartite heightening over the three sub-verses ("Plorans . . . non est . . . omnes amici eius").[22] Although this may seem simply like anaphora, del Río used the technical term *gradatio,* even if the Lamentations verses do not employ the classical technique, associated with this category, of word repetition among the parts of the rhetorical structure. Evidently he simply meant as an internal structure of intensification, with most if not all the twenty-two verses of chapters 1–2 being tripartite and thus displaying a double heightening. This ternary structure is also shared by the twenty-two groups of three one-sentence verses of chapter 3; each group is thus analogous to one verse in the preceding chapters. In contrast, the bipartite verses of chapters 4–5—often used for SS/L2 and 3—make their effect in a shorter span of rhetorical time and with greater contrast (e.g., 4:1, "[a] Quomodo obscuratum est aurum, mutatus est color optimus; [b] dispersi sunt lapides sanctuarii in capite omnium platearum"/"[a] How the gold has darkened, and the finest color changed; [b] the stones of the sanctuary are scattered at the top of all the streets").

Semantic word-tone connections also occur in those verses that suggested the physical and spiritual surroundings of the ritual itself: the darkness of "Denigrata est super carbones facies eorum" (4:8, "Their looks have been blackened beyond charcoal"), or 3:6, "In tenebrosis collocavit me" ("He has placed me in darkness"). In graphic symbolism evident at least to singers reading or memorizing the music—but also to musically informed listeners—such passages were sometimes set to "black" notation (ternary rhythms or meters reduced to binary, with empty note-heads filled in). One example among many is the "Aleph. Quoniam obscuratum est aurum" verse of Tiburzio Massaino's SS/L2 (Venice, 1599). This is written entirely in black notation in all voices except for its first and last words "Quoniam . . . platearum." Other settings of the passage by de Monte, Joan Pujol (E-Bbc, M. 1623), Pedro Rimonte (Brussels, 1607), Antonio Burlini (Venice, 1614), and Antonio Mogavero (Venice, 1623) employ the same symbolism. Outside of Lamentations, the dark opening of Mauro Chiaula's F6/R5 (Venice, 1597), *Tenebrae factae sunt,* referring to the shadows at the Crucifixion, is in literally signifying *color.*

SPECIAL LESSONS

The sacrality of the Latin and the letters in Lamentations was evident throughout the period. But given the intense engagement of Italian circles with vernacular Scripture in the mid-sixteenth century, the reference in a letter of Antonfrancesco Grazzini to Lessons sung "in volgare" by Carlo Lenzoni and Corteccia—the former the vernacular paraphrase, the latter the music—in March 1544 in the circles of the Florentine Academy, is no surprise.[23] Still, the rarity of the experiment is evident in that Corteccia set and published the other Office items—not the Lamentations—in Latin in his *Responsoria omnia,* while the vernacular Lessons have disappeared. Nor is there any trace of Lenzoni's text among his surviving writings, possibly another effect of Roman censorship.[24]

The only surviving polyphonic Lamentations in the vernacular, anywhere in Europe, came from late seventeenth-century Spain, all the more surprising given the strict prohibition of Bible translations in southern Europe, but probably reflecting the sometimes oral literary tradition of *lamentaciones en romance*. This term refers to the practice of singing verses from Lamentations in the vernacular, often in standard octosyllabic poetic meter (see chapter 5). In Catalonia, the Benedictine monk Jaime Vidal (1606–89, active at Montserrat and elsewhere) cast a Castilian version of F5/L1 as a simple strophic *tono* for four high voices, again possibly for female monastic performance or even contemplation: "Ay! Como está ya la ciudad / de la gran Jerusalén sola, y llora de pesares"/"Ah, how the great city of Jerusalem is alone, and weeps from its burdens."[25] Its concluding *estribillo* is a reworking of the "Jerusalem" refrain. Similarly, Miguel Gómez Camargo set a Latin title ("De lamentatione"), no letter, and then what must be a paraphrase recalling 1:6 ("De mis nobles Dios irado hizo justicia severa"/"God, enraged, carried out severe justice on my nobles") for eight voices and harp continuo, probably during his time as chapelmaster at Valladolid Cathedral before 1680.[26] Outside Holy Week, a public devotional event in Lima on 16 October 1630 also heard a "lamentación en romance," evidently in a Eucharistic context.[27] The scattered evidence from cathedral archives points to formal use of these vernacular pieces, and to improvisatory freedom with the texts, sung to the highly formulaic *tonos*. A similar piece, "¡Ay, misera de ti, Jerusalén!"comes out of this tradition, and its dramatic use is discussed in chapter 5.

Beyond the normative structure and tone of verses from chapters 1–4, in almost all the Lamentations cycles and settings the *Oratio* had a privileged place; as noted, it was often was sung to its own tone. As the last reading of SS's First Nocturne, written throughout in first-person plural, its collective voice brought together the woes of Jerusalem and pled for mercy; it also had its own title: "Incipit oratio Jeremiae Prophetae." From Radbertus to Lapide, it was viewed as the *peroratio*, both the "Prayer of Prayers" and the rhetorical summation of the book.[28] Even Orazio Vecchi's 1587 simple Lamentations, set in recitational and strophic *falsobordone* throughout, provided a through-composed setting of the text. For the Franciscan preacher in Tuscany Gieremia Bucchio, writing a commentary on the *Oratio* and the Benedictus in 1573, chapter 1 of Lamentations was the prophet's lament over the city of Jerusalem; 2, another for the kingdom of Israel; 3, his tears over the people of God; 4, his fear and pain for the Temple; and 5, his prayer on behalf of all God's people.[29] Bucchio's preface to his treatise explained the *Oratio* as a model for mental prayer, noting also that singing it led to greater attention to the words than did reading it. Thus it was uniquely appropriate to court settings, as early modern rulers could enunciate penance for their subjects as summarized and musically projected by the Prayer. The treatise, dedicated to Ferdinando de' Medici, thus reflects the family's deeply musical Triduum devotion.

Eventually, the Lamentations verses were not the only ones set to complex music. In late seventeenth-century Naples, some Lessons from Augustine in the Second Nocturne of Matins (L4–6) and those of Nocturne Three from Paul (L7–9) were composed in florid and contemporary style, quite different from the single-pitch reciting formula to which they were traditionally sung. These texts are homiletic and theological, and thus far from Jeremiah's poetry. These new Lessons for Naples were done in the liturgy on the Days closest to the Crucifixion, F6 and SS, and the first ones locally were written by Gaetano Veneziano between 1694 and 1696, although there are individual examples in Portugal earlier.[30] Such items can later be found throughout the Settecento in Naples, later in Venice, Portugal, and Brazil.

Of these musically unusual Lessons, the most disturbing is F6/L6, set locally over a century from Veneziano to Giovanni Paisiello in the late Settecento. F6/L4 deals with Christ's human sacrifice, but L5 focuses the accusation by mentioning the "guilt" of the Jews. L6's text is Augustine's meditation on responsibility for the Crucifixion, and it begins and ends by blaming them directly for the Passion.[31] The saint's relationship with Judaism was complex, to be sure. But this Lesson followed directly on the hyperbolic condemnation of the Jews at the opening of the preceding R5, "dum crucifixissent Jesum Judaei." Given the physical absence of Jews in early modern Naples after their expulsion in 1541 (except for 1740–47), the slur seems to be another case, not of calls to direct anti-Jewish action, but of Christian self-identification through blame of the religious Other. Sadly, this seems to be a wider reflection of eighteenth-century anti-Judaism.

LETTERS AND THEIR MEANINGS

As noted, Hebrew Lamentations consist of sequential verses, each beginning with a word whose first letter follows the twenty-two-letter sequence of the alphabet. Jerome's Vulgate translation included the original letter at the beginning of each verse, but made no other effort to follow the plan. The text of Psalm 118 is organized in a similar way, and, commenting on the Psalm in his *Epistola XXX ad Paulam,* the saint provided complete Latin words, arbitrarily chosen, as equivalent to the letters. He also organized these equivalents into syntactical "connections." Thus the first four letters of the acrostic, "Aleph" (Latin "doctrina"), "Beth" ("domus"), "Gimel" ("plenitudo"), and "Deleth" ("tabularum") were interpreted as "The doctrine of the church, which is the house of God, is found in the fullness of the Divine books (= Scripture)."[32]

Following Jerome, early modern commentators also adumbrated meanings for the alphabet in Jeremiah's book, thus taking on allegorical or moral charge. Jerome's "connections" were repeated for the opening letters of Lamentations verses by the liturgist Timoteo and in Andrade's discussion of the letters just after his explication of Tenebrae. Timoteo's summary reappeared in the largest Italian compendium of earthly phenomena as symbolic figures, Antonio Ricciardi's *Commentaria symbolica* (Venice, 1591).[33] Although this book is best known as a source for the imagery of the *Dicerie sacre* of Giambattista Marino, it provided sacred meanings for many objects, including an explication of alphabets as sequences of symbols.

The letters are repeated over the course of the first four chapters. This quadruple reiteration was taken by Pinto as representing the sins of all four directions of the globe, to which he added a long series of the universal aspects of "four" as the first non-prime number, one with biblical resonance.[34] Pinto's explanation and Ricciardi's tome stand in the tradition of Neoplatonic explications of material phenomena, a late monument to medieval abstraction. To judge from the non-musical evidence, the disappearance of symbolic alphabets around 1600 marked both a crisis in the allegorical representation of reality—as early modern Catholicism turned toward graphic representation of spiritual truth (Federico Barocci, the Carracci, and Caravaggio)—and a decisive move away from medieval meditation.[35]

Yet the emphasis given to the letters in music after 1600 belies the idea of their hermeneutic withering. As late as 1726, the Spanish Benedictine critic Benito Feijóo would refer to them as an "alphabet of penance" as he attacked modern and unsuitable settings of Lessons in his *La música de los templos*. Independent musical sections for individual letters, separate from their verses, are first found in a manuscript copied for Rome in 1600, the only source for Emilio de' Cavalieri's Lessons and Responsories, together with alternate settings of individual verses to be placed inside other Lessons.[36] Such separate letters are also present in an early seventeenth-century French manuscript, in the Newberry choirbooks from a Conceptionist female monastery in Mexico City, and then in works by Charpentier probably for Parisian nuns around 1680, and by Jan Dismas Zelenka at the Dresden court in the 1720s.[37]

The musical lability of the letters should not be considered as a sign of their syntactic meaninglessness, as the amount of time and energy spent on the polyphonic projection of the letters frames their performance as signifiers for contrition in the Passion allegory of the texts and as moments in the ritual of collective penance. In a wider sense, the musically extended letters and titles ("De lamentatione") provide another example of the growth of the paratext in early modern culture, here one embedded inside the ritual text itself.[38] The letters themselves served not only in this capacity but as meditative moments in the rhetorical progression of each Lesson. And the polyphonic unification of titles, letters, and refrain provides these paratextual elements with a remarkable musical charge.

HEARING VOICES, HEARING VERSES

One verse noted above provides a sample of how polyphony could articulate the sub-verses. The second verse of F5/L3 is 1:11: "Caph. [a] Omnis populus eius gemens et quaerens panem; [b] dederunt praetiosa quaeque pro cibo ad refocillandam animam. [c] 'Vide, Domine, et considera, quoniam facta sum vilis.'" The most obvious heightening in this verse is the change of speaker between [b] and [c], as the third-person objective account of hunger turns to Jerusalem herself speaking in affective humiliation. But del Río's *gradatio* from [a] to [b] is clear, as the city goes from simply "seeking bread" to "giving all precious things for food." In Ciceronian/Gilbertian terms, the verse is a double complaint (*conquestio*), in which first the prophet, then the city, depicts the sad situation.

The early modern commentators reacted to the verse in individual ways. Agelli considered Jerusalem as close to death from hunger, condemned by all, while del Río emphasized the change in speaker, considering Jerusalem's words to be a miniature "oratio" foreshadowing chapter 5.[39] In a moralizing vein, Lapide turned the "hunger" of the verse into a condemnation of gluttony, which led sinners even to sell their souls to the devil, and underscoring the utterly degraded state ("vilis"), like that of a worthless servant, to which the city had descended.[40]

This verse also prepares the following 1:12, the emblematic "Lamed. O vos omnes qui transitis per viam . . ." ("O all of you who pass along the way, listen and see if there is any suffering like unto my suffering"), taken as the central personal utterance of Jeremiah. Bernardino Zacchetti's Michelangelesque 1517 fresco of the prophet, in the Benedictine church of S. Sisto in Piacenza, used this verse as its motto (see the dust jacket of this book). But because of its emphasis on personal suffering, 1:12 could easily be heard in the mouths of Christ and of Mary, especially given its use as the opening of SS/R5, sung on Good Friday. Lapide's comments took this triple possibility of speakers (Jeremiah, Christ and Mary) as a cultural given.[41]

Musical projections of 1:11 in the late sixteenth century can be compared with exegesis in settings from cycles by Palestrina (1570s/80s), Lasso (c.1570–80), and Cavalieri (Florence/Rome, in the 1590s; examples 2.1–2.3).[42] Since the three composers were laymen, their settings highlight the understanding of those who presumably would have had less exposure to the technical literature of commentaries. Palestrina set the letters at length, referring to the sixth-tone chant formula in his melodic material for the first letter and verse of this Lesson, "Jod" and "Manum suum." Separated from the verses on either side by a bar-line, but tonally connected to its following verse, "Caph" of 1:11 occupies eleven semibreves (beat units), cycling through a cadential figure heard four times, the first two as half-cadences (*cadenze fuggite*), rather as if the letter were introducing a textual unit without ultimate stability (example 2.1). Palestrina allotted sub-verses [a] and [b] to one musical section, scored for the somber timbre of the four lowest voices, with a half-break (*cadenza in mi*) at the juncture between [a] and [b]. Reminiscent of the composer's litany settings, this section is essentially the repetition of a single melodic cell (G-A-B♭ for "gemens") in the top line, repeated in the next subverse with only the most minimal heightening (B♭ raised to B♮ at "dederunt") in [b].[43] The text comes across economically, with eleven semibreves for the fourteen syllables of [a] and fourteen for the twenty-one syllables of [b].

The major event of Palestrina's verse is the full cadence on the *finalis* after [b], and the separate section for the voice of Jerusalem in [c], a sonic switchover to the three highest voices of the ensemble.[44] Thus [11c] not only sounds high but also begins and ends with the "Phrygian" E-F motion in the cantus, an aural signal of the penitential associations of that mode. Its metric declamation is extended by the repeat of "quoniam facta sum vilis" to such an extent that the beat units (breves) coincide with the number of syllables (eighteen) in [c]. A series of audible gestures takes the verse in del Río's sense—the overwhelming priority of [c]—giving both timbral and pitch signals for the switch of literary voice.

Another example comes from Munich. Unlike his printed five-voice Lamentations, Lasso's four-voice cycle, scored for a low equal-voice (*voci pari*) ensemble, seems to have been kept private for his Wittelsbach patrons, also due to its *musica reservata*-like and madrigalian approach to the text.[45] Since this cycle follows the 1568 Pian breviary and not the readings of the 1570s, "Caph" here is the last verse of F5/L2. Lasso's F5 Lessons are in Mode 6, and this one makes audible use of the Lamentations tone at its beginning, as the bass part of "Caph" is literally the sixth-tone chant for letters, up a fifth (*edcdc*), while above this the voices enter so closely that any sense of overall meter is eroded.

Starting with homophonic declamation and unusual gestures (downward leaps and surprising voice-leading) to set the sighs of "gemens," Lasso also downplayed the [a]/[b] break as had Palestrina, but did so by setting up an expected cadence on F for the end of [11a], which is then deflected and

EXAMPLE 2.1. Palestrina, "Book III," F5/L3, "Caph. Omnes populus."

arrives at its pitch goal only well into [b] (example 2.2). The new sub-verse immediately moves from flat (*mollis*) to natural (*durus*) sonorities, and its cadence features more anomalous voice-leading. At [c], the change of literary voice is marked by a halt in the rhythmic motion contrasting with the sub-verse's following climax, "quoniam facta sum vilis," the latter introduced by cascading entrances of the velar approximant "quo-" on four successive

EXAMPLE 2.1. (*Continued*)

minims. Rather than repeating the irregularities heard at the previous "ge-mens," Lasso then moved the pitch content back to *mollis* territory and again slowed the declamation in order to demarcate "facta sum vilis." More subtly, he imposed musical order on the differing syllable counts of the sub-verses by casting each in eight-tactus units. He thus created an equivalent in musical periods to the exegetical perception of the sub-verses as each representing a poetic line of the Hebrew. Overall, Lasso's music seems to employ methods appropriate to a *carmen*.

At the end of the century, Cavalieri's L3 from his first cycle of Lamentations presents a widely varied pace of text declamation, solos and tutti repeats: a striking and seemingly radical sound in Roman Tenebrae around 1600.[46] But a closer look complicates the picture. Despite its putative Florentine origins, the preserved version sets only the three verses {10–12} typical of Roman polyphony for this Lesson. In his 1:11, Cavalieri also quotes a

EXAMPLE 2.2. Lasso, F5/L3 *a 4,* "Caph. Omnes populus."

version of the standard five-pitch chant formula for "Caph"; this is also the first moment in the whole Lesson at which all five voices are heard, a dramatic gesture followed by the choral repeat of "Omnis populus eius" (example 2.3). Perhaps constricted by the phrase repetition, he introduced a major break (a full cadence on the distant pitch center C) between the sub-verses [a] and [b], followed by fast declamation for "ad refocillandam animam." There is a cadence but no silence before [c], and the full texture continues; thus the sonic change to Jerusalem's voice is not immediately audible. It is evident only in the closing passage, in which the ensemble ends on the *finalis* A, but prematurely at "facta sum," and it is left to the lower voices, in the lower part of their register, to enunciate the full clause including "vilis" in the different technique of *fauxbourdon* (not *falsobordone*), ending back on C. The demarcation is thus at the level of the individual word, not the sub-verse. Perhaps the 6/3 sonorities of *fauxbourdon,* whose use had been condemned by the theorist Gioseffo Zarlino as "non lodevole," were meant by Cavalieri to represent "vilis" directly.[47]

Cavalieri's solo/tutti contrasts and vocal entries presage the gestures of concertato madrigals. In the fast recitation of this Lesson, the large-scale metric units of earlier settings have given way to smaller, word-generated rhythms, and the [b]/[c] break has been overrun in favor of the dramatic effect of the verse's end. The theatricality of the Lesson's close gives some idea of Florentine music as imported to Rome. Heard in exegetical terms, all the laymen in general reacted in different, but internally logical, ways to the threefold overall structure of the verse and especially to the change of voice and extremity of affect in Jerusalem's words, the fault lines of prophetic discourse projected in the music of various stylistic bent. Evidently, some kind of common cultural understanding undergirded these different compositional approaches.

RESPONSORIES, CANTICLES, PSALMS

The constantly changing voice among and within Responsories shows some of the same issues as do Lamentations verses. The almost universal first one of F5, *In monte Oliveti,* provided the mental picture of the Agony in the Garden, the opening of the Passion events:

> On the Mount of Olives, [Jesus (or "I")] prayed to the Father: "Father, if it can happen, let this chalice pass from me. * The spirit is willing but the flesh is weak. But let Your will be done. V. Watch and pray, that you may not enter into temptation."[48]

The transmission of the final sentence in the repetendum, "Fiat voluntas tua"/"Let Your will be done," shows the power of oral tradition. Of an-

EXAMPLE 2.3. Cavalieri, F5/L3, "Caph. Omnes populus."

EXAMPLE 2.3. (*Continued*)

cient origin, it was deleted from the Roman breviary by Urban VIII's 1632 edition, but continued to figure in music north and south.[49] The phrase remained in most Italian settings in the seventeenth century, even the popular and canonical Roman pieces by Bonifazio Graziani (1663), possibly for the church of the Gesù. F. A. Calegari's Responsories dated 18 March 1705 for Padua (in I-Bc) show the phrase first composed, then later crossed out.[50] In Naples, it appears in the cycle attributed to Alessandro Scarlatti (in I-Baf) and was largely retained throughout the Settecento, in sets by Gennaro Manna (1741), Nicola Sala, and Pasquale Cafaro. In Tuscany, Carlo Campion's dramatic Responsories from around 1760 also keep it.[51] North of the Alps, the phrase is almost universal, found in D-Mbs Mus. Ms. 74 of 1654, the Responsories by Stefano Limido copied at the Escorial in 1669, the cycles by Andreas Hofer and J. K. Kerll (in CZ-KR and A-Wm), the incomplete Responsory set by Charpentier, and as late as Michael Haydn's cycle for Salzburg in 1778.[52] In part, this can be explained by its retention in the universal Benedictine breviary adopted by all congregations after 1614.[53]

The exceptions—i.e. musical settings in which "Fiat" was dropped—thus stand out: Erasmo de' Bartoli's double-choir Responsory cycle, probably for the Oratorians of Naples, from c.1640; two Iberian settings, that of Ferdinando de Almeida written for the monastery of Tovar near Lisbon probably also in that decade, and the roughly contemporary version by Marcià Albareda for Barcelona Cathedral; and, a century later, the settings by Francesco Durante for some institution in Naples and by Davide Perez for the Portuguese court.[54] Bartoli's, Almeida's, and Albareda's pieces show composers working directly from the new breviary, and testify to its effect in parts of Iberia. But elsewhere, composers ignored the liturgical book for almost two centuries and worked from a text, either as given in an older chantbook or in other polyphony they would have known or sung.

An English-language Catholic guide to the Week, first published in France in 1670 and then reprinted in James II's London, opened its explanation of the Responsories by underscoring this text's link to Christian patience:

> The Church having represented unto us the Complaints the prophet Jeremy uttered from the very bottom of his heart, in the bitterness of his Grief; she proposes unto us that prayer Jesus Christ made unto God his Father in the heighth of his affliction, being charged with the infirmities of humane nature, and the counsel he gave to his disciples when the Hour of his Passion drew nigh; to teach us, first, that if in the traverses of this life we find that we do not obtain the effect of our prayer, and that any thing should happen contrary to what we beg of God, however we ought to bear it patiently, and give God thanks for all things; and we must no ways doubt, but that Gods will is more for our benefit, than our own desires. Secondly, that if our life be so full of tentation, itself may well be termed a tentation, we then always watch with great care, and pray continually with great fervor and assiduity, to protect us from falling into tentations. *On Mount Olivet . . .* [55]

As the Responsories are linked to the general spirit and events of each liturgical Day, still, given their changes of speaker and literary source, it is hard to read them straight through, in complete isolation from all the other texts, as a separate narrative of meditations or angelic mourning. Three standard ones (F6/R9, *Caligaverunt oculi mei;* SS/R2 and 5, *Jerusalem, surge* [*luge*] and *O vos omnes*) actually quote phrases from Lamentations, thus highlighting the intertextuality of the two liturgical genres. The first glosses 1:16ab ("Caligaverunt . . . qui consolabatur me") and 1: 13b ("Videte . . . sicut dolor meus"), while its verse is the emblematic opening of 1:12a, "O vos omnes. . . ." This case of prophetic voice in the Responsories combines verses of both *indignatio* and *conquestio* according to the *Glossa ordinaria.*[56]

The texts of the polyphonic items of Lauds, at first hearing, come off further removed from the overall affect of mourning. The exultant Benedictus, appropriate for Lauds, which was "joyful" on occasions outside the Triduum, presents a particular problem. But a connection between Passion devotion and the canticle's rejoicing can be found in Denys the Carthusian's commentary on Luke, printed throughout the sixteenth century across Europe. His *Expositio* took Zacharias's words as thanks to God, not only for Christ's embodiment as celebrated in the canticle, but also for the future Passion and its saving work: "Christ's incarnation was the beginning of our redemption and salvation, which were completed in the Passion." The idea of the upcoming Passion runs throughout Denys's entire paraphrase of the Gospel text, and he concluded by exhorting his readers to sing the "relatively brief" (as canticles go) and "sweet" text "most devoutly, with a grateful and affective spirit."[57] The commentary on Psalms and Office canticles by Agelli also linked the "redemptio" of the canticle's opening to Christ's "paying the price" for redeeming His flock from the devil's power.[58] Even later, Maurizio Cazzati's 1668 print of music for both the Benedictus and the Miserere presumed that his audience would be thinking about the Passion, presumably at Tenebrae, as his dedication notes that "the wailful sound of my compositions should have as its listeners the pitying followers of the suffering Christ."[59] To sing the Benedictus in this context was also to commemorate the Passion.

Both the canticle and the Miserere had long and authoritative traditions of *falsobordone* and *alternatim* settings. These straightforward musical projections were open to complex and affective ornamentation when sung by skilled professionals. A popular *falsobordone* for Psalm 50 by Fabrizio Dentice was printed in 1593, while ornamented versions of Gregorio Allegri's Miserere for the Cappella Sistina continued this tradition into the Ottocento.[60] Until composers (e.g., Charpentier) began to set the canticle in through-composed style around 1670, the antiphonal nature of both texts came through strongly. Since two verses form one "unit" in antiphony, both the major ritual moment in the canticle—the extinguishing of the altar lights at v. 7—and the thematic break in v. 9 as the subject shifts from Christ to John the Baptist both coincided with the kind of music beginning each antiphonal verse pair.

Sorting out the Cinquecento meanings for the Miserere, outside of the specific devotional and musical tradition linked to Savonarola's meditation on the psalm, is difficult.[61] The text in itself, the most accessible and universally applicable among the Seven Penitential Psalms, is written (in David's voice) entirely in first person, with absolutely no mention of any kind of redemptive suffering by others. Still, it was used by Catholic exegetes to justify most church teaching, ranging from the seven sacraments to the basic doctrine of justification by both faith and works. Robert Bellarmine's *Explicatio in Psalmos* (1611) took v. 3, "Amplius lava me" as a reference to Baptism, and the last verse (20), "Tunc imponent super altare tuum vitulos," not literally as "calf sacrifice," but as a proof text for the necessity of good works for salvation.[62] In his polemics, the Jewish convert Eustachio equated the "sacrifice" of the psalm with the Eucharist, and explained the text's threefold invocation of God as proof for the Trinity.[63]

One of the most popular explications was Cesare Calderari's *Concetti scritturali intorno al Miserere* (Naples, 1584), thirty-three discourses originally given at S. Maria Annunziata in Naples—a place with later evidence for Triduum music—in 1583. Reversing the usual descriptions of genre between the Benedictus and the Miserere, Calderari noted Psalm 50's nature and the way it had been—and was to be—sung musically:

> The Hebrew text says, not a psalm, but a canticle of David. Even though sometimes the two names get confused, it differentiates between "psalm" and "canticle," since what was called a psalm was sung by human voices together with musical instruments; a canticle was sung by voices alone. But the Hebrew says "canticle" to show that David sang this psalm without any instruments. For the sounds which normally make the soul happy were not appropriate to the penitent that he was; rather, [the text] was sung with dolorous and wailing voices, and today you will not see this canticle being sung with organs, as are the others.[64]

Singing the Miserere without organs is obvious in Holy Week, although Calderari implies that it was never sung with instruments on any occasion. Its simplicity is reflected in Roman musical practice of the Cinquecento.

The preacher avoided specific references to any given liturgical occasion, and the popularity of his book testifies to the psalm as a text for all seasons and all cultural levels, with many different penitential uses. But in his *Lezione* 6, commenting on "Quoniam iniquitatem meam ego cognosco" (v. 5), the Lateran Canon evoked Christ weeping over Jerusalem and described the ruin of a sinning soul, bringing Christ's lament into the here and now via the psalm text:

This city of Jerusalem is our soul; Christ sees it and its miseries, how many sins it harbors; he sees how devils, our cruelest enemies, have surrounded it with barriers and trenches of a thousand wiles, and continually assault it . . . when the Devil has conquered it, he leaves no stone atop another [cf. Lam 4:1 "dispersi sunt lapides sanctuarii," and 2:8], i.e. no virtue atop virtue; the whole spiritual edifice falls to the ground; Christ weeps, since He Himself can no longer weep, he makes you see that this is something worthy of weeping.[65]

USING TEXTS

Although the exact choice of Responsories was sometimes local, at least in northern Europe until about 1570, the texts themselves are fairly stable, and the choice more limited. Scholarly interest has focused on the selection of specific Lamentations verses in Lessons as a sign of the local in this universal ritual. But the disjunctures between breviaries and musical texts are present throughout the sixteenth century, even though there is much more to be done.[66]

From a liturgically determinist perspective, the problems are numerous: no exact correlation among the verses in many Italian Lamentations cycles, north and south (thus composers did not copy their texts from earlier polyphony); different verse selections between composers working in the same institution, city, or diocese; and longer selections in the breviary sources than can be found in most polyphonic Lessons. The most likely places for similarity between breviaries and music are the beginning (F5/L1) and the end (SS/L3) of cycles, although the choice of *Oratio* verses can differ greatly. The situation of the northern Italian print market around 1560 is typical: breviaries of 1559 and 1562 and a text-only OHS of 1566 printed in Venice all give different selections for the Triduum Lessons, and no precise correlation with any of them is to be found in any of the printed or manuscript polyphonic cycles printed in the 1560s. A special case is the use of "Cervicibus *nostris*" in SS/L3 (5:5); found in the Vulgate, the pronominal adjective is largely absent from liturgical sources until the 1572 OHS (where its printing suggests it was added at the last minute), but then almost universal afterward. Still, the word is missing in all the sixteenth-century Roman musical sources, most Italian printed and manuscript Lamentations, and even Guidetti's 1587 chant guide. It does appear in all northern European settings and four printed Italian cycles.[67]

Selections that arrange verses in backward succession relative to the Vulgate, something never done in the breviaries, point to the inclusion of specific (sub-)verses so as to connote some kind of specific meaning. All these cases recall de Martino's lapidary formulation of how southern Italian mourners in the mid-twentieth century engaged their texts: "In Lucania, 'to lament' means, above all, to remember the appropriate textual modules, choosing among those available to the cultural memory of each (female) lamenter, [modules] which tend to exhaust, as it were, the fundamental *topoi* of the possible situations of mourning."[68] At least up to 1580, the role of personal and social choice of texts was quite conceivable.

In the wider world, present political events were close to Jeremiah's words. Figueiro recounted the wounds and defeats of the Roman Church across all Europe in his opening comments on the book, likening the current state of the Church defined as the "city of God" to the solitary city of 1:1.[69] Lapide prefaced his commentary by recalling the memories of his youth, the ongoing suffering of his homeland, amid the destruction of the wars of religion:

> Thus Jeremiah gives us here the model, example, and poem, which in so many words we employ for the overthrow of cities, kingdoms, republics, and the Church, [and] for public calamity and ruin, so many of which things we have seen, and continue to see, in these present years in Belgium; so that we, with the deepest affect of compassion and in bloody tears, may bewail bitterly to God these massacres of bodies, but even more of souls.[70]

The musical expression of such sentiment dates back at least to Guillaume Du Fay's lament for Constantinople in 1453 that famously cites the sixth-tone recitation formula. Finally, the ruin of cities for other reasons could easily be read into Lamentations. Commenting on 1:4 ("Viae Sion lugent"/"The streets of Zion mourn"), Andrade recalled the plague that affected his Évora along with the rest of Portugal in 1598, noting specifically the lack of music and ceremony at his cathedral:

> Who of us, at the time of the plague, saw the church of Évora solitary and deserted, without song, without organs, without its canons, without its ceremonies, with new-grown weeds on the doors of its entrances, and with sheep grazing in its halls, and could have restrained control over our tears?[71]

GENRES, SOUNDS, GEOGRAPHY

The differences of genre among items were codified in their overall scoring. In the Cinquecento, norms for Lamentations cycles changed: four voices up until the last few decades, then more frequently five voices thereafter (the first surviving five-voice Italian cycle is in G. F. Alcarotto's OHS of 1570, although there are previous individual Lessons *a 5*). Palestrina's five/six-voice settings survive only in manuscript, while his sense for the marketability of editions led him to the four-voice Lessons printed in 1588, an edition targeted at smaller or monastic institutions. The most widely preserved Lamentations of early modern Europe, Victoria's OHS and Lasso's Lessons (both 1585), are for four and five voices respectively (again, Victoria's *Oratio* is for six moving to eight in the refrain). Northern Italian cycles requiring larger scorings are noteworthy and only slightly later: Giuseppe Guami's 1588 *Lamentationes* for six voices (with another *Oratio a 8*), and double-choir editions by Gregorio Zucchino (1604; lost) and Valerio Bona (1616). After 1600, solo Lessons are found in Italy (Cavalieri's, and a 1620 edition by Annibale Gregori in Siena) and Spain (Zaragoza).

Responsories were often set for four voices without obbligato instruments (not counting continuo), from the very first surviving settings by Pisano all the way to those of Michael Haydn and Paisiello around 1780. The exceptions include several unusual late-Renaissance sets for five to eight voices, the most famous of which are Carlo Gesualdo's, the only surviving Responsories for six voices. As noted, melody instruments are found in some *concertato* versions, starting with Cavalieri's; the eight F6 Responsories by Francisco de Santiago for Seville Cathedral, perhaps around 1620; Andreas Hofer's set, possibly for Salzburg Cathedral; and some of Charpentier's later ones.[72] The first printed sign of this development was the optional companion volume, consisting of instrumental preludes and interludes, to the 1706 Responsories by the Florentine cathedral organist G. M. Casini, who had published his vocal settings in January of that year.[73] But on many fronts—texts, scoring, even style—Responsories were a far more fixed genre across time than Lamentations.

On a geographic scale, the distribution of Holy Week polyphony from about 1590 to about 1750 is remarkable. If one were to trace a line following the Rhine upstream all the way to the Alps, there emerge different patterns west and east of the river, corresponding to both the linguistic division and the old Eastern/Western break in the Holy Roman Empire. West of the line there are many surviving Lamentations, but almost no Responsories outside Seville and the monastic foundations (El Escorial, Montserrat). East, there are some Responsories, but few Lamentations outside the sixteenth-century Imperial and Wittelsbach courts. In the viceroyalties of Mexico and Peru, the general tradition of Spain seems to have been followed, with the exception of a few Responsories, preserved in Puebla as Lenten motets.[74] But in Portugal, there was a far stronger tradition of polyphonic Responsories, as early as the thirty settings of fourteen different items (all from F5 and F6) by de Cristo for Figueiro's house of Santa Cruz in Coimbra, the seven settings in Manuel Cardoso's OHS of 1648, or Almeida's for Tomar.

In Seville, an exception to the Spanish norm, the first Responsory on each Day was to be sung in chant, followed by polyphonic ones set by the chapel-master Santiago.[75] This testifies to the cultural weight of chant Responsories. Conversely, the chant formula for Lessons in central Europe seemed to have a kind of sacrality. Starting with G. A. Bernabei's Munich cycle (1716), even "modern" Austro-German Lamentations for voices and continuo are simply instrumentations or harmonizations of rhythmicized versions of the sixth-tone chant formula, an approach also used by Zelenka in his simplified second Lesson set of 1723. Thanks to the spread of the Tone-6 formula in Catholic central Europe, it became both a symbol of the Passion and a mark of confessional identity.

As ritual, Tenebrae provided a highly structured vehicle for collective enunciation of penance and meditation, one whose music increasingly became the only variable element. It did not achieve absolution, but it was a necessary preparation for the rites of rebirth and resurrection enacted around Easter. Its texts, central to its meaning, included aspects of both the "performative" and the "illocutionary" in the now-classic formulations of Jürgen Habermas, as it did not finish the process of forgiveness but rather served as a discursive moment in the performance of penance.[76] It therefore incorporated continuity, habitus, and not least individual performance for a given community.

Its geographical differences highlight the tension between the musical reproduction of tradition—in a context where processions, *sepolcri,* the Mandatum, or the Adoration of the Cross all represented seemingly unchanging reenactments of what a community had done for a long time—and the desire for/danger of innovation in the expressive means of ritual which runs through the entire period. Textual understanding gave a range of penitential and Passion meaning, but different musical styles pointed to specific sonic articulation of the words. Some conjunctures between Tenebrae polyphony and its immediate context help trace both continuity and change in the cultural meaning of this music.

Chapter 3

Devotion, Models, Circulation, 1550–1600

Tenebrae music projected Passion commemoration and penance. Thus, a devotional context for the growing number of musical editions after 1560 can be sought in learned poetry and popular spiritual literature that treat these *topoi*. In a high literary register, sacred neo-Petrarchism was propagated throughout Italy in such verse as Girolamo Malipiero's rewriting of the *Canzoniere* as *Il Petrarca spirituale*, (1536). Among his poems on the Passion, Malipiero's version of Petrarch's *Rime* 17 described the lyric speaker's tears in visualizing the Cross, followed by rapture after the "laments."[1] Later in the century, however, Gabriele Fiamma's collection of sacred verse, his *Rime spirituali* (1570), marked a turn toward a different kind of subjectivity. Fiamma had to justify his departures from neo-Petrarchism by providing a self-commentary on his sonnets and *canzoni*. Although many of his glosses use New Testament citations, his remarks on his *Canzon IV* ("Sommo Signor, io piango," on penance) quote the Miserere. His explication of his Sonnet 47, on redemption ("Signor, se la tua gratia") cites a verse (53:5) from Isaiah, but in its wording as the repetendum of F5/R3, *Ecce vidimus eum,* not from the Vulgate.[2] Thus Tenebrae texts were present in the new religious lyric.

In meditative literature, the works of the Spanish Dominican Luis de Granada circulated throughout Catholic Europe from the 1560s onwards, displacing earlier formulations of Passion sentiment. Granada focused on the concrete visualization of specific images or moments in Scripture or salvational history, thus turning away from medieval traditions of abstract or allegorical meditation. In Italy, such works as his *Guía de peccadores, Introducción del símbolo de la fe*, and *Memorial de la vida christiana* found massive circulation (seventeen and eighteen Italian editions for the latter two, respectively, between 1564 and 1580). The fifteenth-century *Speculum vitae humanis* was also published in Italy under his name, as *Specchio della vita humana.* The Triduum Office is also present in Granada's texts; the *Memorial* mentions both Lamentations and weeping in its "treatise" (= chapter) 2 of part 1, "On penance." The section of the *Introducción* on prophecies of Christ refers to Jeremiah's laments. And one chapter of the *Specchio* glosses 1:4 ("Viae Sion lugent") as it refers to the "magnitude of the pains that the Lord suffered in his Passion and death."

Thus the aesthetics of the emerging written polyphony, attempting to standardize oral practice, can be measured against these changes in piety. Some of the compositional complexity at mid-century mirrors the importance of the liturgical texts. The sites of production for Triduum music include in a literal sense the practice of religious orders, basilicas, and local cathedrals, but in a wider way also the mercantile diffusion of the print world. Office polyphony became a wider presence in public devotion, first because of its embellishment of the Passion, but later through its standardization in major churches and its propagation via print. At century's end, the forging of a Roman repertory for the Week embodied many of these features. The new music in the Papal city replaced the Lessons of Eleazar Genet/Carpentras, and those of Costanzo Festa and Morales, even if Carpentras's massive cycle, printed in 1532, had been produced as a self-proclaimed attempt to clean up the "errors" of Papal singers' performances and to achieve a kind of hegemony in the Triduum repertory.

MODAL PLANS, MODEL CYCLES

Since sixteenth-century Lamentations share their high poetic register with other genres susceptible to modal ordering (motets, madrigals), an examination of the plans used in cycles is revealing; one might expect a large presence of Mode 6 in the polyphonic Lessons, since it has the same *finalis* and reciting-tone as the common chant formula. The reality is more complex (appendix, table 2). First, there are those cycles that use the same mode for all three of their Days, the strictest being those with a single one for all nine Lessons (both of Paolo Ferrarese's sets, but also later that of Costanzo Porta and the cycle of the little-known Pietro Giacobetti). A subcategory of this pattern, derived from chant practice, changes mode for the *Oratio* only (cycles by Stephan Mahu/Pierre de la Rue, and Jacquet of Mantua). A different affect generates a single alternative mode for any one Day: F5 (Gubbio cycle 2), F6 (Giovanni Contino in 1561, Giovanni Alcarotto 1570, but also G. D. Montella 1602 and more loosely Michele Varotto 1587), or SS (Lasso *a 5* 1585).

Other cycles provide a different mode for each single Day, as in Bivi's (Aretino) of 1546, with later examples by Jan Nasco, the Cassinese-Benedictine monks Falconio and Chiaula, but also Asola's Lessons of 1584 and loosely

Ingegneri's. A constructivist subcategory (Fabrizio Dentice 1593; Tiburzio Massaino 1599; Serafino Cantone 1603; Carl Luython 1604) is the choice of the first three or four modes over the successive Days in order of numerical ascent. This seems related to the exegetes' understanding of the four chapters of Lamentations as embodying the four directions of the globe.

But to step back from individual cycles is even more revealing. For a genre that grew out of, and coexisted with, chant, the number of Mode-6 Lamentations settings—about twenty percent of these roughly five hundred Lessons—is strikingly low. The frequent representation of *deuterus* modal choices—however Modes 3 and 4 might be differentiated—in Lessons is equally evident. Nor was correspondence with the following Responsories crucial. The most widely circulated chants for the latter are in Modes 8 and 5 (F5/R1–3 are commonly in Modes 8, 8, and 5; those of F6 in 3, 2, 8; SS in 4, 5, 5), the former of which is rarely found in polyphonic Lamentations.[3]

Cycles without strict modal order include some of the best-known or most prestigious works of the century. In the passage on how to compose in accord with the weeping of Lamentations in his *Ragionamento di musica* (Parma, 1588), the theorist-composer Pietro Ponzio considered both rhythmic appropriateness and choice of pitch structure. As if counseling novice composers, Ponzio recommended—but only after a discussion of rhythm—the "naturally sad" Modes 2, 4, and 6, but quickly added that experienced composers could use any mode, and compensate by varying rhythm in the vocal parts.[4] The Neapolitan theorist Pietro Cerone echoed him, adding that Mode 6 should be *durus* (with a natural signature), thus implying the diminished fourth *f-b♮*.[5] Some of the cycles that eschew modal unity or ordering would seem to be demonstrations of such virtuosity on the part of their composers. These include several of Palestrina's cycles, Victoria's OHS, and Lasso's four-voice settings.

In his prescriptions, Ponzio pointed to the style of Magnificat doxologies and the "Et incarnatus est" sections of Credos as models for Lamentations settings, recommending dissonances set against longer values (semibreves) on both the downward and upward gestures of a *tactus*.[6] The example in his treatise, probably taken from his own lost Lessons, also includes one of these (example 3.1); although the voice-leading includes a minor second, it was the slow enunciation of this interval, lasting a minim, and not the fairly standard pitch relations that conveyed the affect of the passage. The declamatory rhythm of the text as underlined by dissonance seems to have characterized the gesture, suggesting the elements of "weeping" music. If composers were successful, Tenebrae public or private must have been marked by the highly audible sobs of tears. Ritual crying was a socially conditioned and polyphonically evoked response to the texts of the Lessons.

EXAMPLE 3.1. Ponzio, *Ragionamento di musica* (1588), "Incipit lamentatio."

ARTIFICE AND SYMBOLISM AT MID-CENTURY

Again in line with the exalted register of the texts, some pieces for court Triduum around 1550 are quite complex. Francesco Corteccia seems to have begun composing a Responsory cycle and Lauds items for the Medici chapel around this time. Certainly the dynasty's preference for virtuoso but intelligible performances was evident in a court order of 1550 that four singers be sent by Corteccia from Florence to Pisa for that year's Week (the Medici often spent Holy Week in Pisa). The previous spring, the ducal family had heard Tenebrae with court singers in a mendicant church so as to avoid the "scordanza della musica" (improvised polyphony?) by the forces of Pisa Cathedral.[7]

Corteccia's works, printed later in his *Responsoria omnia* of 1570/71, responded to ducal taste by replacing Pisano's earlier settings, these latter dating possibly from the 1520s. Besides its problems in rhythmic declamation that Corteccia noted in the dedication of his own works, Pisano's set is entirely cast in a single mode (1tr). The first three Responsories of Corteccia's F5 music are in Mode 6tr, hence characterized by highly flat sonorities, presumably because of the Tone-6 recitation for the First Nocturne's Lessons. But his R4–6, not answering the Lamentations tone, shift to Modes 6 (untransposed), 1, and 11; thus the settings are new in both declamatory style and pitch organization. In the verses, scored according to tradition for a reduced number of three voices, Corteccia's edition includes a punning cue for the silent part; e.g., in R1's verse "Vigilate et orate," the rubric for the resting alto reads, "Vigilate, ego dormiam"/"You people stay awake, I'll sleep [during the verse]." Thus the composer worked something of the common spirit of singers into these high-culture pieces.

Beyond the Responsories, Corteccia's three canticles are through-composed, not *alternatim,* and florid. The last Benedictus of his edition, evidently for SS, is the most complex (table 3.1).[8] Corteccia's structure revolves around the text's praise of Christ in its first eight verses, and that of John the Baptist in

TABLE 3.1.

F. Corteccia, *Benedictus Dominus Deus Israel* (1571), verse structure

v. 1	Choir I: Psalm-tone 6 in Tenor
2	II: free
3	I: opening of tone cited in Alto
4	II *a 4-5:* canon at the fifth, Bass/Tenor
5	I: canon by inversion Canto/Tenor
6	II *a 3:* canon at the unison Canto/Alto
7	I: [canon at the fifth, Bass/Tenor]
8	II: double canon in retrograde Canto/Alto
9	I: canon *super voces musicales* at the lower fourth Canto/Tenor switches at half-way point to Tenor/Canto at half the temporal distance ("Qui natum est preibit ante me, et ego ante illum preibo parare vias eius")
10a	II: canon three in one, with Bass in inversion ("Tres sumus in Unum, sed Unus contra nos, et nos contra illum")
10b	II: alternative verse, canon at the unison Canto/Alto
11	I: free
12a	II: canon at the unison
12b	II: alternative, non-canonic, Alto *ad vocales*
12c	II *a 5:* as 12b doxology optional, although not so noted

the final four. The low cleffing (C4/C4/C4/F4) for the voices signals the seriousness of the work, sung after the Deposition on Friday afternoon. Its citations of the sixth canticle chant-tone are very much in keeping with other settings.

As would be expected in a major festal piece on a text concerned with Christ and the Precursor whom He followed, and in accordance with a long musical/exegetical tradition, canonic procedures flow through many of the verses, starting with v. 4 (canon TB), leading to a canon by inversion (v. 5) and one at the unison (v. 6).[9] Only "Ut sine timore" (v.7) is free, as if expressing the text's "freedom from fear" by means of a momentary relaxation of the canonic strictures.

The thematic if not physical midpoint of the canticle's text is v. 9, as Zacharias turns his praise from Christ to his own son John, "Et tu puer, propheta." In order to set up this change in the subjects of the text, Corteccia laid out v. 8 with a top line whose retrograde is sung by the alto (the rubric reads "Tecum ego, et tu mecum; tu, a fine, et ego a principio canam"), and by the midpoint of the verse its entire text, along with the pitch content, has been stated in these two voices. In this way, another common procedure in music for the Baptist—a symmetrical mirror structure of leading and following reflecting the two children's future roles—came into play at the transition in discourse from one to the other.

At the change in subject, v. 9 is rubricated explicitly as a double canon, in which the leading/consequent voice-pairs again switch halfway.[10] In order to balance the total amount of printed (if not sung) music given to Christ and to John, Corteccia provided one alternate setting for v. 10 and two for v. 12. The most complex gesture is in the first version of v. 10, a 3-in-1 canon for T1/T2/B with the bass in inversion, thus again recalling the symbolism of leading/following.[11] The first treatment of the final v. 12, "Illuminare his qui in tenebris sedent"/ "To illuminate those who sit in the shadows," turns back to the relative simplicity of a canon at the unison, and the alternative vv. 10 and 12 are settings *ad vocales* in the alto without canonic procedures.

With this piece Corteccia created an artifact of symmetrical complexity, at the opposite extreme from the perceived chaos of improvisation disliked by his patrons, and the inclusion of the doxology suggests that he meant it also for use outside the Triduum, perhaps on feasts of St. John. The elaboration of the verses points to Florentine civic invocation of the Baptist. But the kaleidoscopically contrapuntal devices also mark this as a kind of *summa* to Corteccia's work for the entire Week, the last complex polyphony sung in the Office. Although the canticle was important everywhere, here the composer interwove urban sanctoral intercession with Passion meaning in ways doable only by the complex polyphony. And Corteccia's musical references to the saint fit well with the Medici's self-positioning as the custodians of both the Baptist's cult and of Passion piety in Tuscany.

One of the independent *Oratio* pieces not connected to a cycle is Dominique Phinot's. Its verse selection {5:1–8} is rare in breviaries, but it is the same as the first of two Prayer settings in Carpentras's 1532 Lamentations.[12] Although printed in Phinot's 1548 motet collection, the scope of his Prayer's scoring—it is evidently the first piece of obbligato eight-voice Triduum music— and the collective first-person voice of this chapter suggest that this piece involved the resources and devotion of his sometime employer, the della Rovere court of Urbino, whose duke Guidobaldo was prominent in the early circulation of Responsories.[13]

TABLE 3.2.
D. Phinot, *Oratio Jeremiae Prophetae* (1554), verse structure

TITLE	ANTIPHONAL, *A 8*
v.1–2	antiphonal, imitative *a 8*
3–4	high voices, *a 4*
5–6	low voices, *a 4*
7	duets over lower-voice "grids" *a 8*
8	antiphonal, imitative *a 8*
refrain	imitative, *a 8*

Carpentras had structured his Lesson by increasing the scoring (from duet to quartet, then duet-quintet, then duet-sextet) over the course of his Prayer. Given the simple two-choir antiphony or the slightly more complex *salmi spezzati* of Willaert and Jacquet of Mantua's 1550 psalms to which he would contribute, Phinot might have composed a straightforward antiphonal setting, with a tutti conclusion for "Jerusalem, convertere."[14]

Yet his structure is more subtle (table 3.2). Phinot's Prayer is framed on either end by large tutti sections setting the title and "Jerusalem," thus rhetorically an *exordium* and a *conclusio*. The eight verses are grouped in pairs, a plan possibly derived from his decision to use the four high voices of the ensemble (C1/2, A1/2) as a sonic symbol for the "orphans" of v. 3 ("Pupilli facti sumus") and the four low ones (T1/2, B1/2) analogously for the "humiliation" in v. 5 of the yoke on Jerusalem's neck ("Cervicibus minabamur"). Thus the presence of the whole ensemble in vv. 1–2 and vv. 7–8, along with the parallel antiphonal writing used in vv. 1 and 8, provides a wider symmetry. In another framing gesture, an audible citation of the sixth-tone chant formula also links the beginnings of the exordium and the conclusion, "Incipit" and "Jerusalem" (mm. 1 and 223). Even the opening breve of "Incipit" features the same kind of minor-second voice-leading (here a minor ninth, between C1/B1) in the same harmonic rhythm that Ponzio would recommend to produce tears in listeners.[15]

As symmetrical as the structure seems, the musical events are far more varied. First, the eight-voice antiphony is unpredictable, setting individual words ("oratio" or "versa est") or phrases ("Recordare, Domine / quid accederit nobis"), not entire verses or sub-verses. Second, the actual working of the *fugae* is anything but exact; v. 4a, "Aquam nostram" uses four different hexachordal combinations for its imitation. In addition, the verse incipits are elided in both vv. 3–4 and 5–6; the overlap with the end of the previous one ("quasi viduae") makes the beginning of "Aquam nostram" almost imperceptible. A further element of declamatory *gravitas* is provided by the long iteration in the exordium of "Jeremiae prophetae" (thus emphasizing prophetic voice), and by the twenty breves in the conclusion—almost a tenth of the entire piece—spent on the single word "Jerusalem."

The eight-voice passages are anything but simple antiphony. The opening of v. 7, "Patres nostri peccaverunt," turns quickly from homophony to a texture of two simultaneous florid duets ("et non sunt"; C1/T1 and C2/A2) over a four-voice chordal grid (in A1/B1/T2/B2) written in far slower notes (breves, mm. 168–175). The end of the second half-verse ("iniquitates eorum portavimus") goes this one better by using two simultaneous florid trios over two slow voices. In the conclusion, the refrain's final call to penance "Jerusalem, convertere" works a double canon (C1B1/C2B2; mm. 228–233) into an eight-voice texture, as if the setting came around to using all its structural and contrapuntal resources in the service of evoking contrition. It is no wonder that the piece was copied late in the century as far afield as Stockholm (StockholmKB 229) and Rome (RomeBN 117–121), testifying to its ongoing presence at a time of changing aesthetics.

CIRCULATING AND SPONSORING THE REPERTORY

A surge in Triduum prints in the 1560s came against the background of devotional change, and also formed the context for the testimonies of Guidi, Alcaraz, and Vergerio (see chapter 1). Between Contino's OHS and Jacquet's Lamentations (1561–67), three different Venetian publishers produced some ten surviving editions of different genres of Triduum music, compared to three in the preceding twenty-three years. The interplay of devotion and salability also expressed itself in the prints. The Lamentations issued are of variable size and thus represented different kinds of investment in paper: the most important ones of the 1560s, Jan Nasco's (sixty-four leaves) and Jacquet's (sixty-two), contain more than just Lamentations (Passions plus Benedictus and their antiphons for the former, Compline for the latter). Compared to earlier Office prints, such as Bivi's Responsories (Scotto, 1544) and Lamentations (Gardano, 1546; each forty-eight), these are more imposing; the latter was reprinted by Scotto in 1563 and squeezed into thirty-two leaves each, evidently to undersell the growing competition. The two *Lamentationi di Morales* prints of 1564 (by Rampazetto and by Gardano; both fifty leaves) contained only Lessons; these volumes, with more actual music by the unmentioned Festa than by the Spaniard, must have been an attempt by the two different printers to play off the popularity of the Spanish composer's Magnificats. On the expensive end, Paolo Ferrarese's book, with 176 leaves needed to make up a complete set of partbooks, dwarfs any other single volume produced in the 1560s (not only Office music). Its way had been prepared by a more modest but evidently successful product; the sixty-eight leaves of Contino's OHS represented the second-smallest stock of paper that Scotto employed among the composer's eight-volume collected works of 1560/61, less than the composer's hymns or Introits (both ninety-six).[16]

Reading the requests to the Inquisition in Padua for printing privileges shows how long the process, and how intense the competition, was for producing Holy Week volumes at this moment. On 19 April 1561 Padua approved both Lamentations and Responsories by Nasco as well as an edition of Morales' Lessons at the request of the Gardano firm.[17] The dedication of the late Nasco's Lessons by his widow is dated 20 September of that year (and hence his Responsories, if ever printed, have not survived), while Gardano's "Morales" volume, also approved, was held off until 1564. In late 1561 Gardano solicited another privilege for "le lamentationi et risponsori della settimana santa poste in musica da Giacopo Cherle," i.e. an OHS, probably in two volumes to judge from later inventories that give either the Lessons or the Responsories, by Jacobus de Kerle. In August 1563 there was approval for "le lamentationi di Gieremia in canto figurato a 4 voci" and an "opera di Paulo Aretino in Musica." These are probably two editions of 1564 by the printer Rampazetto: Morales/Festa's Lessons for four voices, and the combined set of Bivi's old and new Responsories.[18] The hitherto unnoted Kerle volumes seem part of the composer's effort to publish his way through all the major liturgical genres as a showy career move. His Responsories, listed in both the 1591 Gardano catalogue and the 1598 inventory of music at S. Maria Maggiore, Bergamo, were not the famed *Preces speciales* for the Council of Trent in 1562 but rather Triduum pieces.[19] The totality suggests that the printers targeted a substantial market of institutions that wanted both Lessons and Responsories as standard but modern repertory.

The first two OHS volumes to appear, by Contino and Paolo Ferrarese, represent different approaches to covering the Week's items. The former's comes from his work at Brescia Cathedral, and includes Responsories for only the Third Nocturne, a plan which spaced polyphony throughout the entire span of the two Hours (Lessons at the beginning of Matins, Responsories at its end, Benedictus and Miserere at the end of Lauds). The forces required are expansive: the L3 of each day is scored for five voices and there is an extra Prayer *a* 6. Contino's florid if *alternatim* canticles contrast with the simple Misereres, another sign of the importance of the Benedictus even outside Florence (appendix, table 3 gives OHS contents over the century).

Comparing Contino's collection with a later OHS, Alcarotto's *Lamentationes Jeremiae, cum Responsoriis, Antiphonis, et Cantico Zachariae,* issued in Milan in 1570, is instructive. This latter goes the Brescian composer one better by setting all its items for five voices and by including all twenty-seven Responsories (plus six *falsobordone* formulae each for the Benedictus and Miserere). The net result was a costly print, probably a total of ninety-six leaves. The scoring is not the only similarity to Contino's: Alcarotto's modal choices for the Lamentations are parallel to the older composer's (the frequently notated but not signed B♭s in Alcarotto's F6 Lessons cloud the distinction between Modes 10 and 4tr). In contrast to Contino's carefully delimited sub-verses, and brief letters, the younger composer's Lessons are more continuous, more extended, and sometimes chromatic.

Alcarotto's Office displays another connection among social meaning, public penance, and Triduum music: it is the only Holy Week print dedicated to a convicted teenage murderer. The young and evidently profligate Andrea Marino (1549–c.1571) was the son of the Genoese financier Tommaso Marino (c.1475–1572), resident in Milan, whose palace (still standing in Piazza della Scala) had just been completed.[20] Although the dedication utterly misrepresents Andrea's moral character, at the time of publication he had just been released from four years of house arrest, a reduced penalty for killing a servant of his brother in 1563 (at age 14), and a sentence essentially bought for him by his father.[21] A few years previously, Tommaso himself had only narrowly escaped prison for having hidden the child of his elder son Nicolò, who had killed his wife and fled to Genoa. Thus Nicolò had been disinherited in 1565, and Andrea would have had sole access to the family's immense fortune after that date. According to his inscription, Alcarotto had considered dedicating a madrigal book to the young man, but claimed to have changed his mind in favor of the OHS volume; given the expense of the Triduum edition, this was probably a wise move.

Alcarotto was the priest at the Genoese church in Milan, S. Giovanni Battista at the Oratorio dei Genovesi, and his ties to the financier were close ("the kindness of your illustrious father urged me on," as the dedication to Andrea reads). In 1554, Tommaso himself had built the simple oratory for his fellow Genoese living in the city. In a further link to Triduum ritual, he founded a flagellant confraternity based there whose members carried the Cross in Milan's Holy Thursday procession.[22] Also, probably in the 1560s, Tommaso commissioned the church's altarpiece, a *Crucifixion* by Bernardino Campi (now Fiesole, Badia Fiesolana) which prominently features the financier kneeling at the foot of the Cross, against a background of the urban tumult from which he had emerged and against which his palace was designed to insulate his family.[23] Alessandro Lama would praise this painting for its depiction of the Crucifixion, which brought the patron to contemplate the Passion.[24]

Thus Alcarotto's OHS was the final step in a series of links among the family, the church and Passion devotion: architecture, ritual activity, visual imagery and finally sound. The composer had no musical post at the time of its issue, and would only leave the city in fall 1570 for the fairly humble job of organist at Como Cathedral; thus this large edition of fairly complex pieces seems to be a public gesture and not a reflection of immediate performance, as there is no record of a musical chapel at the oratory. The title page gives the family's traditional coat of arms, not the slightly different one of Tommaso. Hence the edition was clearly Andrea's, a final public act of penance after the young man's release from confinement, spoiled only by his death shortly thereafter.

MARKETS, SCORINGS, TRENDS

A number of prints around 1560 are scored for the low equal-voice ensemble, with a limited overall vocal range known as *a voci pari*. There is a wide version, with a range of two octaves plus a third (Jacquet's Lamentations, along with some pieces by Festa or Morales, the four-voice *Oratio* in Ferrarese's print, or Corteccia's F5 Responsories), and one with a narrower tessitura (two octaves or less, in other Lessons by "Morales," and some 1544 Responsories by Bivi). Such products were targeted at churches without choirboys or even falsettists, and monasteries male or female. The widespread use of equal-voice scoring in the Office music sets it apart from other repertory of the 1560s.[25] Only a few *voci pari* editions were produced by Scotto and Gardano in other genres, and printers seem to have bet that religious houses and smaller churches would buy this kind of music for the Triduum, even if that was their only occasion for polyphony. But the sonic ethos of the Week also required muted sound, sometimes intensified by downward—and hence flat—transpositions of modes. The convergence of the commercial and the decorous resulted in the omnipresence of low scoring.

There are some extreme examples. The bass *ad aequales* writing found in Bivi's 1544 Responsories for F5 (cleffing F4/F4/F4/F5) anticipates, in scoring if not in technique, such pieces as Rore's famed *Calami sonum ferentes* (F3/F3/F3/F5).[26] Bivi's Lamentations and Responsories were bought for Siena Cathedral even in the early Seicento; since there were two purchases at different prices of the latter, presumably both the larger 1564 edition and that of 1544/63 were acquired. Although few institutions would have had the singers to perform it at written pitch, this ensemble in 1610, with its four basses, could just have handled the 1544 scoring.[27] Putting together Bivi's

(a)

(b)

EXAMPLE 3.2a–b. Bivi (Aretino), F5/L1 (1546), end and F5/R1 (1544), opening.

editions of Responsories from 1544 and Lessons from 1546 shows how low Triduum sonority could be, as the combination of the conclusion of F5/L1 and the opening of F5/R1 points up (example 3.2a–b).

In comparison to the set of 1544, the 1564 Responsories demand a wider voice range (e.g., the C2/C3/C3/F3 cleffing of the F5 items, something like two octaves and a third), declaim their text in shorter note-values, and are generally more concise (F6/R2, *Velum templi*, takes up thirty-six breves in the 1564 version as opposed to the fifty-two of the earlier setting). Their modal choices are also different, and given that Bivi's new cycle was indeed recent ("queste mie nuove fatiche musicali," as the dedication put it), the overall sense is of targeting new institutions in a competitive market for Responsories, doing so with more animated music.

The further pace of Holy Week prints proceeded after a seeming break around 1575. In this new moment, at least six complete OHS came out in a decade (Floriano Canale 1579, Falconio 1580, G. M. Asola 1584, Ingegneri 1588, and Contino's new treatment of the texts in his 1561 volume, issued posthumously in 1588). In Rome, the first printed Holy Week music was Victoria's OHS of 1585, whose brief Lessons do follow the outline of the 1572 OHS textual revision, and thus would have been written in the span of 1573–84.[28] In a similar hurry, within seven years in the 1580s, still-extant Lesson cycles by Alessandro Romano, Pietro Vinci, Paolo Isnardi, Michele Varotto, Orazio Vecchi, Asola (two, *a 4* and *a 3*), Giuseppe Guami, Palestrina, and Vittorio Orfino were produced, while north of the Alps Lasso's and Jacob Handl's editions also appeared.

Ultimately, to explain these punctuated bursts in production involves eschewing the standard invocation of Tridentine reform. It was not clear to anyone until 1563, when Giovanni Morone took matters in hand, that the Council would ever lead to any results, and although some sort of breviary change might have been anticipated, the results of Pius V's commission, shepherded into publication by Cardinal Sirleto, were not evident until 1568 (and not always popular even then), taking some time to spread throughout Europe. No surviving Triduum edition mentions either Trent or the new breviary on its title page. In a wider sense, the rhythm of publication has also to do with Passion devotion. Around 1580, as Granada's and Fiamma's innovations for devotion and its aesthetics had become popular, there began another spurt of prints, and it seems no accident that the major early modern exegetical commentaries on Lamentations also began to be published in that decade.

STANDARDIZING ITALIAN CATHEDRALS

Print circulation also aided the codification of Triduum music in smaller centers. The 1561 Lamentations by Nasco, the recently deceased chapelmaster of Treviso, seem to have been popular in cathedrals. All his Lessons were copied later in the century as the second cycle in a manuscript for Spoleto cathedral (I-SPd9).[29] A composer with ties to the Accademia Filarmonica of Venice, and thus influenced by mid-century academic culture in the Veneto, Nasco was at pains to respect and highlight the divisions of verses and subverses, separating the latter by rests, or even "barlines" in all voices.[30] The "Jerusalem, convertere" refrains repeated literally across all three Lessons on each Day link the settings, while more subtle touches, such as the citation of the sixth-tone chant formula only at "Plorans ploravit/Non est qui consoletur" among all the F5 Lessons in that mode, highlight the freedom of Nasco's approach. The modal planning (essentially Modes 6, 9tr, 3 over the three Days) and high style of these pieces—and their use of local effects

such as an augmented fifth at L1's "inter angustias"/"in narrow places"—
seem linked to the culture of the academies, and ultimately to the sacred neo-
Petrarchism of Malipiero.

But Treviso Cathedral had other repertory available. The incomplete
part-books in its library (TrevBC38) first give anonymous Triduum items
(Passions and seven Lessons with all twenty-seven Responsories), then pieces
for the Office of the Dead, a manuscript echo of the "exequies of Christ"
idea. The relation of this source to the now-lost choirbook TrevBC 20 and
to the "tre libri . . . da lamentation . . . per la settimana santa" mentioned in
the cathedral's 1574 inventory is not clear.[31] BC 38's simple contents supplemented the earlier Lamentations cycle by Nasco's predecessor, Maistre Jhan,
contained in BC20; the surviving incipits show this latter to be the set that
had been printed in 1551 by Gardano. In 1557, someone then added Nasco's
F5 Lessons to Jhan's cycle in manuscript, the same pieces that would open
his 1561 print.[32] If the cathedral also had access to Nasco's now-lost Responsories, this suggests the ownership of two sets of Office items.

The strategy of paired books, one with multiple cycles of Lamentations
and one with Responsories, allowed for switching during Matins (or perhaps
in alternate years, or when the available singers changed). In Fermo, the acquisition of Nasco's Lessons went along with the addition of other works:
printed Lamentations by a "Giovanni Tresea," a now-lost set of six-voice
Lessons by Contino and possibly local pieces. Bivi's Lessons were purchased
for Spoleto Cathedral in 1573 (no copy survives there) and the new Responsories from his 1564 print were copied there, without attribution, into I-SPd
10 around 1580.[33] Around 1570, Todi Cathedral owned duplicate Lamentations and G. B. Corvo's Responsories, issued in 1556. The 1598 inventory
of Bergamo's S. Maria Maggiore gives the two volumes of Ingegneri's OHS
plus Nasco's Lessons and Kerle's Responsories, another complete duplication of genres.[34] Even in Poland, the 1572 list of the court's musical holdings
includes Szamotuł's Lessons plus a book of two-voice Lamentations; the former were sung into the eighteenth century.[35]

Again for a small musical chapel, the surviving partbooks of Holy Week
music for Gubbio Cathedral show duplication, here local works.[36] Two anonymous Lesson cycles for equal voices use two different sets of verse selections,
neither matching anything in the surviving repertory elsewhere, the first in
transposed Mode 4; the second, Mode 6. In addition, five-voice settings of
the *Oratio* by Alessandro Romano and the local maestro Desiderio Lacheneth
separate the two cycles. The various Lessons are followed by a two-choir
Benedictus in *falsobordone* plus canticle antiphons by Vincenzo Ruffo. A date
of around 1580 is suggested by the watermarks for these two sources. All
this music, plus the 1579 print OHS by the cathedral organist Canale (still
preserved in the archive), must have been available to this modest ensemble.

The emphasis on Tenebrae polyphony recalls several Passion paintings commissioned for Gubbio's Duomo just previously, including works by Virgilio Nucci and Dono Doni.[37]

Triduum practice over generations in Pistoia began with the first documentary evidence for any kind of polyphony in the cathedral, found in payments to the priest Domenico Ricciardi and his colleagues for singing Lamentations and Passions. These range from 1520 to 1536, with polyphonic "Sponsi" (Responsories) mentioned in 1532. On Holy Wednesday 1524 the singers were given eight *soldi* "to buy a bottle of sweet wine each evening so as to sing the Lamentations well," a mark of real community. Later, it is just possible that the "libbro di musica per la Settimana Santa" commissioned by two canons in October 1583 and paid on 28 June 1584 could be the surviving choirbook I-PSac 215.[38] This source contains music by the current maestro Simone Giovannini, Ruffo (Passions, and Lauds items; he had been chapelmaster in 1573–77), Corteccia (Responsories), Carpentras, Morales, Layolle, Festa, and Matteo Rampollini, thus mixing local, Florentine, and pan-Italian items. But its production, based partially on printed sources, also seems to mark the end of the kind of improvised Tenebrae that had been led by figures like Ricciardi, and the beginning of a new canonization of repertory.

MODELS BY AND FOR REGULARS

Traditional religious orders, and their members, also diffused new Triduum music in the last third of the century. Both the Benedictines—historically Office specialists—and Franciscans attempted to reclaim a public presence in the face of the new active orders (Jesuits, Capuchins). Some regulars preserved diversity in chant, even after the seeming systemization of the Lamentations tone at the hands of Guidetti's *Officium*. Besides its formulae for the Lamentations Lessons, Banchieri's *Direttorio monastico* of 1615 also included a florid *Oratio*. This monophony had been written for Olivetan use by the former lay musician turned evidently difficult monk, Alessandro Romano. In his theoretical considerations on chant Lessons, Banchieri reasserted their penitential nature, mandated that they be sung "distinctly and devotedly" by a solo soprano or tenor (thus allowing for both nuns and monks), and warned against audiences being dazzled by feats of improvised vocal ornamentation, even in chant, so as not to obscure the penitential goals of the music. As late as 1661, the Olivetan Alfredo Bovio reprinted a condensed version of Banchieri's and Romano's monophony, adding separate formulae for the Hebrew letters, another sign of their "detachability."[39]

Among the mendicants, the Conventual Franciscans were one of the most important orders for music in general, and, given their popularizing and Passion-related devotion, the Responsories (a genre also set by the or-

EXAMPLE 3.3. Porta, F6/L2, "Lamed. Matribus suis."

der's composers for other feasts) were appropriate to their devotional ethos.
But a Lamentations cycle was written by the premier Franciscan composer
Costanzo Porta and transmitted in a copy made by a Canon Regular of Ss.
Salvatore (a small Augustinian-rule order, henceforth CRSS) in mid-Lent
1605. Certainly the "irregular" verse selection marks the set as pre-1590, and
the textual choices, ignoring the beginning of chs. 3 and 4, are found only in
this cycle.[40] Porta's Lessons reiterate the gestures of Mode 3 throughout, while
the five-part *voci pari* writing adds to the somber qualities of the Lessons.
The cycle is framed by quotes of the *alter tonus* at "Incipit lamentatio" (T1)
and "Incipit oratio" (B2), and by a motto, a *cambiata* figure E-F-D-E. This
latter provides the top voice's pitch content for entire verses: at F5/L2's "Jerusalem"; the opening verse of F6/L1 "Heth. Cogitavit Dominus" (example
3.3); "Caph" of F6/L2; almost all of F6/L3; the end of SS/L1 ("Bonum est
Dominus sperantibus . . . Jerusalem, convertere"); the close of SS/L2 ("Jod.
Ponet in pulvere"); and the first measures of "Incipit oratio." This economy
of motives and scoring seems related to the composer's penchant for creating
pieces within strict compositional limits, possibly also for such ensembles as
the six men without choirboys that he supervised at Padua Cathedral from
1590–95 (and hence not for internal Franciscan use).

    On a larger scale, the Conventual Valerio Bona wrote his eight-voice
Lessons (*Lamentationi della Settimana Santa*; Venice, 1616) for the order's

basilica of S. Fermo in Verona, linking the texts to the Passion of "sweetest" Christ, in a personal Christology far from complex exegetical allegory. As in other genres, the Franciscan use of accessible musical styles written on a large scale (ultimately a reflection of the order's Christian optimism) was quite evident in this collection, consisting of Lessons, *alternatim* canticles (variably florid or recitational) and *falsobordone* Misereres for each Day. Bona's volume figured in several seventeenth-century inventories, and perhaps his now-lost eight-voice Responsories were a companion to this print. He had already produced at least one, possibly two, other Lamentation cycles for smaller forces.[41] Other prints, many lost, suggest that the Conventuals were quite involved in Tenebrae polyphony both at the Santo in sixteenth-century Padua but also in the musical chapels of cathedrals entrusted to them.[42]

But they were far from alone. That a CRSS musician copied Porta's Lamentations hints at the involvement of these regulars in Triduum music; it was the only occasion for polyphony allowed at their 1519 general chapter.[43] In the upsurge of Triduum music of the 1560s, Cornelio of Brescia CRSS published the deceased Jacquet's Lessons in 1567, dedicating the edition to the prior of the house where he was stationed in that year, the rich foundation of S. Salvatore of Venice (with easy access to music printers). This otherwise unknown canon might have had access to the Lamentations via his assignments; in 1551, while Jacquet was still alive, Cornelio was listed in the annual summary of the order's membership as being in residence at the CRSS house of S. Stefano in Mantua.[44] Thus he might have gotten the music—even the changed version he would later have printed—from the composer himself.

Compared with the manuscript version of this cycle in I-Bc Q.23, the print embellished and paraphrased the chant tone, which had been presented plainly in the codex. The 1567 volume also changed the demarcation of the F5 Lessons, redoing the text of L2's opening from "Gimel. Migravit Judas . . ." to "He. Facti sunt . . ." and truncating "Nun. Vigilavit jugum" from the end of L3. Whoever adopted the Lessons for print reduced the musical texture by omitting the top part in sections of the two SS Lessons, and recomposed the "piteous" end of 3:22 ("non defecerunt miserationes") with new chromatic passages. These operations modernized the musical text by providing more audibly "weeping" music.

The next CRSS member to publish was Canale, whose OHS of 1579 is a large, equal-voice print *a 4* (two Passions, Lamentations, Responsories for all three Nocturnes, separate canticles and their antiphons, CFEs, *falsobordone* Misereres). It provided for performance by either *voci pari* or *voci piene* (by allowing for octave transposition upward of the tenor), thus rendering it suitable for religious houses of either sex and churches with or without choirboys. The Bologna CRSS house of S. Salvatore also owned copies (now in I-Bc) of Contino's second OHS and of Asola's four-voice OHS (1584), thus testifying to Triduum music in their own churches. In 1561, the general chapter's resolutions ("De simphoniato cantu") used the precedent of Holy Week to permit polyphony also for Easter Week, Pentecost, Assumption, All Saints, Christmas, and Epiphany.[45] This small order was able to project itself into urban devotion precisely by means of its Tenebrae music, a wedge that led to its use of polyphony for many occasions.

Among the "new active orders," Jesuit exegetical interest in Jeremiah paralleled their musical practice. In certain but not all situations, members of the Society employed polyphonic Lamentations in their Office: as noted above, on the Indian missions, or at the *Collegio Germanico* in the late Cinquecento, which heard variously one Lesson in chant (1583, the others presumably in polyphony), or two chanted and one polyphonic (1591). The Paris college normally used polyphony for at least one Lesson in Triduum liturgy, although chant also featured.[46]

But Michele Lauretano's tenure at the *Germanico* in the 1570s–80s also hosted improvisational singing of Jeremiah in a two-day penitential retreat with other music (including Lasso's locally popular *Deus misereatur nostri*) in 1583. Here the "cantare sull'organo" of "much" of the entire Lamentations shared a Sunday evening's recreation with "melancholy motets."[47] Although how much text was sung (the book contains some 154 verses) is unclear, this must refer to ornamented improvisation on a chant tone—and not florid polyphony—given that something like one hundred verses must have sounded. At least three different polyphonic sets of Lessons were permitted by superiors for informal singing in post-1590 Munich, and the local prohibition of this recreational music from Passion Sunday to Easter again shows that Jesuits must have performed Jeremiah's verses outside the Triduum.[48] On the Paraguay missions, the order later used sung verses during Holy Week processions on the Guaraní reductions to accompany the path of many confraternity members, including flagellants.[49]

Other outwardly focused orders also participated in the diffusion of Office music. Perhaps it was the power of Fabrizio Dentice's *falsobordone* Miserere that led to a 1593 Milanese edition dedicated to the Somascan Gabriele Brocco (a former president of his order) at S. Maria Segreta. For this edition, an anonymous composer/compiler set the Responsories of Nocturnes II–III (the same selection as Victoria's 1585 OHS) almost entirely in choral recitation and issued them together with the long-deceased Dentice's florid Lessons and his formula for Psalm 50.[50] This print advertises the "Lamentationes" of the famed lutenist on its title page but is actually an OHS, including the Benedictus antiphons and two canticles in florid settings, and two other *falsobordone* Misereres. Although the Somascans had only recently allowed polyphony in their foundations, enough musical disorders had already accumulated at this church to justify corrective measures at the general chapter of 1590.[51] Evidently the restrictions had no effect on the dedication of the highly expressive Lessons, and their presumed use would indicate a high level of musical complexity in the pedagogical order. The composer and liturgist G. B. Rossi, a sometimes-unwilling member of the Somascans in Genoa, wrote Lessons in sixteenth-century style published well after their composition, in 1628.

ITALIAN BENEDICTINES AND THE MUSICAL OFFICE

The permission of Holy Week music for the CRSS is a miniature version of the trajectory of the more numerous and wealthier Cassinese Benedictines.[52] Their printed chant anthology, the *Monastici cantus compendiolum*, was first issued in 1506, and includes a note-against-note polyphonic first verse of F5/L1 (also found in six manuscript sources of the fifteenth century, not all of them related to the Congregation). The 1523 and 1535 editions of this book (with a new title, *Cantus monastici formula*) add an *alternatim* setting of the Benedictus for three voices. The printed compendium must have been meant for those male foundations without a strong musical tradition and also for use in female houses that followed the Congregation; certainly one copy of the 1535 edition was owned by nuns.[53] As late as the 1550s, such *cantus planus binatim* was the public face of all polyphony for the Cassinese.

Although the monks' historical specialization in the Office could explain their move toward issuing settings in print, it would have been hard to anticipate what actually came out: the massive volume of Ferrarese in 1565, followed by four OHS editions by other Cassinese between 1580 and 1604: Falconio (working in Brescia, 1580), Chiaula (in Palermo, 1597), Serafino Cantone (Milan, but written at Subiaco, 1603), and Gregorio Zucchino (Venice, before 1604, now lost), and a final set of Lamentations in 1622 (by Domenico Borgo, also in Venice).[54] Tiburzio Massaino's 1609 *Quaerimoniae*, with its Responsories, canticles, antiphons, and Passions, was dedicated to the Cassinese abbot of S. Pietro in Modena, Giustiniano de' Giordani da Este. The same composer's Lamentations of a decade earlier (the two prints perhaps make up an OHS, given that the Responsories are scored for five voices as are the 1599 Lessons) were inscribed to an Olivetan monk.[55] Out of forty-five total editions known to have been published by the Congregation's composers from 1565 to 1630, seven are for Holy Week Offices. No other order displays such an intense connection to all kinds of Triduum polyphony.

The Congregation's history suggests why Pampuro and Guidi might have had Paolo's OHS issued, how its background would have been perceived, and how it fit into a wider cultural offensive.[56] First is their intellectual and artistic center of S. Benedetto Po, where Paolo seems to have worked most of his life and which was under the dynamic patronage of the humanist theologian and devotee of the Daily Office Gregorio Cortese, both around 1510 and again in 1540.[57] The composer seems to have spent his life at the house, and was noted in Pietro Calzolai's *Historia monastica* (1575) only as having composed hymns for the order. Since he was likely born around 1490 and professed his vows in 1505, the contents of his OHS must antedate their publication, possibly by decades, and thus represent a lifetime of his work. Pampuro himself had entered S. Benedetto Po a decade after Paolo, and thus would have known the composer and his work. When Pope Paul III visited the monastery on Holy Tuesday 1543, probably accompanied by Cortese, he could have heard Paolo's music, possibly a St. Mark Passion like the one included in the print.[58] Indeed, the presence of Paolo's F5/R1 (anonymous, but together with a motet by the Benedictine, *Nigra sum*) in I-Bc, R. 142, datable to 1530–50, suggests how old the music might be.[59] The 1565 volume had two complete Lesson cycles, one for two voices and one for three, along with Responsories, Benedictus, and Misereres, all four Passions, plus other items.

The splashy print was one of several public gestures by the Congregation in Venice in this cultural moment: the contract for Veronese's *Wedding at Cana* and Palladio's new church of S. Giorgio Maggiore, both commissioned and executed between 1562 and 1564. The painting represented the order's leading figures among the wedding guests, but also contained such subtleties as the reference to the deceased Cassinese exegete Isidoro Chiari's ecclesiological interpretation of the Song of Songs (the book's *Sponsus/Sponsa* seen as Christ and the Church).

While Veronese's massive canvas was the most complex statement of the Congregation's image, the printing of Paolo's works seems part of a wider plan of reframing the Cassinese on different public fronts; the giant painting cost the order 324 ducats (plus food for the painter), while the printing contract was only 88 ducats, 5 lire, still evidently expensive. Thus the monk's OHS was comparable in expense to another, non-musical edition meant to represent the Cassinese: a three-volume set of sermons by the long-deceased Chiari, printed in 1565–67 with evidently high press runs, also shepherded through the press by Guidi and dedicated to Pampuro.[60] Guidi's first effort, Chiari's sermons on Luke, preceded the music book; but the second volume of homilies contained hidden within its text a translation of the philo-Protestant letter of the Cassinese Giorgio Siculo, his *Epistola alli cittadini di Riva di Trento* (1550).[61] While at S. Benedetto Po in the 1530s, Siculo had developed his ideas into full-fledged heresy before he was executed, and the house was considered the center of his thought. Although Guidi could not have predicted it, the hardline turn in Rome against the Congregation soon made any product of S. Benedetto Po at mid-century suspect. Indeed, the Vatican purged the entire Cassinese leadership, including Pampuro, in 1568.[62]

Guidi's dedication to the music raises as many issues as it solves, starting with why he did not sign it (chapter 1). Pampuro's ostensible words are also problematic; since there were Cassinese houses in both Perugia and Arezzo, either the abbot had neglected his own monasteries at Tenebrae on his 1564 trip, and gone to other churches where he heard the disturbing music, or else the "diabolical" singing mentioned had taken place in foundations for which he was ultimately responsible.

The other odd feature of Paolo's OHS is its scoring for the Lessons. After the Petrucci edition of 1506, none of the Venetian printers put out Lamentations for two or three voices, at least until Asola's of 1588. Nor do the surviving manuscripts contain any duet Lessons. The technique and scoring of the first Lamentations cycle is not qualitatively different from the *discantus*-style Lessons of Johannes de Quadris, composed for Vicenza around 1430 (and thus evidently the first written-out polyphonic settings of complete Lessons). In contrast to his Lamentations, Paolo's Responsories and florid canticles presume normal scoring.

The 1565 edition also contains the first printed *falsobordone* formulae in any polyphony whatsoever, here used for the alternate Benedictus and for the Miserere settings on F6 and SS.[63] While this is one indication of its proximity to unwritten practice, some other pieces tie it even closer to oral tradition. Formulaic practice is evident in the two-voice Lamentations, as many of the letters are almost identical (e.g., "Aleph" and "Gimel" in F5/L1, "Heth" in L2, "Joth" and "Lamech" in L3). But more telling is the presence of such recurrent modules in different verses: "Plorans ploravit" of F5/L1 begins and continues as does "Et egressus est" in L2; the phrase for "O vos omnes" in L3 is repeated four times in the Lesson; and "Sederunt in terra" of F6/L3 is essentially the same as "Matribus suis" in the same Lesson. Perhaps as a sign of another origin, the three-voice Lessons show less reliance on stock models.[64]

More surprising is Paolo's use of formulae in the Responsories. F5/R4 and 5 (*Amicus meus* and *Judas mercator*) employ rhythmically different versions of the same music, as do F6/R6 and 8 (*Animam meam* and *Jesum tradidit*). The repetition is particularly audible in the bass across Responsories for different days (e.g., the opening of F5/R1, *In monte Oliveti* and F6/R3, *Vinea mea electa*), and it is even clearer in this voice for both of the *alternatim* Benedictus settings in Tone 8 for F5 and F6. All this highlights the ancestry of Paolo's settings in the techniques of oral polyphony.[65]

Putting these characteristics together suggests that the modest require-ments of the monk's Lessons targeted smaller churches with less tradition of polyphony, and also venues of informal/domestic singing. The print run of five hundred copies specified in the contract was about ten times the num-ber of the Congregation's houses, and so the public aims of the edition seem clear. The duplicate and sometimes triplicate items are overwhelming in terms of possible uses. Printing this highly formulaic music seems like an effort to bring the Congregation's learning and liturgical decorum to the perceived "chaos" of improvised polyphony sounding widely in Holy Week. Individu-als or institutions who bought the book—like the German Maria Pfaffenperg who acquired it in 1577—were getting the spirit of the Office, a Benedictine musical interpretation of the ritual, and not just the Congregation's internal practice.[66] In that sense, as also with Chiari's sermons, the print represents a past golden moment of the Cassinese, reformatted to attract the devotion-ally changing world of the 1560s.[67]

MODELS FOR MONKS

The OHS of the Cassinese Cantone (1603; 160 leaves), nominally in-spired by his stay in Subiaco during the Jubilee Year of 1600, rivals the size of Paolo's. Not only did it provide most of the Office items (without canticle antiphons, and with the Responsories for only the Second and Third Noc-turnes, as with Victoria's and Dentice's editions), but it also included Passions and other items for Thursday and Friday. Most notably, it also contains full scores for the Lamentations and a duplicate bass part for the Responsories, presumably for study or possibly keyboard accompaniment.

The composer had evidently been invited to Subiaco for a sabbatical by Angelo Grillo, its abbot at the time, the single most prominent figure in Ital-ian sacred poetry. According to the dedication, the Lamentations were the product of the composer's reaction to Grillo's Passion poetry and to the arid mountains around the house. But the unmentioned source for the Lessons had been published in his own city less than a decade earlier: the Lamentations of Dentice. Apart from the Hebrew letters, Cantone's texts for three Lessons (F6/L2 and SS/L1 and 2) line up precisely with the earlier volume (and not with either the Roman or the Cassinese breviaries), three others are almost the same, while two share their initial verse and one its initial sub-verse with the 1593 book.

Like many court cycles, Dentice's features a highly unusual selection of verses, sometimes with the "wrong" letters, and quite short, a Lesson some-times not even comprising two complete verses. The opening of his F5/L1 shrinks two sub-verses into one, omitting "princeps provinciarum facta est sub tributo"/"the prince of the provinces has become a tributary." The sec-

ond Lesson jumps from v. 4 to v. 12bc, going from the destruction of the city
to God's running the prophet/Jerusalem through the wine press. L3 starts
earlier in the book with v. 12a and adds v. 13, thus combining the "O vos
omnes qui transitis" tag with Divine wrath. Most strikingly, Dentice's F6/L3
uses two backward selections {3: 19, 20, 18, 8}, progressing from individual
sin to personal mortality and changing the Vulgate's third-person discourse
into first person, in order to give the sense of individual despair before an
unresponsive God.[68] Finally, his *Oratio* skips from 5:1–2 to 5:15 ("Defecit
gaudium cordis nostri"/"Joy has left our hearts"), the latter verse being a
standard text for personal grief at a patron's death.[69] Alternating between
the city's grief/destruction and an individual's undoing and death, Dentice's
textual choices seem crafted to respond to the passing of an important patron and/or the destruction of a city. They use *conquestio* while eschewing
indignatio. Although the composer's still-mysterious career makes any identification conjectural, perhaps the Lessons responded to the passing of his
Neapolitan patron Francesco Fernando d'Avalos (d. 31 July 1571).

In his own Lessons, Cantone systematically eliminated the references in
Dentice's text to direct physical punishment or death, omitting "vindemiavit
me," "De excelso misit ignem," and the funereal "Defecit gaudium." One difference is at the end of F6/L3: Dentice's text suggesting Divine rejection of
a suffering penitent's prayer was changed in Cantone's to a selection {3: 19,
26} taken from the wisdom *paraenesis* section of the chapter, which closes
with waiting for salvation in silence ("Bonum est praestolari cum silentio
salutare Dei"). The references to quiet seem to mark Cantone's Lesson as
a kind of summation of monastic praxis, certainly more appropriate to the
barren surroundings and contemplative life of Subiaco than to the busy urban environment of the composer's rich Milanese house of S. Simpliciano.[70]

The monk also truncated Dentice's already short verses and put letters
between sub-verses, setting up one Lesson of less than an entire verse (F5/
L3, which has two letters and 1:12bc). If we take every sub-verse and every
Hebrew letter included as a syntactic entity, the overall text of each Day's
Lessons in Cantone's version includes fifteen such units. Utterly disregard-
ing the Vulgate—a remarkable gesture for a monk whose Congregation was
famed for its Patristic studies—Cantone's Lessons of the first two days use
only the same six letters (Aleph, Beth, Daleth, Gimel, Lamech, Sade) in different sequences, while the SS Lamentations omit the last two and use the
other four. Clearly Cantone meant to display the allegorical combinatoriality
of the letters, probably in the equivalences of Jerome's *Epistula XXX* or Gilbert's *Glossa*.

Cantone's F5 Lessons consist of {Aleph, 1:1abc, Beth, 1:2ab = 7 units};
{Daleth, 1:4a, Gimel, 1:4b = 4 units}; and {"Sadech," 1:12b, Sade, 1:12c = 4
units}. This sequence of symbolic letters generates the words "doctrina, do-

mus, tabularum, plenitudo, disciplinae/cordis, justitiae," perhaps "the doctrine of the Church [= "domus," as in Ricciardi's *Commentaria*] is the fullness of Scripture, of [monastic?] discipline [or "of the soul"], and of justice."[71]
That each day's Lessons start with "Aleph" suggests the traditional idea of
Lamentations as doctrine, based on Jerome's equivalent for that letter. The
procedure could function as a projection of the symbolic alphabet through
music, although it would be audible only to those who had read Jerome,
Gilbertus, or Timoteo, first and foremost monks themselves.

There seems to be no other explanation for the willful manipulation of
the letters, even given the model of Dentice's odd verse selection. That each
Day's Lessons set a total of fifteen textual fragments also suggests their totality as the rough equivalent of a spiritual sonnet of fourteen lines. Thus his
texts attempt to match the devotional verse of his host Grillo, one of whose
poems Cantone would set in an anthology published the next year.

Cantone's Lamentations are indebted not only to Dentice's texts but also
to the lutenist's overall modal plan for the three Days (Modes 1, 2 transposed,
and then *deuterus* [Modes 3/4] tonalities for SS; cf. appendix, table 3), again
reinforcing the exegetical tradition of fourfold procedures in Lamentations.
There are certain points of motivic resemblance between the two: among
F5's Lessons, some of Cantone's letters and "omnes portae eius destructae"
(L2) recall Dentice's. But the musical difference is clear. In its use of both
linear chromaticism and vertical cross-relations, along with its frequent use
of grinding suspensions, Dentice's cycle justifies his contemporary renown.
Along with frequent ♭ 6-♯3 sonorities, one passage in his F5/L2, at "De excelso misit ignem in osssibus meis," displays *mixtio modi* extreme even for
the experiments of mid-century.[72] The Lesson is in Mode 1 on D, but this
sub-verse (1:13a) begins, as its preceding letter had ended, around F. Then
the image of "He sent fire in my bones" swings the largely chordal declamation first to *durus* sonorities on D, then to a B/D♯/F♯ simultaneity followed
immediately by G/B♭/D, a progression involving both horizontal and vertical chromaticism (example 3.4). The close of the sub-verse on the distant C
("erudivit me") further complicates any sense of pitch center. Dentice used
similar gestures for the various occurances of "lachrymae" (an A sonority
with major, then minor third, followed by a C with minor third in F6/L2),
with more ♭ 6/♯3 sonorities for "defecerunt prae lachrymas" in F6/L1. The
cycle's overall flavor is that of *carmen*-like expressive composition, a high-
style *musica reservata*.

Of all this there is no trace in Cantone's Lessons. The chromaticism is
entirely absent, the suspensions infrequent and tamed, and the five-voice writing sonorous but almost completely consonant. Whether the monk thought
Dentice's gestures inimitable or merely inappropriate, this cycle projects a

EXAMPLE 3.4. Dentice, F5/L3 (1593), "De excelso misit ignem."

kind of static monumentality far removed from the expressive ethos of its model. Nor does Cantone's music represent any parallel to the innovations in form and imagery that Grillo had brought to sacred poetry. Ironically, the organist's volume seems to have had the widest diffusion of all the Cassinese prints, found as it was in the 1655 list of books sold by the Fuggers to the Austrian Habsburgs and in a 1661 inventory of church music in Annecy.[73] Its score presentation of the Lessons rendered it a kind of monument; among surviving *stile antico* editions, only Antonio Mogavero's 1623 cycle was issued in the same *partitura* format.

Overall, the activity of regulars old and new seems to have contributed notably to the diffusion of Triduum music as Passion devotion in a good deal of northern and central Italy. Although many orders were small and marginal, their practice clearly kept alive the tradition of public male mourning in the "exequies of Christ." Only by viewing the Roman injunctions against female monastic polyphony in Holy Week as a backhand testimony to its ubiquity can one imagine how nuns could carry out a parallel tradition, if on a smaller and quieter scale.

ROME AFTER 1570

A parallel to the upsurge in Venetian prints—but largely in manuscript—is formed by the Roman situation of the 1570s, all the more unexpected as there is little surviving music from the preceding three decades (just two polyphonic Lessons were copied for the Cappella Giulia up to 1570).[74] Certainly the earlier Lessons of Costanzo Festo (copied until late in the century) and Carpentras continued to be important. Even the accounts of the 1575 Jubilee Year omit music in Holy Week.[75] But changes in devotion were evident, one being the "systematic" meditations (Passion or Marian) of the Spanish Jesuit Gaspar de Loarte (1498–1578). In his *Trattato della continua memoria . . . della sacra Passione* (Venice, 1575), Loarte linked contemplation to the seven canonical Hours, beginning with Matins, and one reference to Tenebrae is clear: "For this, and every other thing that You suffered at the hour of Matins, when (as you permitted) the shadows ("tenebre") took command of You, the true light . . . I pray You humbly to illuminate the darkness of my soul with Your grace . . . so that I may love You perfectly."[76]

The Roman corpus is substantial. On the basis of the text selection, Johannes Matelart's F5/L2–3 from his cycle for S. Lorenzo in Damaso (RomeSLD IV/12) must date to 1569–72, as they follow the 1568 Pian Breviary, not the 1572 *Officium,* while most of his F6 and SS Lessons use the later textual recension.[77] Thus the F5 pieces must come from soon after his hiring at S. Lorenzo in 1567, and they began as individual replacements for the Lamentations that the basilica had commissioned from Juan Escribano back in the 1530s—another sign of a changing repertory around 1570.[78] Matelart's Lessons are variably for four and five voices and in different modes and cleffings (except for SS, which are all in Mode 1 transposed); one other clue to dating is the presence of "et" in 1:8 ("ipsa autem gemens, *et* conversa est retrorsum") in both Matelart's F5/L2 and in Palestrina's setting of the same Lesson in RomeSG 59 of the 1570s. This was a traditional reading for v. 8 up to about 1580, found in the Pian breviary but also the 1572 OHS; by 1590, the conjunction disappears in breviaries and music (including in later Palestrina sources).[79]

The rest of the repertory follows the 1572 OHS, at least in its verses opening Lessons, and some of it came quickly (appendix, table 1). If the dating of RomeSG 59's repertory to 1573–77 is correct, then Palestrina began his new Lessons for the Cappella Giulia with the post-1572 breviary selections, and his other cycles must have been done on the same basis.[80] Older Lessons by Morales and others, with texts reworked after 1572, are among the fascicles of CS 198 for the Sistina. Possibly the longer (manuscript) version of Victoria's Lessons (CS 186) also stems from the same time, and, as noted above (chapter 2), Palestrina's cycle in CG XV.21 ("Book III") has been considered to date from these years, albeit on circumstantial evidence.[81]

The presence of other genres is also revealing: clearly Responsories came later, at first limited to the Second and Third Nocturnes, as the earliest surviving ones seem to be in I-Rn 77–88 of around 1580 or in Victoria's edition. There may have been an oral formulaic tradition, witnessed in the simple modules for Triduum Responsories found in RomeSGF 630, a small book for the confraternity of S. Giovanni dei Fiorentini. The presence of the genre is also associated with confraternity churches or private establishments: the Rn 77–88 books; G. F. Anerio's first complete Roman Responsory cycle of 1596 (plus three Passions, *falsobordone* for Lauds, and a few miscellaneous pieces) in Rn 152, possibly for his employer S. Marcello or its confraternity of the Crocefisso, and Felice Anerio's music for the Altemps chapel just after 1600.[82] But the genre was distant from the major basilicas.

Similarly, the lack of complex music for Lauds is patent. Even as late as Bonifacio Graziani's important Responsories of 1663, there is simply a single formula for one verse of the canticle. Only one Benedictus, from the eighteenth century, survives in the Sistina's music library, although CS 205–206 preserves some thirteen double-choir Misereres, composed or gathered in the early Seicento. In Rome, there was nothing like the artifice of Corteccia's or Contino's canticles. Although some versions of the Miserere in Rn 77–88 are set out for large forces, their delivery is recitational. Ever since the early Cinquecento curial unease about any kind of polyphony whatsoever for the Miserere, the Lauds items were supposed to be plain. The lack of complex music suggests that this Hour's music was a showcase for improvised singing and ornamentation of simple skeletal models: that is, it was a moment of carefully controlled performance and not of composition. Rehearsal time for the Sistina must have been used to coordinate (and regulate internally among its always jealous singers) the virtuoso embellishments of the canticle and the Miserere. Thus the polyphonic sound of Roman Holy Week was of composed Lamentations, with older repertory retexted to fit the post-1572 readings, while even new pieces were subject to reworking and shortening.

MAKING CYCLES

Both Matelart and Palestrina seem to have started on individual Lessons, the Fleming first, which then turned into cycles in the course of the 1570s. For the accretions to repertory, the most revealing source is the partial Palestrina autograph, RomeSG 59. An initial group of four pieces called L1s is found on ff. 1v-6, before a section of hymns. These F5/6 pieces are all in Mode 6 and scored *a 4 pari;* they date from the first "writing moment" in the codex.

Some liturgical confusion is evident in the second Lesson (f. 2v), with its F6/L1 title ("De lamentatione") but setting of only {1:8}, a verse never used in Rome for any F6 Lesson. The real F6/L1 text on f. 3v, {2:8–9}, has no title (and its refrain is the first five-voice section in these pieces). It has already been suggested that the final Lesson in this group (f. 5v), an SS/L1 {Heth, 3:22; Heth, 3:23, refrain} without a title and with graphic signs of both the "first" and "second" moments, was supplemented later with the title, letter, and 3:24 that opens the codex on f. 1, the singers' names on which can be documented in the Giulia from 1574.[83] This opening addition is in the same Mode 3 and scoring as the music of f. 5v, and the abbreviation of its second "Heth" from nineteen to fourteen breves may have occurred when the Lesson was extended from two to three verses.

Further on in the codex, an isolated Prayer for eight voices precedes a group of eight Lessons (ff. 28v–42v) that are all either the work of Palestrina's "second writing moment" or of the chapel copyist Pettorini; they are also all for equal voices.[84] This group covers all liturgical slots except for SS/L1, and it marks expansion, as the four-voice writing in its F5/6's L1 and 2s changes to five-voice scoring in the L3s, while the final Prayer is *a 6*. The F6 L1–2 are reversed in scribal order, perhaps evidence of reworking, while the original partial verse selection of L2 {2: 12–13ab} was supplemented by {13c–14} to make another Lesson of three complete verses. The materials at the beginning of the codex were to be used for SS/L1, and thus this section (f. 28vff.) is an entire cycle, brought together only in the late 1570s.[85] The tight *voci pari* sonority of these pieces is notable, and the larger scorings may have something to do with Gregory XIII's expansion and stabilization of the Giulia in 1578. The genesis of the cycle testifies to a good deal of compositional (and singers') work, testing, and assemblage, an artisan-like musical production.

The modal and declamatory variety of Palestrina's cycle in RomeCG XV.21 is thus striking. In Mode 5, its F5/L1 is saturated with the sixth-tone chant formula, usually in Cantus II, but this is the only one to highlight chant. Palestrina's Lessons continue by emphasizing *varietas,* as F5/L2 moves to Mode 1 but without any citation of the "curia romana" tone as given by Banchieri, and switches to homophonic declamation. L3 has been discussed above, but the changing scoring for the last sub-verse, evident in 1:11c, is also in F5/L2 and other F6 Lessons. The cycle's further modal choices (2tr, 3, 1; 9, 7, 5) coincide with varying approaches to text projection, but the "bookend" role of Mode 5 does suggest some unified gestation, even if not necessarily in 1575. One trait that points to some homogeneity is the almost-universal use of reduced four-voice scoring for most internal verses in all Lessons; 1:11c's three voices thus made Jerusalem's plea sound less dense, underscoring the city's weakness. This cycle shares its initial chant citation and internal four-voices verses with the one in I-Rvat Ottob.lat. 3387, but there are subtle differences, notably the latter's Hebrew letters based on a descending-fourth motivicity, and reduced textures inside fully scored verses (F6/L2 at "prophetae tuae").

The simplest of Palestrina's sets (Casimiri's "Book I") was different. It would be printed in 1588/89, but was evidently begun around 1573, given its F5/L1's place on f. 1v of RomeSG 59. In their four-voice scoring, and equal-voice range, the Lessons as published might even represent the composer's attempt to seize a market for which Victoria's 1585 OHS, with its larger and mixed-voice scoring but also massive success, was not suitable. Hopes for its circulation are evident in the estate of a Roman bookseller in January 1590. Giacomo Briccio (Verrecchio) left some 272 copies of Palestrina's Lamentations, 156 of which were evidently this First Book *a* 4. But the other 116 were called "primo secondo," which suggests a combined edition of two cycles, the second of which is now entirely lost.[86] The 1588 Lessons would have success in Catalonia, where their F5 Lessons (BarcOC 11bis) or their L1s (E-Bbc M. 587) were copied into what seem like personal anthologies.[87]

Even if little studied, Palestrina's printed cycle was thus important in a wider world. The texture of the F5 Lessons is uninterruptedly dense, while rests demarcate the sub-verses, and the letters are long. The sixth-tone chant formula weaves in and out with some regularity; in F5/L3 it figures in all three letters and the first verse. The declamation begins to spread out in F6/L1, generated by the textual parallelism of "dissipare . . . dissipatus"; this Lesson also truncates its final verse, unusually for Palestrina. L2 moves to Mode 3 and eschews any audible chant tone whatsoever, as does L3 in Mode 1tr; this Lesson expands to five voices for "Jerusalem," the only moment of sonic change in the cycle. SS/L1 returns to Mode 6 and the block declamation heard earlier, but without citing the tone, while the Prayer reiterates the same mode but declaims its text more imitatively, with an extended final "Jerusalem." The overall modal choices are limited (6, 4, 1tr, 3), and the print's relative simplicity made it a good commodity for small ensembles, as its purchase by the relatively poor chapel at S. Maria Maggiore points up.[88]

OUTSIDE THE VATICAN

Beyond the Sistina and the Giulia, there is a good deal of surviving music for the cathedral of S. Giovanni in Laterano. The contents of RomeSG 58, clearly intended for the cathedral, both testify to the renewal of the Triduum repertory in the cathedral and relate to other Roman repertory. This manuscript contains an F5/L1 originally attributed (correctly) to Costanzo Festa and then reassigned to Morales, seven following Lessons by Stabile, a duplicate SS/L2 by Palestrina, and then Festa's Prayer with an added v.8.[89] The same scribe then entered a Prayer by Palestrina and one in chant. This section is followed by a hastily written one in a different hand, containing shortened and rescored versions of Palestrina's F6/L1, F5/L3, and SS/L1 found integrally in CapGiulia XV.21, along with a CFE by "Anerio." Although this codex has been assigned to 1576–77, again the hard evidence is lacking, and the second section must be from later in the century, given the "Anerio" piece.[90] Perhaps the changes in RomeSG 58 to its concordant works were made to accommodate the Lateran singers' stamina and/or the timing of Tenebrae.[91]

Another Lateran codex, RomeSG 87 raises the problem of three Lessons—F5/L1, F6/L1–2—given to Palestrina in SpolD9 but to the Lateran's chapelmaster G. A. Dragoni as part of a cycle in the Roman source.[92] The most authoritative work uses local practice in Spoleto to attribute the whole cycle to Dragoni, against the view that the copying of unspecified Lessons for the Umbrian cathedral in 1564 and 1573 is an argument for Palestrina's authorship. In addition to this, the openings of most Lessons in both sources follow the 1572 OHS against the 1568 breviary (e.g., the disputed F6/L2 is {2: 12–15}), suggesting a post-1573 origin and hence not related to Spoleto. Gestures in other Lessons (e.g., a case of a B♭ octave moving chromatically to a G-B♮ sonority at "Lamed. O vos omnes" in F5/L3) are more modern than Palestrina's normal practice. Finally, the modal choices (6, 2, 1tr; 2tr, 3, 3; 8, 8, 8) seem not to line up with a pre-existent group by Palestrina; rather, F6/L2 and 3 go together. All this suggests that all these pieces are by Dragoni, possibly from 1578–98.[93] Another cycle in RomeSG 88 is clearly his; whether these were the "Lenten labors" for which he received six *scudi* in 1580 remains unclear.[94] The books' use in performance can be gleaned from the names of singers for the Misereres and canticles at the end of each, among whom the tenor "Don Carlo" [de' Ludovici] started at the Lateran in 1593 and died in 1601, while the others were active throughout the 1590s.[95] Of these two Lateran cycles, that in RomeSG 87 is longer and more florid; its F5/L3's "Vide, Domine" features a sonic switch like the one in Palestrina's "Book III."

The renewal of Triduum repertory was not only a Papal or basilica phenomenon. Besides Matelart's cycle, there is music for SS. Trinità dei Pellegrini (and/or the Chiesa Nuova), found in the OHS manuscript I-Rn 77–88, assembled by Annibale Zoilo, and individual Lessons from SS. Crocefisso.[96] Possibly Pietro Giacobetti's brief (one or two verses per Lesson) cycle in his OHS stems from his time as chapelmaster in 1579–83 at the Jesuit-run Seminario Romano, even though it was not printed until 1601; it would thus parallel the order's cultivation of Lamentations at the *Germanico*.[97] The inventories of the confraternity of S. Rocco include Jacquet's 1567 Lessons, both the 1544 and 1564 Responsories of Bivi, and Marcantonio Mazzone's now-lost Lessons (all these by 1580), with unspecified Triduum music acquired in 1570 and 1588; in addition, singers were paid occasionally for the Week in the 1570s and 80s.[98]

The twelve part-books of Rn 77–88 include a complete OHS inside a much larger collection of liturgical pieces and motets, with the four-voice Triduum music split among the three groups of four part-books each. If Zoilo compiled them with the Trinità dei Pellegrini in mind, they likely date from the years of his Holy Week duties at the church, 1579–82. To order the Triduum items liturgically is revealing:

> Rn 77–80 F5: L1–3; F6: R4–6; SS: R1–3, R7–9
> Rn 81–84 F5: R1–3, R7–9; F6: L1–3; SS: R4–6
> Rn 85–88 F5: R 4–6; F6: R1–3, R7–9; SS: L1–3

Evidently, the Lessons were copied in Day order and the Responsories added haphazardly, suggesting the priority of the former.[99] A generation later, whoever recopied the Responsories, together with another Lesson cycle by Palestrina (Casimiri's "Book IV") and a Benedictus, into an OHS choirbook (now I-Rvat Ottob. lat. 3387) for the Altemps chapel selected only the Second and Third Nocturne items, attributing them to Zoilo.[100] Ornamentation for several passages in the Responsories, given in plainer form in Rn 77–88, was incorporated into the Altemps choirbook.[101]

AN OHS AND ITS APPROACHES

The seeming success of Victoria's OHS, compared to the mixed reception of Palestrina's Book I, is all the more surprising in that the Spanish composer seems not to have had musical duties in institutions with Tenebrae polyphony, except in his years of slightly reduced duties at the *Germanico* (1573–77), a time that coincides with the frantic activity of Lauretano's first period as rector there. But in the years leading up to the book's publication, the composer would have been free from Triduum services. In terms of its content—with its Lessons, Responsories, canticle, Miserere, and various Palm Sunday/F6 items—the 1585 OHS was both traditional and innovative.

The parsimoniousness of the verses set meant that, according to any non-monastic breviary, almost half of each Lesson would have to be chanted. This is not only an issue of overall length, although even with chant added, Victoria's Lamentations come in at between four and six minutes, while the Responsories take no longer (sometimes less) than the chant they replace; the only other Roman set with such limited verses is Giacobetti's with its Jesuit connections. Victoria's setting of the Responsories also shows the effects of concision; F5/R5, *Judas mercator* (thirty-six breves) is about as economical as Bivi's second, shorter version (thirty-four breves) of 1564.

Victoria's F5/L3 {1:10–11} gives a sense of the *brevitas* at work. The two letters ("Jod" and "Caph") are simply counterpoints around a prolonged E and A respectively, and although the Lesson is in Mode 3, the emphasis on the latter pitch also conveys something of the penitential Mode 4. The scoring for five voices allows for local sonic shifts, and none of the sub-verses are set off by a barline or change in voices; rather, some sort of pitch articulation (full cadence, or a *cadenza in mi*) delineates the end of one sub-verse and the beginning of the next. The short syntactical units for small forces (e.g., the duet for "sanctuarium suum" in the middle of 1:10) are not repeated; this procedure simultaneously articulates the verse rhetorically and drives it through economically to its conclusion.

The inclusion of two verses already makes this L3 one of the longer Lessons in the book, and Victoria must have decided at an early point (the text selection is the same between the manuscript version in CS 186 and the print) to renounce setting the charged 1:12 "O vos omnes" so as to let 1:11 summarize the overall affect of the entire Lesson. Its "Caph" is slightly shorter than the preceding "Jod," and "Omnis populus" opens with full scoring but closes with another articulating duet for "et quaerens panem," setting up the dialogic setting of "dederunt" split between lower and upper voices ending on a *cadenza in mi*; the first two sub-verses both end on the *finalis* E. Just when it seems that "Vide, Domine" will repeat this pattern a third time, "et considera" then changes to the top three, not two, voices, and the rhetorical climax of "quoniam facta sum vilis" brings in all five voices for the first time since the opening of the Lesson (example 3.5).

Without using dissonance for the "vileness" of the text, Victoria manages to make the end—not the entirety—of 1:11c into a rhetorical summation, repeating only "facta sum vilis" to echo the repeat of "in ecclesiam tuam" at the end of 1:10c. The verse thus takes on its own dynamic, while the sub-verses are carefully and hierarchically demarcated by pitch, and the subtle syntactic shifts ("Vide, Domine" to "quoniam") are set off by *varietas* in the local musical effects. Whether or not Victoria talked to his *Germanico* colleagues, something of the Jesuit engagement with the text of Lamentations comes across in the setting. Indeed, the entire volume seems to display an aesthetics of concision, points of imitation held under control to provide both an artistically worked object but also one disciplined to make its points and be over. Thus the Ciceronian power of *brevitas,* especially in verses of *conquestio,* also resonates with Jesuit rhetorical theory.

Victoria's Responsories show something of the same procedures. The text of F6/R9, *Caligaverunt oculi mei,* provides a summation of F6's Matins, and

EXAMPLE 3.5. Victoria, F5/L3 (1585), "Omnes populus."

also gave him a chance to set the "O vos omnes" tag that he had eschewed in F5/L3. The citations of Lamentations verses 1:16ab ("Caligaverunt . . . qui consolabatur me"), 1:13b ("Videte . . . sicut dolor meus"), and 1:12a ("O vos omnes") combines *indignatio* and *conquestio*. The chant for this Responsory is set in Mode 5 emphasizing the *f-a-c* division of the characteristic fifth, coming to full cadences (on *f*) at "a fletu meo," the opening phrase, and "omnes populi," the end of the A section. Victoria picked an entirely different mode (1 transposed) with no reference to the pitch content of the chant. His Responsory's first break comes already after "oculi mei," thus overriding the chant's articulation at "fletu meo / quia elongatus." He used a single gesture to make a parallel between "quia elongatus est" and "qui consolabatur me" and came to a full cadence on the *finalis* G after these words, where the chant had had only a half-cadence (on *a*). This creates a kind of motet-like exordium to the piece, one which does not coincide with the liturgical units (AB) of the Responsory text. "Videte" is given to a solo voice, and the beginning of the repetendum "Si est dolor" set off by silence in all voices, followed by a brief canon (Cantus/Bassus) and simple declamation. The verse uses a simple rising 5–6 sequence, followed by a melodic recall of the repetendum's solo "Videte" in order to frame the return to the B section. Victoria thus ignored both the pitch content and the textual parsing of the chant Responsory, which would have been the framework of his own experience. But the eschewal of chant in favor of motet-like rhetoric would have made sense to the Jesuits, without an Office tradition. Again here, the brevity of complaint must have been quite audible.

In its concision, the edition combined rhetorical appropriateness with the very practical needs of chapels. Even the pattern of the surviving copies gives a sense of its Italian distribution: Rome and its dependencies (Loreto, Anagni); Emilia (Reggio, Modena); Gubbio (which already had Canale's OHS plus the anonymous cycles); and Turin, where in 1712 it was still the only book of Triduum polyphony held by the cathedral. In Turin, it had been bought fresh off the press before the Triduum of 1585. Its diffusion in Spain was much more limited, but still it and Lasso's 1585 Lessons are the most widely surviving Triduum editions of the century.[102]

CHANGE FROM FLORENCE TO ROME

Rome already had a large repertory when Cavalieri's pieces were performed at the Chiesa Nuova in or around 1600. Their only source begins with a complete first Lesson cycle on an essentially Roman verse selection, scored for five voices with a short Prayer. Then there are Responsories for Nocturne III only (like Contino's OHS), followed by a partial second cycle of Lessons for a differently scored (two tenors) five-voice group. This second group is unusual in verse choice.[103] It ends in the middle of F6/L3, and is followed by a hodgepodge of alternate settings of verses and letters, and even Costanzo Festa's seven-voice "Jerusalem" from his *Oratio,* possibly as a more impressive alternative to the short Prayer of Cavalieri's first setting. Vittoria [Archilei] is also mentioned by name in these materials, a link to both Florentine practice but also to her Roman sojourns (1593–94, when she sang for Filippo Neri, the founder of the Chiesa Nuova, and 1601–02). The second set of Lessons and the construction materials for others suggest improvisation and selectivity in the construction of an item, again linked to virtuoso and improvised singing.

The overwhelming impression of Cavalieri's Lessons and Responsories, as noted above in 1:11, is their concertato and dramatic nature. The fast declamation of the texts, with its *fusae* (eighth-notes) in such *concitato* passages as "quoniam vindemiavit me, ut locutus est Dominus in die furoris sui" (with "irae" omitted) but also at "ad refocillandam animam" earlier, conveys this sense of representational and rhythmically unpredictable text delivery— rather like the ebb and flow of theatrical speech. Needless to say, it goes entirely against Ponzio's and Cerone's recommendations for declamation.

How might Cavalieri's pieces have sounded to their putative Roman public? Solo singing was already present in the city's churches, and in such practices as the *Germanico*'s "cantare sull'organo." But here, the verses and sub-verses are free from an ornamented chant tone. Similarly, Cavalieri's emphasis on local effects split the constituent syntax of sub-verses; the opening of F5/L2 (first cycle) separates the verbal phrase "et egressus est a filia Sion" from its grammatical subject "omnis decor eius" by apportioning the first to a soprano and the second to a tenor.[104] Even if Palestrina had changed scorings for sub-verses, this disruption goes well beyond anything else to be heard in Rome.

The pitch structures are also unsettling. Chromatic and enharmonic moves are evident already in the opening title of the first cycle, which fills out all the possible pitch-classes between A_4 and D_5 in the top line. In the second cycle, the concluding "bitterness" ("amaritudine") of F5/L2's "Viae Sion lugent" is given a "normal" setting (which includes a necessarily augmented second) and a "henarmonico" alternate, the latter involving motion from an F-C fifth to a C♯-C♯ octave, then to an A♯-D diminished-fourth simultaneity. This had been preceded by a B♭-A gesture (the equivalent inflected pitches sound differently in mean-tone tuning). In all this, the local voice-leading (fifths to octaves, or the reverse, as at the end of "Quomodo sedet sola civitas") is expressive but has little to do with Cinquecento norms.

On the largest level, Cavalieri's first cycle flouted modal organization. The title of F5/L1 starts off on G in *cantus durus,* then switches to *cantus mollis* and back by the time the text of v. 1 has been reached. This first verse alone includes sonorities built on B♮ and C♯ (the latter including an E_4♯ in the vocal line which again is not the same as the many F♮s elsewhere) and then winds up back on G in *durus*. "Plorans plorabit" redoes the title's chromaticism in reverse, and "Ghimel" features two different diminished fifths in its bass part. Somewhat improbably, the Lesson closes on A in *durus,* but not before any underlying sense of mode has been washed away.

Although pitch relationships are not as extreme in the Responsories, the sonic signals of a break with tradition are certainly present. F5/R7, *Eram quasi agnus,* starts with accentuated solo singing that breaks up "quasi" and "agnus," and this setting also erases the norms for Responsory verses, as it is scored for the same two sopranos who feature in the first iteration of the *repetendum;* i.e. there is no audible scoring reduction in the verse. In F6/R7 the scoring for the verse expands (SST) compared to the first *repetendum* (S solo), also the case in SS/R8.

Although most of the Responsories stick closer to a traditional sense of mode than do the Lessons, F6/R9, *Caligaverunt oculi mei,* seems to start as a Mode 3 piece on E only to wind up on A in something like Mode 10. Cavalieri actually read the opening of the text more faithfully than did Victoria, breaking, as does the chant, between "meo" and "quia elongatus." But again the invitation "Videte, omnes populi" is set off, here by a turn to solo singing along with the only notated appearance of the basso continuo line in the piece, and an alternate solo line, filled with vocal *esclamazioni.* The pathos of the Responsory verse "O vos omnes," here "correctly" reduced from four to three voices, is evident in the cross-relations (C♯ vs. C♮). To Roman publics accustomed to traditional repertory—which had just been increased by such works as G. F. Anerio's Responsories of 1596—the importation of Cavalieri's innovations into the Chiesa Nuova around 1600 must have come as a shock.

Across Italy as a whole, the material result of the century's last third was remarkable public prominence for Triduum music. In terms of its devotional environment, clearly one earlier repertory (Contino, Nasco) from the milieu of sacred neo-Petrarchism was quickly diffused, to remain standard in some places. But the changes of Granada's, Loarte's, and Fiamma's approach to Passion sentiment coincided with a wave of new composition based on slightly different rhetorics (Palestrina, Victoria), which would achieve a kind of hegemony into the new century. In any case, the participatory and musically improvisatory Tenebrae typical of late medieval Italy seem to have given way to a ritual more controlled in ways not only musical. For its participants (not exactly publics in a Habermasian sense), Tenebrae was a different experience at century's end.

Chapter 4

Dynastic Tenebrae

Through all the changes of the sixteenth century, Italian Triduum music reflected a wide variety of origins, institutions, and participants. Elsewhere in Europe, the surviving music is limited but evident in courts. International politics, family traditions, and personal piety shaped the Tenebrae music of the Austrian and Spanish Habsburgs as well as of the Bavarian Wittelsbach.

In central Europe, the older communitarian and improvisatory traditions of the Hours had continued up to the Reformation. The ritual life of the southwest German Imperial city of Biberach an der Riss was recalled by its Catholic priest Joachim von Pflummern after the arrival of Lutheranism in the 1530s.[1] In pre-1530 Biberach, Tenebrae had only recently been moved up from midnight to the late afternoon. A stone pillar (not a hearse) held thirteen candles put out individually after the Office Psalms; everyone participated in the actions around the *strepitus,* with all the candles (not just one) relit and brought back afterward; and—at least at Wednesday's and Thursday's services—the town's students sang "vil hüpscher Gesenglin" in Latin and German from various places in the church: younger children from the presbytery and the pulpit, with some on the stairs leading to the organ loft, while the older ones stood in the choir.[2] Biberach's Tenebrae, with the ritual boundaries broken down between laity and clergy, public and sacral space, incorporated clerics and community. Once again, the positive side of Vergerio's "disordered" liturgy seems evident.

INTERIM SOLUTIONS

Given traditions like Biberach's, civic Triduum was important. The 1549 *Lamentationes Jeremiae Prophetae* produced by the printers Johann Berg and Ulrich Neuber in Nuremberg was the first music edition entirely dedicated to Lamentations in northern Europe and a surprising choice for a firm of Lutheran convictions.[3] However, its appearance should be seen in light of

Charles V's Augsburg Interim of 1548–51, which was supposed to restore pre-1530 liturgy and thus created needs for those Reformed cities that agreed to the partial re-institution of the Office.

The print was produced in time to be sold elsewhere in Germany in time for Holy Week, as its dedication to the abbot of Kempten (Wolfgang von Grünenstein) from the Imperial poet laureate and itinerant humanist educator Kaspar Brusch (1519–57) makes clear. It begins with eighteen pieces by a "Johannes Gardanus," probably a pseudonym for a German collaborator of Brusch. These have no titles nor "Jerusalem" refrains and use only the opening verses of chs. 1, 2, and 4; they are also modally organized. The first six, cast in Mode 6, set most of 1:1–7, normally one verse per piece. The next six, also in Mode 6, take up 2:1–7, and include a bicinium (so designated, and possibly a numerical pun) for the setting of 2:2. The final six items, in Mode 12, comprise four tricinia and two final five-voice settings, and use the verses of 4:1–7. The numerological emphasis on the "prophetic" number of seven verses per chapter is striking, and such symbolism seems underscored by the employment of chs. 1 to 4, in line with traditional allegory of the "four directions of the world." These choices seem related to earlier South German practice like that of the Freising breviary, which used ch. 1 in Nocturnes I and II of F5; ch. 2 on F6; and ch. 4 for the first five Lessons of SS (the Prayer is L6).[4] Rather than eighteen Lessons, the "Gardanus" works can be considered as nine motets, each in two *partes;* in that sense they reflect the ordered approach of Brusch, whose interest in humanist education was also shared by Grünenstein. These "reformed" pieces, omitting the non-Scriptural paratexts, might have been meant as items for the new liturgical situation in German cities.

There follow four Lessons by the Imperial choirmaster Thomas Crecquillon, two *a 5* in Mode 6 and two *a 4* in Modes 6 and 4tr. The print continues with Lamentations taken from the 1534 *Liber decimus* of Pierre Attaignant in Paris, and it concludes with four settings given to "Pierre de LaRue." These last pieces had also been issued in 1538 by Georg Rhaw in Wittenberg, without an attribution. The sum total approaches liturgical overkill: a total of forty-one pieces, seemingly enough for four and a half complete Lesson cycles, but without any titles set to music or any texts from ch. 5. Due to the lack of "Jerusalem" closes, it would not have been immediately clear how many "Lessons" are contained in the edition.

The catalyst for this unusual product was Brusch. His precocious Latin gifts had led to his coronation as Imperial poet laureate at the Regensburg Diet of 1541. A passionate amateur musician, he also wrote encomia of Caspar Othmayr, while leading an unsettled life teaching in Protestant *Lateinschulen* across southern Germany, most recently in 1547–48 in Lindau.[5] In late 1548/49 he evidently found himself unemployed in Nuremberg, which would have given him the occasion to work with the printers on the compilation of this edition. The poet would have had access to the settings by Crecquillon if he followed the Emperor in later years to the annual Reichstag, where they were available. Brusch could even have heard some of them when he received his award on Holy Wednesday, 13 April 1541, at the Diet.[6] Even closer to publication, the 1547 Reichstag that confirmed the Interim began in Augsburg on 1 September, and Brusch seems to have taken leave of his job in Lindau in order to attend it. Another of his contacts in the Imperial chapel, the composer Pieter Maessins, could also have facilitated his acquisition of otherwise inaccessible music in Charles's circle.

The presence of the Imperial composers Crecquillon and "LaRue" in this city-oriented print shows the impact and attractiveness of the court's Office music across a variety of German cities. Brusch's dedicatory poem considered Lamentations as a prophecy of Christ's suffering and referred to singing Jeremiah in and out of churches as a penitential act commemorating the Passion.[7] The poet made a direct apostrophe to the Emperor on the power of Crecquillon's music to produce affect, evidently in the Lessons printed here: "And Crecquillon, the Orpheus of our time, [is] often moving your soul, o Charles V."[8] The reference to "often" suggests that the chapelmaster's Lessons were also performed outside liturgy.

The local fate of the edition was mixed, as Nuremberg's acceptance of the Interim was opposed by the reformer Andreas Osiander. While restorative liturgical principles were adopted immediately, Osiander's arguments did at first block the return of the Office (outside Vespers). But evidently a compromise was reached which allowed for anticipated Matins to be sung in Nuremberg during the Triduum and for Ascension, Pentecost, and Trinity Sunday of the coming year. That the city council had to assign guards to protect the first Matins sung under this arrangement in Holy Week 1549 gives a sense of its contentiousness.[9] Brusch may have intended the edition to provide music for such newly reinstituted services elsewhere. Still, the political arrangement of the Interim soon fell apart, and with it Matins in German cities (except Zittau and Halberstadt). Even before the Interim's demise, the report on Nuremberg by the Catholic bishop of Kulm/Chełmno (and future cardinal) Stanislaw Hosius in fall 1549 noted that nothing in religious life had changed from three years before, and that the city "politely pretended" to observe the arrangement.[10]

HABSBURG VOICE, IMPERIAL LAMENTS

For all that the "LaRue" Lessons in the print would have suggested the Burgundian heritage of the Imperial chapel, they later appeared as part of a larger cycle of nine, attributed to Stephan Mahu, printed in the massive

Habsburg motet series *Novus thesaurus musicus* (Book I; Venice, 1568), the public face of sacred music for Emperors Ferdinand I and Maximilian II in Vienna. Here, unlike the 1549 print, the Lessons have liturgical placements for all three days.[11] A close reading of the 1568 texts suggests special selection at work. Four Lessons use verses from different chapters, and four others feature "backward" verses from the same chapter (cf. appendix, table 4). The only seemingly normal texts are the bookends, F5/L1 and the *Oratio*.

The Lessons' rhetoric underscores certain aspects of Jerusalem's misery. Several end by recounting how the city's children have been led into captivity or death by the enemy: F5/L2 (using 1:5) finishes with "parvuli ejus ducti sunt in captivitatem ante faciem tribulantis"/"Jerusalem's children have been led into captivity in the face of the oppressor"; F5/L3's last sentence is a mix of 2:11 and 12, "Matribus [suis] dixerunt parvuli et lactantes . . . cum exhalarent animas suas in sinu matrum suarum"/"The babes and sucklings said to their mothers . . . when they breathed out their souls in the breasts of their mothers"; the final words of F6/L1 are "abierunt in captivitatem"; and F6/L2 ends "facti sunt filii mei perditi, quoniam invaluit inimicus"/"my children are desolute, because the enemy has prevailed" (the end of 1:16). Unusual and highly graphic verses about mothers and children are also worked in (4:10, "The hands of piteous women have cooked their own children" in F5/L3, a verse rarely used and otherwise associated with SS Lessons).

In addition, several verses originally written in third or second person have been shifted to, or combined with, first-person discourse: F6/L2 begins, quite audibly, "Expandi manus meas" instead of the Vulgate's 1:17 "Expandit Sion manus suas," followed by a reworked 2:15 "Plausuerunt super *me* [not "eam"] manibus omnes transeuntes." SS/L2 moves back and forth in ch. 3, from first-person plural (3:41 "Ad Dominum levemus corda nostra") to singular (3:21 "haec recolens in corde meo") to plural, and finishes with "it is good to bear the yoke in one's youth" (3:25, "bonum est viro cum portaverit jugum ab adolescentia sua"), again taken from the paraenetic verses. This choice provides a youthful and first-person voice to the selection.

Finally, Jerusalem's great sins and evil counselors have led to a bloody end for a destroyed city. F6/L3 begins "Complevit Dominus furorem suum . . . Propter peccata prophetarum ejus . . . qui effuderunt in medio ejus sanguinem justorum"/"The Lord has carried out his wrath . . . because of the sins of Jerusalem's prophets . . . who spilled the blood of the just in its midst" (4:11 and 13), while the next Lesson, SS/L1, reads "Erraverunt caeci in plateis, polluti sunt sanguine . . . 'recidite polluti' clamaverunt eis . . . dixerunt inter gentes: 'Non addet ultra ut habitet in eis'"/"They have wandered like the blind in the streets, polluted with blood . . . they cried out to them: 'Depart, you polluted ones' . . . they said among the peoples: 'He will no longer dwell among them'" (4:14–15). These verse combinations go far beyond all the disjunctures between liturgical texts and musical settings in normal practice, returning to the same topoi of *conquestio:* the destruction of children and mothers, the first-person lamenting of a young speaker, and a city's past sins causing a gruesome present. Furthermore, since these textual operations flow through the whole cycle in the *Novus thesaurus,* including Lessons not picked up by Rhaw and Brusch, the 1549 print likely selected excerpts from a pre-existent set of pieces based on such selection.

The 1568 volume includes music by many other (often little-known) figures from Ferdinand's and Maximilian's chapels, for which attributions have never been questioned. If Mahu was indeed the composer, there would also be a context for the cycle. As he is first noted in 1528 as having served the Archduchess Anna of Hungary, the consort of Ferdinand, the reference seems plain: the destruction at the Battle of Mohács of the Hungarian nobility in 1526, first and foremost Anna's brother King Louis II, along with the loss of his entire kingdom to the Ottoman Empire, the enslavement of thousands of Christians including children, and the Turkish occupation of Buda including the arson of the city. Quite literally as in 1:1, the disaster made Ferdinand's sister Mary of Austria, married to Louis, a widow at the age of twenty. Despite a temporary comeback, Ferdinand's claims to the Hungarian throne would be defeated by his rival John Zaponyi in league with the Ottomans, and within three years Suleiman the Magnificent's forces would be at the doors of Vienna.

The selection's emphasis on female grief recalls the situation of Anna and Mary as well as the loss of Hungary to Mother Church. Indeed, the cycle may have been intended as much for the highly musical Mary as it was for Anna/Ferdinand. It thus would link to a tradition of Habsburg elegies for deceased spouses drawing on Lamentations dating back to the anonymous lament *Se je souspire.*[12] The sense of the ruined kingdom, its children and thus its future irretrievably lost, is clear. The tone of the verses is also that of the humanist laments for the loss of Hungary and the plight of Austria, like that of Caspar Ursinus Velius's *Querela Austriae* (Augsburg, 1531). This poetic address to Germany, which detailed the 1526 defeat and the Turks' ravages in Hungary, contained the same kind of graphic description of the suffering and death of children to be found in the cycle: "They hang [children] shamefully from raised pikes, and throw away the tender infants, and even run their small bodies through with spears; here they cut them into bits, there they mow down their heads with swords." If the composer himself was from this region, as has been speculated, he himself might have lost family.[13]

The place of these pieces in Habsburg piety is evident on the index page of the 1568 print, with its Lessons prominent. The changes to Jeremiah's text, involving first-person discourse, raise the problem of voice, seemingly placing the words in the mouths of Ferdinand, Anna, or Mary. Whether this cycle was written for the immediate shock of Mohács's aftermath in Lent 1527, or during Mahu's later tenure in Vienna as vice-chapelmaster (documentable from some point after September 1529), as Ferdinand and Anna struggled to recover from the loss of Hungary, it seems to be a testimony to political and personal loss in the form of Lessons.

The musical setting also points to place. Although different tones circulated in Eastern Europe, the Hungarian tradition of Esztergom seems to have used a "mixed" fifth/sixth-tone formula, with a triadic (*fac*) opening phrase reciting on *c* for the first part of Lamentations verses, and the familiar scalar pattern on *a* for the second part of each verse.[14] Mahu's Lessons 1–8 paraphrase the normal Tone-6 chant formula in various voices. But his *Oratio* is different from the rest of the cycle: unlike all the other Lessons, which began in four voices even if expanding their scoring in later verses, it starts with five voices and ends in four, a textural symbol of loss. It also uses something like the *alter tonus* on *e* as its source of motivic material, beginning *ega*. To judge by its use of chant, this cycle seems first to use a Lamentations tone known to Anna, and to conclude with one known to Ferdinand, born and brought up in Spain and called the "Spanish" Archduke.

If Mahu's settings refer to the Habsburgs' situation, the five-voice pieces by Crecquillon in the 1549 volume take on added resonance. Except for the first verse in Lesson 1, they all have only two sub-verses, and even the opening is missing a word (-[filiae] "populi mei"). The opening two Lessons come from the middle of ch. 2 {2:11abc, 12ac} and {13ac, 14ab}, and the first begins in direct prophetic voice ("Defecerunt prae lacrimis oculi mei"). It turns immediately to the suffering of Jerusalem's children, and finishes with their death ("as they breathed out their spirits in their mothers' breasts"). The second Lesson voices Jerusalem's degradation, also in first-person voice ("Cui comparabo te?"), and again blaming the city's prophets for avoiding penance. Gilbert had given this passage to the *topoi* of *indignatio*.[15]

Lesson 3 uses a "backward" selection from ch. 4 to depict children's suffering {4:4, 2} and, like Lesson 1, it is followed by partial verses that limn the city's shame {1:4ab, 5ab}. The excisions of the sub-verses focus the themes: children's deaths, followed by Jerusalem's disgrace and penance, iterated twice. If Brusch did indeed pick these pieces up around 1541 from Charles's chapel, the settings must have existed by 1540 and thus were not far from Mahu's cycle. The situation with the Ottomans in the eastern Mediterranean, after the Battle of Preveza (1538), was one of retreat and loss, and thus both Ferdinand's court and that of his brother Charles were marked by the reverses of Habsburg Christendom.

The musical parallels with Mahu are most evident in Crecquillon's selective use of the sixth-mode recitation formula (his letters use the *fga initium*). The first extensive citation of the tone is in the second verse of Lesson 1 ("Matribus suis dixerunt"), but it also undergirds "Mem" and "Zain" of Lesson 2, then in canon at the opening of the verse "Cui comparabo te?." Crecquillon created a motivically saturated group, unified by the formula and by a recurrent descending tetrachord. At the very beginning of the first Lesson (whose "Aleph" should be "Caph" and possibly was changed by Brusch to mark the opening of a *topos*), the minor second E-F is clearly audible, suggesting *deuterus* tonal constructs with their association of penance. Crecquillon's Lessons seem a compendium of everything that can be done in Mode 6. But striking turns to E♭ set references to starving children, at "et lactans" in Lesson 1 and "parvuli eius petierunt panem" in 3. The flat sonorities also frame the concluding reference to the city's "missed" penance in Lesson 2: ("nec aperiebant iniquitatem tuam, ut te ad *paenitentiam* provocarent"/"nor did they [the prophets] denounce your iniquity so as to move you to penance," 2:14ab with a deleted final sub-verse in order to end with the theme of penance; example 4.1). Thus the tonal gestures link the death of children to the need for penance, possibly another reference to the Hungarian events.

Charles V's court was nothing if not international, but the possible use of Crecquillon's four-voice Lessons in the Spanish royal chapel is not clear. Miguel Pérez de Aguirre's ceremonial guide originated in court practices of the 1550s, while the composer was still alive, even if written down during Philip II's early years; it mentions Lessons *a 4* evidently accompanied by *vihuelas de arco* (i.e. viole da gamba), possibly doubling the voices.[16] Certainly Crecquillon's five-voice settings seem to carry more personal and political meaning, and possibly these were private works for the sovereign, with the smaller scorings being the public chapel repertory. As noted below, some of the other Spanish court repertory is hard to ascertain.

A generation later, another set of Lamentations that combines confessional agreement with the proximity to Habsburg power is a cycle by Christiaan Hollander. Once again, confessional politics seem to have been implicated in the production of the only surviving source, a presentation manuscript to the new Emperor Rudolf II, dated 1579.[17] The dedication was signed if not written by the Saxon (and Protestant) court singer Michael Echamer, who would have had access to the music when he was a colleague of Hollander's at the Innsbruck court chapel between 1566 (Echamer's arrival) and 1569, when the composer disappeared from the local pay records.[18] Hollander had worked in the Low Countries (Oudenaarde) until joining Ferdinand I's Vienna chapel in 1558, only to be dismissed at the Emperor's death in 1564, as

EXAMPLE 4.1. Crecquillon, Lesson *a* 4 (1549), "ut te ad paenitentiam provocaret."

the newly crowned Maximilian II presumably wanted his own singers. Hollander then moved to the Tyrolese Habsburg court.

For the aging composer, whose motets had a wide European reception, this must have been a step down, and the Innsbruck records note the denial of a raise in 1566, his failing health, and his desperate efforts to get his music printed, including his request for a privilege. He must have been close enough to the Saxon singer to entrust his music to Echamer, who is next found in Dresden (where he would remain) in 1576, whence the dedication was signed three years later.[19] The cycle likely originated in Imperial service, as Hollander's 1549 contract back in Oudenaarde made no mention of Triduum polyphony at the collegiate church.[20] If Mahu's Lessons were still the Vienna repertory in the 1560s, Hollander would not have had occasion to write new ones until his move to Tyrol, where Triduum polyphony seems well documented. At the female Damenstift in Hall near Innsbruck, whose liturgy seems to have been based on local court practice, an order of 1588 required the external male musicians to sing Lessons, Prophecies (Easter Vigil), and Lamentations, according to the Roman breviary, even if it caused a lack of clerics elsewhere.[21] A manuscript cycle of Lessons by Alexander Utendal, working at the Tyrolean court from 1566 onward, was recorded in the holdings of Swabian Catholic Hechingen in 1597.[22]

An important visit to Saxony by the failing Maximilian, together with his chosen heir Rudolf, lasted for some months after Easter 1575, and would have allowed Echamer to have met the Habsburg musicians.[23] Politically, the alliance was key at that moment to the future election of Rudolf as Emperor in light of Maximilian's decline, and the flip side of the agreement was Imperial tolerance of Lutheranism: i.e., Rudolf was to be a "Moderator," with close ties to Dresden, like Ferdinand I and Maximilian II, and indeed he played that role until the late 1580s.[24] These Saxon-Habsburg relations are the long-term context for the gift of Hollander's music. The dedicatory poem manages to praise music as an art, Jeremiah's prophecies as sung by (?Habsburg) ancestors, and Rudolf as leader of Austria and music patron, all within ten lines.[25] But the inscription is silent about the work that it prefaces and its composer, suggesting that Rudolf did not know Hollander and had no contact with his music.

In a wider world, the sense of Hollander's cycle as Habsburg dynastic threnodies raises other questions. Were these pieces sent to Prague in order to provide Rudolf a personal equivalent in his new court chapel to whatever polyphony that he might have heard during his youth in Madrid, or to the previous repertory of the Austrian court? Certainly the Emperor's own piety, later quite suspect, was still at this point directed towards Triduum liturgy, as a 1577 letter from the Papal nuncio Giovanni Delfino praised his participation in Holy Week processions.[26]

The example of Mahu's Lessons again warrants a close look at Hollander's text selection, coincident with no breviary and not even similar to any northern set of Lessons (appendix, table 4). It completely omits any verses from chs. 2 and 5. Also noteworthy is the absence of titles on F6 and SS, which suggests either that Eichamer excised them or—more likely—that the pieces were intended by Hollander also to fit into non-liturgical performances in a tradition going back to Brusch's references to Crecquillon's Lessons "often" pleasing Charles V. In this case, not only is there no evident breviary source, but several small variants without any liturgical or Vulgate tradition suggest that the selection was done from memory.[27]

Hollander's F5–6 Lessons use a total of 12 verses, all from ch. 1. The opening of ch. 3 provides verses for SS/L1–2 and that of ch. 4 for SS/L3. The texts of the first Day portray the destruction and sin of Jerusalem, in third-person narration; F6's Lessons move to first-person plural, as "nostram" replaces the Vulgate's "meam" in 1:9. The Lesson at the cycle's center (F6/L2) is the emblematic one of the prophet/Christ ("O vos omnes . . .") and the only one of *indignatio,* with all the others of F5/6 being *conquestio.* F6's Lessons end with another switch from third to first person, the destruction of Jersualem, and the prophet's calling on friends who, however, sought their own good and not that of the city ("Vocavi amicos meos"). Finally, SS's texts begin with partially rearranged verses of first-person suffering from ch. 3 ("Ego vir videns . . . "); they end with the destruction of the city and the image of the "daughter of my people ruined like an ostrich in the desert" (an image worthy of a Habsburg *Wunderkammer*).

The frequent "wrong" letters may be mnemonic, although only two of the six for the F6 Lessons are liturgically correct. Positing a deliberate allegorical substitution like Cantone's and using Jerome's equivalences, this Day's letters read {Aleph, Daleth, Lamech, Ain, Zain, Daleth}, or "domus, tabularum, disciplina/cordis, fons/oculus, haec, tabularum," something like "the house of Scripture is the discipline and source of these writings" or "the house of Scripture is the source of the heart of these writings," a hidden meaning that implies the music itself as the "writings" to which the allegorical code would refer. In light of the Lutheran channels by which it came to Prague, the cycle cannot have a confessional meaning—also excluded by the tolerant attitude of Maximilian and Rudolf—and thus probably refers generally to human sin. The death of Emperor Ferdinand (along with that of Habsburg infants) in 1564, and Hollander's own failing health, give immediate personal meaning to the selection.

Still, the textual emphasis on false friends and the destruction of the city does recall the war against the Ottomans, even though Maximilian's abortive anti-Turkish campaign in 1566 would actually be deserted by Hollander's employer Archduke Ferdinand of Tyrol.[28] Hollander's modal choices also do not line up with text selection or exegetical plan. Four Lessons (including all L2s) are in Mode 6, but three others use Mode 3 and the remaining pair 1tr. The chant recitation tone is sometimes quite clear (F5/L3's opening, in the bass) but none of the Lessons are permeated by the formulae as are Mahu's. Ultimately, the cycle makes sense as private Lamentations for one or another emperor.

The long-term effects of Echamer's gift in Rudolf's Prague chapel are not clear; Fynes Moryson, not always the most musical of foreign observers, recorded only "mournefull tunes" during his observations of the Triduum in the city.[29] Jacob Handl's Lesson cycle of 1587, printed in Prague as part of his *Opus musicum* series, also are largely generated by recitation formulae (both the Tone-6 version and the *ega* initium), albeit less completely than Mahu's. Although the 1517 Prague breviary has been seen as the source of Handl's verses, the readings in an earlier breviary of 1502 show even closer agreement with Handl's choices than does the 1517 book (appendix, table 4).

The correspondences of Handl's cycle with the older breviary include the "Et factum est" preface; the correct Hebrew letters and the presence of 1:9 in F5/ L3; the correct letters in F6/L3 (although Handl omitted 3:34–35); and the use of 4:16 in SS/L2, none of which are in the 1517 book.[30] Although there are minor phrasing differences, and one inverted verse-pair, Handl's pieces seem to have been written from the memory of the 1502 breviary. This could have either been for a Prague church that still used the book, or with a view towards the future printing of the *Opus musicum*. In any case, they seem to be urban, not court, pieces, as none of the earlier Habsburg cycles seem to be based on such local readings.

LATE HABSBURG LAMENTATIONS

Given the dynastic tradition of Lessons, the unusual text selection in the printed cycle by Rudolf's last chapelmaster Carl Luython (1604) is no surprise. This set is also the only one of the Habsburg Lamentations, Austrian or Spanish, to have received treatment in the literature.[31] Luython's F5 Lessons portray the ruined city, then move to the two central verses for L3, {1:11–12}, "Caph. Omnis populus . . ." and "Lamed. O vos omnes. . . ." (appendix, table 4). F6's texts are three sets of three verses each from the latter part of ch. 3, treating three topics: Divine wrath and first-person plural penance; the search with clouded vision for God, in first-person singular; and a thankful recollection of an individual who has called on the Lord, and been heard ("Ne timeas"). Finally, the SS Lessons reiterate this trajectory with two sets of contiguous verses from ch. 4. L1, on the swiftness of the city's persecutors and the "Spiritus noster Christus captus est" verse (an obvious reference to the Passion), is followed by L2, one of the most joyful Lessons ever set in polyphony, "Gaude et laetare, filia Edom," ending with Divine forgiveness of the city's sins. The reference to the remission of sin is clear ("iniquitas tua completa est . . . discooperuit peccata tua"). The concluding Prayer then sets only the first five verses of ch. 5.

The dedicatee, the powerful Catholic baron Georg II von Oppersdorf (c. 1547–1607), was not known as a patron of music. In the tradition of Mahu's settings, court connections are suggested by the text of each Day's L3, which ends in first-person singular or plural, also used for F6/L1–2 and SS/L1. The references to Divine wrath destroying cities, but also the hopeful mentions of God's hearing pleas and His forgiveness, might refer to the Habsburgs' "Long War" (1593–1606) against the Ottomans in Hungary and Romania, which saw several victories against the Turks in the 1601– 04 campaigns. Certainly Hans von Aachen's monumental series of victory paintings, done for the Emperor, commemorated Imperial successes in the conflict.[32]

Whatever the political implications, the references to the Passion and to penance are quite clear. The structured progression of texts is also reflected in Luython's modal choices, again employing the succession of Modes 1–2 (transposed)-3 over the days, again reflecting the importance of number in exegesis. But the surprisingly joyful conclusion of SS/L2 suggests that the devotional ethos of this selection marks a meeting among Passion meditation, numerical symbolism, and Christian optimism.

The possession of the volume at Hechingen around 1610 suggests the cycle's use in courts. Along with Pedro Rimonte's 1607 Lessons, it also appears in the German book fair catalogues, joining Lasso's 1585 cycle and the Cinquecento prints of Contino, Paolo Ferrarese, Festa/Morales, Nasco, Bivi, and Palestrina.[33] But the ownership of the copy, now surviving in Freiberg in Saxony (D-FBo), by the Protestant town's Kantor Christoph Demantius (1567–1643) also suggests interconfessional appeal. Demantius would have been familiar with Latin Triduum liturgy from his earlier post as cantor at the Gymnasium in Zittau.[34] When Demantius started his new job in Freiberg on Holy Thursday 1604, Luython's cycle would just have been published.

The durability of earlier repertory is evident in other Austrian Habsburg courts. The 1673 list of the Graz court music, presumably acquired under Archduke Ferdinand at the beginning of the century, included now-lost pieces such as a print of eight-voice Lessons by Francesco Stivori. In addition, the twelve-voice cycle by Georg Poss mentioned in a local inventory of 1611 must have been used there.[35] Yet Triduum music in Vienna, codified after Ferdinand II's move of much Graz repertory to the capital in 1619, includes none of this, based as it was on unspecified (but sixteenth-century) Lessons and Ingegneri's Responsories.[36] The 1665 list of the Innsbruck court chapel lists a chantbook and much polyphony, all Italian and all later than Hollander and Utendal: Orfino's Lamentations (1589), Dentice's OHS (1593), Paolo Magri's Lessons (1597), G. B. Montella's two-volume OHS (1602), Tommaso Pecci's Responsories (1603), Gesualdo's Responsories (1611), Mogavero's Lamentations (1623), and Barnaba Milleville's Responsories (1624).[37] But it is unclear how much of this music was actually used.

IBERIAN SOVEREIGNS AND THEIR LESSONS

By comparison to the Austrian Habsburg court, the situation in Philip II's chapel seems clearer liturgically but more lacking in surviving music.[38] One ceremonial suggests that four or five court singers performed only the first Lesson on each Day in polyphony, along with the whole ensemble for the Benedictus and Miserere in *fauxbourdon* (or *falsobordone?*). This would explain the limited number of codices with Lessons in the earlier 16th-century inventories from the court. Some of the copying records line up with this emphasis, for instance the two five-voice L1s by the chapelmaster Georges de la Héle written in 1585. But others show expansion around the same time; an eight-voice Lesson the same year, after the copying of three Lessons in 1582, was followed by two more in 1586, presumably all composed by the chapelmaster even if listed anonymously. Although the records are spotty, three more unattributed Lessons were copied after Philippe Rogier's death, in 1597; none of this repertory seems to survive.

Adding some pieces from the court known only from João IV's Lisbon inventory of 1649 also points to larger scorings in the 1580s: three L1s by Englebert Turlur (active in the chapel 1586–98), and an equal number of L2s for nine or ten voices, along with an F5/L1, by Geert de Ghersem, presumably done during his time as vice-master (1598–1604). Some of this seems to be blocs of Lessons that expanded the traditional opening Lamentation in polyphony around 1600. It is not clear how many Triduum pieces, surviving or not, by the vice-masters in the early seventeenth century, Gabriel Diaz Bessón and Joan Bautista Comes, might date to their time in Madrid. And some Italian music might also have sounded: Ghersem left behind the Lamentations of Dentice, presumably the 1593 Milan edition, when he inventoried his goods before departing for the Low Countries in 1604. Five more Lessons by Dentice, including an eight-voice Prayer, were in the Portuguese collections and thus circulated in Iberia.[39]

As for performance, the practice mentioned by Pérez de Aguirre of gambas to accompany four-voice Lamentations was revived or continued in the practice of the choirboys around 1600, who learned the instrument and played it to accompany Lessons.[40] For all that the repertory was growing incrementally around 1600—and this might explain the reports on Tenebrae from Valladolid in 1604, although Joly only specifically mentioned music in darkness (i.e. Lauds)—none of this involves single-composer cycles of Lessons.

As late as 1640, the differentiation between L1, sung by the whole ensemble, and more flexible scorings for L2–3 continued.[41] Some Responsories were sung in polyphony, and the master of court ceremonies at that point, Manuel Rivero, recorded the removal of the altar candles at v. 7 of the Benedictus. Rivero had noted just before this that "los responsorios cantan nel choro los cantores de canto llano,"; evidently there was ambiguity about the regular use of polyphony in the Responsories, which corresponds well to the source situation. But he was more concerned with the precise moment and manner

that the chaplains and the singers were to make obeisance to the King, speci-
fying this even before his rules for polyphony.[42] The only surviving candidates
for surviving court Responsories are those of Stefano Limido, again possibly
chamber works given the composer's appointment to the court instrumental
band; the settings are largely simple and homophonic.

At other sites patronized by the Habsburgs, Triduum music was important. For the Jeronymites of the Escorial, Matins had been anticipated at
some point between 1456 and the customary of 1527. In the later sixteenth
century, the services were recited slowly, lasting some 180 minutes, and *falsobordone* was used for the psalms of both Hours. Some Lessons from around
1600 survive, while a 1746 ordinal, evidently traditional, mandated chant
Responsories for Nocturne I and for R9, the others in polyphony.[43]

HABSBURG CONNECTIONS ACROSS EUROPE

At the Brussels court of Archduchess Isabella Clara Eugenia and Archduke Albert, a site which united Iberian and Austrian Imperial traditions,
there is little trace of Triduum before 1600. Neither the 1598 nor the 1607
inventories of court music mention Holy Week pieces.[44] The occasions for the
Brussels musician Pedro Rimonte's six-voice Lamentations cycle (printed in
1607 in the same edition with motets for penitential seasons) are not clear. If
he had not started it in his previous job in Zaragoza, he might have written
it in the Spanish Netherlands, perhaps for the first Triduum that the newly
married Archdukes would have spent in their new residence, the Jubilee Year
of 1600.[45] Given the local lack of Office music, possibly it was meant to provide Isabella with the kind of complex Lessons that, as her father's favorite
daughter, she would have heard at Philip II's court during her young adult-
hood. Indeed, the sheer scale of the forces required—the only six-voice Italian printed cycle had been Guami's of 1588, while four of Palestrina's eight
Lessons in the same scoring are *Oratio* settings—was impressive. Rimonte's
Lessons must be roughly contemporaneous with Luython's.

The print's dedication to Philip III is hidden on the verso of the title-page,
and Rimonte's long and learned inscription about the sacred power of music seems to refer only in the most indirect ways to the contents: motets for
Advent and Lenten Sundays, a Salve Regina and Penitential Psalm, and the
Lessons as both prophecy and Passion music, recalling Echamer's inscription
of Hollander's Lessons to Rudolf II.[46] The printer Phalèse had published no
other Holy Week music. In addition, the Passion piety of the Brussels court
was centered on the Cross as object and not on allegorical enactments or
texts; the major guide to its ritual makes no mention of Tenebrae polyphony.[47]

In 1607, the actual chapelmaster was van Ghersem, who had arrived in 1604 and pushed Rimonte into the lesser job of master of chamber music. With its dedication and its seasonal motets, the 1607 print seems targeted to Spain, perhaps to keep its composer in public profile in his homeland. Still, the resources of the Archdukes' chapel could have just handled his eight-voice *Oratio*.[48] Rimonte switched mode in every Lesson; in the ones on A (Modes 9 and 10) the references to the *egaa* formula are subtle. In F5/L1, the formula, transposed to *d,* opens the "Incipit" title. Setting the text in florid counter-point conditioned the limited choice of verses, normally three per Lesson except for those drawn from ch. 3 (F6/L3 and SS/L1, with five and eight re-spectively) and the Prayer, set in its post-1572 liturgical entirety (appendix, table 4).

Although the readings of the Albarracín manuscript that preserves most of the cycle are sometimes questionable (the print survives in only one part-book), Rimonte's F5/L3 gives a sense of the procedures at work.[49] The only setting in Mode 6, this Lesson cites the *fga initium* at its beginning, middle, and end ("Jod," "Mem," and "Jerusalem"), in the latter two cases as imita-tion in all the voices. Thus, like Mahu's, the cycle actually employs two dif-ferent tones, Iberian and Germanic. The crowding of *soggetti* into small imi-tative space is evident at "De excelso misit ignem." Here four entrances of a subject limning the modal compass are squeezed into three breves, followed by a fivefold entrance of the same idea, this time within two breves (at the textually suggestive "conversit me retrorsum").

Rimonte's florid counterpoint also intersects with the articulation of the sub-verses. The Lesson sets {1:10, 12, 13} (omitting the "Caph. Omnes popu-lus" verse). Rimonte separated the [a] and [b] sub-verses ("desiderabilia eius / quia vidit," "attendite et videte / si est dolor," and "et erudivit me / expan-dit rete"). In 1:10, the opening "Manum suum" leads to a clear cadence on the *finalis* at the end of the [a] sub-verse. But the connection between sub-verses [b] and [c] "quia vidit gentes ingressas sanctuarium suum / de quibus perceperis, ne intrarent in ecclesiam tuam"/"The Lord has seen people enter His sanctuary / whom you were told not to let into your church" is not only elided, but finishes with repetitions for the verse's final words, "in ecclesiam tuam." Here all six voices repeat a stretto set of entrances, as the cantus I part briefly goes far out of its modal range (nominally no higher than C_5) to enter on the only high F_5 that it sings in the entire Lesson (example 4.2). This climax underscores the text's sense of the violation of ecclesial space by the ungodly. The reference for the Brussels court, still engaged in a war (until the truce of 1609–21) with the United Provinces over the territory and confes-sional affiliation of the Low Countries, must have been clear. The conflict's

EXAMPLE 4.2. Rimonte, F5/L3 (1607), "[ne intrarent] in ecclesiam tuam."

front line was some eighty kilometers away from Brussels, and its ravages would be mourned by the southern Netherlander Lapide in his commentary on Lamentations (ch. 2).

The next printed Habsburg cycle for Spain evinces some parallels and some differences. In the service of the Austrian legate to Venice from around 1590, the southern Italian Antonio Mogavero had also run the music at the patriarchal seminary there before moving to Madrid, probably around 1615. While in Venice he also had contact with the Spanish ambassador, and at some point published four-voice Responsories.[50] His now-lost edition of Masses and dialogue motets in 1604 had included pieces for both branches of the Habsburgs, among them Queen Margaret of Austria and a prayer for the newborn future Philip IV.

His large and expensive Lamentations, published in Venice in 1623, consisted of six-voice Lessons plus a through-composed Benedictus and *alternatim* Miserere both *a 8*, along with a full untexted score. It was dedicated to the fourteen-year-old Cardinal-Infante Ferdinand (Philip IV's brother), and

Mogavero mentioned both his 1604 edition and his personal service to the House of Austria in the inscription. A separate preface to readers stresses the "croma-laden [i.e. filled with *cromae,* modern eighth-notes] and varied invention by which the force of the words may be expressed, and the pious together with the learned may be refreshed in spirit through these allurements of polyphony." Mogavero referred indirectly to the full score as a means to experience the music's sweetness by reading at the keyboard, and suggested vocal performance with doubling by six viole da gamba together with a large harpsichord (e.g., not a spinet) and a theorbo, to be performed slowly. The advice resonates with Italian practice and also recalls the tradition of gambas accompanying Spanish court Lamentations over the previous century, including their more recent use by choirboys at Philip III's court. Mogavero thus mapped earlier Venetian traditions onto an ongoing Madrid practice.

Still, the edition's relation to his musical activity in Spain is not clear. He was not the court chapelmaster, as Mateo Romero was firmly in that position, nor the deputy (Comes). Nor does he appear in the payrolls of the *capilla española* in the first third of 1623, and a very general letter of recommendation for him from Ferdinand II of Austria to Philip IV dates later, to January 1624.[51] Perhaps the print aimed to position him for Habsburg patronage, not so much the chapelmaster post in Toledo, where the relatively young Juan de la Bermejo had just taken up a spot in 1619, as the Capilla Real in Granada, where the aging maestro Manuel Leitao de Aviles was coming to the end of his tenure. Recent work has shown that he sent copies to both cathedrals.[52]

Mogavero's F5/L1 shows some of the procedures at work. As with Rimonte's cycle, he omitted some verses, here 1:5. This sixth-mode piece is driven by the tension between its F-centered opening/close and the pitch centers of vv. 3–4 on D. Its *gravitas* is clear even in the opening "lamentatio," where an F♯-F♮ cross-relation (over D) both shades the tonality and presages the multiple pitch centers (example 4.3).

This tonal polarity is also evident in the other F5 Lessons. Mogavero's F5/L3 gives a sense of his "varied invention." "Jod" begins with two superimposed *soggetti,* a descending pentachord D-G and its inversion, a rising D-A, also suggesting that the piece is in Mode 9tr (on D). The first of these motives opens every section of the Lesson (as a tetrachord at "Caph," "O vos omnes" and "De excelso"), while the second is run against it again at the openings of these three sections. Mogavero systematically varies the counterpoint against the pentachord; although there are few *chromae,* the opening seminimins in the second *soggetto* underscore the rhythmic motion to which the preface refers. And the extended Hebrew letters (fourteen breves for the opening "Jod") work as audible loci for the counterpoint.

EXAMPLE 4.3. Mogavero, F5/L1 (1623), "Incipit lamentatio."

For all the constructivism, still traditional rhetoric and exegesis are audible in the Lesson. The trajectory of 1:11 starts with another long "Caph," turning at the sub-verse [b] "dederunt pretiosum" to E♭ sonorities (another case of a semitonal relationship with the local *finalis* D; example 4.4). The only moment of complete silence in the Lesson, a semibreve rest in all parts, demarcates the change in speaker at "Vide, Domine, et considera." Mogavero stated Jerusalem's plea chordally, then repeated the climax "quoniam facta sum vilis" thrice in each voice, employing three four-breve blocks of

EXAMPLE 4.4. Mogavero, F5/L3, "Caph. Omnes populus."
Continued on the next page

EXAMPLE 4.4. (*Continued*)

declamation and cadencing on G. The emblematic "O vos omnes" is declaimed by the four high voices in close contrapuntal imitation, again limning flat sonorities, echoed by the sixfold statement of the descending tetrachord within three breves' space at "Mem." Another superimposition of the two subjects at "De excelso" turns to triple time for the image of "He set fire in my bones"/"misit ignem in ossibus meis."

The end of the Lesson also repeats some of the previous gestures: the turns to *mollis* for the sorrow of "tota die maerore confectam" and another threefold repetition of this phrase, like "quoniam facta sum vilis." Finally, "Jerusalem, convertere" saturates the voice-leading with the descending tetrachord gesture, reinforcing the emblematic quality of this simple contrapuntal tag. Perhaps to provide modal unity across the Day's Lesson, the refrain moves away from D to finish on F. The complexity of Mogavero's procedures seems more schematic but no less artificial than Rimonte's. Both prints seem to show off contrapuntal virtuosity as a public gesture, but also as suitable to the House of Austria.

DYNASTIC DEVOTION IN MUNICH

The private Triduum music of the Wittelsbach over the last decades of the 16th century stood in some contrast to Habsburg practice east and west. Lasso's four-voice Lamentations in manuscript for the court, noted above for their directly affective nature, use the verses of a source found nowhere else in the repertory: Pius V's 1568 breviary (cf. appendix, table 4).[53] The composer's printed and more contrapuntal five-voice cycle (1585) employs a verse selection that begins identically to all Lessons of the four-voice set, but in almost every case halves their number, something to be expected of a product meant for institutions with a wider range of singers' mnemonic ability and perhaps less time for Tenebrae. The seventeen surviving copies of the 1585 edition plus the four of its Parisian reprint testify to the music's diffusion throughout Europe, including Spain and Italy.

The employment of liturgical books is also suggestive. The Triduum readings of the Freising breviary used in Munich are quite different from the Pian ones, and were current at court and in the diocese up through the 1570s.[54] A 1571 text-only OHS, probably from Munich, contains the long-standing local Lessons. Lasso's double use of the new Pian breviary reflects a Wittelsbach or Jesuit initiative to project readings directly from Rome, sweeping aside the past and the local. The dating, however, remains problematic; all Roman/Venetian breviaries after 1572 contain the shorter recensions of the Lessons, while recent work has suggested the early 1580s for Lasso's published cycle, and, surprisingly, a later date (1588–1591) for the manuscript

Lessons.[55] The composer could have encountered the post-1572 readings already during his 1574 Holy Week spent in Rome, and so the reasons for his textual choices are not clear.[56]

But one possible source is a variant 1579 Roman OHS, apparently preserved only in Munich, which contains the pre-1572 selection (although it does have later marginal notes for deletion of the extra verses). The one surviving copy belonged to the Jesuit College in Munich, and hence was close to the rulers and the composer. If Lasso used this "rogue" edition, he must have begun his project in 1579 or 1580, as the 1581 Munich reprint of the OHS already corrected the Lessons to the norm of 1572.[57] The composer's recourse to some liturgical book (or memory thereof) is clear, as both his settings of 1:8 contain the extra "et" ("gemens *et* conversa est") noted above (chapter 3).

Lasso's choices also resonate with his Roman, not local, annual hymn cycle from 1580–81.[58] This trend continued with the more aggressive activity of the Cologne Jesuit Walram Tumler at court between late 1581 and 1583.[59] Tumler's first Holy Week of 1582 induced the Wittelsbach to long meditation at the *sepulcrum* during the Triduum. As has been noted, the Jesuit's drastic efforts to "reform" liturgical and musical life at Wilhelm V's court included requests to the *Germanico* for music, although a close reading suggests that music for the clerics, not the polyphonic singers, was imported: psalm-tones, responses at Mass, and Holy Week music only in the form of Passions.[60]

The newly created repertory was larger than merely Lessons. The copying of D-Mbs 2749, containing anonymous versions of the "lesser" (Mark and Luke) Passions as well as the Responsories for Nocturnes II and III, took place in the two months before the 1582 Triduum, finishing with the Responsories in Passion Week.[61] Modern scholarship has attributed all these pieces to Lasso. It is not clear if the idea of setting only the Nocturne II-III Responsories originated with him, or with others who used a similar plan, like Victoria or Zoilo in Rome, whose music he could have heard during the 1574 stay. Of Lasso's other Office items, the Lauds pieces are preserved in sources dating between 1585 and 1590, while the dedication of the printed Lessons is before Lent 1585, in time for sale in advance of the Triduum.

The updating of court piety might have occasioned the Responsories, the Passions, and possibly the four-voice Lessons, recopied along with the Lauds items later in the decade. This massive OHS-like production recalls the *Germanico:* both Lauretano's cultivation of Triduum polyphony, and Victoria's OHS, whose pieces might have been tried out at the college in the 1570s. A Bavarian effort toward homogenous Tenebrae repertory seems in line with the Wittelsbachs' push for all matters Roman.

MARKING THE TRIDUUM IN MUNICH

Lasso's printed Lessons of 1585 are remarkable for their free invention, evidently not using a reciting-tone anywhere. The direct musical representation of words or phrases is also more infrequent, compared to the manuscript cycle, although in F5/L1's first verse Lasso combined a solmization pun with a sudden moment of solo singing for "sola civitas."[62] The emblematic 1:12, "Lamed. O vos omnes" begins F5/L3 in both the print and the manuscript cycles, and Lasso parsed the sub-verses in similar ways: equally long letters, a full cadence at "viam" whose declamation slides into "attendite," and another break separating "videte" from "si est dolor" (a *cadenza in mi* in the five-voice cycle). The "pain" of this sub-verse generates a prolonged E♭/D relationship in the five-voice Lesson, while the declamation is faster in the four-voice cycle, but includes a more chromatic *ductus* of the top line. The gestures for "quoniam vindemiavit me" are similar between the Lessons, but the five-voice setting features metric disruption inside the *tactus* by means of the 10 off-beat entrances on the fricative "furoris," while the syncopations are fewer and shorter in the four-voice piece.

Tones mark parts of the manuscript cycle *a 4*, for instance the Tone-6 formula in the F5 Lessons, which serves as a cantus firmus in L1's 1: 1 and 2a. It is cited at the opening of every other verse except v. 4, used in the letters and "Jerusalem, convertere" of the other two Lamentations of the Day, and again quoted in verses of L2 (1:7a) and L3 (1:12a and 14a), thus creating a refrain effect. But no chant formula seems present in the F6 and SS Lessons. Whether the employment of the Tone-6 motives was a Romanizing symbol, like the use of pre-existent material in the Magnificats, depends on more precise dating.[63]

Across the cycle, one group of chromatic pitch relationships is generated by the references to "tears," which also override the importance of the chant citations in the F5 Lessons. At "Plorans ploravit" of L1, D/E♭ relations begin to color this strongly Mode-6 piece, and at "et lachrymae ejus" the tone is abandoned and the semitone inflection takes over all voices except the tenor. A similar juxtaposition is heard at "Defecerunt prae lacrymis oculi mei" in F6/L1, in which the flats are even more audible as the piece is based on A (a rare example of Mode 9 in a composer normally considered as using an eight-mode system). The next Lesson features a similar semitone relationship in the passage from "Ain" to "Fecit Dominus quae cogitavit," followed quickly by an analogous pitch choice (A-B♭) for "et laetificavit super te inimicum, et exaltavit cornu hostium tuorum," the enemy's defeat of Jerusalem. Local rhythmic disruptions underscore the derision of "deriserunt" (F5/L2) and "stulta" (F6/L2), while the gleeful hooting of the city's enemies, "We will devour [her]; behold the day which we awaited; we found and saw her" ("Devorabimus; en ista est dies"; 2:16), employs triple time.

Some of the contrapuntal *durezze* also give this cycle its word-oriented flavor, including the ♯-♭ relations at "et circumdedit me felle et labore" (F6/L3). As a climax, the widest pitch juxtapositions are saved for the SS Lessons. At the beginning of L2, the "Quomodo obscuratum est aurum" verse, Lasso chose, not notational symbolism, but the complete range of pitch mutations for the idea of "mutatus est color optimus" at the end of the first sub-verse. The verse begins with *durus* sonorities for "Quomodo . . . aurum," ranging as far as D♯. The setting of Jeremiah's "change of the best color" moves to A♭ and E♭, then returns to the *finalis* G (the Lesson is in Mode 8). In the Prayer, a slow declamatory setting of the verse "Patres nostri peccaverunt" begins innocuously on the *finalis* but reaches an F♯ sonority within two breves, before the half-verse is even over, making sure that the chromatic gesture for "our fathers sinned" was marked, perhaps as an intercessory gesture for Wittelsbach ancestors.

The Responsories work in different ways. In Mode 1tr, as are all three items of this Nocturne (the chants are in modes 5/6), Lasso's F6/R9, *Caligaverunt oculi mei,* shows a different kind of economy from Victoria's. It opens homophonically, moving quickly from G to a clear cadence on the reciting-tone D at the end of the first clause ("a fletu meo"), and declamatory elision carries through to the end of the A section, a half-cadence again on D. Since this is an R9, the repetendum is sung thrice, and in it Lasso juxtaposed *durus* and *mollis* for "si est dolor." Most remarkably, he evaded a well-prepared cadence on B♭ twice within the space of two breves at "dolor similis," turning quickly to the *finalis* for "sicut dolor meus" and thus suggesting that nothing could substitute for Jeremiah's/Christ's suffering (example 4.5). After all the avoidance of the B♭, the Responsory's verse finally provides it at "per viam," but not before introducing two irregular dissonances, first a fourth quitted by leap in the lower voice and then a grinding minor seventh; this is paralleled by a licit but still harsh minor second towards the end ("et videte"). For the *Glossa ordinaria,* this verse represents *conquestio;* if the dissonances were meant to provoke tears, in Ponzio's sense, they could not have been more audible.

Lasso's three through-composed Benedictus, all for Holy Week and all for nine voices in two choirs, display greater weightiness than his single Miserere—a feature also typical of his other Office canticles, the many Magnificat (Vespers) and fewer Nunc dimittis (Compline) settings. They do not share the intertextual references of these other genres, but they do have pre-existent material, namely the canticle tones: 3 (ending on *a,* as was the composer's practice in the Magnificat and Nunc dimittis), 4 (on *e*), and 1 (on *d*). That

EXAMPLE 4.5. Lasso, F6/R5, "Si est dolor."

the three of them were copied together with the other items for the Week suggests that they were meant for F5, F6, and SS, respectively; only the last accords with the canticle's antiphons, all three of which are in chant mode 1.

Both their scoring and their nature distinguish these pieces. Of contemporary settings in Italy, only four—by Paolo Ferrarese (1565), Corteccia, Falconio (1580), and Asola (1584)—are full settings of all the verses. Many are in Mode 6, with Lasso's choice of Mode 4 shared only by one of Contino's, while Modes 1 and 3 are not found at all. Those of Alcarotto (1570), D-Mbs 2747, and PistAC 215 are the only ones for five voices; the large-scale repertory comprises Falconio's eight-voice setting and a nine-voice piece by Palestrina, in which the only time when the entire ensemble is heard is for a few bars at the end of the last half-verse ("pedes nostros in viam pacis").[64] Nowhere else in Europe would the end of Lauds have sounded as it did in Munich of the 1580s.

The template for Lasso's three settings was simple: in the even-numbered verses from 2 to 10, the canticle tone is stated as a cantus firmus in the second choir, usually but not always in T2.[65] The odd-numbered verses, for choir I, are free, except for v. 1 in the Tone-3 and Tone-1 pieces, which use the tone. In the former, the chant is carried by C2, while the Tone-1 setting splits the formula between the two choirs (T2 and C1, respectively). If the overall plan seems schematic, its execution is marked by the seemingly endless contrapuntal invention on display. Some moments reflect meaning, as in the literal scoring for the choirboys singing v. 9 alone, "Et tu puer," in both the Tone-3 and 4 canticles.

The climax of the text is v. 12, "Illuminare his qui in tenebris et in umbra mortis sedent; ad dirigendos pedes nostros in viam pacis"/"To illuminate those who sit in darkness and the shadow of death; to direct our steps into the way of peace," set in all cases by Lasso for all nine voices enunciating the full text. Again the *Glossa ordinaria* on Luke are suggestive, given their use by German Jesuits. Their comments, taken from Bede and Nicholas of Lyra, provided moral meaning: Bede considered the "tenebrae" as sin, and "directing our steps" as the conversion of the heart that drives good works ("steps") along the route to the "house of perpetual peace," heaven.[66] Nicholas made a break in the first half-verse between "in tenebris" and "in umbra mortis," seeing those "in darkness" as the patriarchs in Limbo whom Christ came to redeem immediately after the Passion, while "those sitting in the shadow of death" meant all living humans illuminated by Christ's preaching. The moral gloss interpreted the "way of peace" as the fraternal and heavenly path to which those liberated from original sin were directed by the gift of divine grace.

Lasso's three approaches to this verse reveal affinities beyond their scoring. The first similarity is the declamatory separation of "Illuminare" from "his," setting off "to illuminate" from "those in shadows." In all three pieces, "his" gets a single chord, answered by the other choir; in the Tone-4 canticle, the word is set with a remarkably low scoring in choir II with a D_2 in the bass. Lasso kept the rest of the clause "qui in tenebris . . . sedent" together, taking the break at the half-verse after "sedent." But in the Tone-4 piece, "et umbra mortis" is prolonged by 5 ½ breves compared to the other versions (example 4.6).

The ending of the canticle also differentiates the Tone-3 piece, with its single-choir declamation of "ad dirigendos pedes nostros" followed by a concise "in viam pacis." The other two settings split "ad dirigendos" and "pedes nostros" between the choirs, with a long extension (eight breves) for "in the path of peace." The Tone-1 canticle, presumably meant for liturgical SS, climaxes in the long four-breve *supplementum* (as Joachim Burmeister would call it) on the *finalis* D in the lowest voice of choir I and the top one of choir II. Lasso's settings echo the *Glossa*'s moral explanation, but their separation of the verse's first two words from each other is not found in exegesis and seems to refer to the Wittelsbach past and present.

One of the sharp contrasts at the Munich court was between Wilhelm V's taste for liturgical splendor and the increasingly penitential tone of court life in the 1580s. The scoring and the seriousness of the Lauds items reflect this. Lasso's long-term engagement with all liturgical canticles as texts for

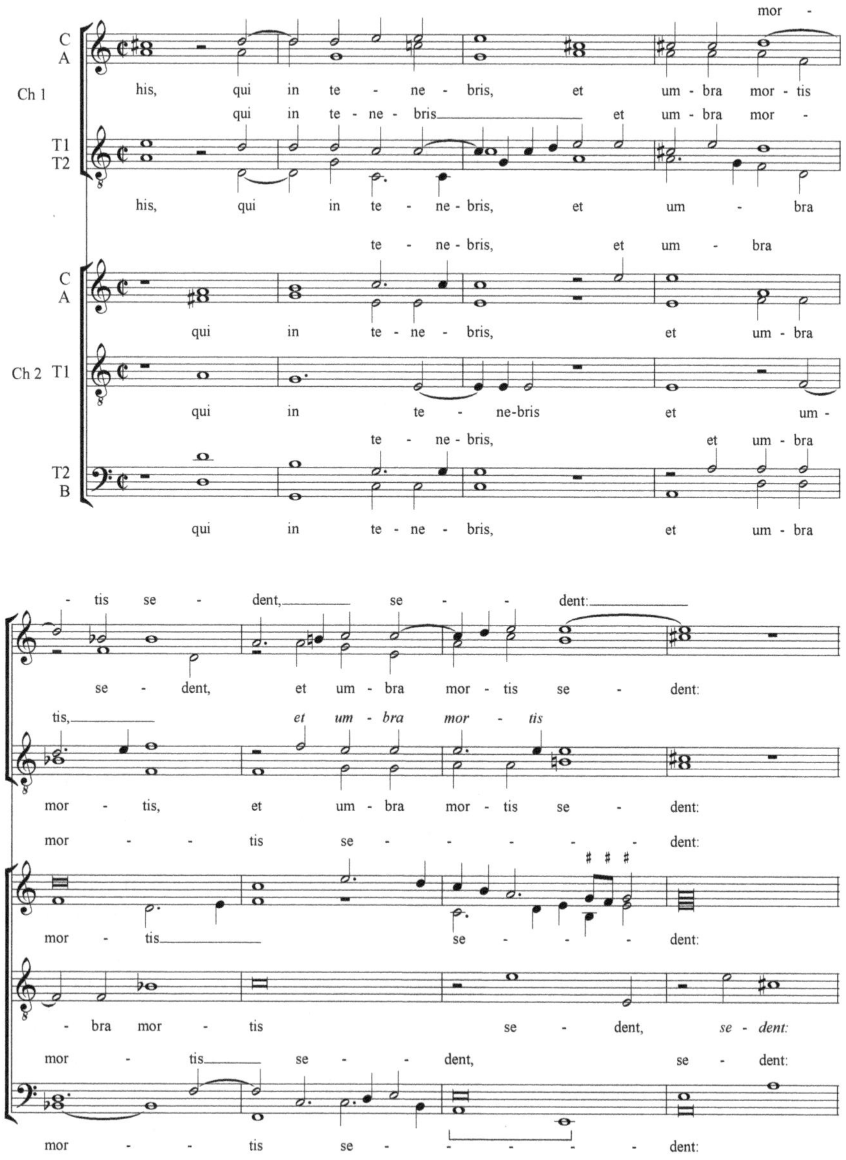

EXAMPLE 4.6. Lasso, Benedictus *quarti toni,* "Illuminare his."

experimentation and contrapuntal play found another outlet here, although without the relationship to previous polyphonic models in the Vespers or Compline pieces. The musical underscoring of "to illuminate those who sit in darkness and the shadows of death"—quite literally the ritual moment of the Benedictus, with all but one candle gone from the hearse—resonates with the concern of the composer and his patron in the late 1580s with age, end-of-life introspection, and personal justification. And the Tone-1 canticle's emphasis on D, also the *finalis* of SS's antiphon *Mulieres sedentes,* links it to the scene of the Three Marys at the Tomb, and thus to mourning but also resurrection.

The remarks of Fiamma—whose sacred verse Lasso was setting in his 1585 and 1587 madrigal books—are suggestive. Commenting on the fifth stanza of his own double sestina on the Passion "Quando, per dar al mondo eterna vita," the poet explained his lines addressed to the souls in Limbo, waiting for Christ to come: "Behold the bright day, happy for you, which will lift you from the center of the earth, and out of the obscure shadows of death." This reference to the first effect of the Passion—the Harrowing of Hell, imagined as taking place after the Deposition and thus during SS's Lauds—was justified for Fiamma by the prophecy: "Illuminare his, qui in tenebris. . . ."[67]

The Benedictus works were the final contribution to the growing weight of Munich's Tenebrae, pieces that balanced the complexity of Lasso's Lessons and shared in the compressed expressivity of his Responsories. The Wittelsbach heard original contributions to all three major Office canticles during the last two decades of Wilhelm's reign and Lasso's life, and all seem to have held lasting value. The next surviving Triduum works associated with Munich are possibly J. K. Kerll's Responsories from around 1670 and certainly G. A. Bernabei's Lessons and Responsories (1716).

Comparing Habsburg and Wittelsbach practice also suggests familial preferences. Although all were associated with Lessons, only the Austrians seem to have heard them outside of liturgy, as a kind of prophecy suited to the rulers' status. They, along with the Bavarians, were presented with items in neater packages—Lesson cycles or Lauds—as opposed to the more gradual accretion of individual Lamentations, with wider preservation of earlier works, among the Spanish. But Munich and Madrid quickly adopted the Roman Lesson texts, a development postponed in Vienna until the arrival of Ferdinand II in 1619, with an evidently codified Graz repertory in tow. As opposed to the ritual weeping of the Italian repertory, court decorum at these sites seems to have encouraged works for personal listening or meditation, not culturally conditioned emotion. The preservation of repertory across new devotional trends and changing social situations is one side—but only one—of the changes in the coming century. Still, there is a certain tension in the repertory between the universality of the liturgical texts and the personal resonance of the settings for sovereigns. In a social sense, the shrinking of Tenebrae from community to court, from collective to private meaning, is all too evident.

Chapter 5

Static Rites, Dramatic Music

In a new century given to affect, Lapide's prolegomena to his commentary on Jeremiah underscore the emotions behind Tenebrae Lessons:

> Lamentations were written by Jeremiah from urgent and pressing feeling, and thus they are full of affect . . . here Jeremiah indulges in these affects and his sorrow, without order or ordered discourse, heaping up his sentences in a rush, according to how his pain pours them out.[1]

This dynamic view of the words stands in sharp contrast to their ossifying projection, as the ritual was fixed by the gradual adoption across Europe of the Roman liturgical books and their standard selection of Lamentations verses, seconded by the seventeenth-century ceremonials describing unchanging local enactment of the Hours.[2] But the possibilities for more labile emotion were inherent in the new musical styles, and meant that the changing affect of verses could find audible expression in the settings, beyond the structures of the previous century.

In central European devotion, the fifty-third "mode" of meditations on Christ's sufferings by the Polish Jesuit Gaspar Druzbicki (1589–1662) provided a capsule table of events of the Passion and, in a parallel column, the corresponding verses from Lamentations 1–4: "In this way the entire Passion of Christ can be found in the prophet Jeremiah, and indeed in just the first four chapters of his Lamentations; in this way Jeremiah gives an admirable interpretation and illumination to the words of the Gospel story, and conversely he receives the same illumination from the Gospel."[3] For instance, the Flagellation ("Tunc apprehendit Pilatus Jesum et flagellavit") was linked directly to 3:1 and 3:3 ("Ego vir videns . . . Tantum in me vertit," also the opening of F6/L3). First printed in 1652, Druzbicki's *Tractatus de variis passionem . . . meditandi modis* was reissued in 1657, 1660, and 1664.[4]

The concept of darkness also took on new meaning in European spirituality. Lesson verses such as "Me minavit, et adduxit in tenebras, et non in lucem . . . In tenebrosis collocavit me"/"He has led me and brought me into darkness, and not into light . . . He has placed me in dark spots" (3:2 and 6, also F6/L3), besides the obvious reference to the Passion, resonated with personal experience.[5] The need for "darkness" as part of introspection and penance was evident, and so musical settings of texts invoking "shadows" could have positive meaning for individual spirituality.

The spatial environment reinforced the lack of light. Of all the places discussed here, only Paris (1667, roughly contemporary with Charpentier's first Lessons) and Vienna (1688) would introduce street lighting; elsewhere, the service continued to let out into the darkness of the early modern city.[6] Obviously, the political crises of the century also figured in the fields of meaning, although it is difficult to relate surviving Lesson cycles to any specific catastrophe.[7]

THE PRACTICE OF THE OFFICE

The ceremonials from major sites vary in their specificity. The guide by M. A. Mattei (*cerimoniere* 1652–1700) for public ritual in S. Pietro in Vaticano and its Cappella Giulia did not prescribe the exact items to be sung in polyphony. Rather, it emphasized the placement of the hearse, the lack of any other visual stimuli, and the reverences that the singers were to make to the altar and the canons.[8] Giuseppe de Fide's 1636 overview of the basilica's ceremonies had also mentioned polyphony in only a general way.[9] The actual diaries of the chapel, however, show a good deal of chant for L1/2 and unspecified polyphony for L3. In 1607 and then in 1615–18, Andrea Amici noted this pattern, and in 1616 he recorded that the majority of the Responsories were sung to new settings by the chapelmaster Francesco Soriano, music that seems not to have survived.[10] But given the Giulia's Cinquecento history—the surviving manuscripts still in its archive include two Palestrina Lamentations cycles and one simple set by G. M. Nanino, along with a print of Felice Anerio's Responsories of 1606—this was a remarkable scale-back, one paralleled in other basilicas.[11] Palestrina had written all four of his Lesson sets during the twenty-three years he ran the ensemble, and to have only three Lessons per year sung meant a shift toward Responsories and/or chant Lessons. It is striking that none of the Giulia's chapelmasters during the century—Soriano, Paolo Agostini, Virgilio Mazzocchi, Orazio Benevoli—left surviving Triduum Office polyphony. This parallels the often-cited stagnation of the Sistina's ritual after 1600, where the diaries record little change in the routine of Tenebrae, normally the L1 only in polyphony and always sung by soloists, with the major surprise being the popularity of Allegri's Lessons even over Palestrina's, and normally only the first Lesson sung in polyphony.[12] Stefano Landi's monophonic rewriting of the chant Responsories in 1631 caused the Sistina's singers to remark that the new versions were "too short and not devout," and in 1633 Landi's versions were rejected by Urban VIII's order.[13]

An important prelate's own international experiences, including Rome, are in the Italian-language diary of Ernst Albrecht von Harrach, archbishop of Prague from 1623 to 1667. Starting in 1647–49, he recorded Triduum polyphony, whether at his cathedral of St. Vitus or on his travels. In 1647, despite the evident problems of Prague's musical chapel, he heard Lessons, the Benedictus, and the Miserere (specified as the second iteration of the psalm) in polyphony.[14] The next, more charged year—in the presence of Emperor Ferdinand III and with the Swedish army soon to begin its siege of the city—Harrach reported that Lamentations, Responsories, the canticle *alternatim*, and the Miserere were sung in St. Vitus at 4 p.m., probably performed by the Viennese court ensemble.[15]

The following year, after his capture and release by the Swedes, the archbishop was on one of his longer journeys, again together with the royal family but this time in Trent, where he was amazed by the Habsburg disinterest in Wednesday's Tenebrae and by the participation of the pregnant Empress Maria Leopoldine in the Washing of the Feet ceremony on Thursday. Finally, on Good Friday, he wound up at the Observant Franciscans of S. Bernardino da Siena on the outskirts of the city, where he recorded the friars' "good but extraordinarily unusual" ways of singing Lamentations, especially the *Oratio* and the Second Nocturne Lessons. This may be a reference to the Trentino Franciscan traditions of either *canto fratto* (rhythmicized chant) or improvised polyphony; if so, it is a testimony to the survival of these orally-transmitted practices in a major ecclesiastical center, and to their intersection with figures from "high" culture.[16] From then on, Harrach noted his attendance at musical Tenebrae at St. Vitus in following years, and then in Rome during the conclaves of 1655 and 1667.[17]

In late seventeenth-century Seville Cathedral, the polyphonic singers were to sing the Lamentations and all the Responsories, minus the verse, on Wednesday. The entire choir performed L1 and then smaller ensembles or soloists took the other Lessons; this is the same practice as in the northern cathedral of León.[18] The CFE was sung in polyphony, and there was some latitude for the choirmaster in terms of the selection of the Miserere. On Friday, however, the Responsories were all sung in chant, and the Miserere strictly *alternatim* (and hence there are no SS Responsories). The surviving Responsories for F5/6, with obbligato instruments in the latter, by Seville's chapelmaster Francisco de Santiago (there 1617–43) seem to have replaced a choirbook of sixteenth-century pieces.[19] Santiago's eight-voice items for F5 (R2–9) are largely antiphonal, while the three instruments in the F6 pieces include small dulcians (*bajoncillos*), although the top line as transmitted in the copy of 1772 goes up to C_6 and D_6 outside the standard seventeenth-century ranges of the soprano dulcian (G_5, according to Praetorius).[20] The indication in the parts of a "muta" instead suggests the use of a kit violin, otherwise called "sordina" in Spanish dramas that use it often, not least in some passages that cite Lamentations.

Although the Seville inventories do include a manuscript with three L1s by Alonso Lobo (of which only the SS/L1 survives) and make no mention of Santiago's four now-lost Lessons recorded in the Lisbon catalogue of 1649, the liturgical guide suggests that the whole First Nocturne was sung.[21] In mid-century, the destination of the surviving Lessons by other *maestros* is not clear, and the overall lack of extant L2s seems to contradict the ceremonial.[22] At the end of the century, Diego José de Salazar's two L1s in the cathedral's holdings are *a 8* but with some verses for solo or duet voices with three *bajones* as used in Santiago's F6 Responsories; they were probably composed during his tenure as chapelmaster, 1685–1709 and could have replaced Lobo's Lessons on F5–6.

What the Hours might have been like in a civic basilica is evident in the ceremonial for the Papal legate in Bologna's S. Petronio in the 1630s. The Lamentations were sung by professional singers and the other Lessons by clerics in order of seniority; the indications for extinguishing the candles and the *strepitus* correspond to other Italian practice.[23] The basilica's repertory from this decade does not seem to have survived, although the guide provides a background to later music by Maurizio Cazzati (Lamentations and Lauds, opp. 44/45, 1668) and G. P. Colonna. To judge from these composers' production and from the copying records, from the 1660s onward Lessons included solos with both continuo only and with string accompaniment, while the Lauds items were for four/five-part voices with instruments.[24] Besides his printed cycle for solo voice and continuo of 1689, eight different Lessons by Colonna survive in manuscript (A-Wn), of which two (F6/L3 and SS/L2) have five-part string accompaniment. These were probably copied in Bologna for Leopold I's *Schlafkammerbibliothek*, but not necessarily for liturgical performance by the Vienna Hofkapelle. In 1696, as G. A. Perti took over the depleted establishment after Colonna's death, the chapel's codex (I-Bsp A. 21) of anonymous Responsories from 1585 was refurbished. Tenebrae at the basilica would have been long, impressive, and polystylistic, and the participation of instruments provides a link between the north Italian practice studied by Baroncini and Padoan around 1600, and Settecento

orchestrally accompanied Lessons that influenced young composers study-
ing in Bologna, such as Giacomo Puccini sr. (1712–86; see chapter 7 below).

As in the previous century, Tuscany and Rome continued to be important centers. The practice of S. Petronio would have been in the Florentine
poet Jacobo Cicognini's ears when he wrote his poetic paraphrase of Lamentations, the *Lagrime di Gieremia profeta* (1627). He was in the service of
Cardinal Luigi Capponi, legate in Bologna in 1615, but had already been
involved in Florence producing innovative texts for musical setting, most recently the opera *Amor pudico*.[25] His reworking of Jeremiah is in five sections,
corresponding to the book's chapters, each generated by their twenty-two-
verse structure. But, unlike earlier paraphrases, Cicognini's also includes the
"Jerusalem, convertere" refrain from the Office, placing it after sets of stanzas throughout the entire text.[26]

Cicognini's paraphrase resonated with the Medici tradition of the Hours,
which he would have heard in Pisa or Florence. From 1600 onward the court
chronicler Cesare Tinghi recorded polyphony ("mattutino") every year with
multiple choirs and the court's best virtuosi.[27] In 1602 Giulio Caccini led the
musicians (including his teenage daughter Francesca) in three-choir pieces
for Wednesday's Office at S. Nicola in Pisa, with its corridor connecting to
the Palazzo Ducale. The following year, this scoring was repeated on both
Wednesday and Thursday, with Vittoria and Antonio Archilei.[28] In a few
years there were smaller-scale performances, occasionally without the female
singers.[29]

In Florence, the Office took place in S. Felicita, the ducal church with
Vasari's corridor to the Uffizi. In this case, the public nature of Florentine
Tenebrae is evident from the space, with its ample nave and the gallery of
the corridor above the entrance; hence the choirs upstairs would have alternated with the ensemble placed in the crossing. In contrast, S. Nicola's smaller
size, and the placement of its gallery in the south transept, would have meant
more proximity for the ensembles and less projection of the sound throughout the church, contributing to the more private effect of the music. It is possible that the seventeenth-century project (never completed) to install a flat
wooden ceiling at the Pisan church was conceived for Tenebrae's acoustical
needs.[30]

The overall pattern would last well into the 1630s: three-choir performances on Holy Wednesday and the same or slightly smaller ensembles for
the other Days, largely at S. Nicola, with blocs of years in Florence when the
Medici did not travel (1617–21 and 1626–31). In 1606, cardinal Ferdinando

Gonzaga arranged for the Caccinis, the Archileis, and Jacopo Peri to sing in Holy Week in S. Nicola, repeated the following year and in 1610. The first time this was done in the more public spaces of Florence was in 1612, as the three-choir ensemble sang on Wednesday at S. Felicita until an hour after sunset, one choir up in the corridor and the others below, with a large audience in the church.[31] In 1614 the ensemble was expanded to four choirs, and this was repeated at S. Felicita in 1618, with two choirs upstairs and two in the church, in a year that had already seen Cicognini's *L'Andromada* performed during Carnival. This set of Office music was crucial in the court's perception of Francesca Caccini's remarkable abilities. In 1619, she prepared her female students by having them learn music by rote for two weeks during Lent, as her letter of 19 March, Monday in Holy Week, testifies.[32] The result was Wednesday's Office at S. Felicita with three choirs, repeated with instruments the following year.

For the first time in 1622, the music was specified as being by Muzio Effrem (Wednesday) and Peri (Thursday), and the latter provided music for a four-choir Office in S. Nicola the following year.[33] After a Carnival featuring Francesca Caccini's *La liberazione di Ruggiero* in 1625, she again led the three choirs in S. Nicola for Wednesday's and Friday's Offices, and the performance of her female pupils seems to have repaid her earlier work.[34] For Caccini and her students, Tenebrae was a major venue of public singing. Even in the year of Cosimo II's death, when all theatrical entertainment was shut down, the service continued, perhaps with resonance of ducal mourning.[35] Later less massive, polyphony still ran through the diary; in 1633, Girolamo Frescobaldi provided Wednesday's music, and G. B. da Gagliano Friday's.[36] Although the difficulties of the 1630s led to occasional years without polyphony, still music is recorded up to the chronicle's end in 1644. In its regularity and sheer scale, the polyphony outpaced theater music, and the Medici Triduum was one of the few places in Europe, outside female monastic foundations, to hear women sing the Office.

But a close reading of the diaries indicates subtle changes in court piety and its reflection in musical repertory, especially in the last years of Cosimo II's reign (1618–20), with a stronger emphasis on vernacular music. Already on Good Friday 1619 "fu dalle dame cantato salmi di passione e *Stabat mater dolorosa*," and the year after, Princess Margarita sang "alcune laude" on Friday together with two singers of the archduchess.[37] Even before the Regency (1621–28), the large-scale music was reserved for Wednesday afternoon (less crowded with other events), as music in different cultural registers (*laude*), more obviously related to the Passion, was sung on Friday.[38] This presages the discomfort with the Office to appear more widely among European royalty in the coming century.

The actual repertory performed is hard to track. Possibly Cavalieri's works from the 1590s were performed into the new century. Peri's large-scale music in the 1620s, not an output traditionally associated with the composer, is lost.[39] Caccini's rote learning of 1619 suggests recitation formulae serving as a basis for improvisation; there is also a sense of the composer herself worrying about Medici perception of such practice. The surviving *voci pari* Responsories for four voices published by Marco da Gagliano in 1630 seem in style and scoring to be Duomo music, distant from what this repertory must have been. Ironically, in view of the large-scale nature of the music, the one surviving candidate is Frescobaldi's solo-voice F5/L3, preserved in the mid-century Roman manuscript I-Bc Q. 43, and possibly for the 1633 Tenebrae for which he had written pieces. The Giulia's diaries seem to exclude the piece from S. Pietro's practice, where he was active before and after his time in Florence.

One textual clue is the omission of "irae" in Frescobaldi's 1:12 (thus "in die furoris sui"). Although the word appears universally in Italian breviaries and in all the Giulia's polyphonic Lessons that the composer would have known earlier as organist of S. Pietro, it is missing in one post-1590 source: Cavalieri's first cycle of Lessons preserved in the Vallicelliana manuscript. Either Frescobaldi took his text from hearing Cavalieri's music in Rome, or the omission represents a Florentine variant of the verse.[40]

The surface chromaticism and ornamentation of Frescobaldi's Lesson have parallels in his solo motets of 1627.[41] Despite the general perception of the composer's lack of education, his F5/L3 is rhetorically clear. Cast on D/*durus*, the Lesson demarcates verse structure by pitch; in 1:11, the sub-verses move to F, then A, with another weak cadence back to D at "facta sum vilis," without grinding dissonances or solecisms. Precisely at "O vos omnes" and "si est dolor sicut dolor meus" of 1:12, Frescobaldi turns to chromaticism, saving the highest vocal register around the high G_5 and followed by an anabasis (A_4-D_5 chromatically) for "De excelso misit ignem" (example 5.1). Although not the most difficult piece in Q. 43, Frescobaldi's setting shares its irregular passage-work ("locutus est Dominus") with other Florentine repertory.

Outside the court, Responsories followed Tuscan traditions, as with the *Responsoria omnia* (Venice, 1607) of the Augustinian Girolamo Bartei, working in Volterra, for four *voci pari,* and including the Lauds items. The eight-voice anthology *Responsoria hebdomadae sanctae* (Venice, 1612), compiled by the otherwise unknown Ruggiero Argilliano, features composers from Lucca, including the Guami family. But the volume, dedicated to Pellegrino Bertacchio, the new archbishop of Modena and the former archpriest in Argilliano's hometown of Castelnuovo di Garfagnana, goes beyond local repertory.[42] It includes composers from Emilia, Genoa (Simone Molinaro), and

EXAMPLE 5.1. Frescobaldi, F5/L3 (Q. 43), "Mem. De excelsis."

the Veneto (four by the recently deceased Giovanni Croce, Pietro Lappi, and Viadana). Despite the scoring, the style of these Responsories is traditional, as is Bartei's.

On the other hand, the title—*Musici modi in Responsoria Divini Officii*—of the Sienese nobleman Tomaso Pecci's 1603 four-voice set points to its "aesthetic," not functional, conception. The dedication, shot through with the language of the Song of Songs, is to St. Catherine of Siena, mentioning only her intercession for the composer and his city, with no reference to the Passion.[43] Pecci's Responsories are as unconventional as his madrigals and canzonettas. The cycle opens with an F5/R1 *In monte Oliveti*, written with close attention to the change of literary voice from "oravit ad Patrem" to "Pater, si fieri potest." Between the two phrases, there is a full cadence, double-bar, and then a simultaneous declamation of "Pater" with unusual voice-leading. Pecci's response to direct emotion is clear at the opening of R2, as "Tristis est anima mea" generates chromaticism between the first two sonorities, along with grinding cross-relations (B♭/♮ for "mea") and a minor/major third duality at "usque ad mortem" that must be a sign for Christ's own agony in Gethsemene. Although the rest of the Responsory is not quite so unstable, still "fugam" occasions two different *fugae*.

There is a good deal of surface chromaticism and unusual voice-leading in other Responsories. The most charged passages, whether or not Passion-related, also are underlined by unusual pitch relations; the initial perfect

fourth gesture of *Plange quasi virgo,* for instance, is immediately repeated up
a step up but diminished (B-E vs. C♯-F♮), and *O vos omnes* reiterates a D-E♭-D
figure a semitone higher. The opening of *Tenebrae factae sunt* is generated by
the darkness of the Crucifixion that it sets: cast in Mode 2tr (on G), as will
only become clear at the end of the repetendum, it begins with *mollis* sonorities on E♭ and a bass line leaping down an octave for the "shadows." But in an
uglier way, Pecci emphasized the "guilt" of the opening sentence's "Judaei"
via chromatic heightening and a full cadence with bar-line (example 5.2).
This musical attack by anaphora is not found in other settings of this text
across the peninsula—apart from Gesualdo's Responsories of 1611, whose
setting also reiterates the word, underscoring it again by pitch relations.[44]
It is not clear if Gesualdo imitated Pecci, but given their lack of obligation
to patrons or institutions, this seems to have been a personal choice on the
part of the two nobles, a sign that anti-Jewish sentiment was not confined to
lower classes.

Another set of Responsories, geographically close to Argilliano's and
Pecci's but stylistically quite different, gives a sense of Triduum in smaller
places. After a checkered career through church posts in and out of his Olivetan order, Barnaba Milleville was brought to the small cathedral of Sarzana (north of Massa and Carrara) as the organist on 26 February 1623. The
Duomo seems to have had no regular singers, and musicians were imported
for the major feasts of Trinity Sunday and the Invention of the Cross (3 May).
In Milleville's first Holy Week, he incurred extra expenses, probably vocal-
ists from elsewhere.[45] Later that year, he was reprimanded for this evidently
too-frequent practice, and there are no records of Triduum payments until
his 1626 departure.[46]

But in 1624, he published his Responsories under a title referring to the
"exequies" of Christ, with a dedication to Stefano Salvago, a relative of the
local bishop G. B. Salvago.[47] The scoring includes fourteen items *a 4* (C/T1/
T2/B), 6 *a 3,* and 7 *a 2,* all with continuo; there are also solos and duets inside the four-voice pieces, and Milleville indexed oral practice by his use of
falsobordone in eight Responsories. The combination of reduced scoring and
recitational writing results in undemanding soprano and bass parts, suggesting that the trustworthy singers were the two tenors. The note in the index
that these parts could be sung by sopranos allowed for female monastic performance (e.g., at S. Vito in the composer's native Ferrara, or S. Chiara across
the street from Sarzana Cathedral), while the title-page's suggestion of the
contents as motets for Forty Hours' devotions showed their utility.

The opening F5 items immediately provide the collection's range. *In monte
Oliveti* is almost entirely in *falsobordone,* but *Tristis est anima mea* eschews

EXAMPLE 5.2. Pecci, F6/R5 (1603), "Tenebrae factae sunt."

the technique. The latter starts off as an expressive solo for one of the tenors, with *mollis* gestures at the opening. In a complete reversal of all scoring norms for the genre, most of the text is a solo, but the verse ("Ecce appropinquat hora") is for tutti. In the repeat of the B section, the full ensemble joins in only for the last words ("immolari pro vobis"). Milleville thus made this text into a dramatic motet.

In other items, pitch expression takes the place of scoring or texture; *Plange quasi virgo,* another tenor duet, starts in a C/*mollis* sonority, turning via a chromatic anabasis to E/*durus* and eventually G/*mollis*. The piece does not reach what will turn out to be its F tonality until the end of the repetendum; at the da capo, Milleville rewrote the chromaticism, ending the Responsory after the repetition of the A section and before the liturgically necessary third iteration of the repetendum. Thus the last words heard are "wail, shepherds, in sackcloth and ashes." The local synodal restrictions on the *strepitus* had been reissued by the bishop Salvago in 1618, warning against peasants who "disrupted"—in their terms, commemorated—Tenebrae with noise-makers, horns, and agricultural tools, and limiting wooden sticks in Lauds to the size of the little finger. For the prelate, as for Guidi, such ruckus was Satan's work.[48] Milleville's edition replaced the rural *charivari* racket with stylized music, just as it ultimately substituted improvised song with notated polyphony.

Finally, two printed Lesson cycles point to solo singing in Siena. Annibale Gregori's *Cantiones ac sacrae lamentationes* (Siena, 1620) mixes Lessons and motets, as does Alessandro della Ciaia's *Lamentationi sagre e motetti* (Venice, 1650); both have been well studied.[49] Like Milleville's Responsories and G. B. Rossi's Lessons, Gregori's settings include late examples of solo *falsobordone* along with "accentuated" singing and melismas often placed at the end of sub-verses.[50] Both editions almost entirely eschew direct reference to the Tone-6 chant formula.

The 1650 edition testifies to nuns' practice of the Tenebrae Office, as its composer noted its origin as music for female houses. The unexpected and quite difficult melismas are not restricted to the ends of verses, while the letters are highly elaborate; a "Jod" in della Ciaia's SS/L1 features simultaneous metric proportions (C against 12/8). The shifts of *mollis/cantus* system (F5/L2's "Peccatum peccavit") and local chromaticism with hexachordal uncertainty requiring use of the *quadro* sign ("Non esset auxiliator" in the same Lesson, or "Vide, Domine, et considera" in L3's 1:11c) highlight the charged nature of the settings. Amid the striking chromaticism and dissonances of della Ciaia's Lessons, the Prayer seems to have been meant as a rhetorical summation, as in the exegetical tradition. This is most evident in its internal pitch relations among verses; at the very beginning (v. 1b), its exordium on G/*mollis* swerves suddenly to markedly flat regions in the middle of the sub-verse for "respice *opprobrium nostrum,"/*"look upon our reproach," cadencing on Ab. The following v. 2, "Hereditas nostra" immediately changes system from *mollis* to *durus,* arriving at the very distant A♮. Of the 11 verses, only three end on the same pitch on which they began, and the reference to ancestors' sins in v. 7 ("Patres nostri peccaverunt") led della Ciaia to the widest pitch contrast inside any verse, as the opening on A /*durus* leads to C♯ and then back to a *mollis*-inflected B♭ by verse's end. That these traversals of the widest possible parts of the tonal spectrum should occur twice in the Prayer highlights the text's role as climax. Overall, della Ciaia's idiosyncratic Lessons provide one benchmark by which to measure other solo pieces around 1650.

ROME AT MID-CENTURY

In Rome, the Triduum also produced both devotional literature and polyphony. The poetic paraphrase of Jeremiah by Niccolò Strozzi (1590–1654; *Parafrasi delle Lamentationi di Ieremia*, Rome, 1635) was based on the liturgical Lessons in their sung form, as the author noted in his dedication to Cardinal Antonio Barberini.[51] It was accompanied by short moralizing commentaries. With his version of F6/L3, Strozzi turned to the Passion, as he linked

3:2 ("Me minavit et adduxit in tenebras et non in lucem") to Christ's sacrifice: "In His Passion, Christ was brought by His Father into the shadows of pain, without any light of comfort."[52] The poet continued the "darkness" imagery in his remarks on both the "optimistic" verses of SS/L1 (3:22ff. "Misericordias Domini") and the gloomy L2 (4:1ff; "Quomodo obscuratum est aurum"): "God's mercy, like morning light, illuminates ['stenebra'] the night of our misfortunes . . . The gold of justice is darkened by the shadows of sin."[53]

Strozzi's paraphrase provides a context for mid-century Roman Lamentations, which largely come from two sources, the local manuscript I-Bc Q. 43, and the roughly contemporary printed *Lamentationes Jeremiae Prophetae* (Rome, 1653), the first publication of Pietro Cesi (c.1630–1703). They both seem to reflect the practice of smaller or national churches outside the major basilicas. Among musical visitors, Harrach recorded only the Papal singers' ornamentation of psalm verses on Holy Wednesday 1655. On this occasion, cardinals from the ongoing conclave came to the Cappella Sistina, although almost no one stayed to the end of Tenebrae. On Thursday, as the cardinals mixed with the singers on their balcony, Harrach noted Lamentations and the Miserere without comment.[54] The prelate's remarks inaugurated the long tradition of outsiders' reports on the music for the psalm in the Sistina.

Cesi's op. 1 is dedicated to Giannicolò Conti (1617–98), the new Referendary of the Tribunals of the Apostolic Signature. It was signed by an unnamed cleric at the Roman house of S. Pantaleo, and this must mean someone from the circles of the disgraced Piarist order, which had been dissolved by Innocent X for its misdeeds.[55] Possibly the inscription was meant to enlist Conti's support in a rehabilitation campaign, the first step of which would be taken by Alexander VII in 1656. The dedication referred to the "religiosa familia" that the congregation had been forced to become after being stripped of its status as order in 1646. But it noted that the pieces had been sung at S. Pantaleo and were now being printed.[56] The edition also includes an appendix transposing its soprano vocal line into alto and tenor range with instructions for altering the continuo part.

Cesi's own links to the Piarists dated to his education by their founder, Joseph Calasanz, through the agency of his father, Giovanni Federico Cesi, the third Duke of Acquasparta. However, he became a priest after the order had been degraded and could not admit new members; hence he was technically not part of the congregation. Still, the Piarist chronicler Giancarlo Caputi noted his training by Calasanz, his ordination, musical and rhetorical studies, later residence at S. Pantaleo (along with teaching music to poor children as if he were a member of the order), and his use of a substantial patrimony to fund music for the church's titular feast.[57] Cesi's will in 1703 gave the Piarists his musical instruments as well as money to perform (exclusively) his compositions on the feast of St. Pantaleon, the titular celebration of the now-rehabilitated house.[58]

In the order's troubled days, one cause for scandal was regulars who played instruments and sang secular music. The only Piarist allowed to teach music in the order's schools was a "Domenico Antonio," banished from Rome for his offenses in 1642.[59] Even the 1665 restatement of the 1659 general chapter presumed only chant for Tenebrae.[60] The choice of Lamentations as an op. 1—the first edition of Lessons in Rome since Palestrina's in 1588 and the only one printed thereafter in the city—carried social meaning as well. Given the penitential character of the genre, the print was both a public act of atonement for the order's offenses and a symbol of Tenebrae's spread to this previously unmusical congregation.

The repertory in manuscript is suggestive in different ways. With its twenty-three Lessons, Q. 43 continues the "repository of Lessons" tradition as opposed to neat cycles, here all solo settings except for two duets for soprano and mezzo (C1/C2 cleffings). About half the contents are anonymous, with three by G. F. Marcorelli, and two settings each by Giacomo Carissimi and the architect/musical amateur Carlo Rainaldi. Single Lessons are attributed to Frescobaldi, Carlo Caprioli, and "M.M.," probably Marco Marazzoli; the other thirteen have no composers and no concordances, and the music must date from the middle third of the century.[61] The source is related by paper types to other cantata manuscripts in I-Bc; the best recent study gives those found in Q. 43 to Rome after 1650.[62] The Lessons are followed by six Passion/penance pieces in the vernacular (including a contrafactum placing Monteverdi's *Lamento d'Arianna* in the voice of Mary Magdalen), and six early oratorios; given the six weeks of Lent, this suggests a *quaderno di Quaresima,* a book with all the extra music for the season.

Its assembly may be reflected in its structure (table 5.1). Lessons by Carissimi, Rainaldi, Frescobaldi, Marcorelli, and "M.M." are all contained in different gatherings, suggesting they were obtained separately. Multiple anonymous items in a single fascicle include pieces for more than one Day (e.g. F6/SS on ff. 35r-42v), while others are organized by Day (three SS Lessons at ff. 48r-55v). The volume seems to have come about piecemeal; possibly the anonymous works were by a single person with a personal relationship to its owner. Although the opening three Lessons for F5 seem to be a set by Carissimi and Frescobaldi, there are five extra items for the Day. For F6 there is an additional L1 but no L3 at all, and SS has six settings for its L2 and a duplicate Prayer.

Practicality is evident, both in the uncorrected scribal mistakes in Frescobaldi's Lesson or in an anonymous, technically difficult, F5/L3 (f. 33), but

TABLE 5.1.
I-Bc, Q. 43, Lessons and fascicles

FASC.	FOLIO	COMPOSER	LITURGICAL PLACEMENT	*FINALIS*/SIGNATURE
1	f. 1r	Carissimi	F5/L1	D *durus*/F *mollis*; transposition; chant citations
	5r	" I.C."	F5/L2	B♭ *mollis*
2	7r	Frescobaldi	F5/L3	D *durus*
3	11r	—	F5/L3	E or A *durus*; transposition
4	15r	—	F5/L1	A or C *durus*; transposition
	16v	Carlo del Viol	F5/L1	incomplete
5	23r	Rainaldi	F5/L3	E with ♯
	27r	Rainaldi	F5/L2	F *mollis*
	30r	—	F5/L2	E *durus*
6	32v	—	F5/L3	A or C *durus*; transposition
7	35r	—	F6/L1	G *mollis*
	37v	—	F6/L2	F *durus*
	40r	—	SS/L3	F *mollis*; chant
8	43r	—	F6/L1	F *mollis*; chant; like f. 53r
9	48r	—	SS/L1	C *mollis*
	50v	—	SS/L2	G *mollis*
	53r	—	SS/L1	F *mollis*; chant
10	57r	"M.M."	SS/L2	E *durus*; *a 2*
11	61r	Marcorelli	SS/L2	G *mollis*
12	65r	Marcorelli	SS/L2	G *mollis*
	67v	—	SS/L2	G *durus*
13	70r	Marcorelli	SS/L2	G *mollis*; *a 2*
	76r	—	SS/L3	F or D *durus*; transposition

Total: 23 Lessons = F5: 3/L1; 3/L2; 4/L3; F6: 2/L1; 1/L2; 0/L3; SS: 2/L1; 6/L2; 2/L3 also in the transposition indication for four items. Like the voices of the two duets, these are related by thirds: Carissimi's opening F5/L1, notated on D/ *durus*, has instructions for performance up a minor third on F/*mollis*. More mystifying is the case of four anonymous Lessons (ff. 11r, 15r, 32v, 76r), whose notation seems to make no sense until it is read as a combination of two different pitch levels written on a single system. All four have an odd G-clef (G4) for the vocal part and a sometimes differing transposition signature in the continuo. On f. 11, either the vocal part must be read in G2 clef but down a fourth, with the continuo at pitch, or the bass up the same interval with the top line at pitch in treble clef. Elsewhere (ff. 15, 32, and 76) the transposition is a third (either the voice taken down or the continuo up). In this setup, accidentals are read according to the inflected pitches in the transposed clef. The procedure points to singers of different tessitura, as in Cesi's edition.

On the other hand, the volume covers liturgical needs haphazardly. Since there are no items for the end of F6 Matins, its owner might have been accustomed to leave Thursday's Tenebrae early, so as to organize processional music elsewhere, and the quantity of SS Lessons indicates multiple occasions for the Friday service. Ultimately, Q. 43 seems a personal collection of Lessons for someone who had responsibility for accompanying them.

Two L1s, one for F6 (f. 43r) and one for SS (f. 53r) show strong similarities: their titles are essentially the same, and their letters alternate simple gestures derived from chant with much more florid moments. The former uses recitation over a static bass in 2:8–10, a procedure also found in the latter's 3:24 ("Pars mea Dominus"). In both these F/*mollis* pieces, the later verses (F6's 2:10–11; SS's 3:28–29) turn to the pitch center D; finally, the "Jerusalem" refrain in both, reaching up to the high G_5 in the vocal line, is essentially the same music. The similarities point up the continuing power of improvisatory models in this seemingly highly stylized repertory.

The two duets by "M. M." and Marcorelli form part of the large SS/L2 group, and share their C1/C2 cleffing but not their pitch centers (E *durus* and F *mollis* respectively). The former Lesson separates its sub-verses by declamation (4:1 goes from recitation to imitation) and includes a florid conclusion for vv. 5–6 of the Lesson, both verses firmly on the *finalis* E. Marcorelli's version uses more theatrical declamation (repeating "Quomodo" from 4:1a before "dispersi sunt lapides sanctuarii" in 4:1b), wanders further afield tonally, and uses the image of the "cruel daughter of my people" in 4:3b to swing the music around to *mollis* regions on E♭. His solo setting of the same verse resorts only to surface chromaticism in a stable tonal structure (f. 62; example 5.3). As might be expected from a composer who had spent time in Umbria and Rome before working at Rome's Chiesa Nuova in 1646–47

EXAMPLE 5.3. Marcorelli, SS/L2 (Q. 43), "Sed et lamiae."

(whence the piece might stem), Marcorelli's approaches to this Lesson are less virtuosic but more varied rhetorically.[63]

A PROPHET ENVOICED AND OUTCAST

Several factors brought Lamentations closer to dramatic music, as can be seen in Lessons' proximity to oratorio in Q. 43 and in the "theatrical" Medici practice of the Office. The first case of the prophet as a singing role was probably the 1671 Passion *sepolcro* for Vienna, *Il Trionfo della Croce,* with a libretto by Nicolò Minato and music by G. F. Sances. However, the character of Jeremiah does not paraphrase Lamentations in this piece, the case also for another libretto by Minato including the prophet, *I frutti dell'albero della Croce* (with music by Antonio Draghi, 1691).[64] At the end of the important oratorio by G. A. Bergamori and G. P. Colonna, *La caduta di Gierusalemme* (Modena, 1688), the prophet foretells his future lamenting without reference to the book or the Lesson tone.[65]

But in the anonymous *Lamenti profetici nella Passione di Cristo,* produced for the Accademia dello Spirito Santo in Ferrara in 1676 and repeated seven years later, Jeremiah does indeed cite both his books. These are three short cantatas, with characters and a narrator, serving as *introduzioni* to the Miserere on the Days, one each evening. Possibly the now-lost music was by Giovanni Legrenzi, if it is indeed the same piece sent by an Oratorian in Fano to Venice in 1700.[66] Here, four prophets—also including David, Ezekiel, and Isaiah—foretell the Passion, glossing verses both from their "own" and from other prophetic books. Jeremiah turns to a Lamentations verse only in the second strophe of his aria in the Wednesday piece.[67] In a later recitative, the "Spiritus oris nostri Christus captus est" verse from ch. 4 was reworked to include penitent tears, followed by a concluding tutti that presages the "Amplius lava me" verse of the Miserere. [68] But overall, the Ferrara piece uses the Tenebrae Office sparingly.

The most remarkable appearance of sung Lamentations in their liturgical form on the seventeenth-century stage was a passage in Pedro Calderón de la Barca's last *auto sacramental, El cordero de Isaías* ("Isaiah's Lamb"), written in the final months of his life (1681); its music, evidently by Manuel de Navas, does not survive.[69] However, the prophet's text was first invoked in an early *comedia* by Calderón, *Origen, pérdida y restauración de la Virgen del Sagrario* (1616–29). In the older play, concerning three moments in the history of a Marian image in Toledo, Lamentations' opening is paraphrased as a song at the end of the "Jornada segunda," as the city is on the verge of falling to the Moors. The Christian lord Godmán and others gather in a cathedral chapel the night before the city's capture to take and hide the image, and their final procession is accompanied by a sung version *en romance* of 1:1, "¡Oh, cómo está la ciudad / sin consuelo y sin placer!" Godmán comments on the appropriateness of Jeremiah for this moment of sadness, and the act ends with a repeat of the song.[70] Again, oral tradition was present in Calderón's use of standardized poetic meter and the *romance* tradition.

In the 1681 *auto* for Corpus Christi, the "lamb" is literally a sheep taken to Jerusalem for sacrifice by Behomud, the Ethiopian eunuch baptized by the deacon Philip according to Acts 8:26–40; symbolically, it represents Christ and the Real Presence in the Eucharist. Candaces, a queen and Behomud's sovereign, waits to hear the report of his journey, which is menaced by the devil. The play opens with an earthquake, a symbol of Good Friday, and after initial dialogues for the main characters, Behomud leaves for Jerusalem. The scene changes, and Candaces, in dream-like confusion, reappears on a float representing her palace—but metaphorically, the house of *Anima*.

Two court ladies begin this moment by singing a paraphrase of 1:1, and they are answered by a solo female musician, picking up 1:12c fused with the "Jerusalem" refrain: "Oh, how the empress of peoples lies prostrate, without comfort or pleasures, and all who see her cry 'Jerusalem, Jerusalem!' [solo:] Since there is no suffering like your suffering, turn back to your Lord and God, the greatest good! [tutti:] Jerusalem, Jerusalem!"[71] Turning to spoken octosyllable quatrains (*redondillas*), Candaces asks for clarification, and one of the singing ladies gives the source: "What sad song is this? [Lady:] One which I read in one of your books. [Candaces:] Which one? [Lady:] *Lamentation* by Jeremiah."[72] After the queen expresses her confusion and melancholy at hearing of Jerusalem's ruin, pleading for her fears to be eased, Faith enters, lulling her to sleep, and promises her aid until Behomud has accomplished the sacrifice. The interlude ends with more music, as the ladies sing a combination of 1:1 and 2, and the soloist repeats the vernacular equivalent of "Jerusalem, convertere."[73] Hence the citations were identifiable not only as Lamentations but specifically as parts of Lessons.

The penitential meaning of the passage is clear, as Candaces is still waiting for salvation to be enacted through the sacrifice of the lamb/Christ. The fragments of the Lesson are sung during her confused, dream-like state to urge personal *metanoia*. The long tradition—since Macrobius's *Commentarii in somnium Scipionis*—of prophetic communication in the liminal state of dreams seems to underlie Calderón's use of Jeremiah, and the queen's presalvational waiting for the sacrifice also mirrors the role of Lamentations as preparation for the Passion.

In performance, the excerpts were sung by three women, probably from the company of Manuel Vallejo which seems to have performed the *auto;* its leading actress Manuela de Escamilla specialized in portraying musicians, and she thus probably did the refrain's paraphrase, with the verses done by two of the four other women in the troupe.[74] This use of a Lesson as a penitential lullaby must have been underscored if Navas used the audible signal of citing chant. The words of the prophet, here projected in the vernacular by musical actresses, were ultimately linked to the apotheosis of the Passion around the performance of the *auto*, Corpus Christi's celebration of the Eucharist in the theaters and streets of Madrid.

The link between dreaming and penitential prophecy is also evident at the opening of Francisco Antonio de Bances Candamo's *El Austria en Jerusalén,* written for the Spanish court in the early 1690s and set during the Crusades' conquests of Jersualem.[75] *El Austria* opens with another sung Lesson, this time to the sleeping Crusader Emperor Frederick II, besieging the city (in the Sixth Crusade of 1229). The aged Jeremiah and Lady Jerusalem appear, the latter in Ottoman costume and in chains, inside small grottos to the dreaming Frederick. They begin with another text as a *lamentación en romance,* "Ay, misera de ti, Jerusalén!." Its music is indicated as an echo piece, accompanied by the standard theatrical combination of a "hoarse" drum and kit violins, used more widely in *comedias* to convey mourning or loss.[76] After the Emperor awakens, he explains that he had been reading Lamentations, and several sentences in his long monologue give some idea of the book's effect on seventeenth-century readers.

Jeremiah and Jerusalem open their scene with a "weeping" version of "Jerusalem, convertere" ("Llora, suspira, gime . . . conviértete al Señor, procure el llanto"). Then the Lady sings a vernacular version of 1:1ab ("Cómo yace triste y sola . . . viuda entre lutos se ve!") as a *copla* about herself, answered by Jeremiah expanding 1:1c ("La Reyna de las provincias tributo paga") and closing with the "Ay, misera" *estribillo*. Frederick answers sleeptalking ("Jeremiah, I have already seen your Lamentations fulfilled; Jerusalem, I have learned of your captivities and wept"). Jeremiah then follows with a version of 1:2a, Jerusalem with one of 1:2b, and the two collaborate on a repeat of the opening tag. The quasi-Lesson ends with free references to 4:1c and 1:6a in the final two solo *coplas* and a repeat of the entire refrain. Bances's freedom in mixing the vernacular text with the Vulgate seems a legacy of the oral literature tradition. The playwright must have taken the idea of the dream lullaby "Lesson" from Calderón's *auto,* but he put it into the mouths of Jeremiah and Jerusalem simultaneously. The laments over the lost city, and the Crusade setting, also evoked the ongoing campaign of the 1684 Holy League (including Spain) against the Ottomans. The signs of Tenebrae were the musical opening of this play.

The early eighteenth-century Novena theatrical songbook holds music for this version, set economically and with voice/continuo parts only (perhaps the kit violin lines were improvised). The text also had wider distrubution, a tribute to the interplay of oral tradition and theater. Another setting is attributed to Miguel Ferrer in another theatrical collection, and a version different in its *coplas,* attributed to a "León," is also in the former Barcelona Cathedral holdings (now E-Bbc M. 1679/31), rubricated to be sung "after the Miserere," perhaps a final piece after the *strepitus.* Thus all the versions held ritual and penitential meaning.

A duet setting of "Ay, misera!" by Juan de Serqueira is found in Valladolid Cathedral, probably for the institution's use in or out of the Triduum. The *tono* as set by Serqueira has eight *coplas,* different from Bances's; these are more personally penitential, and first rework 1:1–3 each into two stanzas, continue with stanzas glossing 1:3b, 6a, 3c, and then conclude with 1:4a in a tropological vein ("Lloren de Sión las calles / cuando desiertas se ven / de virtudes, oh alma mía, / copia de Jerusalem") and a final strophe on weeping for sin.[77] Although he did not cite a chant tone, Serqueira signalled the affect of the text in the opening phrase of his *estribillo,* with a diminished fourth $F_4\sharp$-$B_4\flat$ horizontally in the top line, followed by a grinding minor ninth as the tenor enters on A_3 underneath, echoed by the succeeding horizontal diminished sevenths in the same part. The related texts of Bances and Serqueira continue the long-standing connection between Lamentations and tears in ritual theatrical and liturgical.

PARAPHRASE IN ROME

As with most poetic versions since Cicognini's, Benedetto Menzini's *Lamentazioni* of 1704 were generated by the Lessons and not the book as a whole.[78] Over the course of its nine sections ("*Trenodiae*"; thus not chapters but equivalents to liturgical Lessons), verses correspond to varying amounts of text. In the first section (= 1:1–5, F5/L1), three tercets roughly equal three sub-verses, while *Trenodia* 2 is comprised of four-tercet groups corresponding to L2. In later sections, the numbers are more varied, and sub-verses are re-arranged; Menzini's version of F6/L2 (= 2:12–15) is built around groups of three to six tercets. It opens with direct speech, including echoes of Dante's Count Ugolino, by the suffering children of 2:12: "a terra cade / Il pargoletto: e sembra dir cadendo: / 'Madre, di me non muoveti pietade?' / O simulacro spaventoso, horrendo!"/"The child falls to earth, and seems to say in falling: 'Mother, are you not moved to pity for me?' O frightful and horrible scene!" The Passion and penance are only implicit, but the dramatic impulse is clear. Although denunciations of composed Lamentations for their supposed theatricality would resonate from Rome to Paris to Oviedo throughout the new century, the continuity in the musical-dramatic representation of the prophet's book is also present in this product of Arcadian circles, dedicated to Pope Clement XI.

Its projection of Jeremiah did not go unanswered, however. The Roman diarist Francesco Valesio reported on Holy Wednesday 1706 (31 March):

> [Pietro] Cardinal Ottoboni wrote . . . a beautiful oratorio for music, dedicated to St. Philip Neri, and the literary material was the Lamentations of Jeremiah, translated by His Eminence into Italian, sung by the best musicians accompanied by many instruments, including six muted trumpets.[79]

More precisely, in the first half of his *(Per) la Passione Di Nostro Signor Gesù Cristo: Oratorio a tre voci* Ottoboni paraphrased, not the entire book, but rather Wednesday's three Lessons, weaving a penitential dialogue among his three characters Guilt, Penance, and Grace (Colpa, Pentimento, and Grazia) in and out of the Jeremiah-inspired sections.[80] This *parte prima* represents the Old Testament, while the second part of the oratorio makes explicit references to Cross theology and the New Testament, using as its liturgical foundation the Improperia (thus Good Friday's liturgy), and indeed the entire oratorio ends with a paraphrase of *Dulce lignum/Crux fidelis*.

As evident from the printed libretto of 1706—which does not name Ottoboni—the music was by Alessandro Scarlatti, and the dedication was to the cardinal's favorite saint. The visual experience of the premiere also emphasized darkness and the Cross, as the room was draped in black velvet, illuminated only by pseudo-porphyry vases with candles inside, while the lights for the musicians' stands were covered by screens depicting scenes of the Passion. The central feature was a large crucifix and below it a representation of Neri in meditation; a similar portrait of the saint was the frontispiece to the printed libretto. All of Ottoboni's oratorios that year attracted a large crowd of the nobility.[81]

This relatively well-known piece—even though there is no accessible modern edition—formed part of a broader concern with Jeremiah that occupied Ottoboni for a decade. In the Jubilee Year of 1700, the cardinal had organized musical Lamentations for a public including the dowager Queen of Poland on Tuesday of Holy Week—thus not part of the liturgical Office.[82] Scarlatti's six Lessons for voice and instruments (I-Baf) may relate to this occasion. In 1702 the prelate commissioned Scarlatti to set the verses of F5/ L1–2 in the vernacular—the first Italian evidence of this since Corteccia's lost experiments in the 1550s noted above—and had them performed in his palace.[83] It is possible that this became the nucleus of the 1706 oratorio.

A week before the premiere of *Per la Passione,* the Seminario Romano had staged a repeat of a 1705 oratorio treating the prehistory of Jerusalem's fall, Filippo Fabbri and Scarlatti's *Sedecia.* The seminary dedicated the performance to Ottoboni; a year before, the Oratorio del Crocefisso had produced a Latin oratorio on the subject (music by G. B. Borri). Although neither of these previous pieces featured the prophet as a character, the background to Lamentations was present in Rome even as the cardinal arranged for Jeremiah's words to resound.

Ottoboni pulled out all the stops for the first performance of his oratorio, and pushed the piece with a passion unusual even for him. It was repeated in 1707, prefaced by an entirely new dramatic work without reference to Jeremiah, the *Introduzione all'Oratorio per la Passione per la Feria Quinta,* whose New Testament characters personalized Christian grief at the Passion, with text again by the cardinal.[84] The music for this, probably by P. P. Bencini, is lost, but to judge by the text, it would have added another forty minutes to a seventy-minute performance. Unusually, the 1706 oratorio was done again in 1708, together with the prologue, and both evidently were revived in 1725 for the Crocefisso, with a translated Latin text printed alongside the original in the libretto; that is, they were sung as Latin contrafact oratorios. Another Roman performance of the original version, sponsored by the prelate, dates from the last Holy Week that Ottoboni would live to see in 1739; it was heard by the travelling Saxon-Polish Prince Fredrick Christian along with twelve cardinals.[85]

After three consecutive years of staging his own texts, in 1709 Ottoboni commissioned yet another oratorio textually generated by Lamentations, but actually historical. *Il Trionfo di Tito per la Distruzione di Gerusalemme espressa nelle Lamentazioni del Profeta Geremia* featured a libretto by the cardinal's protégé A. D. Norcia and music (now lost) by the cellist Filippo Amadei and by Ottoboni himself, possibly his only known composition.[86]

This musical enactment of the destruction of the Second Temple portrayed Titus Vespasian along with a Jewish Priest and Mother, and again it paraphrases Jeremiah's verses, this time the F6 Lessons. It may be a political allegory of the temporary defeats of Clement XI at the hands of another emperor, Joseph I, in the War of the Spanish Succession.[87] Ottoboni's obsession with Lamentations seems not to have lasted past 1709, but the depth of his engagement with the book is striking.[88]

The liturgical Lessons undergird the 1706 text. Although the piece was intended for Holy Wednesday, as the date of its premiere and its use of the F5 items suggest, Guilt's opening aria sets the dark scene of Good Friday's Crucifixion, another link between the poetry and the black backdrops to the performance.[89] This aria does not use Jeremiah's words, the case also for her following recitative, which specifically describes Christ crucified as visualized in personal meditation. Then, a duet for Guilt and Penance is followed by the first citation of Lamentations, Penance's paraphrase of 1:1–2 in *versi sciolti* set as recitative, "Come sola rimane / L'infelice Sion; non d'altro piena / Che di Popolo infido, empio, e crudele!"/"How unhappy Zion is left alone, full of nothing but pagan, impious, and cruel people!" Penance's following aria, "Spinta dal duolo," reworks 1:3, and Guilt continues with a version of 1:4–5, "Le strade di Sion neglette sono"/"The ways of Zion are abandoned." Grace then completes the "Lesson" with an aria, "Gerusalemme pentita," which rephrases "Jerusalem, convertere." This points to the liturgical items, not the Biblical book, as the embedded text for the libretto.

Grace continues, momentarily eschewing Lamentations, by re-evoking darkness and shadows in yet another reference to the Passion, and is answered by Guilt and Penance, turning to the joys of Christian remorse ("Oh fortunato pianto!") and to a duet that sings the happiness of tears. Guilt sings an extended solo paraphrase of L2: "La Figlia di Sion non ha più in volto l'usata maestà"/"No longer does the daughter of Zion have her past majesty on her face" equivalent to 1: 6–7; an aria "Gerusalem non ha dove posare il piè"/"Jerusalem has no place to step" like 1:8; a parallel to 1:9ab, "Passegia per sentiero sordo, e impuro"/"She walks on a deaf and impure path"; and then an aria for the city's direct speech of 1:9c, "Mira, Signor, deh mira il dolor mio"/"Lord, look at my suffering." Again Grace returns with the "Jerusalem" refrain, a different aria ("Gerusalem, Gerusalem, ritorna").

With two Lessons completed, Penance inaugurates another free transition by reversing the darkness into both the light of Grace and the inflamed heart of standard Christological devotion ("Prenderò dal tuo lume, Grazia superna e bella, quel sentiero"/"O heavenly and beautiful Grace, I will follow that path by your light").[90] After this lyric moment, and without any preparation or thematic shift, Guilt begins another solo paraphrase ("Vidde Sion rapirsi dalla nemica destra i suoi tesori"/"Zion saw her treasures stolen by her enemy") of the entirety of L3, with some verses (e.g., 1:11) shortened.[91] Then, for the first and only time, the third iteration of "Jerusalem, convertere" interacts with Ottoboni's text, as Grace's statement of the refrain ("Gerusalemme ingrata figlia riedi al tuo Padre, e Signor, che ti richiama"/"Ungrateful Jerusalem, return to your Father and Lord Who calls you") is the A section of a da capo trio, with Guilt and Penance's B section not derived from the liturgy, and this closes the oratorio's first part.[92]

Most of the Lesson paraphrases are set as florid recitative in *versi sciolti,* but the three arias reworking Jeremiah's text are set off by unusual (and different, suggesting that Ottoboni did not intend them to correspond to a single "original" pattern in the Hebrew) metrical choices: "Spinta dal duolo" (=1:3) in *decasillabi;* "Gerusalem non ha" (1:8), in *settenari tronchi* and "Mira, Signor, deh mira" (1:9c) in a combination of *settenari* and *quinari.*[93]

The *Introduzione* that Ottoboni produced for the next year is a long dialogue among Mary, the Magdalen, St. John, and an Angel (one more singer than for the 1706 oratorio). The cardinal's anonymous preface to the reader stressed the "introductory" nature of the piece.[94] In its first part, the thought of Christ's upcoming suffering leads Mary to affective recollection of her life, while John looks for light amidst the shadows ("tenebre," hence yet another reference to the ritual). Between the Angel's attempt to ease her pain, and John's praise of her future, Mary expresses her sorrow, followed by the Magdalen's expression of her own devotion to Christ.

In the oratorio's second part, following a long tradition of Marian laments dating ultimately to one version of the fourth-century *Acts of Pilate,* the Virgin swoons from grief. This idea had been criticized by episcopal theorists of art around 1600, such as Gabriele Paleotti and Federigo Borromeo, as inappropriate to the Gospel accounts of Mary's steadfastness. But its importance for Ottoboni is evident in three paintings executed around 1700 by his resident painter Francesco Trevisani, all of which feature the unconscious Virgin consoled by the Magdalen; the cardinal seems to have owned all three.[95] In the *Introduzione,* the Madonna returns to consciousness and is consoled by the Angel, who then conveys the Crucifixion by using the words of Tenebrae Responsories.[96] The shock of the news brings Mary to declaim the exact opening, not of *Per la Passione* as a whole with its references to Good Friday, but rather Ottoboni's gloss of 1:1 ("Come sola rimane . . ."). The Magdalen interrupts her to indicate the upcoming performance of the 1706 piece as sinners' penance, linking it to the Madonna's intercession, and the *Introduzione* ends with an aria for the penitent saint (and not for Mary, the focus of much of the text).[97] This mimetic ending, pointing to the earlier work by both description and quotation, links it inseparably to *Per la Passione*.

Norcia's 1709 *Il trionfo di Tito* is similar to the 1706 oratorio in its dependence on the liturgical Lessons. Its preface explains how its characters of the Priest and the Mother use the F6 texts to depict the destruction of Jerusalem in 70 CE, including a reference to Josephus's *Jewish War* as a proof of historical verity. *Il Trionfo* begins with Titus victorious over the destroyed Jerusalem, and a despairing dialogue between the two Hebrew personages. At about the same point in its Part I at which F5/L1 had been introduced in *Per la Passione,* Norcia's Priest refers to the prophecies of Jeremiah, and then begins a gloss of the opening of F6/L1, "Cogitavit Dominus dissipare murum Sion" as "Dissipar l'eccelse mura di Sionne Iddio pensò"/"The Lord thought to destroy the lofty walls of Zion."[98] His following recitative reworks 2:9, which gives way to a "free" colloquy among Titus and the two Jews describing the city's ruin. Then, the Mother's recitative and aria represent 2:10–11, thus ending the passages generated by F6/L1.[99] In another expansion of vocal resources, this scene continues with a chorus of Jews who sing a paraphrase of the opening of L2 ("Madre, il cibo, e la bevanda / per noi miseri dov'è?"/"Mother, where are food and drink for us miserable ones?" = "Matribus suis dixerunt"), moving the third-person narration of Lamentations into first-person plural *conquestio,* as Menzini's poem had done. The citation of Lamentations in Part I ends, not with the conclusion of F6/L2, but rather with a recitative by the Priest rephrasing 2:13 ("Cui comparabo te?") followed by a free solo aria, duet, and concluding trio for the Priest, Mother, and Titus.[100]

Part II of *Il Trionfo* begins by completing the paraphrase of L2, with two recitatives for the Priest and the Mother corresponding to 2:14–15, each followed by a free aria (the Mother's recalls 1:12 in a way that subtly points to the use of "O vos omnes" in Marian devotion).[101] The Priest describes his own misery by reworking the opening of F6/L3 (= 3:1–2), upon which a chorus of victorious Romans enters and again interrupts the Lesson paraphrase.[102] The Mother's following recitative depicts her suffering (= 3:3–5, but here in a female voice, not that of the male prophet), followed by a "darkness" aria generated by 3:6, "in tenebrosis collocavit me."[103] Another "free" passage (Titus's victory aria and a trio) leads to a brief dialogue gloss of 3:7–8, followed by the Priest's aria that finishes the paraphrase of L3 by reworking 3:9 without the "Jerusalem" refrain, which is thus missing in all three "Lessons."[104] The concluding colloquy of the Mother and the Priest mentions the Crucifixion and prophecies the downfall of Jerusalem and the future glory of Rome as the center of Christianity. As opposed to *Per la Passione,* the liturgical Lessons generate both halves of the oratorio text, but the omission of the "Jerusalem" refrain must be due to its dramatic inappropriateness here.

Ottoboni's libretto of 1706 was evidently meant to have value in its own right. Thus the 1725 Latin translation for the Crocefisso does not use the words of the Vulgate in its rendering of the passages corresponding to Lamentations verses. One can imagine the entire text of *Per la Passione* as taking place in the interior theater of the meditative Christian mind, in front of the Crucifix, as the engraving in the 1706 libretto portrays Filippo Neri. Indeed, Penance's introductory recitative ("Ma per render più grave") to Guilt's reworking of L2 refers to the lamenter as female and thus *Anima:* "Continue, o Guilt, the lament of her who became so unhappy and wretched through your cause."[105] One example of the meditative subject for the original audience could have been the cardinal himself, as he heard his musicians against the totalizing backdrop of the Crucifix, with the contemplative experience aided by the scenes of the Passion on the lampshades.

The *Introduzione* also shows an interiority removed from the action of the Passion, and both these pieces focus on individual sin, not any kind of corporate guilt. Sad to say, *Il trionfo*—not written by Ottoboni, born into the multicultural world of Venice—brushes more closely up against the classic accusations of Jewish "responsibility."[106] It is just as well that the music is lost.

VERSES IN MUSIC

Tracking the original performers and expenses of *Per la Passione* is difficult, due to the missing lists of musicians and payments for 1706–13, but certainly the 1725 revival included a trumpet, timpani, and two horns, of which there is no trace in the two surviving scores.[107] These sources are both in Germany, and possibly the Dresden (D-Dslb) version was acquired from a Neapolitan or Roman source sometime around 1738–40, for a performance at the Saxon court.[108] The other manuscript, in the Schönborn-Wiesentheid (D-WD) collection, has different music for some sections, although Ottoboni's text was not changed. Many lines paraphrasing the Lessons—including the ariosos in which Scarlatti cited the Tone-6 chant formula—are the same in both. But three musically free arias are quite different: "Gerusalemme pentita" (the "refrain" of L1); "Gerusalemme non ha dove posar il piè" (from L2/1:8) and "Mira, signor, deh mira" (L2/1:9c). In all cases, the Wiesentheid version is slightly longer than Dresden; in the first case, a fast 12/8 movement of forty-eight measures in WD is replaced by a 3/4 section (forty-three bars) in Dslb, while all the da capos in this latter source are written out. "Gerusalemme non ha" is a continuo-only aria in WD, a scoring not found in the

Saxon version. The Dresden manuscript uses the wrong vocal clef (C3 instead of C1) in passages of "Le strade di Sion," while it contains a pitch error in Penance's recitative leading to Guilt's "La figlia di Sion."[109] Finally, the opening of "Vidde Sion" in WD has an Allegro instrumental introduction, of which only the last note remains in Dslb. This all suggests that Wiesentheid must be closer to the Roman original of 1706, and Dslb a later redaction with fewer earlier-style movements, corresponding to "exported" Neapolitan taste in the 1730s. WD is thus the basis for the musical discussion here.

In a piece generated by the Lamentations text, Scarlatti could only have used the sixth-tone chant formula, at least for paraphrase sections. He did so, though, taking the tone as both motive and artifact in the sections corresponding to Lesson verses. These are set, not as simple recitative but accompanied arioso, normally citing the chant *initium* at the beginning of sections, with often-dramatic instrumental accompaniment in the string band. As a "verse" continues, it normally abandons direct chant citation in favor of a more varied *ductus,* with melismas at the ends of poetic lines contrasting with the otherwise syllabic declamation. Much of the piece's success must have been due to the variety of Scarlatti's music, not least the use of chant on a wide variety of pitches and in different tonal constructs.

At the entrance of the paraphrase verses, Penance sings the equivalent of 1:1 with strings alone (no keyboard), and the "halo" effect thus provided for the Prophet's text recalls the treatment of Christ's words in various Passion settings, including Scarlatti's own St. John version.[110] The duet leading to this first citation had cadenced on F, and one might have expected the citation of an *fga initium* harmonized clearly in F major to follow. But in WD, a tonal catabasis prepares a vocal line using the chant but starting unexpectedly on $E_4\flat$ and harmonized on C/*mollis*. The chant citation continues through the *mediatio* half-cadence, thus here on G (example 5.4; there is a signature problem in the Dresden source).[111] Motivically, the tone recurs in this first section on pitches all over the flat/sharp spectrum: $D_5\flat$ (harmonized on B♭; "quasi vedova"), D_5 (on D; "piange l'intera notte") and finally its "proper" F_4 (on F; "ne vè chi la consoli"), a rhetorical climax via the return to the aural expectation of the "correct" pitch for chant citations.

The tone's pitch lability is also evident from its next recurrence, sung by Guilt, starting on $B_4\flat$ harmonized in G/*mollis* at the arioso for 1:4, "Le strade di Sion." Grace's version of the refrain, "Gerusalemme pentita," is free from chant citations, but the *initium* of the tone is picked up again as the opening of Guilt's aria-like declamation of 1:6 that opens the section generated by L2's text, "La figlia di Sion." Scarlatti's music oscillates between musically "free" sections and those generated by the chant as declaimed on changing pitches: an aria without citations for the paraphrase of 1:8 ("Gerusalemme

EXAMPLE 5.4. A. Scarlatti, *Per la Passione* (1706), pt. 1, "Come sola rimane."

non ha dove posare il pie"); another reiteration of the recitation formula starting on B$_4$♭ harmonized on G/*mollis* at the parallel to 1:9ab ("Passagier per sortir"); and then "free" arias for 1:9c ("Mira, Signor, deh mira") and the "Jerusalem, convertere" refrain.

Tonal variety is also audible in the passage for Guilt that corresponds to L3. After all the previous *mollis*-inflected iterations of the tone, she begins by starting the citation on B$_4$♮ harmonized on G/*durus* ("Vidde Sion"), while the *ductus* of the vocal line lacks the references to the *mediatio* cadences found in L1's paraphrase. Although the opening of this paraphrase section is set in *durus* regions around B and A, the switch in literary voice to Jerusalem at 1:11c ("Ah, quanto io sono fatta vile") moves the tonal spectrum back to B♭ harmonized on G. Scarlatti also changed tempo (andante) at this point, linking this sub-verse directly to the following "O vos omnes" quote of 1:12, and followed quickly by *concitato* gestures that set the paraphrase of "quoniam vindemiavit me," God's fury. That the tonal motion in the "Lesson" continues to oscillate between A and B♭ precludes further citations of the chant formula, and indeed the closing iteration of the "Jerusalem" refrain omits any references to the tone.

Comparing these approaches with the corresponding passages in Scarlatti's two liturgical Lessons for F5 (as noted, preserved in I-Baf) is instructive; the latter, like contemporary Neapolitan pieces by Caresana and Veneziano discussed below, do not employ the recitation formula. Thus the chant-generated passages of *Per la Passione* have no counterpart in Scarlatti's L1 or L3. But even the "free" sections diverge; the title, "Quomodo sedet," and "facta est sub tributo" sections of Scarlatti's F5/L1 begin with minor, not major-third, motives (their only, distant, gesture towards the chant *initium*); and the Lesson's closely spun four-voice canon for "Migravit Juda propter afflictionem" (1:3) is nothing like the 12/8 Lento *siciliana* (on C with two flats) that sets the equivalent aria in the paraphrase, "Spinta dal duolo." There are analogous differences between the rest of this Lesson and the oratorio, and between Scarlatti's L3 and the end of *Per la Passione*'s first part. Partially because of Scarlatti's desire or obligation to use the chant tone in the oratorio, and partially due to the divergent aesthetics of the genres, the two projections of Lamentations turned out dissimilar. Whatever the temporal or geographical distance between the Lessons and *Per la Passione*, Scarlatti used an entirely different rhetorical and gestural vocabulary for the occasions on which he encountered the prophet's words.

VIENNESE ECHOES

At a generation's distance, the appearance of Jeremiah in Apostolo Zeno and Antonio Caldara's Viennese court oratorio *Sedecia*, first performed well before the Triduum (27 March; Fourth Sunday of Lent) in 1732, updates the approach of Ottoboni's pieces. In forced Venetian retirement from Austria, but still continuing his series of libretti (often based on prophetic books) for the court, Zeno must have known the Roman works. In 1711, there seems to have been a Viennese performance of Fabbri/Scarlatti's *Sedecia*. Given Caldara's close ties to Ottoboni during his Roman years, the composer was probably aware of Scarlatti's music, both for the eponymous oratorio of 1705 and *Per la Passione*. His own piece for the Habsburgs featured Farinelli singing the title role; it was clearly an important work. Besides the autograph, there are two fair court copies.[112]

Zeno's text changes Roman traditions, as the prophet here is a major character, sung by the famed alto castrato Gaetano Orsini. The librettist saved his reworking of 1:1–4 for the end of the first part, as Sedecia has defied his mother Amital and the prophet by fleeing Jerusalem and refusing to surrender to Nabuco, king of the Babylonians. The latter recognizes and esteems Geremia, and sings an exit aria commenting on the fate of prophets at court ("I profeti in corte fanno," perhaps a veiled allusion to Zeno's own exile from Vienna). Geremia turns to his servant (perhaps Baruch), takes his lyre, and prophecies—not laments—the future destruction of Jerusalem in a long aria of four five-line stanzas paraphrasing the opening of Lamentations:

[recitative]: Dammi, o buon servo, / La mia cetra lugubre: ond'io qui assiso / In flebil concenti / Faccia al ciel risuonar Treni dolenti.

[aria]: Ahi! come quella un tempo / Città, di popol piena, / Deserta or siede in solitaria arena! / Quasi vedova fatta egra e meschina / Ella di genti in pria Donna e Regina . . . [113]

Good servant, give me my woeful lyre, so that seated here, I can make my sad lamentations resound to the heavens. [aria:] Ah, how that city, once full of people, now sits in the solitary sands! She who formerly was the lady and queen of the peoples, is now exhausted and wretched like a widow . . .

Zeno varies the moment by not having each biblical verse generate a single stanza (the equivalent of 1:2 begins in the middle of the second strophe) and thus omitting or condensing some sub-verses of the original. Geremia's preceding *secco* recitative does indeed cadence on F ("Treni dolenti"), and, given the mention of "sad lamentations," Caldara could have produced a string-accompanied vocal citation of the *fga initium*. But evidently moved by the idea of the "cetra," he wrote a ten-minute aria for Orsini with a brilliant obbligato for *salterio* (hammered dulcimer) and its Viennese court virtuoso Maximilian Hellmann. He probably surprised his original audience by casting the piece in D/*durus* (no signature, but with flat inflections), not F major, marked "Larghetto," and by eschewing the chant reference and string "halo." In line with a long Viennese tradition for important arias in sacred drama (and perhaps inspired by something like Lapide's sense of the book as *carmen*), he set the text strophically, repeating the music of stanzas 1–2 for 3–4, and took special care to set off the lyre-like timbre of the obbligato instrument by silencing the harpsichords in the continuo except for a brief passage where the *salterio* rests.[114] The prophet's vocal line is relatively simple, projecting the paraphrase as lament, as the spectacular filigree of the dulcimer part runs throughout the aria, providing a constant reminder of Geremia's lyre.

Thus Caldara created a spectacular double display piece, an aria that his royal audience would not soon forget and one that marks a clear climax to the first part of the oratorio. As Part II moves to its tragic denouement of Sedecia's defeat and Jerusalem's ruin, Lamentations make no further appearance, although reworkings from the Book of Jeremiah are present in the prophet's final aria with another special instrument, the viola da gamba, "Esca dall'Aquilon." *Sedecia*'s musically representational moment moves from the prophet's citation to Jeremiah himself singing his laments in a theatrical context.

The dramatic envoicings of the prophet gave more immediate expression to Tenebrae sentiment. But the plays and oratorios also used Jeremiah to convey penance, while the plot (Calderón) or social context (Ottoboni) of the performances delivered Passion meditation. Like the poetic paraphrases, the stage texts used liturgical Lessons with the "Jerusalem" refrain, not just Lamentations verses, to invoke the sounds and meanings of the rite. It might seem that the migration of Jeremiah to theater reacted to a stagnant musical repertory for an already-codified ritual moment. But listening to European Tenebrae around 1680—Calderón's senectitude and Ottoboni's adolescence—provides a different picture.

Chapter 6

❦

European Tenebrae c. 1680

Across the continent, the last quarter of the seventeenth century witnessed the creation of much Triduum music, ranging from Naples to Paris to Spain. Even in central Europe, new Responsories were written by Andreas Hofer (possibly for Salzburg, in CZ-KR) and J. K. Kerll (probably for Vienna or Munich, in A-Wm). The diversity, national only in part, reflected the vitality of the ritual's music and new developments in sacred aesthetics at century's end.

ROME IN THE LATE SEICENTO

A generation after the Lessons of Q. 43 and of Cesi, surviving pieces or descriptions of Tenebrae in Rome are scattered. The *Rituale* of the archconfraternity of the Sagre Stimmate di S. Francesco, to which both musicians and the nobility belonged, allowed for the two major Passions (Matthew and John) and Lamentations to be sung in Holy Week.[1] Some churches tried to limit their expenses; at S. Antonio dei Portoghesi in 1693, only the Miserere and CFE at the end of Lauds were performed with five voices and strings, perhaps by musicians who had come from Matins elsewhere.[2]

One edition circulating in and out of the city was Bonifazio Graziani's Responsories, op. 9 (1663), reprinted in 1691. With over ten preserved copies, including a corrected reimpression, it was one of the most valued Triduum prints since Victoria's OHS.[3] Its dedication to the rector of the Seminario Romano says nothing about the music or its origin, although the Jesuit connections are clear, not least in the composer's years of service to the church of the Gesù. Almost all its pieces are in *durus* on A and D, the only exception being the central *Tenebrae factae sunt* on G/*mollis,* which also uses the traditional black notation for its opening phrase. Other local Responsories must have had a market, as in the case of the Franciscan Michelangelo Falusi's cycle with Lauds items, op. 1 (1684), of which a copy survives as far as Por-

EXAMPLE 6.1. Berardi, F6/L3, "Aleph. Ego vir videns."

tugal.[4] These pieces were published during the composer's time at Ss. Apostoli, although they also may reflect his previous experience in Assisi. These two prints mark a change in the traditional Roman diffidence toward polyphonic Responsories.

Even if most of it was written for various cathedrals elsewhere in the Papal States, Angelo Berardi's sacred music was bequeathed to S. Maria in Trastevere, his last job at the end of his career in the 1690s; it include one Lesson (F6/L3), seventeen Responsories, and Lauds items, evidently in the composer's autographs.[5] Despite the presence of Graziani's and Falusi's volumes in the church's archives, Berardi's Responsories were important enough to be kept at S. Maria. His Lesson for solo bass is quite modern, with clear divisions of the verses, and a linear tritone shift after the opening "Aleph," as the prophet/Christ narrates his own punishment ("Ego vir videns"; example 6.1). The dark sonorities, low vocal register, *durus* pitch orientation, and often enigmatic voice-leading of this piece provide an immediate sonic counterpart to the situation of the text's speaker, and stand in some contrast to the procedures of Q. 43.

Alessandro Stradella's two Triduum items, a duet Benedictus and a solo F5/L2, mark new ways to set these texts. Although the source evidence is not clear, they might well date from his years in Rome up to 1677, and the alto voice in both suggests his close friend, the castrato G. B. Vulpio.[6] Stradella's through-composed fifteen-minute canticle is cast on C/*durus,* with no reference to any chant formula, and it articulates the ritual by means of a long imitative duet at v. 7, "Ut sine timore," as the altar lights would have gone out.[7] Vv. 1, 4, and 11 are also duets, symmetrically flanked by solos that often group two verses in contrasting meter (vv. 2–3 for soprano, and 5–6 for alto, in duple/triple and triple/duple, respectively).

Against traditional exegesis, Stradella bridges over the thematic switch from Christ to the Baptist in v. 9 by including both it and v. 8 in the same solo. John is given further equality via the long melismas in vv. 10 and 11, as "plebi eius," "Dei nostri," and "oriens ex alto" are extended. In the last verse, Stradella's unexpected swings to *mollis* regions (E♭ and A♭ in the vocal lines) signal the "shadows" of "Illuminare his qui in tenebris et umbra mortis sedent." They are balanced by strong *durus* sonorities and extrovert *soggetti* for the joy of the concluding half-verse "ad dirigendos pedes nostros in viam pacis." There is no Roman canticle like Stradella's; perhaps its long praise of the Baptist was designed to suit the local confraternity of S. Giovanni dei Fiorentini, which sponsored his oratorio on the saint in the Holy Year of 1675.

The traits of Stradella's solo F5/L2 mark the same kind of innovation. Whether or not the composer had contact with Carissimi, the latter's setting of the same Lesson in Q. 43 provides some points of comparison for how settings could change over a generation. There are three important textual points in this Lesson's text: the invocation of memory at the beginning of v. 7, "Recordata est Jerusalem dierum afflictionis suae"; the sense of turning around in 8c, "conversa est retrorsum"; and the switch from third-person description of Jerusalem's woes to first-person despair at 9c, the end of the Lesson, "Vide, Domine, afflictionem meam, quoniam erectus est inimicus."

Carissimi's Lesson had featured the chant formula in most letters, the openings of every verse and the "Jerusalem" refrain, gestures completely missing in Stradella. Cast on B♭, the older composer's piece turns to even more *mollis* regions at the reference to memory in v. 7, setting off the last two sub-verses by long melismas and repeating the switch to flat sonorities at the change to first-person voice in v. 9c.

But citations of the tone are avoided in the younger composer's Lesson. The first audible novelty of Stradella's L2 is declamatory: the widespread repetition of sub-verses as well as of individual words, which lengthens it to ten minutes (Carissimi's comes in between six and seven). The choice of G/*mollis* as tonal structure gave Stradella the occasion for large-scale descent. Already in the first sub-verse 6a the pitch center moves to F, and, by verse's end, markedly flat sonorities (D♭ for "ante faciem tribulantis") bring the piece around to E♭, before any significant change of voice or affect in the text. This acceleration of tonal distance inside a Lesson is a less obvious but equally important marker of change.

"Recordata est Jerusalem" takes the *topos* of memory as the occasion for another tonal catabasis, from E♭ to D via the *durus* G♯s in the vocal line that are different from the A♭s of the previous verse (example 6.2).[8] The triple

EXAMPLE 6.2. Stradella, F5/L2, "Recordata est Jerusalem."

declamation and long melismas of "deriserunt sabbata eius" underscore the enemy's profanation of the city's holy days. Then the pitch trajectory of v. 8 ("Heth. Peccatum peccavit"), starting on G, literally enacts the text of the last sub-verse, as its "conversa est retrorsum" moves back to the D on which v. 7 had cadenced. This procedure continues with a return to a stable, triple-time E♭ (as in v. 6bc) for the first two sub-verses of v. 9 ("Sordes eius"). Although there is no surface disruption of the declamation at the switch to first person in v. 9c ("Vide, Domine, afflictionem meam"), the sub-verse does regress to the F heard previously in v. 6a. The following "Jerusalem" reaches up to the alto's high D_5 some five times, and uses this *ductus* as a pivot to restore the original G-centered tonality. Thus the "conversa est retrorsum" idea generates a palindromic iteration of the *mollis* G-D tetrachord and back, spread out among the verses of the Lesson, reaching its most distant and *durus* point on D as a kind of tonal analogue to the city's memory ("recordata"), before working its way back to the awful reality of "quoniam erectus est inimicus."

Another major site for Triduum music was at the Spanish national church of S. Giacomo degli Spagnoli, part of the church's role in the ritual life of early modern Rome.[9] Originally its Tenebrae were not as important as its Easter procession with music in Piazza Navona, an annual event which highlighted its function as a noble urban auditorium for spectacle as produced by Spanish Rome.[10] Its Passion decoration, a *sepolcro*, was noted even in the late Cinquecento.[11] In 1705, the old monument was replaced by a new one, evidently a miniature church holding the Eucharist, housed in the chapel of the Resurrection. Still, the financial situation led the diarist Valesio to note that it was skipped "to avoid expenses" in the hard year of 1709.[12]

Although much Seicento music at S. Giacomo was for the patronal feast or other national festivities, the earlier layer of Triduum Lessons now in the church archives includes ten pieces attributed to the organist Giuseppe de Sanctis, active there from 1668–1702.[13] Two others bear his initials, one an F5/L2 dated 1697. A further six are anonymous but in the same general scoring for solo voice, two violins, and continuo, and in the same hand. Of these eighteen Lessons, fourteen are for canto solo, with three for alto (F5 and SS), and a single duet Prayer for CB. This is dated (or simply copied) 1709, despite the problems with the *sepolcro* that year. The pieces add up to duplicate Lessons for each slot over the three Days, and so this seems to be two different but complete cycles, all by the organist, and created in the century's last decades.[14] The lack of Responsories seems also to echo Spanish practice.

Several settings, attributed to de Sanctis or not, use a descending gesture in the continuo to open L1s and L3. One F5/L1 starts with a diatonic form, while the other Lesson for this slot employs a chromatic version; in the two Prayers, the motive is again diatonic.[15] Another common trait is a tonal catabasis for important sub-verses. The v. 11c of one F5/L3, for instance, moves from G to F for the change to Jerusalem's voice, while in the other setting of this text, the turn-around of 1:13b ("Conversit me retrorsum") also descends more drastically from B♭ to A.[16] This latter piece, a large-scale setting for soprano, is filled with florid letters and dramatic pauses, notably a complete silence preceding the final sub-verse, "posuit me desolatam." Its "Jerusalem" is set as a *fuga a due soggetti* involving voice and violins.

Some sense of the organist's approach to verses and structure is evident in an SS/L2 for soprano and violins.[17] Cast on C/*durus*, the Lesson's affect is set by its opening: dramatic octaves and a fast instrumental ritornello imitated by the voice. But the images of the first sub-verse (4:1a, "Quomodo obscuratum est aurum, mutatus est color optimus") led de Sanctis first to darken the tonal system by turning to *mollis* on C for "obscuratum," and then to provide a *mutatio toni* at "mutatus est," the C sharpened and leading temporarily to D (example 6.3). The sub-verses are minimally punctuated, and the letters are either independent sections or attached to the preceding verse. Still, there is change inside any given verse, as the unaccompanied recitative for the thirst of sucklings (v. 4, "Adhaesit lingua") leads to *concitato* gestures at the closing reference to the lack of anyone to break bread for children. Jerusalem's crimes, greater than Sodom's in v. 5, are declaimed in accompanied recitative. The verse ends with de Sanctis's reiteration of the last phrase "et non ceperunt in ea manus"/"and no hands were laid on her [i.e. Sodom]." Lapide had explained this idea as Jerusalem's greater punishment by prolonged physical sacking than was Sodom's, which had been burned immediately by fire and brimstone. Still, the Jesuit could not come up with a spiritual interpretation for this phrase, and thus the musical underlining seems a purely dramatic

EXAMPLE 6.3. de Sanctis, SS/L2, "Aleph. Quomodo obscuratum est aurum."

gesture by the organist.[18] Despite the interest of these pieces, and their later circulation, the Roman Lessons repertory as a whole between 1680 and 1700 is oddly evanescent. Perhaps it was this lack that led Ottoboni to his decade-long engagement with Jeremiah at the beginning of the new century.

CHANGES IN SPANISH CATHEDRALS

Spanish practice of the 1670s and 1680s is evident in a number of places, but understanding it is more difficult. One problem is relating the largely polychoral corpus of Lessons to devotional understandings of Lamentations (there are almost no Responsories and few Misereres) or to exegetical works read in late seventeenth-century Spain. The most striking pieces before 1650 are polychoral F5/L1s: one of the earliest ones, that of J. B. Comes, was likely for Madrid (1618–28) or Valencia (1608–17 or 1627–42). Vicente García Velcaire's (1593–1650) three-choir piece was conceivably used in Valencia Cathedral, the Encarnación in Madrid, or Toledo; Sebastián Romeo's (d. 1649) ten-voice setting (possibly from Tarazona or more likely Zaragoza), and the fourteen-voice Lesson by Urban de Vargas (1606–56, active in Pamplona, Calatayud, Zaragoza, and Valencia) add to the total.[19] Vargas' SS/L1 *a 11* was copied in 1649, when he was in Zaragoza, again underlining that cathedral's place in innovative Lesson production. In Madrid, the destruction of the royal chapel in the 1734 fire of the Alcázar means that court repertory is lost, unless Comes' total of three Lessons date from his time there. Certainly the Escorial's repertory grew, as the eight-voice set of L1/L3s by Pedro de Tafalla from mid-century were joined by same items as composed by his Jeronymite colleague Diego de Torrijos a generation later in the 1680s.[20] One feature of the Spanish repertory up to 1700 is the continuing importance of the chant tones, notably the *acdd* or *egaa* versions, as a source for motivic material and indeed overall structure. Indeed, Irízar wrote a Mass on the Lamentations formula.

Although there was a good deal of new composition, some institutions held tight to tradition; the Barcelona Cathedral choirbook (E-Bbc M. 1623) of Joan Pujol's Lessons from c. 1620 includes the signatures of the *escolaris* (choirboys) from 1673–1704, perhaps a mark of their having learned the pieces. The early eighteenth-century "Manual del Cabiscol" cathedral ceremonial referred to unspecified Lessons sung in polyphony, but with Responsories in chant.[21] Other items, including an SS/L1 and a Miserere both *a 8* by Joan Barter, active first in Lleida and then Barcelona, are preserved in the late seventeenth-century holdings from the musically active collegiate church in Verdú (80 km west of Barcelona) along with a manuscript copy of Palestrina's 1588 F5/L1.[22] The Roman Lamentations had circulated almost a century earlier in Catalonia (E-Boc 11altre and E-Bbc 587); thus this community had access to the new and the old in its Tenebrae.

In Girona, the hiring of Francesc Soler in 1682 led to his writing a new F5/L1, scored *a 9* with a *bajoncillo* in choir I, to mark the opening of his first Triduum the next year. In the rest of his tenure until 1688, he added an F5/L3 for two high voices using echo effects and an SS/L1 for two *seises*. His successor Josep Gaz (1690–1710) wrote an F5/L2 in modern style with an obbligato violin and bass violin.[23] At Valencia Cathedral, the L1s were sung by the full choir, and the other two as solos with instruments, while at the Seminario de Corpus Christi (the Patriarca), by the early eighteenth-century chant was preferred, in evident contrast to previous practice there.[24] Still, in the last third of the seventeenth century, Gracian Babán, Antonio Ortells, Aniceto Baylón, and Máximo Rios all contributed Lessons, large and small, to both Valencian institutions.

Clearly, though, the northern cathedrals matched Catalonia. Zaragoza, Segovia, Valladolid, Burgos, Zamora, Salamanca, and Santiago documentably all heard new compositions, and this is not a complete list.[25] The situations of Segovia and Valladolid seem oddly parallel: Miguel de Irízar (twenty documentable Lessons, some datable 1671–83) and Miguel Gómez Camargo (about the same number, from 1660–84) were contemporaries in the two positions, followed by their respective successors Jerónimo de Carrión and José Martínez (del) Arce (twelve and fifteen Lessons). In both institutions, the overall production is for a widely varying number of voices; it includes at least one L2 in the works of everyone but Carrión.[26] The tenuous condition of their transmission (e.g., on the backs of letters written by Irízar) also connects the social world of these Lessons.

To judge from a note on one of them, Juan Pérez Roldán's two three-choir L1s must have been written during his service at Segovia Cathedral, 1667–70, and sent back to the chapter after he left for Zaragoza; there are also eighteenth-century duplicates of both, suggesting they were used for some time, even after the production of his successors Irízar and Carrión.[27] Roldán's F6/L1 is scored for ten parts, all notated in high clef combinations, while the SS/L1 is for twelve, adding extra C2 and C3 parts. In both, the lowest (C4) parts in choirs II and III are untexted, and the eighteenth-century copy of the SS Lesson (56/45) mentions the *bajoncillo*, while the accompaniment for the former is "clavichordio." Thus the F6 piece involved eight singers and the SS piece ten. Both Lessons are on A *durus,* and the *acdd* formula is omnipresent, woven into imitative counterpoint even in the letters of the F6 piece (example 6.4). Roldán's pieces employ a high tessitura, with the top parts ranging to C_6 and D_6; either these are *chiavette* works or there were remarkable *seises* in Segovia.

EXAMPLE 6.4. Péerez Roldan, F6/L1, "Heth."

Still, the century's last decade marks some distance from the use of tones. Salazar's scoring for his two Lessons in Seville around 1690 recalls that of Santiago's Responsories in the same cathedral two generations earlier: one choir of four voices only, and one of voices each doubled by a *muta* or *bajón/ bajoncillo*; neither choir cites the chant formulae. Salazar's solo and duet verses are accompanied by various combinations of instruments, e.g., F5/L1's "Plorans ploravit" for *tiple* plus *muta* or treble *bajoncillo,* as Jerusalem's tears receive direct timbral expression through the sonority. Although this scoring with the muted tone of dulcians seems typical of Seville, still Máximo Rios, chapelmaster at Valencia's Patriarca (1686–1705) wrote an F6/L2 for voice and three dulcians. Similarly, Matias Durango in northern Spain produced an F5/L3 for the same forces. Thus the dark timbre with the dulcian ensemble seems to have symbolized Tenebrae in a number of Spanish churches, but it was balanced by high lines like Santiago's and Roldán's.[28]

NUNS AND TRIDUUM PRACTICE

Another sonic change is represented by repertory from women's foundations across the Catholic world. On one hand, the dedication of della Ciaia's Lamentations from 1650 testify to nuns' performing the Office in Siena, but elsewhere such singing could be contested. A note from the diocesan curia in Parma around Holy Week 1675 complained of sisters, taught by young married men, who ate meat during Lent so that their voices would be in good shape for the Triduum, and who sang all the Office items only so as to be appreciated by their male admirers.[29] Parma asked for a total prohibition of nuns' music during the Days, although the fate of the request is unknown.

In Naples, the Franciscan female houses were active in Tenebrae: S. Maria Donnaregina had received permission from the Congregazione de' Vescovi e Regolari for Holy Week polyphony in 1593, but only if done by its nuns, while a similar request from the Benedictines of S. Gaudioso in 1599 was turned down.[30] A report on a 1673 scandal at S. Maria Maddalena claimed that the Franciscans had done Tenebrae for a large public, and that individual musical Lessons had been applauded "excessively."[31] In the famed monastery of S. Chiara the same year, a group of Franciscans complained that the practice of ornamentation and solo singing with harpsichord of Lamentations by their sister nuns had led to dissoluteness rather than devotion.[32] But the nature of these Neapolitan Lessons, with the liturgy interrupted for "inappropriate" applause, again shows the interaction between religious orders and the city during the Triduum; evidently some clapping was considered normal. Already here, the move from the community Office to Tenebrae for an early modern public is evident.

Despite the battles, the musical evidence for Naples' female houses seems clear. Nun singers are found in the inscriptions of Triduum pieces by Donato Ricchezza (1648–1716) and Gaetano Veneziano (c. 1660–1716) from the 1690s. These include four Lessons by Veneziano for "Suor Chiara" and "Suor Maria Giuseppa" in a Dominican house (on the basis of the verse selection), probably one of the order's eight female foundations in the city; two Lessons for Suor Giuseppa Conti and a verse of the Miserere for "Suor Eugenia," both women in the female conservatory of Santo Spirito where Veneziano worked as *maestro* in 1701 (the first hard evidence for music in girls' educational foundations here); Veneziano's Third Nocturne Lesson for a "Suor Colomba"; and Ricchezza's F5/L1 for a "Suor Antonia"; neither of these latter were Dominicans.[33] These eight pieces are about a quarter of the total high-voice Lessons by the two composers.

Pending a closer study of castrati's activity, it seems unlikely that men could have covered all the high-voice pieces in Naples, including some for Nocturnes II/III; the city's leading composers, Cristoforo Caresana and Veneziano, each seem to have left about twenty Lessons for canto or alto, with or without strings, and Ricchezza a further eight. In addition, the Responsories (Nocturnes I and III only) by Antonio Nola (c. 1650–1716, in I-Nf) are scored for CCAA plus violins and thus again suggest nuns' ensembles, collaborating or not with the much-prohibited outside male musicians. Works for sisters represent a reasonable share of the emerging repertory in late Seicento Naples, and the tradition would be continued a generation later in the works by Porpora, Leo, and Hasse for the members of the d'Andrea family in the Lateran Canoness house of S. Maria Regina Caeli (see chapter 7).

Elsewhere in Catholicism, attempts at restricting nuns' Tenebrae would have run into traditions established earlier in the century. The book of service polyphony compiled in 1633 for the Spanish Franciscan house of S. Clara in Carrión de los Condes includes four anonymous Lessons clearly meant to be sung by the sisters, three high voices and probably a *bajón* player for the bass line.[34] The book's dedicatee, the abbess Sor Luisa de la Ascensión, had political and devotional links to the Habsburgs, and polyphonic Tenebrae seems not to have been a problem. Around the same time, the Newberry choirbooks contain a Lesson by Juan de Lienas, part of the repertory evidently for the Mexico City Conceptionist house of La Concepción; in this source, there are also a version of Victoria's Prayer from 1585, an anonymous Lesson, and a setting of the Hebrew letters for F5/L3. All these pieces are like the Carrión de los Condes works in that they could have been performed by female singers plus *bajón*.[35] In the 1670s, also in La Concepción and another house of the same order (Jesús María), Mexican nuns were paid extra to sing Holy Week

Offices, and this must mean Tenebrae, while their foundations spent money on male clerics, evidently of varying musical ability, to sing the Passions.[36]

During the 1630s in Lima, F5 Tenebrae was regularly heard by the vice-regal court at the church of the female Augustinians of La Encarnación on Wednesday, while the Hours on other Days sometimes took place in its daughter foundation of La Concepción. In part this may be a reflection of the Spanish tradition of hearing the Office in female monastic churches performed by men, but both of these houses boasted nun musicians and their participation cannot be ruled out.[37] Tenebrae on Thursdays and Fridays in Lima otherwise took place in the cathedral.

In France, the first hard evidence is the music in F-Pn V*ma* Rés. 571, evidently compiled for the Benedictine house of Montmartre in the 1630s. The Guise servants who sang some of Charpentier's Lessons in the 1670s may have done so at this same house, replacing the resident Benedictines, given the family's ties to the abbey.[38] Most imposingly, the twelve Lessons and nine Responsories (H. 96–119) written by Charpentier and contained in two adjacent fascicles of his autographs have traditionally been given to singers among the female Parisian Cistercians of l'Abbaye-aux-Bois, also on the basis of a report in the *Mercure de France* of 1680. Charpentier first entered almost a complete cycle, eight Lessons (H. 96–98 and 102–106), in his *cahier* 26, then gave three different indications for the concluding Prayer to be found in other manuscripts. There follow a substitute F6/L2 for solo voice (H. 107) based on an earlier duet version of the text, and then a set of substitute L3s for all three Days (H. 108–110), these latter being large-scale works for two *haute-dessus* and *haute-contre*. These trios rework pieces from the quasi-cycle of H. 96–106 or from earlier in the composer's production. The Miserere (H. 173, in the same scoring as the new L3s) that opens *cahier* 25 might also be added to this, rather as if Charpentier had first written a new Lauds piece and then the Matins items in the same scoring.

The texts of the composer's F5 Responsories follow the earlier Use of Paris, not the French Cistercian breviary nor Paul V's universal *Breviarium monasticum* (1613). As is well known, Charpentier stopped writing what was intended to be a complete three-Day set after the Parisian 1680 breviary revisions, when he had finished only the F5 pieces. Given the close ties of the abbesses of the Bois to the local archbishops, who had supervised their move from the provinces in 1655 and presided at a translation of relics in 1667, the Cistercians could well have sung liturgy according to local, not monastic, Use.[39] Charpentier's music would have advertised the urban presence of the recently arrived nuns; it would also have resonated with their church's now-lost altarpiece, a *Descent from the Cross* by (?Jean-Baptiste de)

Cani.[40] These spectacular Lessons and Responsories—among the highlights of seventeenth-century Tenebrae music anywhere—are real tributes to these women's abilities.

Whatever the sixteenth-century restrictions might have been, by 1690 nuns seem to have sung Lessons despite curial interference, and this marks a sonic shift in ensemble pieces from low *voci pari* to high voices. It also represents Tenebrae as performed by "supraprofessional" musicians, outside the normal labor force of male church singers.

CHARPENTIER: BACKGROUNDS AND GENRES

The role of female monastic singers also raises the question of the immediate devotional context for Charpentier's entire Triduum corpus. One temporally close reworking of Lamentations was Louis Charpy's de Sainte-Croix's (1610–79) *Les saintes offices de Ténèbres* (Paris, 1670), which provided the Latin text of Matins plus vernacular explanations of the Psalms. It also included moral remarks on the Lessons (some taken from Lapide's exegesis) and a poetic paraphrase of their text. There is a similar commentary for all the Lauds items, plus translations (but no paraphrase) of all Responsories and antiphons; that is, it is a presentation of the whole service and not just the Lessons. In his preface, Charpy noted the omnipresence of Tenebrae polyphony, while criticizing those who went only to hear the music. Through his own efforts at restoring something of the original Hebrew meter, missing in the Vulgate, he aimed to bring his readers to the sadness and penance that music should—but evidently did not always—induce. The poet's tropological approach to Lessons is evident in his comments on 1:1, directed to Jerusalem as the figure of the individual sinning soul.[41]

It is hard to link specific exegetical or devotional literature to Charpentier's patrons. Certainly his relations with the Jesuits in the late 1680s and 1690s means that their exegetical literature—first and foremost Lapide, but also the Jesuit Jacobus Tirinus's *Commentarius in Vetus et Novum Testamentum* (Antwerp, 1632)—had formed Parisian Jesuits' ideas of Jeremiah. The biblical commentary that might have been known by his important patrons from the Guise family is less clear, perhaps something like the *Commentarius in universam Scripturam* of the French court preacher François Carrière (Lyon, 1663).[42]

The overall chronology of Triduum music in Paris depends on a more precise dating of Michel Lambert's two Lesson cycles for voice and continuo, traditionally considered as intimate settings for the court. If these are from the 1650s, then they are the first surviving examples, but if they stem from the end of the composer's life (c. 1690), then a good deal of Charpentier's

music had already been produced, including many solo pieces.[43] It is also unclear how publicly the royal repertory circulated; perhaps the earlier works
of Antoine Boesset for Montmartre in Rés. 571 would have been more familiar to local audiences.[44]

Another corpus of music that the young Charpentier would have heard
during his student years in Italy was the Roman repertory, thus Lessons like
Cesi's or the works of Q. 43; given their omnipresence, it would have been
hard to miss Graziani's Responsories. Among Roman Lamentations, it is hard
to find a single verse in either Cesi or the Bologna miscellany that displays
the same kind of consistent motivic work—as opposed to simple citation or
rhythmicization—with the chant formula as does Charpentier's first surviving Lesson, H. 91. Similarly, the Responsories of Graziani display a textural
homogeneity not found in Charpentier's settings. In the Triduum pieces (unlike his *histoires sacrées*), his student years seem not to have affected his production.

Much of Charpentier's output can be grouped into four large moments
or patronage situations, differentiating between the works in the "Arabic"
and in the "Roman-numeral" cahiers. In the "Arabic" volumes, there is a first
group of four scattered Lessons plus a Miserere in the early 1670s, some if
not all probably for the Guise household; a second chunk consisting of the
Abbaye-aux-Bois pieces c. 1680 and their reworkings; then a pause of a decade before a third group of six Responsories followed by a set of solo L2s,
around 1690, possibly for the Jesuits. Finally, in the "Roman-numeral" fascicles of outside commissions, there seems to be one group of three L1s, one
for each of the Days, and then three groups of three L3s, all these pieces dating from successive years around 1690–94. Although the items in the first two
groups sometimes use obbligato instruments, larger-scale orchestral writing
is more important in the works of the 90s, as it sets local affect and provides
rhetorical structure by demarcating letters and verses in the Lessons.

From the perspective of rhetoric and genre, Charpentier's Lessons are
novel on any number of counts: their sheer length, first and foremost. Not
only are the Hebrew letters long, but their antiperiodic structure renders them
unpredictable. A second kind of freedom is the possible, but not inevitable,
division of the sub-verses by tempo, scoring, and affect. In addition, the motivic interplay of either an active continuo line, or in some cases of obbligato
instruments, renders the texture complex. The articulation of verses by the
use of repeated or new patterns in the instrumental bass expands the expressive lability of the basic procedures at work.

The relationship between chant formula and polyphonic structure in the
Lessons was detailed in a still-underappreciated book of 1966 by Theodor
Käser, which painstakingly showed the generative power of the Tone-6 for-

mula (often pitched on G) in every verse of many Lessons, centered on the H. 96–105 group. This analysis also caught the importance of the sub-verses, each made up of groups ("Phasen") of melodic cells, these latter variously ornamenting and expanding the simple gestures of the recitation tone into rhetorical climaxes for each verse. While not downplaying the affect and impact of individual words, Käser highlighted how the formula-generated structures were basic to Charpentier's conceptions, and even how they were retained or expanded in the reworked Lessons of the early 1680s, H. 108–110.[45]

Two larger points are a logical extension of Käser's analysis. First, this view of the Lessons' vocal nature implies that their musical conceptions are horizontal; some of the more striking vertical simultaneities ("dissonances") are actually the result of each line's logic, and in that sense the Lessons are both profoundly polyphonic, not chordal, and ultimately a high-level manifestation of oral-"formulaic" composition. Second, the later Lessons of Charpentier move away from the omnipresence of the chant-tone-generated cells/ groups in favor of freer invention. In a wider sense, the Lessons of younger composers (Lalande and Couperin) work in very different ways from those of Charpentier.[46]

Another issue in the Lessons, so tied to chant, is that of their tonality, and here again Charpentier's earlier pieces differ somewhat from his later ones. Eight (plus three reworkings) of the early group are on G with no signature (= G/♮), and two others feature a sharp. Only two early Lessons are on F, with one on C/♮. But the sets of three Lessons from the 1690s differ notably: two are on F, one is in the C/♮ system, with one on C with two flats, and another on G with a ♯.[47] Obviously, all the tonal types with a major third allow for the audible use of the Tone-6 recitation formula, on whatever pitch. However, the large-scale (double-choir in the refrains) L3s (H. 135–137) from the same decade, evidently an outside commission (*cahier* LX), are written on C with two flats. Hence their minor-third tonality permits citations of the tone only in a few Hebrew letters and the opening of the Prayer.

Beyond Lamentations, the partial Responsory cycle H. 111–119 with voices and continuo separates its tonalities by Nocturne: G, A, and E (all no signature), while the Responsories H. 126–134, for voices and obbligato instruments, written around 1691, present a less homogenous tonal picture. The earlier set breaks with tradition, not only in the frequent scoring for solo voice or the flouting of reduced-ensemble texture in the verses, but in its theatrical approach. The opening gesture of F5/R1 (H. 111) shows an unrecognized aspect of Charpentier's use of chant outside the Lessons. Pitched on G, it outlines the incipit of the chant Responsory, moving gradually from G_4 up to D_5. Taken up canonically in the three voices, this idea leads to a full stop in the middle of the A section. Christ's prayer, "Pater, si fieri potest" is given to the solo *haute-contre,* turning strongly to C/*mollis* for the "chalice to be drunk" ("transeat a me calix iste"). Still cast as a solo, this leads to the repetendum back on G/*durus* for the "willingness of the spirit," pausing on D at the "weakness of the flesh" ("caro autem infirma"). Finally, Christ's resolve ("Fiat voluntas tua") picks up a subject first stated in the continuo, and is declaimed twice.

Against common Responsory procedures, Charpentier then brings back the entire ensemble for the normally reduced-scoring verse, here "Vigilate et orate," which also takes up some twenty-eight measures, in contrast to its typical brevity. The end of the verse is elided into a rewritten version of the repetendum for the whole ensemble, starting with the original *haute-contre* solo line but assigning to the first *dessus* a gesture presented originally in the continuo. "Caro autem" is largely similar to its first iteration, but the ending of "fiat voluntas tua" is rewritten for the whole ensemble so as to articulate the words some four times, emphasizing conformity to Divine will in emphatic ways. Not for the last time would dramatic declamation and sonic contrast trump the norms of genre familiar to Charpentier.

Some pieces are more traditional: R2, *Tristis est anima mea,* goes from two singers to one (marked "celle que a chanté la première leçon," hence a nun) for its verse. But R3, *Amicus meus,* repeats its opening words ("my friend") at the end of its A section, rather as if Christ was speaking in incredulity that a friend would betray him.[48] If the Lessons and Responsories were done together, this piece would have come immediately after an F5/L3, either the trio H. 107 or its models H. 92 or 98. Finally, the R9 *O Juda,* a reproach to the apostate Judas Iscariot, uses its opening words as a refrain, like *Amicus meus.* That it was even set in polyphony contradicts the Parisian ceremonial of 1662, which specifically demanded that the celebrant sing it slowly and only in chant, without figured music.[49] This strongly *durus* piece, set on E, drives forward to a *passus duriusculus,* a kind of emblem of the bitter betrayal of Christ at the end of the verse, "et lingua tua concinnabat dolos"/"and your [Judas'] tongue produced only deception." The voice-leading for this phrase embellishes a doubled leading-tone *cadenza in mi* on B♭ using C♮ and A♯, and the augmented-sixth sonority along with the "duplicate" cadential motion emblematizes Judas's duplicity.

The early Misereres (H. 157 of perhaps 1673, and H. 173 for the same three-high-voice ensemble familiar from the Lessons/Responsories of c. 1680) deserve their own consideration. The former is followed in *cahier 6* by a Prayer (H. 95).[50] Charpentier's innovation even in the scoring is clear from the two recorders in some of these works, evidently the only Triduum music in Europe outside the Spanish Lessons with *bajones* to call for obbligato wind instruments until the next century. H. 157 stays close to its tonic A (most of the twenty verses cadence on A or E), recalling the polyphonic implications of psalm-tone 4 (reciting on *a* and ending on *e*).[51] Its closing indication is "Suivez au Recordare," i.e., the immediately following *Oratio,* H. 95. The vocal and instrumental forces are roughly the same between the two pieces, and the implication is that they were performed together, with the Prayer displaced from its normal liturgical position and concluding the entire service.[52]

Here the emphases of H. 95 are suggestive. It is relatively concise (266 measures for its title, twenty-two sub-verses, and refrain, about twelve minutes in performance), and so repetition and unusual pitch gestures have important weight. Among the verses, v. 1ab ("Recordare, Domine, quid acciderit nobis"/"Remember, o Lord, what has happened to us"), 3ab ("Pupilli facti sumus absque patre, matres nostrae quasi viduae"/"We have become orphans without fathers, our mothers like widows"), 4b ("ligna nostra pretio comparavimus"/"we bought our wood for a price"), and 5b ("lassis non dabatur requies"/"for us weary ones there will be no rest") are each declaimed twice, with a diminished octave in 3a at the mention of "fatherless" Jerusalem. In v. 7a the reference to ancestors' passing gets a striking metric switch and chromatic inflection ("Patres nostri peccaverunt, et non sunt"/"our fathers have sinned, and are no more"), while in the second subverse, their sins weighing on children is also repeated ("et nos iniquitates eorum portavimus"/"and we carry their sins"), underscored by slower motion and grinding 7–6 suspensions. Finally, the shame of Jerusalem's women in v. 11 ("Mulieres in Sion humiliaverunt"/"they oppressed the women in Zion") is set to a chromatic descending tetrachord in the continuo line, again a sign for lament.

Previously, the concluding vv. 17–20 of the Miserere emphasize individual penance and salvation: an anaphoric duet at "Domine, labia mea aperies," major compositional reworking evident in the autograph at "holocaustis non delectaberis," repetitions at "cor contritum et humiliatum, Deus, non despicies," and a long closing verse "Tunc acceptabis sacrificium justitiae." The closing section thus begins with "Lord, open my mouth," continues with "You will not delight in animal sacrifices" and "God, You will not despise a contrite and humbled heart," and finally "Then You will accept the sacrifice of justice": a series of penitential actions resulting in forgiveness, opened by a speech-act. The two pieces are presented in the source, against liturgical order, so as to conclude with the collective tone of the Prayer, and they both seem to emphasis mourning and penance. This Tenebrae would have culminated in the *Oratio* after the almost twenty-minute-long Miserere, thus totaling a half hour of funereal polyphony, emphasizing "fatherlessness" and the plight of Jerusalem's surviving females. The combination points to intercessory music for the deceased fathers of women, possibly Charpentier's Guise patronesses.

Charpentier's only Benedictus was written in the mid-1680s when he seems not to have been concerned with new Tenebrae music; it is as much of a departure from convention as Stradella's (and the two could well have known each other in the Rome of the 1660s).[53] Scored for a large Guise ensemble (six voices/two violins), it is cast on G/*durus,* perhaps a memory of Tone-6 canticles transposed up a step. In some ways, Charpentier played off the conventional structural articulation of the Benedictus as *alternatim;* in order to create an odd number of sections, vv. 3–4 are fused as a long solo, and the opening six sections alternate kaleidoscopically changing textures, including Roman-style two-choir writing at v. 5 ("Ad faciendam"). The moment at v. 7 of extinguishing the altar lights, "Ut sine timore," is marked by an accelerando and the return of imitative texture; it also moves in the sharpest directions (around E) heard thus far.

Zacharias' turn to addressing his son ("Et tu puer," v. 9) is tonally linked to G, but its florid vocal solo with echos in the violins signals the change in the canticle's subject. After more two-choir music and a solo (vv. 10–11), Charpentier set the final verse "Illuminare his, qui in tenebris et umbra mortis sedent / ad dirigendos pedes nostros in viam pacis" as a long conclusion, some eighty-six measures. Given that the canticle has twelve verses, and there are a total of 447 bars, "Illuminare" takes up about twice its allotted length.

Starting as a trio without a clear break from v. 10, "Illuminare"'s opening half-verse gradually builds, with only the slightest of natural inflections (F♮) for "in umbra mortis," to large-scale imitation and polychorality for its second half. The entire verse is then re-stated in antiphony moving to imitation, as voices enter from high to low, and then a third time, from low to high. This dissolves into an octave D heard only in the instruments, and then silence, before a fourth iteration of "ad dirigendos nos" in stretto rounds off the canticle. In this verse, Charpentier built an ensemble *scena,* with emphasis on moving "into the way of peace." If the piece was written against the background of the troubled political times of 1686–87, as the League of Augsburg took shape against Louis XIV, the allusion makes sense. But the canticle also marks the joyous commemoration of the Passion for the Guise after the years of mourning, and for good reason Charpentier's nephew, Jacques Edouard, noted in his 1726 catalogue that "cette pièce est extraordinaire."

LESSONS: WORKS AND REWORKINGS

The new three-voice versions for the ensemble of female Cistercians, H. 108–110, based on earlier Lessons also illuminate the large-scale rhetoric

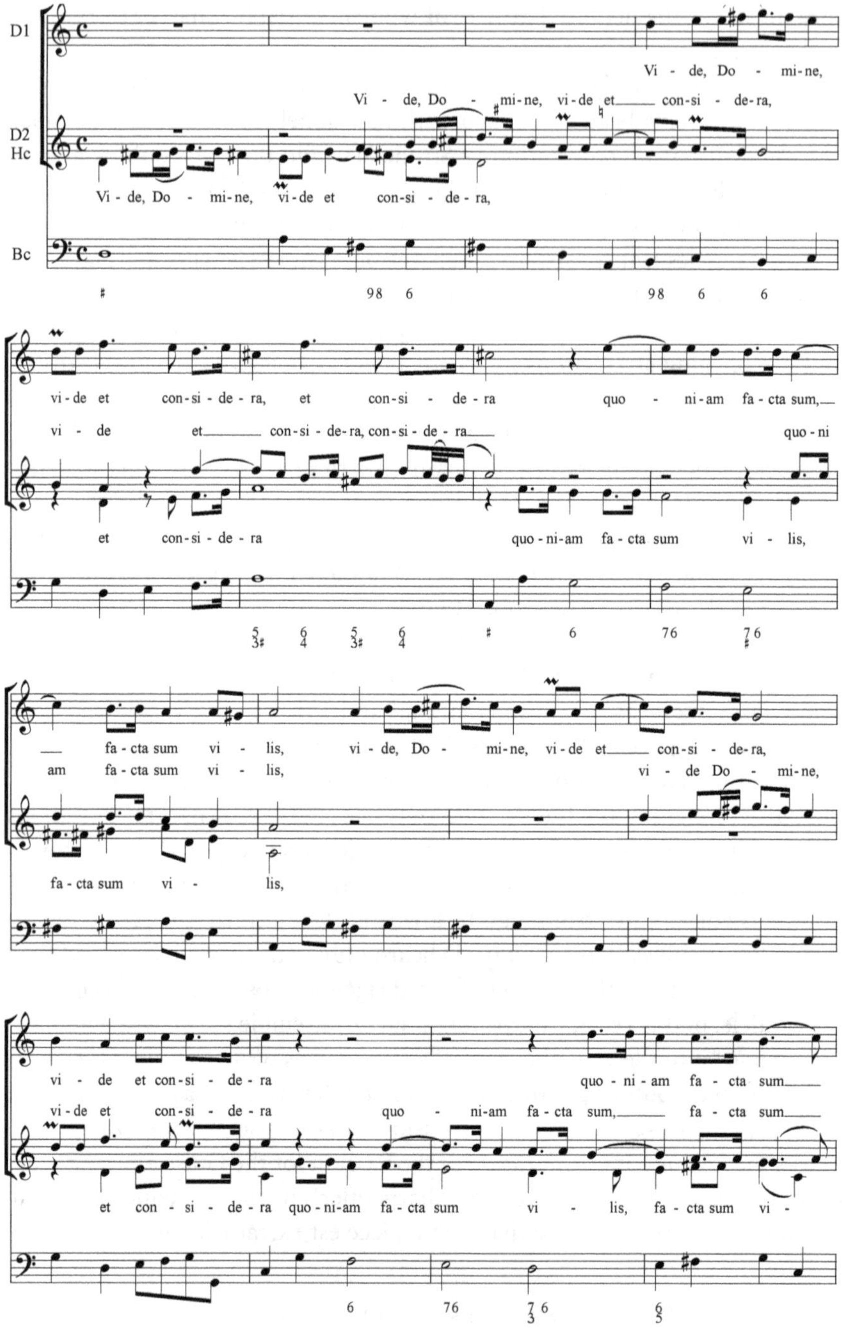

EXAMPLE 6.5. Charpentier, F5/L3, H. 108, "Vide, Domine."

EXAMPLE 6.5. (*Continued*)

of their models. In the case of F5/L3, H. 108 engages much of the music of H. 92 and H. 98, two Lessons that are almost identical; for F6/L3, H. 109 revisits some of H. 104 but is less dependent on H. 93. The new Prayer (H. 110) begins with the "Incipit oratio" title as set in the Lesson of mourning, H. 95. But then it weaves in and out of intertextuality, citing and reworking some of the earlier setting, while changing both the musical text and the declamation of verses and sub-verses.

To examine the three related F5/L3s provides a sense of the fixed and the mutable. The opening "Jod" is similar across the two earlier Lessons, while H. 108 adds a new top line. The first major change is at 1:11c; whereas the earlier pieces had simply repeated the declamation of "Vide, Domine" in triple time, the trio setting first expands the "sighing" of "gemens" in 11b with a long vocalization in all parts, then demarcates 11c with a double-bar and a return to duple time, neither present in the earlier versions. This leads to an entirely new double period organized around a descending figure for "quoniam facta sum vilis" (example 6.5).

In v.12a, H. 108 also re-sets "O vos omnes" for the *haute-contre,* the only solo apportioned to her. The *concitato* duet for the following sub-verse, symbolizing the "wine-pressing" of 12c's "quoniam vindemiavit me," adds to the contrast. Another solo meditative letter, "Mem," similar across the three settings, interrupts this affect, while the "fire in the bones" sub-verse (1:13a) recalls 12c via another soprano duet. A further entrance by the *haute-contre* marks H. 108's imitative reworking of material from the earlier Lessons at "expandit rete pedibus meis"/"He spread a net for my feet." Again the third sub-verse gets special attention: 1:13c was rewritten in duple time, compared to H. 92 and 98, as the affect changes back to yet another descending passage for the reversal articulated by "convertit me retrorsum." The verse ends quietly, with a homophonic ensemble for Jerusalem's "desolation" ("posuit me desolatam") and 9–8 suspensions for the sorrow of "tota die maerore confectam."

Charpy's comments and paraphrases of these sub-verses give some idea of the possible resonances and reasons for the changes. For 1:11, the poet took his comments on the city's hunger directly from Lapide's tropological sense of Lamentations, while his verse paraphrase extended the description of Jerusalem's misery. At 1:11c, Charpy moved beyond "vilis" to death: "O Dieu! Considerez quel est mon triste sort / Et rendez moy la vie, ou donnez moy la mort."[54] At 1:12, he noted that the words of "O vos omnes" were normally applied to Christ directly, and his gloss for 1:13c read "Que souffrir sans morir, c'est tout que je puis." Hence death and suffering lie behind the two sub-verses that were so drastically changed.

The final verse of H. 108, "Vigilavit jugam," opens and closes in recitation by the same soprano who had begun v. 10, with a middle phrase "a demy voix" continuing the muted tone of the previous verses. Finally, the "Jerusalem" refrain is expanded from seventeen measures in the solo versions to twenty-four in the trio; this is laid out in three large declamatory periods, of which the third is extended. Here the opening gesture limns the C-F motion recalling the Lesson chant formula as pitched on *c;* as if this were not enough, the tonal motion also arrives on C, not on the tonic G, at the seeming end of the refrain's third iteration. Once again introduced by the *haute-contre,* an extension of "convertere" is set to the "modal fourth" D-G, at last returning to the *finalis* while rearranging the liturgical text, as it comes before "Jerusalem." The same refrain also serves for the two other new trios.

Similar issues obtain in the trio reworking of F6/L3, H. 109, set on G/♮ in all three versions. The individual subjectivity of this Lesson ("Ego vir videns") was explained by the exegete Carrière in a triple sense: the prophet, the suffering Jewish people, and Christ Himself describing the Passion.[55] For the preacher, the verses corresponding to L3 had to do with the "imprisonment and chains done at night by the cohort and tribunes," with v. 3, "Tantum in me vertit," referring to the chaining of Christ's feet and His interrogation.[56] This differs from Druzbicki's connection of these verses to the Flagellation. The earlier solo version, H. 104, is similar to the trio in vv. 1, 4 and 8, but each of the three Hebrew letters in H. 109 features new material. Unlike the earlier duet setting, H. 93, they are simply repeated on each iteration. All three Lessons turn to *mollis* regions in v. 5, but here H. 93 and 104 are largely independent from each other.

The most novel moment in H. 109 is 3:3, "Tantum in me vertit, et convertit manum suum tota die." The duet version had moved to the distant pitch center E here, and H. 104 expanded its material. Both the prior versions ar-

ticulated the verse between "vertit" and "et convertit," as would seem logical
from the binary structure ("Only against me did he strike / and re-strike his
hand all the day"). But in revising for the nuns, Charpentier read the text in
a different way, eschewing the monodic writing of the earlier versions, and
replacing it with a 39-bar *fuga a due soggetti* for all three voices. The two
fugal subjects are apportioned to "Tantum" and "in me vertit et convertit,"
respectively: "Only / against me did he strike and re-strike his hand . . ." (example 6.6), while the long values of the first subject are also set off by the
detaché (dot) ornament. The contrapuntal contrast is thus unlike anything
in this or other Lessons; the division of the verse suggests the singularity of
Christ's sufferings, while the cycling quarter-note counterpoint seems to represent the back-and-forth blows directly, similar to the linkage in contemporary exegesis of this verse to the Chaining or the Flagellation.

This revised parsing of 3:3 seems to have had long-term effects for the
composer: one of Charpentier's late Lessons, an F6/L3 for three low voices
and orchestra (H. 136, from the large-scale and theatrical H. 135–37 set),
also apportions long values to "Tantum," separates it from the rest of the
verse, runs the two gestures together in counterpoint, and then repeats the
entire musical period. It seems that the composer used the modules first developed in H. 109 for later settings. In 3:3, Charpy's verse paraphrase simply
stressed the personal suffering of the prophet, in a different binary fashion:
"Il assemble sur moy les traits de son courroux, / J'ai predit tous nos maux,
et je les souffre tous."[57]

LATER OFFICE MUSIC

The Triduum works of the 1690s are obviously different, but it is not
clear how much of this is due to the new spaces or singers for which Charpentier was writing. Given that he was working for the Jesuits, the order's
exegesis and projection of Lamentations that had accumulated by this time
seem to be reflected in these more extrovert works. Again, 1:11 provides an
example. Charpentier's thirteen-bar deletion in the F5/L3 (H. 123) for solo
basse-taille (here the singer is named as "M. Beaupuy") suggests how the
composer articulated verses.[58] The Lesson is marked by its "semiotic" use of
the instrumental ensemble, notably in the long preludes to "Jod" and "Jerusalem." This sense of instrumental structure is most audible in the last letter
"Nun," two pitches only in the voice at the mid-point of a thirty-one-bar
orchestral movement.

H. 123's declamation of 1:11a moves away from G to B, then back to
G for 11b. The sub-verse "Vide, Domine" is set off by its own double-bar
and a move to D, a pitch center hitherto unheard in this G-mode piece. Je-

EXAMPLE 6.6. Charpentier, F6/L3, H. 109, "Tantum in me vertit."

EXAMPLE 6.6. (*Continued*)

rusalem's plea migrates to E, as the phrase itself is fragmented and repeated between "Vide, Domine" and "quoniam facta sum vilis" (example 6.7). As he was composing the verse, Charpentier evidently decided to demarcate "Vide, Domine" not only from the two preceding sub-verses but more subtly from the following letter "Lamed." He deleted a 13-bar passage featuring the winds originally meant to accompany "quoniam facta sum," wrote new counterpoint in the violins, and only then introduced the full orchestra over a descending ("lamenting") tetrachord E-B as a preface to the Hebrew letter and to presage the *conquestio* affect of the following verse, "O vos omnes."

The directly representative nature ("theatricality") of the later Office music is clear from such use of the instrumental ensemble for rhetorical articulation.[59] It also highlights a new distance from both the direct citation of the Tone-6 formula and from chant's generative function in the Lessons. Another set of L3s, H. 141–143, even though cast on F, cites the chant *initium* only at the opening of the F5 and SS pieces.

Certainly the Responsories H. 126–134 must have been written for a church of regulars following Roman rite, since their texts differ from both the pre- and post-1680 Parisian breviary.[60] In these pieces, a new sense of drama

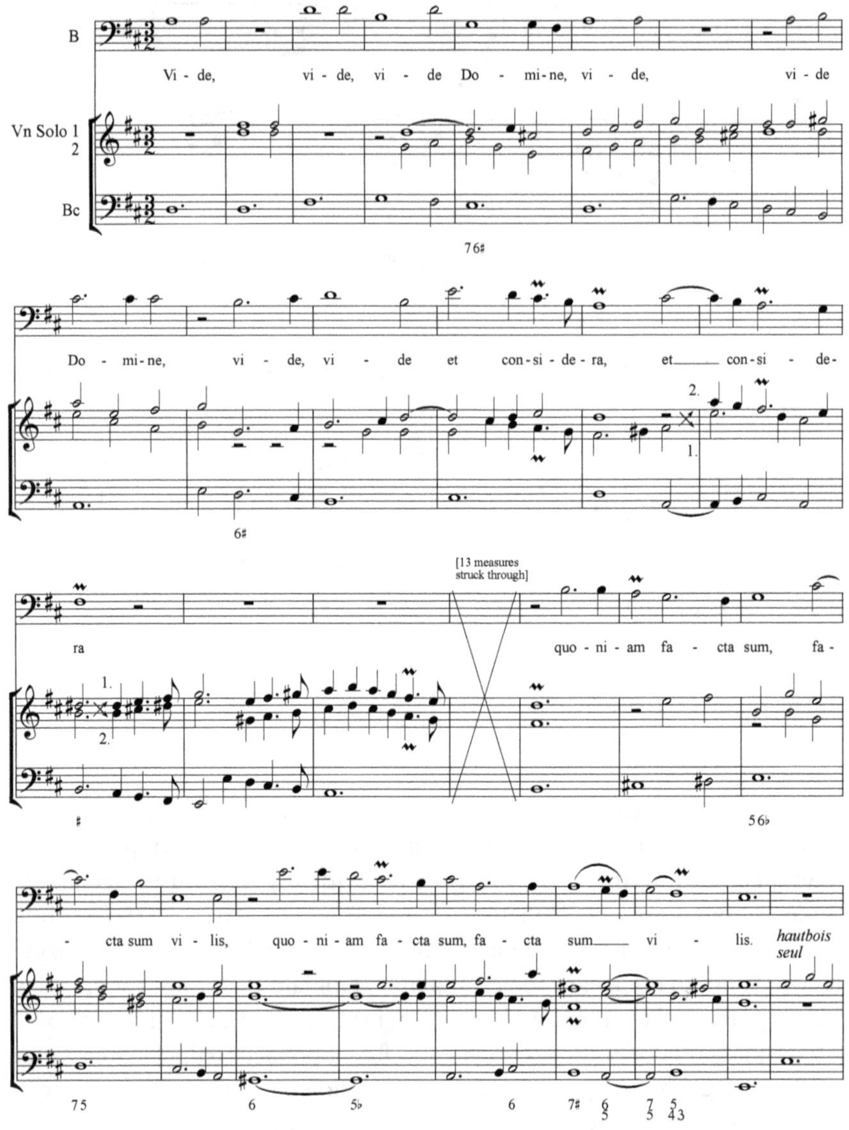

EXAMPLE 6.7. Charpentier, F5/L3, H. 123, "Vide, Domine."

led to formal solutions unlike the high-voice Responsories of c. 1680. One of the most memorable is the F6/R2 that recounts the marvels at Christ's death on the Cross, *Velum templi scissum est,* H. 130. It begins with a *concitato* instrumental ritornello for violins and recorders, and the upward runs that follow in the piece's three male voices correspond to the ripping of the Temple's veil. The muted string tremolos that represent "et omnis terra tremuit"/"and the whole earth shook" in the Responsory's repetendum could be expected. But then the text changes its narrative voice, as the Good Thief begs for salvation ("Memento mei, Domine, quando veneris in regnum tuum"). Again here, Charpentier breaks with tradition by reducing the scoring at the end of the repetendum, not in the verse. Thus the Thief's plea—the desire of every Christian at death—is projected and repeated by a solo tenor. There follows an instrumental postlude to the repetendum on a rising motive, symbolizing but not declaiming Christ's here-unspoken answer (Lk 23:43): "Amen I say to you, today you will be with Me in Paradise," a text that listeners would have supplied mentally even though it is not in the Responsory.

Charpentier then takes the semantic echo between the opening of the verse, "Petrae scissae sunt" and that of the entire Responsory ("Velum templi scissum est"), as an occasion to return to the original full texture and affect of marvel, again cutting against the tradition of reduced scoring in the verse. All the more surprising is the verse's second half, describing the resurrection of the sleeping saints from their tombs ("et multi corpora sanctorum qui dormierant surrexerunt"; example 6.8). In a gesture that indexes transcendence, the ascent of the sanctoral bodies is set to an upward sequence, over a bass line that rises by step from $B_2\flat$ to $B_3\flat$, the repeated 7/5 sonorities collapsing into sixths, an effect as remarkable as the event it narrates.

In yet another departure from liturgical propriety, Charpentier's following return to the repetendum omits all text after "terra tremuit" (thus excising the Good Thief), but rescores the opening phrase by combining the original vocal parts simultaneously with the instrumental tremolos. Finally, the Responsory ends with a new postlude anchored by a final low $B_1\flat$ in the continuo. In retrospective hearing, however, this has the effect of placing the Thief's plea theatrically at the center of the whole piece, and of imposing a symmetrical five-part structure with an emblematic solo at the center—not unlike the Lesson H. 108 of a decade earlier—in place of the normative ABAB pattern.

On a European scale, there is no corpus of Triduum music as original, varied, and remarkable as Charpentier's, for whichever patrons the various items were composed. It stands in stark contrast to the music of the French court chapel, with its large-scale Triduum psalms by Jean-Baptiste Lully. Most familiar are Lully's items for F5 (*Notus in Judea,* LWV 77/17), and

EXAMPLE 6.8. Charpentier, F6/R2, H. 126, "Et multa corpora sanctorum."

EXAMPLE 6.8. (*Continued*)

F6 (*Quare fremuerunt gentes?*, LWV 67), both without doxologies. According to the court ceremonials, Lessons were often sung in simple chant and there is no mention of Responsories, but clearly polyphony clothed other liturgical items.[61] In the same vein Charpentier wrote three extensive Matins psalms for the Triduum of 1699, as he took up his job at the Sainte-Chapelle (H. 228–230). At Lauds, other doxology-less and hence liturgically possible psalms in his manuscripts include *Benedixisti, Domine* (conceivably F6/P3; H. 181), and *Bonum est confiteri* (SS/P2; H. 185), this latter has the same scoring and named group of six singers required in the Benedictus for the Guise, H. 345.[62]

NEAPOLITAN PRACTICES

The devotional appropriateness of French court Tenebrae, however, was not evident to foreign observers. This was the impression of the Neapolitan traveller G. B. Gemelli Careri on his visit to the Royal Chapel on Holy Thursday 1686. Gemelli criticized not only the singers, presumably conducted by Lully, but also the lack of *durezze* in the pieces themselves:

> The voices were not the greatest thing in the world; and the composition was not only different from Italian taste, but set out with so little artistry, and so short on dissonances and suspensions, as required by the words of these Days, that our wise and learned Tommaso Carapella would have laughed for more than a day.[63]

Gemelli relented somewhat the next Day, but the different aesthetics of composition are clear. Up to the 1680s, the Neapolitan musical tradition that Gemelli implicitly considered as a model survives largely through Responsories. Printed cycles of this genre by G. D. Montella (1602), Pomponio Nenna (1607 and 1622), G. D. Viola (1622), and Gregorio Strozzi (1655) represent an older tradition, while the manuscript sets by Erasmo de Bartolo, Scipione Dentice and Giovanni Salvatore reflect Neapolitan Oratorian practice from 1620 to 1650 (the former two) or conservatories/city churches a bit later (the last). There were also now-lost pieces by G. M. Trabaci, Nicolo Tortamano, and Cesare Rosa. What the Lesson repertory might have been, besides the four-voice pieces in Montella's and Strozzi's OHS publications, is unclear.

Jeremiah's text continued to be present in early modern Naples. In vol. 4 of his *Lettere ecclesiastiche* (Venice, 1716, dedicated to St. Augustine), the Apulian bishop and frequent resident of the city Pompeo Sarnelli (1649–1725) discussed the Hebrew letters and verse structure of Lamentations, using authorities from Jerome onward eclectically. His remarks took each letter as prefixing three poetic lines of the original, each sub-verse thus equivalent to a line. Sarnelli also reiterated the book's four chapters as symbolizing the sins of the four parts of the world (and explicitly not just of the Jews), then repeated Jerome's glosses and syntactic combinations of the letters.[64]

In his *Lezioni scritturali . . . sopra i Threni del profeta Geremia* (Naples, 1707), Sarnelli also considered the moral implications of the books of Job and of Lamentations.[65] His twenty lessons paraphrased Jeremiah's text in two senses, "mystical" (tropological) and symbolic, referring to the soul ruined by sin and to Christ, respectively, noting that the Church sang it at Tenebrae in a "wailing" tone to represent the Passion and to move all to compassion.[66] The bishop took ch. 1 as an allegory of Christ weeping over Jerusalem, with the city like a soul abandoned by God, and referred to the letters as an alphabet of personal penance. Finally, the prelate considered the Prayer as the model of a rhetorical summation.

Before Gemelli Careri's comments, the earliest surviving pieces in modern style locally are the eighteen Lessons *a 1–3* with instruments by P. A. Ziani (I-Nf), evidently performed if not composed for his final years after arriving in Naples to take over the Royal Chapel (1681–84), probably two annual cycles.[67] The earliest dated Lessons by Caresana and Veneziano, organist colleagues in the viceregal ensemble and elsewhere, are from shortly thereafter; the numbers are impressive, each composer having left about twenty-five surviving examples. Caresana's are roughly split between solos with strings and those with continuo only, whereas most of Veneziano's are for voice and instruments. The expansion of Lessons into the Second Nocturne readings is also evident; three for SS by the latter (1694–99) are discussed below. Why Augustine's texts should have been singled out for musical emphasis, beyond the truisms of the seventeenth century as a golden age for his thought, must have to do with figures like Sarnelli and with the desire to treat the Passion and salvation directly, not allegorically.[68]

The accessible production of the two organists is marked by the sharp differences in their settings, even though the dated pieces of both were evidently created within the same decade.[69] To take only works with instruments, Caresana's use of four-part mid-century string scoring (cleffed C1/C1/C3/F4) contrasts with Veneziano's modern ensemble (two violins, viola, and cello on the same staff as the continuo), the latter used in almost every sub-verse of his Lessons. Formally, Caresana's open designs stand apart from the formalized structures in Veneziano's verses, e.g., the frequent use of the 12/8 *siciliane* with solo violin, contemporary with similar movements by Alessandro Scarlatti.

A solo Lesson by Caresana is probably the earliest dated one (1685). This virtuoso F6/L2 (I-Nf, Inv. 529) for bass begins by setting up a pattern for the first two verses (2:12–13): Hebrew letters for voice and instrumental band

EXAMPLE 6.9. Caresana, F6/L1, "Sibilaverunt, et moverunt."

EXAMPLE 6.9. (*Continued*)

which share motivic material, alternating with declamatory verses without strings. The verses end in short melismas but maintain their musical and affective unity, at least until v. 14. Here the instruments enter during the verse, and the reference to penance at the end of 2:14b ("ut te ad poenitentiam provocarent") generates the first of four vocal explosions across the singer's entire tessitura, brought to a sudden stop at sub-verse [c] ("viderunt autem tibi"). In turn, 2:14 ends in another irregular burst of melisma, symbolizing directly the word "ejectiones" ("banishments"). The process of fragmenting the sub-verses is then extended in v. 15, where a direct vocal representation of "hooting" ("sibilaverunt") highlights 15b. Finally, the derisory question with which the Lesson ends, "haecine est urbs . . . gaudium universae terrae?"/"This is the city which was . . . the joy of the whole earth?," shows its "universality" in a two-octave solo flourish, ranging downward to the lowest C possible for the singer and visiting both flat and sharp sides of the local tonality (example 6.9).

In contrast, an undated F5/L3 for soprano and instruments (Inv. 846) by Veneziano works in discrete if strongly contrasted sections, in which the strings play throughout. On A/*durus,* its "Caph" is a long and vocally virtuosic Allegro, arrested by a switch to a 3/8 Adagio moving to E. The sub-verses of 1:11 [a] and [b] are clearly demarcated in this slow section, and Jerusalem's own voice in [c] is marked by another change, an "a tempo giusto" ostinato aria on C for "Vide, Domine." "Facta sum vilis" is declaimed some four times without symbolic solecisms, and the verse concludes with another long letter "Lamed." In this Lesson, the sub-verses often become closed sections of sharp contrast as opposed to their more irregular treatment by Caresana.

Two dated settings, both for soprano and strings, of the charged F6/L3 ("Ego vir videns") by Caresana and Veneziano (Inv. 913 and 848; 1688 and 18 March 1698, respectively) provide further differences between their approaches.[70] Sarnelli's explanation would link these verses directly to the Passion.[71] Caresana's Lesson is cast on F/*mollis,* beginning with an instrumental prelude which repeats and adds the vocal line for the first "Aleph." The verses are set in a pattern similar to his 1685 Lesson in its scoring and vocal emphasis on the ends of verses (v. 1, "indignationis eius"; v. 3, "tota die"; v. 4, "ossa mea"). In 3:3, whose "vertit et convertit" Sarnelli would compare to the repeated blows of a blacksmith hammering metal again and again, Caresana's setting juxtaposes an imitative "Aleph" with an unpredictable melisma for "tota die," while Veneziano did justice to the "reiterated blows" by repeating "convertit" four times and then linking the passage to the following "Beth."[72] Overall, Caresana's eschewal of repeating verse text and his demarcation between letters and verses lend a measured decorum to the musical declamation.

The technical difficulty of Veneziano's Lesson would have been compounded by the mere nine days until Holy Thursday in 1698 that performers would have had to acquire and learn the piece. On E, its first half is split into three large sections, each articulated by a half-cadence on a Hebrew letter. Thus v. 1 is linked to the following "Aleph," vv. 2–3 to the following "Beth," and v. 4 again to the "Beth" of v. 5. In contrast to Caresana, Veneziano repeats all the words or phrases of every verse, and often emphasizes the verbs rather than the nouns (e.g., the dance-like 3/8 meter for "Me minavit, et adduxit in tenebris" of v. 2). In this sense his declamatory approach is like Stradella's F5/L2.

The imagery of v. 5 ("He has built around me, and encircled me with bile and labor") led Caresana to his first use of instruments in a verse, with the kinds of *durezze* that Gemelli had desired to hear in French Tenebrae two years earlier. Veneziano broke this verse in the middle, casting "et circumdedit me" as a Largo based around the sharpest pitch regions of the Lesson. Caresana's v. 6 ("In tenebrosis collocavit me") turned to flat sonorities, while the "darkness" of this verse evoked a repeated chromatic catabasis in Veneziano's piece, first through a fifth and then an entire octave, taken up by the violins and voice, and necessitating a cancellation of the sharp with which the Lesson had originally been signed. V. 7's idea of "building around against me so that I might not escape" also generated Veneziano's gesture of a two-voice (unison violins together with cello/lute) instrumental capriccio in imitative style, over which the voice declaims the words. Evidently the "invention" of the capriccio symbolized the "building around" idea.

Veneziano followed with a frantic v. 8 ("Sed et, cum clamavero et rogavero, exclusit orationem meam"), in which the prophet's desperate pleas in the face of Divine deafness are symbolized by increasingly frequent and uncontrolled scales down and up in the voice and instruments. Sarnelli's *Lezioni* would refer to this verse as the "extreme misery of one afflicted, besieged on all fronts, having God and man against him." Veneziano's v. 9 is a *siciliana* with solo violin, moving back to *durus* areas. For these verses, Caresana had returned to *mollis* regions (v. 8), and then employed an uncharacteristically long melisma on the final "semitas meas subvertit" of v. 9 before the refrain. In both Lessons, "Jerusalem, convertere" is the longest single section, Caresana's in triple time and Veneziano's with a contrast of two tempi ("un poco animato"/"a tempo lungo"), but also recalling the energy of his v. 8 with another set of virtuoso string figurations. The two Lessons thus have decidedly different rhetorics of *conquestio,* Caresana's in discrete and carefully declaimed units that separate verses and letters, while Veneziano's are based on local contrast, less predictable verse declamation, and a directly representational role for the instruments. Although changing affect is evident in both, Veneziano seems to have taken Lapide's insistence on the "disorderliness" of prophetic expression to highly audible extremes.

Veneziano's music for nuns is not qualitatively different from his other Lessons. The F6/L3 (Inv. 861) of 1700 for "Suor Chiara," an alto, was finished well in advance (18 February) of the Triduum that year, and it sets the {2:7–9} prescribed for the Lesson by the Dominican breviary. Cast on E/ *durus,* its concision derives from the short overall text, reinforced by vv. 8 and 9's use of passing cadences to set off the sub-verses without double-bars or changes of affect/tempo. A long opening 2:7a ("Zain. Repulit Dominus altarem suum") contrasts with triplets in the rest of the verse. The following "Heth" and its verse "Cogitavit Dominus dissipare" culminate in long melismas for "dissipatus est" but surprisingly move to D, all in triple time. After this, v. 9 sets the implosion of Jerusalem's gates ("Defixae sunt in terra portae ejus") to a flashy violin solo and downward vocal leaps. Finally, a lengthy *a tempo giusto* "Jerusalem" refrain balances the extended opening of the Lesson. Even if Suor Chiara needed a good deal of Lent to learn this piece, her technique was quite professional.

Three Second Nocturne pieces (L4, 5, 6, all for SS, from 1694, 1699, and 1695 respectively) by Veneziano take different approaches to their texts, which are Augustine's reflections on Ps 63:7. Here, the saint gave an allegorical interpretation of the psalm verse as prophesying the scene of the Priests and Pharisees asking Pilate to post guards at the Sepulchre (Mt 28:11–15). The affect of 1695's L6 (Inv. 933) is conditioned by its narrative placement after the Resurrection, even though it was to be sung on Good Friday afternoon. Its stable opening A tonality (two sharps) and triadic leaps lend a martial air to Augustine's affirmation of Christ's rising, while setting the idea that the guards could have testified to the miracle if only they had told the truth ("miracula facta sunt talia . . . si vellent vera nuntiare").

But the Lesson then recalls the opening of the Passion, Judas's greed and betrayal, and its symbolic repetition in this episode: namely, the guards also gave in to a bribe from the Scribes to report that the Apostles had stolen the

EXAMPLE 6.10. Veneziano, SS/L6, "Vere tu ipse."

body while they were asleep. This linkage of the Passion's entire trajectory displaces the tonal centers to D, B, F♯ and finally back to A for the central ironic paradox of the "watchers who failed to watch" ("Vere defecerunt scrutantes scrutationes . . . o infelix astutia"), and a condemnation of the "unhappy cunning" of a world blind to the Resurrection. Indeed, the saint's emphasis on correct sight here evokes a key passage on introspection in the *Confessions,* in which Augustine pointed to "divine light" and "seeing rightly" as part of his own conversion experience.[73]

These same tonal regions are revisited for the text's parallel reiteration of the lie that the guards were told to repeat ("vobis dormentibus, venerunt discipuli eius"). Augustine scornfully finishes by taking "sleep" as a metaphor for rejection of Easter's message: "Dormientes testes adhibes? Vere tu ipse obdormisti, qui scrutando talia defecisti"/[addressed to the Scribes:] "You use sleeping witnesses [the guards]? Really, you yourself fell asleep as you failed in examining such events." Veneziano used this rhetorical question as the occasion for a triple-time *a tempo giusto* peroration, whose ending provides a literal representation of "failed"/"defecisti" by thrice avoiding a full cadence on octave As between vocal line and continuo. This case of musico-rhetorical *abruptio* leaves the instruments to finish off the Lesson by themselves (example 6.10). Veneziano's changes of local affect, motivicity, and pitch centers stood him in good stead to follow Augustine's paradoxes and intellectual shifts.

The new expressive range of these Neapolitan pieces, even if they seem not to have circulated outside the city, set up a wider set of possibilities for Lessons, based on contrast between and even inside verses. This freedom would be useful, and audible, in the Triduum music created for a later, changing devotional environment. But the vitality of Tenebrae in a wide range of situations in the late seventeenth century is quite evident.

Chapter 7

༻❈༺

Ad honorem Passionis

Triduum Music and Rational Piety

Tenebrae after 1700 was sung amid new currents of devotion and social life not necessarily favorable to the allegories and emphases of its texts. Despite some recent work, eighteenth-century Catholic piety as a whole is still unclear, and the implications for the heuristic analysis of the century's sacred music are also only beginning to emerge. In Italy and central Europe, a newly direct spiritual discourse made its appeal to the "reasoned" Catholic, while in France the idea of "natural" religion was a wider attack on traditional practice. But in the same decades as these changes in spirituality, innovative Lamentations and Misereres were created, as much for courts as for cathedrals, with some notable examples in the 1740s discussed below, and the impact of some mid-century works provided a musical counter to the wider crisis of the Office. The renovation of the repertory is epitomized by a tribute to the Passion, the closing inscription at the end of an apparently autograph F6/L1 by Francesco Durante (GB-Lcm 176): "Ad honorem Passionis D[omini] N[ostri] J[esu] C[hristi]." This concept from the fourteenth-century *Speculum humanae salvationis* received devotional and musical expression in the middle of Enlightenment Europe.[1]

INTELLECTUAL AND SOCIAL PRESSURE

That Tenebrae's traditional meanings had to be defended can be inferred from an encyclopedic guide, the 382-page *Ufficio della Settimana Santa*, first published in 1704 by the bishop of Montefiascone, Alessandro Mazzinelli. Even its preface, beginning with a reiteration of the very concept of sacred seasons, pointed to the fading of temporal sacrality.[2] Mazzinelli underscored Holy Week as the culmination of Lent, and claimed that the faithful universally attended its denuded services as acts of penance. In what seems to be wishful thinking, the Church removed "all sweetness of song" from its Offices. Thus the words and actions of the Week united prophecy and history, image and reality, light and shadow.[3]

The prelate remarked the Lessons on each Day, linking them not to the Passion as a whole but to Calvary in particular, and emphasizing the tears of Lady Jerusalem as a response to the Crucifixion, a new feminization of Passion sentiment. The most modern aspect of Mazzinelli's explanation of Lamentations was his mention of the personalized penance of the sensitive listener, like the Three Marys at the Tomb.[4] Again, Passion piety was related to female agency. In his view, the first-person discourse of Tenebrae psalms reflected variably the sinner or Christ, while the bishop highlighted the theology behind the readings from Augustine and Paul in the Second/Third Nocturne Lessons. By contrast, the Responsories and Benedictus not only lacked commentary but were barely mentioned. In line with the guide's introspective attitude, the noisiness of the *strepitus* was downplayed, and its meaning as representative of Nature's chaos during the Crucifixion included the continuing "hard-heartedness" of the unbelieving Jews, another sign of continuing anti-Judaism. The guide clearly targeted a wider public than simply clerics, as its audience would have included courts, cardinals, and princes male and female whose Triduum devotion was increasingly being channeled into other forms.

Still, some traditional modes of understanding continued elsewhere, especially among the regular clergy. An extreme case is the three-thousand-page commentary, on chs. 1–3 alone of Lamentations, by the Bohemian Discalced Carmelite Modestus a S. Joanne Evangelista, which subsumed most church doctrine and Scriptural understanding under its enormous weight of learning, as it gave literal, allegorical, and moral understandings of the book.[5] Other exegetical books excerpted Lapide's ideas, while *Il Direttorio mistico* (1754) of the Jesuit spiritual counselor G. B. Scaramelli used ch. 3's "Ego vir videns" in the tradition of spiritual "darkness," as spoken by the miserable soul aware of its sins.[6]

Among the various streams of devotion in eighteenth-century Catholicism, Mazzinelli's efforts found varying levels of echo. Despite the bishop's efforts to save the Hours, the "regulated" approach of Ludovico Antonio Muratori emphasized the Mass, not the Office, for the enlightened believer. Muratori's famed *Della regolata divozione de' cristiani* (Venice, 1747) makes no mention of the Hours whatsoever, while its only citation from Jeremiah is not from Lamentations. Earlier, Valentin Larson's *Theatrum dolorum Jesu Christi . . . in augustissimo sacrificio Missae apertum* (Augsburg, 1709) posited only the Mass as re-enacting the Passion. In a wider rationalist framework, Bernard Picart's massive compendium of world religious ritual, *Céré-monies et coutumes religieuses de tous les peuples du monde* (Amsterdam, 1723), summarized Tenebrae without providing an illustration, dismissing its chants as "useless to give in detail which could interest only priests."[7]

Besides their liturgical projection, the texts themselves lost prominence, at least in Italy. Alfonso Maria de Liguori's *L'amore delle anime* (1751), a guide to individual meditation on the Passion, cites the Song of Songs six times and Lamentations only thrice.[8] Positive spirituality led Liguori to emphasize Christ's love (hence the Song), while individual sin and its destruction of the soul retreated into the background. The future saint's own musicality, even if in a lower cultural register than Triduum Office music, and the omnipres-ence of musical Tenebrae in his Naples, stand in sharp contrast to his down-playing of Lamentations. Another popular publication, Liguori's vernacu-lar paraphrase of all Office psalms and canticles, also did not mention the Triduum's use of the Benedictus and Miserere.[9] Extended sonic projections of allegorical texts presented problems to the new directness of eighteenth-century piety and its emphasis on the Mass, not the Hours.

The changing social nature of physical darkness also counted. In central European courts, dining (normal after Tenebrae) and entertainments were increasingly moved from the late afternoon into the early night hours.[10] The sense of the service as the end of daily activities began to wane. Beyond de-votion, even the music provoked problems. From the Buen Retiro in Ma-drid on Good Friday 1744, Philip V's consort Elisabetta Farnese wrote her son sarcastically that the Triduum had exhausted her, since "the Office was very long and M. Courcelle [the chapelmaster Francesco Corselli] was so kind as to have three little nanny-goats sing who bored me," while in 1749 the Infanta wrote back to her mother that "Tenebrae went on forever, and then there was a Miserere composed by Courcelle which lasted half an hour; you would have been quite tired, since these are three terrible days."[11] The former must refer to the new Lessons for 1744's Friday, Corselli's SS/L2 for tenor (E-Mp, #342) and an *Oratio* for ATB (#343), while his 1749 Miserere, unsurprisingly given the royal reaction, has not survived in the Bourbons' musical archive, unless it was a repeat performance of his eight-voice work of 1748 (#166). In 1750 his deputy José de Nebra did the Miserere (#897). Elisabetta's distaste is all the more striking in that she herself had brought Corselli from Parma to Madrid shortly after her marriage in 1734.

A generation earlier on the other side of Europe in Dresden, Friedrich August I made his court composer J. D. Zelenka omit a Miserere because of the length of the new Office music in 1722.[12] On F5, the First Nocturne alone that year at the Saxon court would have lasted an hour, if Zelenka's two new Lessons (ZWV 53, ~ 25 minutes total) and all three Responsories

(~ 19 minutes) were sung. The length would have amazed the Elector's new daughter-in-law Maria Josepha, an Austrian Habsburg, who had had quite different experiences while growing up in Vienna, as she would have been used to the First Nocturne's *falsobordone* psalms, chant or Renaissance-style Lessons, and Ingegneri's Responsories, taking about half the time.

Part of the reaction in Dresden was also due to custom, as polyphony had built up only slowly in the court's Office; in 1710, the local Jesuits in charge of the mission asked Rome for polyphonic Responsories, but only one Nocturne and Lauds were sung in polyphony, using the Italian court musicians. In 1718 this was expanded to all three Nocturnes, and Lamentations are mentioned for the first time as performed, including the Benedictus and Miserere the next year; it is not clear if these were florid settings.[13] The order's report on the 1722 Triduum noted, besides the excessive length, that Zelenka's Lessons and other items required transposition of the organ into the lower-pitched *Kammerton,* which would have been used for the winds called for in his Lamentations (oboes, traversi, and a chalumeau). In 1723, with the royals away, Zelenka set the SS Lessons for solo voice and continuo in a simpler syllabic style paraphrasing the Tone-6 chant formula, without obbligato instruments (ZWV 54). In addition to its length, the musical complexity of Tenebrae sometimes evoked only ennui among the very sovereigns it was supposed to edify.

The problems were not restricted to the nobility. A memorandum from around 1755 at the Escorial tried to correct senior canons who left choir after the musically florid First Nocturne, using the excuse of watching out for disturbances, and then ate dinner without returning. This document also specified that the chapelmaster alone was responsible for the performance of the Lessons, suggesting previous attempts to delegate it.[14] A post-1721 discussion of timing the Hours in the Cappella Giulia questioned Tenebrae's starting time in S. Pietro, and also musicians' habit of running to different churches after Matins in order to augment their income by performing at Lauds.[15]

The service's place as musical ritual also began to weaken in comparison to its dialectical and seasonal pendant, *opera seria,* and to oratorio, which portrayed penance and/or the Passion directly, as in Ottoboni's case.[16] Unlike the modernity of musical theater secular or sacred, the Office had the long psalmody (and sometimes Responsories) with only chant; hence the pressures, both for audiences and musicians, to depart after the polyphony of the First Nocturne. Even among less rarified social circles, public attention focused on genres that were more obviously linked to contemporary devotion: oratorios, to be sure, but also the Marian-mediated Passion reflection of the Stabat Mater, and the first-person voice of the Miserere.[17] The latter was increasingly performed outside the Triduum, while the former was often used on the Feast of the Seven Sorrows in Passion Week or elsewhere during Holy Week. One obvious example is the rocket-like popularity of Pergolesi's *Stabat mater,* although the devotional space for its prominence had already been created well before 1736, through oratorios and motets on the Virgin's Sorrows. Settings of "O vos omnes" with Marian meaning independent of liturgy also spread, especially in the Hispanic world.[18] Passion piety simply took other forms, the six Latin duets on meditative texts composed by Nicola Porpora for the court of Maria Theresia in 1754 being just one example.[19]

The emergence of Second/Third Nocturne Lessons from the 1690s onward also corresponded to less allegorical devotion, since their texts treated the Passion more directly. Socially, the demands of singers in and out of monastic foundations also led to composition of these texts. After Veneziano, Second Nocturne items in Naples by Nicola Conti and Gennaro Manna were possibly for nuns, while Nicola Sabatino set some seven such texts at mid-century. Later, such Lessons for all three Days were composed by Bonaventura Furlanetto and others for the Venetian *ospedali.*[20] In the highly Neapolitan culture of eighteenth-century Lisbon, José Joachim dos Santos produced L1, 4, and 7 of the entire Triduum, not as solos but *a 4,* together with L9 of F6 and SS, thus ending Matins on the most charged Days with complex music. A generation later in 1794, Luis Xavier dos Santos set L4, 5, and 7 for F5 along with L5, L7 and 8 of the other two Days. Contemporary Triduum repertory from Ouro Preto around 1800 by Joao de Araujo and Jerônimo de Sousa Queiros also includes Lessons from later Nocturnes.[21]

CRITIQUE AND CREATION

As the social pressure on the Hours increased, the discomfort in traditional circles about inappropriate music also found expression. One important formulation was in Benito Feijóo's famed letter on the state of liturgical music, "La música de los templos" (1726), Discourse XIII of his *Teatro critico universal.* The Benedictine minced no words in his attack on "unsuitable" Lessons:

> In printed Lamentations I have seen the exact same changes in movements, denoted by name, which are used in cantatas. Here it reads "grave," there "airoso," and over there "recitado." What! Can't everything be grave, even in a Lamentation? And must the brief airs of theater be found in the representation of the saddest mysteries? If there were tears in heaven, Jeremiah would weep again to find such music applied to his laments. Is it possible that in those sacred complaints, where every letter is a sigh, in which, according to their various meanings, we mourn not only the ruin of Jerusalem by the Babylonians,

not only the ruin of the world through sin, not only the affliction of the Church Militant in persecutions, but finally also the anguish of our Redeemer in his sufferings—precisely there must we hear "airosos" and "recitados"? In the Alphabet of Penance, as some commentators call the Lamentations, must banquet tunes and serenatas resound? . . . In the same way, even worse, I saw in one of the Lamentations cited above the marking "airoso" for the phrase *Deposita est vehementer non habens consolatorem* [from F5/L2]. [sarcastically:] How appropriate is "airoso" for the lamentable fall of Jerusalem, or of the whole human race, oppressed by the weight of sin, and moreover lacking consolation in its misery! But that adverb "vehementer" was to blame, since the expression of vehemence seemed to the composer to require lively music. So at this point he speeded up and used some forty eighth-notes in octave leaps to set "vehementer." But this word, looked at by itself, required very different music, for in this context it means the same as "gravissime," energetically expressing that weightiness and sorrow with which the city of Jerusalem, burdened by the overwhelming load of her sins, fell to the ground, temple, houses, walls and all.[22]

Although his targets were anonymous, Feijóo then criticized Sebastian Durón's general penchant for such word-painting independent of context, and possibly this attack was aimed at a setting by Durón (although no F5/L2 by him survives). Since the Lessons were printed, Feijóo must have been referring to a product of José de Torres' *Imprenta de Música* in Madrid, the only music press in Spain (again here there are no extant Lessons). Other Spanish settings of F5/L2, for instance one by Pere Rabassa (E-VAc 51/6) possibly for Valencia around 1720, eschew such display at "vehementer."

Pope Benedict XIV's reused Feijóo's passage in his 1749 apostolic constitution on sacred music, *Annus qui*. The pontiff turned to the "abuse" of Triduum music in the section concerning instruments, employing the monk's criticisms against the "flowery" music so often heard in Lamentations.[23] After general prescriptions for church music, Benedict also dredged up Pius V's injunctions of 1571 against the use of instruments during the Week in regulars' churches in Lucca, pointing to it as a still-valid norm. One often-forgotten point is that the text was meant to apply to Rome, during the upcoming Jubilee Year of 1750; how much it affected music elsewhere will be seen below. In an immediate echo, the curia in Benedict's old see of Bologna excluded concerted music already for the Triduum of 1749. Its "Decreto sopra le musiche" was issued in Passion Week (26 March) and reiterated that the constitution "prohibits these sinfonias, arias, and recitatives in churches when singing Holy Week Lamentations, in which variously the destruction of Jerusalem by the Babylonians, the slaughter of the world through sin, the affliction of the Church Militant through persecutions, and the anguish of our Redeemer in His sufferings are lamented."[24] The wording of this local decree derives almost precisely from Feijóo's remarks of a generation earlier, as cited in the apostolic constitution.

But even before his election the pontiff had defended tradition. In his *Delle feste di Gesù Cristo nostro signore* (Bologna, 1740), the then-archbishop Lambertini spent a chapter on Triduum Matins/Lauds, paraphrasing F6/L3 ("Ego vir videns") and the SS Lessons as reflective of the prophet's and of Christ's sufferings.[25] This began the prelate's hundred-page explication of the whole Triduum, which he used to attack Gallican clerics who would reduce liturgical ceremonies to "purely natural" actions. In his passionate defense of the symbolism of Tenebrae's sounds and gestures, Lambertini reiterated Mazzinelli's defense of the Hours against the onslaughts of natural religion.

BOLOGNA, VENICE, NAPLES

Despite the problems in devotion and aesthetics, the musical production continued unabated, not least in Lambertini's Bologna, as witnessed by the group of fifty manuscript Lessons (nine anonymous pieces for solo voice and strings, the others by some fourteen different composers, almost all with only continuo) compiled for the Oratorians of S. Maria in Galliera, probably over some decades in mid-century.[26] Eight of its composers were local, while four worked in and around Venice; there is also a complete cycle by Giovanni Maria Clari, from his years in Pistoia or Pisa (possibly the former, given the Oratorians' presence in that city). The activity of the composers represented spans some eighty years (1680–1760). Although this might suggest accretion, planning is evident: overall, the collection contains five L1s and L3s for F5/6, eight L2s for each Day, but only two Prayers. Thus the church had almost five different cycles and a high number of L2s (as with Q. 43).

Lessons by composers working directly for the Bolognese Oratorians include pieces by G. A. Perti from his decades of service to the church, followed by his coadjutor L. A. Predieri and then A. A. Caroli who took over in 1750. The links to its sister house in Venice must have led to the acquisition of works by Antonio Lotti, Porpora, Giovanni Porta, and A. B. Coletti. An original nucleus, covering most of a liturgical cycle without duplications, is evident in the items by the three composers (G. A. Aldrovandini, Bernardo Sabbadini, F. A. Pistocchi) who died before 1727. Possibly these pieces came with Pistocchi, who had become a member of the order after a career as a singer/composer and spent his last years in Bologna, 1718–26.

Various Lessons project the texts in notably different ways. Perti's SS/L2 for solo bass (#60) sets all six Hebrew letters as short but florid vocal variations over a *ciacona* bass; together with its bright D-major tonality, the contrast with the affect of the verses ("How darkened is the gold . . .") is marked. Some declamatory sections override the sub-verses (vv. 2, 3, 5, 6) while other arias respect it entirely (v. 4, "Adhaesit lingua," the centerpiece of the work). In contrast, Lotti's setting of this Lesson for soprano (#59) changes the tonality and declamatory placement of all letters, while employing local harmonic color to illustrate the sub-verses. His v. 3b, "filia populi mei crudelis," uses a diminished 7th-tritone-diminished 7th progression found again in 5b at "amplexati sunt stercora," a different approach to musical recurrence.

Lotti's piece testifies to Venetian practice, surviving fragmentarily elsewhere. Benedetto Marcello's almost-complete Lesson cycle for solo soprano and continuo (missing the L3s of F5–6, with the SS/L2 as a soprano/bass duet) seems to be the pieces he left, along with Lauds items, to the church of S. Sofia in Venice, although the surviving copy is now in Hamburg.[27] One aspect of Marcello's famed vernacular Psalms not present here is the recourse to traditional Hebrew melodies; the Lessons are modern, not least in their use of *siciliana* movements to signal sadness (in F5/L1 at "Viae Sion" and "parvuli eius"). Marcello separated sub-verses minimally, but several short phrases evoked individual gestures: the angular octaves leaps for the walls falling down ("et murus pariter dissipatus est" in F6/L1), the hooting over Jerusalem ("super filiam Jerusalem" in F6/L2) set as a high pedal F_5 in the voice, or the chromatic anabasis for the thirsting sucklings' tongues in SS/L2, at "Adhaesit lingua."

Another Venetian puzzle is Tenebrae Lessons in the *ospedali*. The Triduum in these foundations was separate from musical activity on the three days from Palm Sunday to Holy Tuesday, which featured motets, *introduzioni* to Misereres, and oratorios. Even before Porpora's six solo Lessons with continuo for the young women at the Derelitti (Ospedaletto), evidently composed in 1745 (F5/L1–2 plus F6/SS/L2–3s), Antonio Pollarolo had written a now-lost cycle for this institution in 1730, while the visiting Prince Frederick Christian noted Office music there on two Days in 1740.[28] Porpora's 1745 pieces were produced quickly, as his list of compositions from March that year do not include them, and the Triduum was 14–16 April.[29]

Outside the *ospedali,* other commissions to Porpora led to six other extant Lessons for solo voice and continuo, either in Naples or Venice (one from 1732 must be for the former, for reasons explained below). Furthermore, Porpora's five solo Lamentations with strings for F5 (L1–2) and F6, extrovert works without recitatives, look to both places. They survive in a Neapolitan copy now in London, but three seem to be reworkings of Lessons by Porpora with continuo only, two from the Derelitti set of 1745.[30] These pieces with instruments have always been linked to the composer's last years, specifically Florimo's report of his Lamentations in 1760 as sung at the Neapolitan Arciconfraternita della Trinità dei Pellegrini by Caffarelli (Gaetano Majorano, soprano castrato) and Anton Raaff (tenor), but the Venetian origin of some argues for a more complex genesis. The London works are for soprano, and hence the tenor ones, if indeed this was the same set, are lost.[31]

The Neapolitan repertory continued to grow through all the political changes in the city. Triduum Office polyphony in the viceregal ensemble had been publicly noted as early as 1694 under the Spanish Habsburgs, in 1718–23 during Austrian rule, and in Bourbon Naples from 1734 onward.[32] The chapel's repertory of the early Settecento is not clear. Its master at many points up to 1725 was Alessandro Scarlatti, but his six Lessons use a smaller string band than the Seicento pieces for the same ensemble (Ziani, Caresana), and his authorship of a Responsory cycle (I-Baf) has been questioned. No Triduum items survive by his deputy and successor Francesco Mancini, the case also for Mancini's own successor Domenico Sarri. Either the chapel held to the Seicento settings, or much music has gone lost.

The solo Lesson cycle with continuo of Leonardo Leo, created along with other seasonal items for the chapel in 1744, thus marks a new moment in Neapolitan practice. His Lamentations and F5 Responsories were performed in services reported by the *Gazzetta di Napoli* as having been attended by Michele Reggio, the Bourbon lieutenant temporarily in charge of the city.[33] One early manuscript containing this repertory, given as a *quaderno di Quaresima* by Farinelli to Ferdinand VI of Spain in early Lent of 1757, has largely escaped attention.[34] This source, with its "originali" if not holographs, is in Washington; it holds the complete cycle of Leo's Lessons, with its L2s for alto and the others for soprano; it is the only source with datings of completion for each Lesson. There is also a set of R4–9 for F5, scored for SATB and continuo (ff. 71r-101v and 55r-66v, respectively). The other items in it include an eight-voice Miserere in C minor with non-detachable doxology for earlier in Lent, and Mass Propers for Lenten Sundays; both of these and the Lessons, unlike the Responsories, survive elsewhere. All this must represent the frantic work that Leo carried out in his first and only Lent to provide a new repertory for the season. One clue is that all the Lessons are dated March 1744 in US-Wc except for SS/L2, marked April; the Triduum that year was 1–3 April, and so Leo must have raced against time, finishing the *Oratio* first so as to have a concluding Lesson no matter what, and completing the SS piece only as the Triduum began, with no space to write Responsories for the other Days.

As a gift, the manuscript seems more a treasure than something for actual use in Madrid's Royal Chapel, which normally heard Lessons with orchestra.[35] But an early biographer of Farinelli claimed that he had been charged with regulating sacred music by the Patriarch of the Indies at some point in the 1750s. The castrato reputedly procured tightly guarded Roman repertory for Holy Week, and this gift to Ferdinand VI may be further evidence of the singer's efforts.[36] The dedication of the Wc manuscript suggests an important, but still feudal, servant laying model music at the feet of his patron, as the inscription actually reads.

Leo's Lessons trace a *stile di mezzo*, not entirely arioso, with traits of recitative and aria. Most of them move in *mollis* tonalities with "transposed" key signatures (one flat less than modern practice) except for the last to be composed, SS/L2 on E (i.e. *quarto tuono* without a signed sharp). The overall pitch centers are [B♭, G minor, C minor]; [G minor, D minor, F minor]; [C minor, E "Phrygian," B♭], suggesting partial mirror symmetry. Especially in F5/L1, the sub-verses are well demarcated, and although some do tilt slightly towards pure declamation or florid vocality, none employ exclusively one or the other. Rather, textual units are driven by intense motivicity shared by voice and bass, whose gestures may or may not portray verbal content; indeed, F5/L2, with its high continuo line and low alto vocal part, sometimes sounds like an imitative bicinium.

The most obvious gestures of these Lessons are the local enharmonic changes in F5/L2–3 and SS/L3. In 1:8 of L2, "Peccatum peccavit Jerusalem," the E♭ in a V7/B♭ sonority at "quia viderunt ignominiam eius" is re-interpreted as a D♯, swinging the end of the sub-verse to A (example 7.1). In 1:13 (L3), the motion is in a *mollis* direction, as the C♯ in a V4–2/d sonority for "tota die maerore confectam" becomes D♭, with the bass descending from G to F and thus setting up a B♭minor 6/4. Finally, the first sub-verse of the Prayer's 5:7 "Patres nostri peccaverunt" ends in C minor; then a move to B♭ minor at the second sub-verse, "et nos iniquitates eorum portavimus," sets up a prolonged D♭, recast as a C♯ harmonized on A, which leads to a D-minor cadence. The semantic triggers are "shame," "sorrow," and "iniquity," and the tonal derailment generated by the switches goes both ways across the *durus/mollis* divide (flat to sharp, sharp to flat, flat to sharp).

Thus Leo's gestures work at the level of the sub-verse or even the individual verbal phrase. The title of F5/L1 outlines a florid version of the Tone-6 chant formula, here on B_4♭ with recitation on D_5 throughout, and this contrasts with much Neapolitan repertory since Caresana and Veneziano which had eschewed the tone. But several other features in the opening have implications for the rest of the Lesson and even the cycle: the surprise turn to minor (and thus D♭s, with a G♭ prolonged at "Aleph") already at "Jeremiae

EXAMPLE 7.1. Leo, F5/L2 (US-Wc), "Peccatum peccavit."

prophetae," and an eighth-note bass figure which provides irregular harmonic rhythm and which in various guises runs throughout the entire Lesson (example 7.2). The sense of citing chant is heightened by the number of sub-verses which also elaborate the D_5 as the reciting-tone (vv. 1a, 1b, 2a). The opening gestures of L1 both index tradition and introduce the cycle's intense motivicity.

Some of the letters in this Lesson are separate sections ("Beth," "Ghimel," "Daleth") while others are attached variably to the preceding or following verse ("Heth" and v. 5a). Silences and fermatas demarcate even smaller syntactic units, as with "omnes portae eius destructae" that has its own Presto moment with *concitato* gestures. But in general Leo repeats or extends the final sub-verse of any given verse (vv. 1c, 3c, 4c, this last underscored by a semitone gesture in bass and voice for "et ipsa oppressa amaritudine"). Both letters and obvious words get chromatic heightening ("Beth" and "inter angustias"), but the final v. 5 ("Facti sunt hostes") returns to the chant tone, with the *initium* beginning all its sub-verses. Its last word "tribulantis" generates the same turn to tonic minor, closed off by the same continuo postlude, that had been used in the "Incipit" title. Leo created an internally rounded piece requiring close listening to the sub-verses, evidently presuming attentiveness on the part of Reggio and the court.

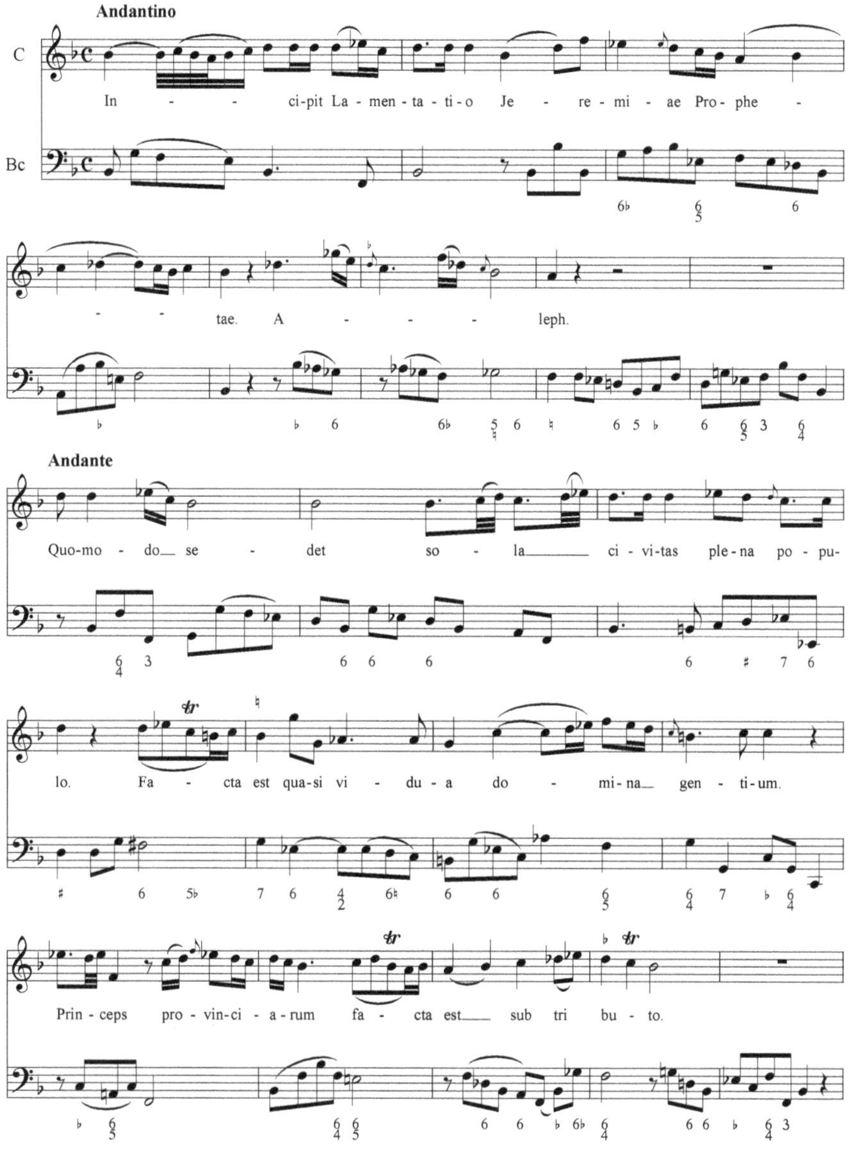

EXAMPLE 7.2. Leo, F5/L1, "Incipit lamentatio."

Some of these structural features also obtain in F5/L3. Here, 1:10a and c are both built over a long octave bass descent from the tonic C, with the final unit again emphasized by the vocal leaps for "ne intrarent in ecclesiam tuam." The sub-verses of 1:11 are all separated by silences, with diminished intervals for "gemens," and the move to Jerusalem's voice in 11c is marked by double declamation of both "Vide, Domine" and "facta sum vilis" along with a turn from F major to G minor. "O vos omnes" invokes the flat regions of B♭ minor, followed by theatrical gestures in 12c ("in die irae furoris sui"). The recitative setting the next verse, "De excelso," slides into arioso at "conversit me retrorsum, tota die maerore confectam," and the enharmonic gesture noted above at "maerore" is a kind of rhetorical climax.

Leo's two last Lessons for SS echo other moments in the cycle. L2's second letter "Beth" has the same chromatic descent that had been used in F5/L1, and the opening vv. 1–2 erase the bipartite structure of the sub-verses. V. 3's mention of the "sea monsters suckling their young" generates extended parallelisms throughout, including a series of downward leaps for "quasi struthio in deserto," the city as an "ostrich in the desert." An even more literal depiction comes in the next verse, as the lack of anyone to break bread for the city's children ("non erat qui frangeret eis") is set by "breaks" of eighth-note rests in both voice and continuo. Finally, after a v. 5 moving from G major to minor, the "greater" sin of Jerusalem over that of Sodom ("et major effecta est iniquitas populi mei peccato Sodomorum") is set to yet another chromatic anabasis, followed by the only unison phrase between voice and continuo in the Lesson. Again here, as in de Sanctis' setting of the same verse, the lack of exegetical explication for these words suggests a purely musical climax and thus a distance between sonic projection and learned understanding.

Some gestures in the vocal line, notably the use of octaves (descending, at "et respice" or ascending, at "cervicibus nostris minabamur") heighten the sense of Leo's Prayer as peroration. He set off the "orphans" of v. 3 with a fermata and a turn from B♭ major to the parallel minor, its first appearance since F5/L3. The same gesture is picked up at "et nos iniquitates" of v. 7b, with its enharmonic reinterpretation leading to V/D minor. The downward jumps of SS/L2's "quasi struthio in deserto" are echoed semantically and musically at the Prayer's v. 9b ("a facie gladii in deserto"), and then heightened rhetorically by the even wider leaps used in the short Presto section of 10c ("a facie tempestatum"). The final v. 11 ("Mulieres in Sion humiliaverunt") returns to B♭ minor, and this shading of the tonic is echoed in the last iteration of the "Jerusalem" refrain, again recalling the opening of the entire cycle.

On the other hand, what Reggio would have heard in Leo's Responsories that Wednesday afternoon invokes local tradition dating back to Giovanni Salvatore's Seicento set. Several begin with short points of imitation (R5) or

use the technique in their repetenda, while solos and duets are not only al-
loted to verses but also begin pieces (R6). The Responsories are concise, but
Wednesday's Matins in the chapel, even if everything else was sung in chant,
would have included about an hour of Leo's new compositions. These are
some of the most intense continuo-only Triduum pieces of mid-century, and
Leo's eschewal of the full forces of the Chapel in favor of soloistic writing
concentrates attention on the verse declamation.

The appeal of Leo's cycle did not, however, limit further Tenebrae production in Naples. After 1750 the father-son pairs Gennaro and Giovanni
Manna, and Giovanni and Gian Francesco de Majo produced Lessons over
two generations, followed by Felice Fenaroli, Francesco Ricupero, Francesco
Frezza, Nicola Grillo, and Paisiello.[37] Particularly active was Alessandro
Speranza (1724–97), with Lessons for all three Nocturnes. Responsories survive in lesser numbers, but include a set by Gennaro Manna from 1741, and
a later cycle by Carlo Contumacci (both I-Nc). An undated group by Nicola
Sala (1713–1801) features contrapuntal textures.[38] There is a complete Responsory set by Paisiello, which may be related to the 1794 Miserere and
Christus he wrote for the male Benedictine house of Ss. Severino e Sassia.[39]

RENEWAL AND ITS PUBLICS

Tuscan cities also changed Triduum repertory between 1720 and 1750.
In Pistoia, the confraternity of S. Maria Maddalena Penitente commissioned
Lessons from Clari and Ludovico Giustini in the 1720s. Although the local
bishop Colombano Bassi (1660–1732) came to hear a cycle by the former
on two afternoons in 1726, everyone (including the prelate) left after the
music, sung by an Augustinian tenor, Flavio Torelli, and the secular priest
Cosimo Bui.[40] This move from community Office to musical spectacle was
also evident two years later (24 March 1728), when a local chronicler noted
both the confraternity's *sepolcro* and the Lessons by Clari and Giustini it
had ordered.[41] This music might have been like the former's cycle in Bologna's Oratorian holdings, with its its elegant melodic lines, highly tonal in
a modern sense, with minimal separation of the sub-verses, and continuo
preludes/postludes framing verses. It is no wonder that the tradition of public applause for the Office continued, even in the presence of the bishop; far
from the contested Tenebrae of female houses, here male regulars performed
not as clerics but as virtuosi.

Slightly earlier in nearby Lucca, the patrician Lateran Canon Pompeo
Orsucci (1665–1725) had written various Lessons for all three Days for solo
voice. Orsucci's two SS pieces, an L1 and an L3, employ prominent cello
parts, L1's somewhat simpler, but both flout Pius V's 1571 injunction against

instruments in the city's Tenebrae.[42] His *Oratio* opens with a repetitive cello obbligato in 16th-notes and a vocal line that projects a simple version of the Tone-6 recitation formula, pitched on G (not F), over a descending bass line. This first section (5: 1–2, "Incipit oratio . . . extraneos") comes back as a ritornello whose music sets all the even-numbered verses, turning the piece into a rondo, with the five episodes being declamatory settings of vv. 3, 5, 7, 9, and 11. The yoking of this form to the Prayer is nothing if not original.

A generation after Orsucci, Giacomo Puccini *senior* created a local repertory in the 1740s which would remain static over the four decades that he was chapelmaster to the Republic of Lucca (late 1739–1781).[43] Thanks to Fabrizio Guidotti's comprehensive account of music in the Settecento, it is clear that the Holy Week works held an important place in Lucchese ritual life.[44] According to the composer's diaries, the Cappella Palatina—singers and a string band with a single oboe—performed Tenebrae on Thursday and Friday at the male Olivetan church of S. Ponziano at the city's east walls, the audience including the Republic's leadership.[45] The entries from 1748–60 and then again from the last decade of Giacomo's life (1770–80) repeat the evidently normal practice: six solo Lessons with orchestra over the two Days divided among three singers, with eight musicians for the Responsories. These latter survive in the family manuscripts: four-voice Roman settings (First Nocturne only) by G. O. Pitoni, originally written for the Cappella Giulia in the early Settecento, with string parts added for the local players. In all, Giacomo left at least ten Lessons, of which eight were for the Palatina's forces (with two for nuns discussed below).

The origins of these services—which also contradicted Pius V's ban on instruments—are not clear. The 1701 obligations of the Republic's Cappella, as copied by Giacomo in 1743, do not include functions at S. Ponziano.[46] Yet two sets of Triduum Lauds items for voices and strings by Giacomo's predecessor Giuseppe Montuoli (1667–1739), preserved in the Puccini family's holdings and dated 1715 and 1719, clearly state their use at the church.[47] The earlier of these was copied on order of the priest and composer Domenico Saminiati (c. 1650–1721), and so the practice must be an early Settecento move to make Tenebrae part of the Republic's ritual life, a kind of civic Passion devotion in a church of regulars linked to the state and not the bishop.

Giacomo's seven surviving Lessons with orchestra (along with an F5/L1 for voice and continuo) consist of two F5 items from 1739 and 1741, a complete set for F6 (1745–48 with one undated), and two for SS (L2–3, from 1740 and 1751).[48] Six are for soprano or alto (two of which have alternate passages to suit either voice-type) and one for bass, while the diaries around 1750 mention two Lessons each for F6-SS sung by soprano, tenor, and bass, and those of the 1770s soprano, alto, and tenor. Some of his music has evidently not been preserved, while the F5 pieces might have been meant for Wednesday's "Notturni concertati" performed in the church of S. Girolamo, as they are not for S. Ponziano. Outside Lamentations, the conservative repertory is clear; for Lauds, he composed a new *alternatim* Benedictus in 1741 which he reused into the 1770s, and another in 1745. In 1758 Giacomo specified the order of the Hour: on Thursday, the canticle and then the Miserere, while on Friday the first Miserere was sung polyphonically before the Benedictus.[49]

As a student in Bologna, Giacomo would have heard the Lessons by his teacher G. M. Carretti (1690–1764), Perti, and others. Already in the F5/L1 from 1739, he used a basic structure followed in almost all the S. Ponziano pieces: occasional declamatory recitative, but largely florid letters and verses set either in accompanied recitative *a battuta* or in melismatic arioso, these latter two with dramatic and virtuoso string lines. In v. 1a, the first arioso begins already at "Quomodo sedet sola," while "Omnes portae eius destructae" (4a) is set *con sordino* and with triple/quadruple stops in the violins. His SS/L2 of the next year uses similar gestures at 4:3, for "Sed et lamiae," Jerusalem's depravity greater than that of sea-monsters. Similarly, the 1745 F6/L1 depicts the implosion of Jerusalem's walls ("dissipare muros filiae Sion") mimetically by its fast violin runs.[50] Puccini normally linked letters to the preceding verse, and he modulated unexpectedly between verses, often by unrelated thirds; in the 1739 Lesson, vv. 3–4 wander from D minor through B minor and G minor to E♭ major. V. 5 begins with a B♭ major arioso, but switches to measured recitative in D minor at "parvuli eius ducti sunt," returning to the tonic A minor for the "Jerusalem" refrain. His 1745 F6/L1 has an alternate text to make it usable for F5/L1, and its vv. 2:10–11 go from C major to G major, but via a recitative in B minor at 10c, "Abiecerunt in terra," as the idea of the "virgins of Jerusalem hanging their heads to the ground" generated a temporary tonal catabasis. Although the forces required were moderate on the annual scale of musicians' activity, still the well-crafted vocal lines and difficult violin obbligati highlight just how much labor went into public Tenebrae in Lucca.[51]

As the composer aged, he prepared his son Antonio to take over while holding to old pieces; in 1775, Giacomo repeated his Miserere of 1740 (not extant) and his Benedictus from 1741 (which does survive), while the younger Puccini wrote a new Lesson (not preserved in this form) with viola and cello obbligati. This latter part had to be played on a small double-bass by Domenico Baldotti, for lack of players and space on the *cantorie*.[52] Although the local Olivetan abbot's desire to have horns in the ensemble (contradicting two of Benedict XIV's injunctions) was not to be realized, Baldotti faithfully recorded in his own diary playing in Tenebrae at S. Ponziano from 1777 on-

ward.[53] Thus Giacomo's Lessons presumed the skills of the local instrumentalists, including Leopoldo Boccherini who played contrabass in the 1750s,
and the fixity of the local traditions that he established lasted past his death
into the Ottocento, in utter disregard of *Annus qui.* This suggests that the
patrician Republic wanted continuity, not innovation, in its public Office, in
sharp contrast to the new Tenebrae production of Naples.

The use of cello obbligati in Lucca (Orsucci and Puccini) to symbolize
the melancholy of the Lessons was part of a wider phenomenon, evident in
the scoring for one or two celli in Lamentations by Zelenka, J. H. Fiocco (for
Antwerp, around 1733), Durante and Sabatino in Naples, F. S. Giaj in Turin,
Carretti in Bologna, Vallotti in Padua, and F. P. Ricci (preserved in Como), or
low strings and bassoon in two Lessons for Dijon by Joseph Michel (1735).
In Corselli's output for Madrid, there are difficult cello obbligati in some 10
settings ranging from 1741 (#355) to 1774 (#273), including one (#350 of
1773) for two instruments. The solo Lessons of F. X. Richter for Strasbourg
(1773) employed an obbligato cello in seven items, along with violas, flutes
and bassoons, eschewing violins entirely.[54] As late as 1793, the Tuscan court
composer Christian Joseph Lidarti would write an F6/L1 for vocal bass and
bassoon, making him the only known figure to have set both Hebrew liturgical music as well as Lamentations for the Catholic Office.[55] Thus the mel-
ancholic nature of the low instruments pointed directly to textual affect.

LESSONS FOR NUNS

Besides his Easter Vigil music written for the Lateran Canonesses of
S. Giovanetto in his home town, in 1752 Puccini made copies of two of his
Lessons for a nun from the Monzone family of Lucca, one (or both) of two
sisters who had professed in 1749 in the noble Franciscan house of S. Chiara
in Massa, a foundation under the patronage of the local Cybo rulers.[56] Both
Lamentations, an F5/L1 and an *Oratio,* are vocally difficult. He also set the
Dominican version of the *Oratio* (all twenty-two verses beginning "Oratio
Jeremiae Prophetae," to be sung after L9 at the end of the Third Nocturne)
for two singers and organ in the female house of S. Michelotto down the
street from S. Ponziano. In 1771, he produced an F6/L7, also with only keyboard, for an unnamed soprano in Genoa.[57] Neither of these latter pieces are
as virtuosic as the Palatina repertory sent to Massa, but they underscore the
possibilities of Tenebrae for nuns in central Italy.

In Naples, the Lessons commissioned by two aunts and a niece in the
Lateran Canoness house of S. Maria Regina Coeli stand out. These women
were all members of the d'Andrea family: Isabella (b. c. 1690) and Marianna
(b. 1699) were daughters of Gennaro d'Andrea (1637–1710), the first Marquis of Pescopagano, and nieces of the Neapolitan jurist Francesco d'Andrea

(1625–98).[58] They took vows around 1705 and 1714, respectively, and were soon joined by their niece, another Isabella, born in 1710 and professed in 1729, followed by yet another, Teresa Maria, in 1734.[59] These latter two were the daughters of Diego d'Andrea (1688–1748), the second Marquis. Marianna took the religious name of "Maria Chiara," and one or the other Isabella must have changed her name to "Anna." Chiara (an alto) received the inscription of an F5/L3 by Leo in 1720, as well as an *Oratio* by Hasse, who was in Naples from 1723 to 1730. The two sopranos were Isabella, the dedicatee of a Lesson (also F5/L3) dated October 1732 by Porpora (in Venice at this point), and Anna, for whom Hasse wrote an F5/L2.[60] Three of the four items are L3s, and so the settings would have provided dramatic endings to the First Nocturne in their house.

The cloister had a long tradition of independence, if not uncontested, from episcopal authority. Some time before the d'Andreas entered, the nuns' choir had been raised to clerestory level and set behind the altar at the east end, allowing for direct visual and aural contact between singers and the public, and for greater interaction with the ritual of lights during Tenebrae.[61] In 1737, the *Gazzetta* reported a moving Miserere performed there during Holy Week, possibly written by Nicola Conti, in charge of music after 1733.[62] Certainly some of Conti's seven surviving Lamentations and/or his five Second Nocturne Lessons, all for high solo voices, must be for women in the house, most likely an SS/L1 for soprano dated 1734 (I-Nf).

Hasse's SS/L3 for Chiara (I-Nf 481–2) is structurally regular but also minds the singer's abilities. Set in E minor, it faithfully alternates recitatives and arias, saving the latter for vv. 1, 3–4 (combined), 7, 8, and 11; all the single-verse arias repeat their entire text, in a way similar to typical *Kirchenaria* form, and the two sub-verses in each are clearly demarcated by rests and internal cadences. In all of these, plus the title and refrain, there is a written-out cadenza at the end of the vocal line. The recitatives predictably set up the dominant of the following aria and move quickly through their text (one combines vv. 5–6 with minimal breaks); the effect is of a sequence of similar arias. The Lesson's tessitura is revealing; C_4 is touched on only once, and most of the writing, including the difficult cadenza passages, is above the C3 staff, ranging up to the high F_5. The Lateran Canoness must have had a good high register and a weaker chest voice. Another Prayer by Hasse (for soprano, 481–1bis), not specifically designated for a nun, is similar in its written-out cadenzas but more florid vocally, eschewing strict alternation (vv. 4–5 and 6 are two successive arias).

Hasse's F5/L2 for Anna (I-Nf 481–1) is a more complex and virtuosic piece. Cast in C minor, the verses touch a wide range of other tonal centers, with only the opening verse (1:6) set as a single movement, and even here [a] is separated out. The lengthy text of v. 7 ("Recordata est Jerusalem") led

EXAMPLE 7.3. Hasse, F5/L2, "Peccatum peccavit."

to three contrasting movements for the sub-verses, all virtuosic: an opening
Moderato in B♭ with a recurrent dotted figure and wide vocal leaps; a triple-
time Allegro for v. 7b, emphasizing "non esset auxiliator," and moving to G
minor; and a very long 7c back in the local tonic, with elaborate vocal figuration generated by the "mocking" of "et deriderunt sabbata eius." A similarly
tripartite v. 8, "Peccatum peccavit," uses tonal contrast, generated by the text
"propterea instabilis facta est . . . conversa est retrorsum" (example 7.3). Its

EXAMPLE 7.3. (*Continued*)

[a] sub-verse, in G major, moves from florid passages to a tonally unstable recitative for the sub-verse [b] in E minor, and finishes with a concluding Andante [c] in G that moves back to E minor at "conversa est retrorsum." Yet again, v. 9 is set out as aria-recitative-aria, with the first-person speech of 9c ("Vide, Domine, et considera afflictionem meam") as peroration. For all the d'Andreas' vocal abilities, still the written-out cadenzas in the various Lessons suggest that they had not had the opportunity to learn improvisation as professionals.

Finally, Porpora's F5/L3 for Isabella was originally in G, but also survives a tone lower in Bologna's Galliera collection, suggesting that Porpora used it later for a different singer in Venice, whence it made its way to Bologna.[63] Starting with its opening "Jod," virtuosity is foregrounded. No verses or letters are set as pure recitative; passages at the beginning and end are in fast tempi, and—unlike his procedure in the Derelitti pieces a decade later—Porpora even broke the sub-verses of vv. 11–13 into separate movements. The pathos of 1:11 is marked by three successive Adagio sections, while "O vos omnes" is a 12/8 *siciliana* with long melismas on "dolor" and "meus." The final "Jerusalem" is also slow but equally taxing vocally. The overall range is only an eleventh, but again most phrases lie in the upper register.

Porpora's 1:11 begins with a "Caph" as the first Adagio, moving to V/E minor (D minor in the Bologna version) via an augmented sixth. Although "gemens" in the next Adagio (v.11ab) generates long runs, [a] and [b] are demarcated only by the repeat of the initial vocal motive for the new sub-verse, now in relative major. But [b] is enunciated some three times, with repetitions of "pro cibo" and long florid passages for "ad refocillandam animam," emphasizing Jerusalem's desperate state. The third successive slow section,

11c, turns to a Mode-3 tonality (on B with no signature or on A with a flat) opened by the voice alone, the sub-verse declaimed twice and with an expanded reiteration of "facta sum," another way to underline the city's misery (example 7.4). In order to separate the affect of this verse from the slow *siciliana* for "O vos omnes," the following "Lamed" is a fast major-mode period, a contrast more musical than meditative. This bloc of Lessons for the d'Andreas testifies to the ongoing traditions of nuns' Tenebrae, and represents what must be a wider practice in Naples.

Despite the controversies over female Franciscans' Tenebrae earlier, there is also evidence for Lessons at S. Chiara, the largest house of the city. An incomplete F5/L1 in I-Nf (405.4) is marked "per la sig.ra donna Agnese di Gennaro," and this must be the abbess who commissioned a chant antiphoner in 1788 still in the monastery's museum. The Lesson reads "GM" and has been given to G. F. di Majo (1732–70).[64] Yet Agnese was the sister of the Neapolitan literary figure Antonio di Gennaro, duke of Belforte (1717–91), whose works include two cantatas for the clothing ceremonies of novices at S. Chiara, both set to music by Gennaro Manna.[65] A posthumous tribute to Agnese's brother calls her "peritissima nella musica," and thus it is more likely that Manna, not di Majo, is the composer of this piece.[66] One F6/L3 of 1769 clearly by G. F. di Majo (I-Nf 405.10) includes two written-out cadenzas like Hasse's and was also likely for a nun.

A final tribute to nuns' Tenebrae is the collection of the Benedictines of S. Lorenzo in San Severo (Apulia), whose close ties to Naples also preserve some unexpected parts of the Triduum repertory.[67] About 50 Lessons (eight from the Second or Third Nocturnes) clearly from the 18th century survive, with others composed and copied into the last third of the nineteenth century; the earliest are evidently those of Conti and Manna, but the collection also holds some twenty-seven Lessons by Giuseppe d'Avossa (1708–96), with later settings by Nicolò Piccinni, Antonio Sacchini, Fedele Fenaroli, and lesser-known figures. Some of these might originally have been written for Naples, but certainly d'Avossa's pieces, not preserved elsewhere, show links to the house. Several singers' names are on the copies, especially Alba Santelli in the 1760s, and a few Lamentations (including Piccinni's) feature a part for *salterio,* perhaps another sonic reflection like Caldara's of Jeremiah's melancholy lyre.

PROJECTING TENEBRAE IN MID-CENTURY ROME

Despite the profusion of Neapolitan music, it was for Rome that the most influential Lessons for voice(s) and orchestra would be written. In the city, the Triduum was made theater in such *sepolcro* constructions as Filippo Vasconi's "sagro apparato" for Ottoboni's church of S. Lorenzo in Damaso in Holy

EXAMPLE 7.4. Porpora, F5/L3, "Vide, Domine."

Week 1728.[68] The sites with new Tenebrae music seem to have been outside the major basilicas. Still, Prince Frederick Christian was more impressed by the Papal singers in 1739 than he was by the Lessons and Lauds verses at S. Giacomo degli Spagnoli.[69] Evidently the traditional music organized for the Spanish by the chapelmaster Giovanni Biordi, otherwise active in the Papal chapel, could not match the improvisatory skills of the Sistina's forces.

After Biordi's tenure, which ended in December 1742, the efforts at a major turn toward modernity in S. Giacomo's music are evident in its deputies' hiring of the opera composer Domènec Terradellas.[70] In this transitional moment for the chapel, the deputies may have commissioned two solo Lessons (1742 and 1744) with instruments from Ottoboni's former protegé G. B. Costanzi; the earlier one has two SATB interjections like those appearing in Aurelio Aurisicchio's cycle for the church a decade later.[71]

Perhaps less pressed by operatic duties, the Catalan Terradellas seems to have produced large-scale music for the titular and other feasts, but the corporation's effort to get him to write orchestral Lamentations was a miserable failure in 1743–44, and in 1745, as the deputies were coming to the end of their patience, he simply repeated the voices-only pieces of the previous years, possibly Biordi's outdated settings. This, along with other issues, led to his dismissal in summer 1745. The very next year, S. Giacomo took extraordinary measures for Tenebrae (6–8 April). This involved commissioning a Day's Lessons each from Jommelli, Davide Perez, and Durante, based in Venice, Palermo, and Naples, respectively.[72] Jommelli was working at the Ospedale degli Incurabili, and he had just finished his *opera seria Cajo Mario* for Rome, heard at the Teatro Argentino some two months before the F5 Lessons were premiered at S. Giacomo; his Venetian duties did not involve Lessons.[73] Perez, who had produced an opera for Carnival in Palermo but no Lenten oratorio, dated his three Lamentations 28 February, then 6 and 11 March 1746 (on the scores in I-Rcns). It took him about five days to complete a Lesson, and he finished early in Lent, in time for the music to arrive and the pieces to be learned. Durante, without operatic duties, presumably had more time to work on his Lessons.[74] In addition, eight-voice Misereres for each Day were commissioned from three local figures: the Roman Francesco Ciampi, Pedro León (Pietro Leone; a Spanish tenor singing often at S. Giacomo), and an unnamed Portuguese abbot. Ciampi's psalm is also preserved in London and Münster, and was admired by Burney, who owned a copy acquired on his 1770 trip (now in GB-Lcm), while the others remain in the church's archive.[75]

Jommelli's theatrical fame led to his qualitatively higher fee, 45 *scudi* as opposed to Perez' 30 and Durante's 19.[76] Perez had had neither an opera nor church music performed in Rome as of spring 1746, although clearly his Lessons would stand him in good stead a few years later upon his arrival in the city and his search, together with Jommelli, for a job in the basilicas. Durante's church music must have been known in Rome, although he received by far the smallest commission, rather as if the deputies were willing to pay more to the other two for theatrical-style music and thought (correctly) that he would provide more traditional pieces. Only Perez had written a datable Lesson (a duet F5/L2 for Palermo copied in 1738, now in I-Nf), while Durante's complete Lesson cycle and Responsories for SSB and continuo are dated 1751/2 in one copy (GB-Lcm), and are of uncertain origin. Jommelli seems not to have written Triduum music up to this point, a mark of how much the deputies wanted operatic music.[77] Here, a collaborative new cycle of Lessons was intended to make a public statement, in some contrast to Leo's more limited audience in Naples.

What S. Giacomo received from the three were extended Lessons, Matins alone on each Day lasting as long as an act of an *opera seria*. The similar scorings point to a coordinated plan: soprano and alto, respectively, in the solo L1 and L3s by Jommelli and Perez, and duet L2s for all three composers; only Durante was allowed four voices for his *Oratio*. All Lessons used two winds (flutes/recorders doubling oboes), two *trombe da caccia* [horns], strings and continuo. The writing, except for the four-voice sections of Durante's Prayer, is soloistic, and hence the church must have used its normal complement of 12 singers for the Triduum only in the tutti sections of the *Oratio* and in the Misereres. Perez marshalled his forces creatively, asking for normal oboes ("oboi lunghi") instead of the normal high-pitched Roman instruments, and also switching between recorders and *traversi,* thus resulting in a differentiated and somber instrumental spectrum.[78] The horn parts in all three composers' Lessons are relatively demanding; perhaps this wind/brass scoring provoked Benedict XIV's ban on such practice some three years later.

It is not clear if the composers had stylistic or declamatory prescriptions. Jommelli's F5 pieces are set in C minor, F major, and D major; they all feature long orchestral ritornelli, as extensive as the 30-bar prelude to L3's 1:13 ("De excelso"). But his letters vary widely, from the two-pitch "Ghimel" of L1 to the 36-bar duet, based on the chant formula (of the verses, not the letters), that sets L2's opening "Vau." The sub-verses of L1, except for "Viae Sion," are linked, but starting with L2, Jommelli separated the [c] phrase of verses: "Et abierunt" (1:6c) is a fugato in invertible counterpoint, a far cry from the soloistic writing of L1. Highlighting the final sub-verse continues throughout this Lesson and most of L3 (1:10–13), as Jerusalem's "Vide, Domine" of 11c is set off by key and tempo (example 7.5). The sad "posuit me desolatam, tota die maerore confectam" conclusion of v. 13 is given to voice alone without even continuo.

Fresh off the experience of five accompanied recitatives in *Cajo Mario,* Jommelli used the technique once in each of the first two Lessons. The most famous case is that of L1's "Viae Sion," among the several passages in these Lessons recreated by Rameau's Nephew in Diderot's dialogue treatise *Le neveu de Rameau.*[79] But the other *accompagnati* are almost as memorable, as the addition of the *traversi* frames Jerusalem's piteous plea ("Vide, Domine, afflictionem meam") in 1:9c. And L3 employs the technique twice, once in the central "O vos omnes," which swings from G minor to E♭ minor by the end of 12b, followed by a move to the parallel major and orchestral fury for "Quoniam vindemiavit me." Another *accompagnato* sets the situation of the infirm prophet ("infirmata est virtus mea") in the final verse, "Vigilavit jugum." "Viae Sion" must have impressed Diderot for several reasons, not simply its status as "mimetic" accompanied recitative: apart from the title and refrain, it is the only minor-mode movement in L1, and it separates its subverses by both affect and key. It starts in G minor but turns to V/C minor; v. 4b ("Omnes portae") continues in E♭ major and ends in F minor for the

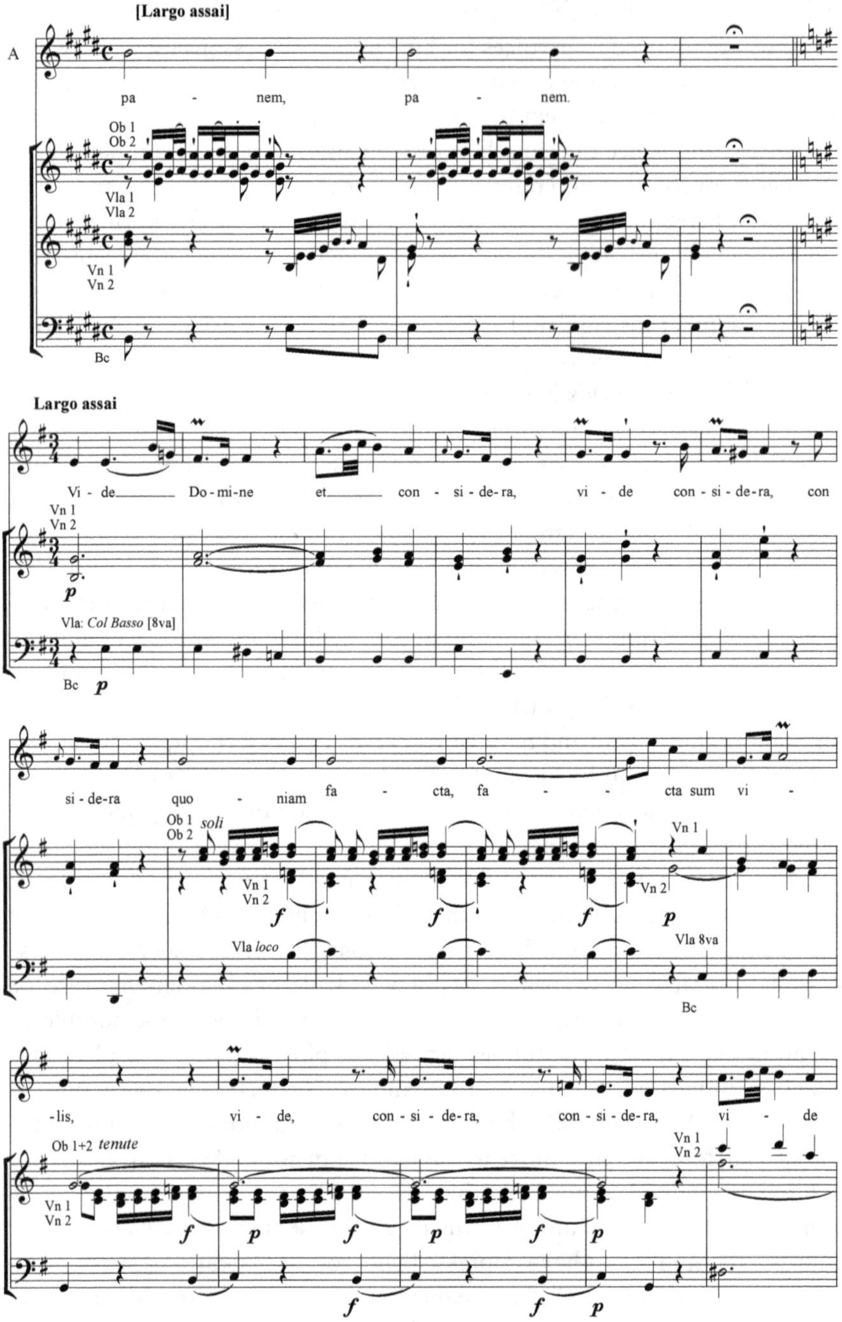

Example 7.5. Jommelli, F5/L3 (1746), "Vide, Domine."

EXAMPLE 7.5. (*Continued*)

Adagio of v.4c, "virgines ejus squalidae," hence adding flats over the course of the verse.

Jommelli's largest-scale structural features come in the contrapuntal L2 duet. An eight-bar gesture in the opening ritornello to 1:7, "Recordata est Jerusalem," recurs so often in 7a that it functions as an emblem of memory, returning at the end of the entire verse ("Viderunt eam hostes"), as Jerusalem seems to be unable to stop thinking about her own misery. This Lesson is also rounded off by its closing repeat of an earlier section's "Jerusalem, convertere," the Adagio that had ended the opening duet on "Vau."

Perez's pieces are equally extrovert, starting with the third verse of L1 (2:10, "Jod. Sederunt in terra"). The "humiliation" of this verse is presaged by the agitated string writing already in the letter and by its turn to F minor (the Lesson is in E♭ major), adding recorders and horns to set the scene of Jerusalem's virgins and priests in the dust. The demands on the violins are repeated in the duet L2, at 2:13 ("Cui comparabo te?") and in L3's ritornello for 3:1, "Ego vir videns," and there is even a difficult horn part in L1's "Jerusalem." Perez's F6 items also tend to separate out the last sub-verse, and the amount of counterpoint is somewhat surprising for such "theatrical" Lessons. Two of his L1 letters ("Teth" and "Caph") feature imitation between solo voice and strings, while "Prophetae tui" (2:14) in L2 and "Beth. Vetustam fecit" (3:4) in L3 are fugatos. Although he is known mainly as an opera composer, the emphasis on fugal technique suggests that either Perez was selected for his abilities in traditional style, or that he wanted to have Rome hear his solid training.

On Good Friday of 1746, Durante's L1 would have continued the expansiveness of the previous Days' Lessons. Its opening ritornello, with prominent flutes and horns, emblematizes a *sotto voce* gesture (*cercar la nota/ subsumatio*) of upward appoggiaturas. Cast in F minor, it moves to C minor for the title and opening "Heth." The frequent Hebrew letters and short verses create groupings by flat/sharp tonalities, as vv. 22–24 form a first tercet around Bb, Eb, and G minor, while the opening verse "Misericordiae Domini" is declaimed twice. The grouping culminates in 3:24, set as a two-part *Kirchenaria* with double declamation of the verse and cadencing in G minor. For the next tercet (vv. 25–27), the "Bonus/Bonum est" verse sequence dealing with waiting and hope, Durante dropped suddenly to E minor, and arranged verses in triple time around the *durus* forms of the pitches of the first tercet: E minor, G major, B minor. Again here the opening verse is declaimed twice ("Bonus . . . quaerenti illum"), while the repetition of the last verse ("Bonum . . . ab adolescentia sua") is fragmented into three phrases.

In order to prepare an extended last verse, Durante shortened the declamation of the penultimate verses, casting vv. 28–29 ("he will sit solitary") as quick accompanied recitative without textual repetitions, still around G major/B minor. But the move to clear Passion allegory, v. 30's "He will give his jaw to those who strike him," is underlined by a return to C minor and a *fugato a tre soggetti* worked through the voice and strings (example 7.6). "Giving" ("dabit percutienti . . . dabit se maxillam") is emphasized at the expense of the liturgical text. The musical declamation thus reiterates the "striking" and hence, in exegetical understanding, the Flagellation. Durante's note of honoring the Passion in his London Lesson here finds specifically musical expression.

Durante's duet L2, with its more somber text ("Quomodo obscuratum est aurum"), relies on motivic and sectional repetition to convey its affect: its "Aleph," "Beth," and refrain all start with similar gestures in the bass, outlining a fourth, and even the soprano line of the letters and [a] sub-verses in vv. 1–2 resemble each other. The first five verses explore various flat tonalities around C minor, while the middle verses are apportioned as solos (soprano vv. 3–4, alto v. 5). Finally, v. 6 ("Et major effecta est") turns literally to G major, and is highlighted as a syncopated duet in simultaneous declamation.

For all the symmetry in the first two Lessons, it would have been hard for S. Giacomo's audience to have anticipated the structure of Durante's

EXAMPLE 7.6. Durante, SS/LI (1746), "Dabit percutienti."
Continued on the next page

EXAMPLE 7.6. (*Continued*)

Prayer (table 7.1). The opening 11-bar ritornello is over a descending minor tetrachord (G-D), which turns into the subject of the G minor vocal fugato setting the title (example 7.7). This falling motive is reused for the words of v. 1a, "Recordare, Domine, quid acciderit nobis," and recurs after the two first verses, characterizing the Prayer as a whole. Durante took Jerusalem's suffering iterated in vv. 3–6 and set it as a single movement in F major for soprano solo, differentiating the verses by tonal goals (C minor, D minor, and back to the local tonic), while troping in a brief return of tutti fragments from v. 1b ("intuere, respice") between vv. 3 and 4.

The next surprise is the following third movement, a large-scale fugue *a due soggetti* that resets the text of v. 1a to different music ("un poco largo") and moves from C to F minor; it is written in *stile osservato* note-values. This is followed by another of Durante's tonal shifts, to D major, for a fourth movement *a 4 concertato* with prominent horn parts at vv. 7–8, the memory of "our fathers sinned, and are no more." Both of these latter verses finish in a more extended troping of v.1b, "respice opprobrium nostrum." V. 9 is a kind of B section, a 3/8 Andante for the same forces, again with v.1b as a postlude, and the da capo indication means that this large ABA structure in the middle of the piece parallels the earlier repeat in the Lesson's opening.

TABLE 7.1.
F. Durante, *Oratio Jeremiae Prophetae* (G minor), verse structure

[Mvt 1]	Title	*a 4,* 11-bar ritornello; descending tetrachord, G minor, Un poco andante
	v.1ab	solo SA + tutti, v.1a ending in E♭
	v. 2ab	SA solo leading to tutti
	v.1a	da capo to 1a, ending in G minor
[Mvt 2]	v.3ab	+ "intuere et respice" from 1b; Largo commodo, S + horns, F major
	v.4ab	C major
	v.5ab	D minor
	v.6ab	F major
[Mvt 3]	v. 1a	*un poco largo,* new *a 4 osservato,* C minor, repeat, cadence in F minor
[Mvt 4]	v. 7ab	Andante *a 4 concertato,* D major, horns
	v. 8ab	+ "respice opprobrium" from v. 1b
	v. 9ab	Andante, 3/8, then "respice," cadence A major, plus da capo to 7ab
[Mvt 5]	v. 10ab	A solo, 3/8, G minor
[Mvt 6]	v. 1a	*a 4,* C minor = Mvt. 3, cadence F minor
[Mvt 7]	v. 11ab	Largo, 3/8, S solo, D minor (no signature)
[Mvt 8]		"Jerusalem" A tempo giusto, SA solo, then tutti, G minor

"The burning of our skin like a portable oven" in v. 10 is an alto solo which returns to G minor and declaims its text twice, followed by a repeat of the third movement, the C minor fugue for v.1a. Given the quality of Durante's counterpoint, however, only the most unmusical of S. Giacomo's deputies would have wondered if this Prayer was ever going to end (its roughly twenty-eight-minute overall length makes it one of the longest Lessons in any repertory). V. 11 again employs solo writing, and the final "Jerusalem" refrain returns not only to G minor, but also to something like the initial ritornello ideas in the strings. Thus Durante's penchant for symmetry articulated both

EXAMPLE 7.7. Durante, SS/L3 (1746), "Incipit oratio."

EXAMPLE 7.7. (*Continued*)

structure and affect, as the two sub-verses of v. 1 were re-inserted across the entire Lesson, with "Recordare" recurring as a formal component and "intuere et respice" as an emblematic trope. Once again the Prayer functioned musically as a closing rhetorical summation to the Triduum.

The virtuosic solo writing and the demanding orchestral parts over all three Days must have made an effect, although there seems to be no record among Roman diaries and newspaper accounts of 1746. Including the various Misereres, the polyphony alone would have taken up to ninety minutes each

Day, as each set of Lessons comes in at somewhere around seventy minutes (presumably the Responsories were in chant, in Spanish tradition). Although Jommelli had gotten the highest fee, the reaction of the deputies after Holy Week was to reward Durante with a tip equivalent to eight *scudi,* and he was then commissioned to write the Requiem for Philip V at S. Giacomo later that year.[80] The original public might not have anticipated the future popularity of Durante's Lessons, especially the Prayer, but they remained present in local memory for a generation. Burney's characterization of the entire cycle, based on his looking at manuscripts twenty-five years later, is generally accurate, although some of the details had been forgotten, such as Perez' use of fugal style, and the dramatic novelty of Jommelli's accompanied recitatives.[81]

Beyond the Lessons, at least one other commissioned piece had long-term effects. Ciampi's Miserere, a polystylistic, eighteen-movement psalm in F minor, must also have come off well, since he was made responsible for all music at the church in 1748. His nine orchestral Lessons might stem from that year, as the date on the autograph of F5/L1 suggests. If so, Ciampi worked hard, as the F6 and SS Lessons are also on the same scale.[82] The idea of a new cycle following the model of 1746 is suggested by the scoring, with Ciampi's L1s set for solo soprano, the L2s for AT, and the final Lessons for SAB, all with strings (violas doubled), horns, and also flutes in F5–6/L1 and SS/L3.[83]

In some cases, possibly to avoid Durante-like lengths, Ciampi abbreviated the declamation: the F5/L2 has a good deal of homophonic writing, and vv. 3–6 of F6/L3 are given to the top voices, with the bass interjecting Hebrew letters seamlessly. Of this set, the F5/L2 travelled as far as Mexico City Cathedral, possibly via Spanish transmission.[84] Still, the F5/L3 is a large-scale vocal trio in C minor with strings and horns, and its long opening ritornello immediately recalls the 1746 pieces.[85] This moves to a fugato for "Jod," and there is a full fugue at 1:13, "De excelsis." Clearly the contrapuntal sections of the 1746 cycle had made a deep impression at S. Giacomo. A violin obbligato sets off the change of voice in 1:11c, while the final verse "Vigilavit jugum" uses the doubled violas to set its affect. The Lesson's exploration of flat tonalities starts with "O vos omnes" in E♭ major, but the verse turns quickly to the parallel minor for "si est dolor sicut dolor meus" (1:12b) and finishes in B♭ minor. Its expressive range and sheer intensity mark it as a worthy companion to Ciampi's earlier Miserere.

It is not clear if Benedict XIV's constitution, or simply a lack of money, motivated the deputies to commission a new cycle of Lessons, this time without orchestra, from Ciampi for 1749; only five singers and a continuo group were engaged, and the set was repeated in 1750.[86] The composer responded with vocally less virtuosic pieces for homogenous forces across the Days, as the Lessons are scored for S, SA, and SAB (with AT for SS/L2).[87] The switches among singers for the Days (five needed to cover four voice parts) also suggest that performers often migrated among Roman churches for different Matins. *Concertato* style is quite present in these pieces, notably the F5/L2 duet in F minor.

Within a few years of Ciampi's Lessons, Aurelio Aurisicchio was being groomed as the older man's successor at the Spanish church, not least by writing a less contrapuntal but more extrovert Lesson cycle with strings (but no winds, also in possible deference to *Annus qui*) in 1752. Of these pieces, the L1s for F5 and SS also made their way to Mexico City.[88] The composer's use of a four-voice ripieno choir for one verse in each Lesson (in F5/L3 it is the last one, "Vigilavit jugum") contrasts with the solo vocal writing and first violin part, even more virtuosic than in the repertory of the 1740s. But in terms of declamatory time, the ripieni verses are economical in their homophony, as at 1:3 in F5/L1 ("Migravit Juda"), or the final verses of F6/L2–3 or SS/L1–2.

The total holdings still in the church's archive can thus be construed as cycles of c. 1697 and c. 1704–09 (de Sanctis), 1746 (the three composers), 1748 (Ciampi with orchestra), 1749 (Ciampi without orchestra), and 1752 (Aurisicchio with orchestra) (table 7.2). These traditions continued; in 1775 two visitors from Casale Monferrato heard music on Wednesday and Thursday in the Sistina, and then in Friday more modern works in S. Apollinare, judging the best singers and instrumentalists to be there and in S. Giacomo.[89] On Good Friday 1780, Antonio Canova went in the afternoon to the Spanish church to hear three Lessons in music, and then in the evening another set of Lamentations at the Congregazione della Morte, the latter sung by the famed tenor Giovanni Davide from Bergamo, who had also performed in operas by G. B. Borghi and Mysliveček that Carnival. This Tenebrae finished, not with the Miserere but with the Stabat Mater, and as late as 10.30 p.m., signs of the priority of modern devotional texts over liturgical prescriptions.[90] In the 1780s, Aurisicchio's successor Filippo Ciampi, probably the grandson of Francesco, wrote ten surviving Lessons for different years, scored variously with and without orchestra.[91]

Even with the gaps, the sum total of S. Giacomo's repertory over a century is remarkable: highly virtuosic and suitably modern pieces, different from the traditional repertory of the Roman basilicas by Pitoni, Girolamo Chiti, or Claudio Casciolini. Around 1750, Tenebrae was renewed frequently: the three-composer cycle of 1746, Ciampi's two sets within three years, and then Aurisicchio's. Although there is little outside evidence, the production shifted S. Giacomo's sonic profile in the city away from the Easter festivities and into Holy Week, two months after the end of the opera season, placing it at the center of modern Triduum devotion.

TABLE 7.2.

San Giacomo degli Spagnoli (Rome), Lamentations repertory to 1752

F5	F6	SS
1. **Lessons with 2 violins and solo voice except for SS/L3: attr. to de Sanctis**		
L1, 2 (1697), 3	L1, 2 (x2), 3 (1704)	L1, 2, 3 (all x2)
anonymous, same scoring		
L1, 2, 3	L1, 3	
2. **1746 Lessons with orchestra (winds, horns) and solo voice except as noted**		
Jommelli, L1, 3; L2 *a* 2	Perez, L 1, 3; L2 *a* 2	Durante, L1 *a 1*; L2 *a* 2; L3 *a* 4
3. **F. Ciampi, Lessons with orchestra (doubled violas) and 1–3 voices**		
L1–3, F5/L1 dated 1748	L1–3	L1–3
4. **Ciampi, Lessons *a* 3 without orchestra (continuo only)**		
L1–3, F5/L1 dated 1749	L1–3	L1–3
5. **Aurisicchio, Lessons with strings, solo with vocal ripieni *a* 4**		
L1–3, F5/L1 dated 1752	L1–3	L1–3

COURT LAMENTATIONS IN MADRID

A royal Spanish tradition is indirectly evident in the luxuriousness of S. Giacomo's Tenebrae, but very patent in the production of orchestral Lessons in the Madrid of Philip V and Ferdinand VI. The overall picture of royal Passion devotion is hard to gauge, but the Spanish guides to Holy Week and Lamentations-inspired literature provide some context. Antonio de Morales (E)Spino's *Manual de la significación de las ceremonias que observa la Iglesia . . . en la Semana Santa* (Madrid, 1746) explained the Triduum for audiences defamiliarized with its allegories by continually citing none other than Durandus, along with occasional references to Beleth and Rupert of Deutz.[92] This medieval touch continued in Spino's explication of the Hours, which gave the historical context of the two destructions of Jerusalem, the fourfold nature of the Hebrew acrostics, a summary of the Second and Third Nocturne Lessons, and the texts and actions of Lauds.[93] Later in the century, Francisco Gregorio de Salas published a vernacular poem in 1772 paraphrasing Lamentations along with the Miserere and Benedictus, again based on the Lessons and not the book as a whole.[94]

The 1734 fire in the Madrid Alcázar and its music holdings necessitated a complete replacement of the whole liturgical repertory, not just the Triduum. The datable repertory starts with the pieces that Corselli composed after his predecessor José de Torres's death in 1738, and it contrasts in some ways with the Roman or Neapolitan works of the 1740s. Corselli's Tenebrae output began in the shadow of slow decline during the later years of Philip V and continued in the improving climate after the accession of the music-loving Ferdinand VI and Maria Barbara in 1746 (table 7.3).[95] Overall, his production went up after a sovereign's succession: three new Lessons in 1747 (despite—or perhaps because of—the complaints by Elisabetta Farnese, no friend of her stepson), and five in 1761 after Charles III's accession. Of these latter, two are designated as "short," in line with the new sovereign's taste for briefer musical liturgy. But the Tenebrae of 1746, 1747, 1749, and 1751 all featured three Lamentations by the maestro. A setting of F6/L3 from 1749 (#351) was indeed cut when recopied, but not until 1775 (#173). His only Lesson without orchestra (#253) dates from 1747 and employs a soprano and a solo cello; it lasts about 10 minutes, just a bit shorter than his earlier works.

After 1734, Tenebrae was normally performed with the royals present, in the church of San Jerónimo, part of the Buen Retiro complex. At the beginning of his tenure, Corselli could count on eight or nine singers plus seven strings and continuo; the resources are evident in his first Lesson of 1739, #154, with its five voices including two sopranos, and strings only.[96] Still, the presence of Torres's twelve-voice Lessons with orchestra (F5-F6/L1 and an *Oratio*) in the post-1734 holdings of the chapel (preserved in E-Mp) led Corselli to write items for other liturgical slots. He began usually with one a year, often for solo voice, until 1744, and there was a notable increase at the time of royal transition. A final replacement of Torres' works could have taken place in 1751, with Corselli's three L1s for eight voices. This would also have meant the end of an earlier style, while the ample scoring of the new works continued the tradition of large-scale opening Lessons.

The Italian began his first Triduum as chapelmaster by clearly differentiating his work from Torres's. Two F5/L1s, the latter's 1720 Lesson *a 12* and Corselli's *a 5* of 1739, stand in sharp contrast, beginning with the older composer's retention of late 17th-century polychoral tradition, mixed with short arias and *fugae* involving four real voices.[97] While Corselli displayed his skill at brief fugal passages, his three solo arias are in Italianate style, thematically differentiated among the sub-verses.

His F5/L2 of the next year, for SAT (#155), is marked by longer verses and contrapuntal letters; it begins with solo flutes (the first appearance of winds in his Triduum output), and its opening "Vau" takes up some twenty-

TABLE 7.3.
Orchestral Lessons by Francesco Corselli (E-Mp)
for the Spanish Court, 1739–1760

Philip V

1739   #154 *a* 5; F5/L1

1740   334 *a* 2, 155 *a* 3; F5/L3, L2

1741   355 *a* 1; F6/L3

1742   255 *a* 2; F6/L2

1743   281 *a* 1; F5/L2

1744   342 *a* 1; 343 *a* 3; SS/L2, L3

1746   190 *a* 1; 256 *a* 1, 156 *a* 5; F5/L2, F6/L2, SS/L1

Ferdinand VI

1747   253 *a* 1 (no orch), 254 *a* 1, 158 *a* 2; F6/L2, F5/L2, SS/L2

1748   212 *a* 1; F5/L3

1749   157 *a* 1, 351 *a* 1, 372 *a* 1; SS/L1, F6/L2, SS/L2; reorganization of Chapel

1750   159 *a* 1; SS/L3

1751   161 *a* 8, 246 *a* 8, 287 *a* 8; all L1s (287 later shortened)

1752   257 *a* 2, 252 *a* 5; F6/L2, L1 [also J. de Nebra, 3 Lessons]

1753   267 *a* 2, 194 *a* 8; SS/L2 SS/L3 [Nebra, 2 Lessons; 1754 Nebra, 2 Lessons]

1757   319 *a* 2; F5/L2 [Farinelli's gift to Ferdinand of Leo's Lessons]

---

four bars as opposed to the nine of 1739's "Aleph." Its tempi change according to grammatical phrases, not even sub-verses (Feijóo would have objected strongly), e.g., an Adagio for alto solo without continuo to set the "lack" of "et abierunt absque fortitudine." The long sub-verses of this Lesson are often differentiated by tempo, and this D minor piece wanders to B♭ minor at "instabilis facta est." The breadth of the orchestral writing is evident at "Zain. Recordata est . . . ," where a forty-bar Hebrew letter leads to an Adagio sub-verse (v.7ab) set out as an alto arioso with a flute duet over unison string figuration; at 7c, the "derision" of "Viderunt eam hostes" generates a sudden turn to a contrapuntal "Vivo" for all three voices. In all these pieces, the florid ensemble singing distinguishes Corselli's Lessons from his court operas of those years. The solo Lessons, starting in 1741, also feature counterpoint, traditional gestures and only moderately repeated declamation; a standard chromatic catabasis sets "dierum afflictionis suae" in the F5/L2 (#281) of 1743. The same passage in a solo Lesson of three years later (#190) was even simpler.

The pieces of 1744 are neither radically longer nor more operatic than what Elisabetta Farnese had heard in previous years (which suggests that she disliked all of Corselli's production). The *Oratio* for ATB groups its eleven verses into five large sections, three of them solos, and concludes with a fugue for the refrain, probably about fifteen minutes in all. The Lessons produced after Ferdinand's accession explore different directions: the F6/L2 with cello of 1747 (#253) is a duet for voice and instrument sharing motivic material, with each apportioned a cadenza. A solo SS/L2 of 1749 with flutes and trumpets (#157; ironically, in the year of *Annus qui*) begins *piano* with muted or pizzicato strings, and half cadences demarcating sub-verses. The letters are all short fugal expositions, and "filia populi mei crudelis" is set off by *concitato* gestures and dynamics. The misery of vv. 4–5 ("Adhaesit lingua . . . Qui vescebantur"; example 7.8) is set off by a difficult violin obbligato *con sordini* over simple declamation of the text, and the mutes come off only for the final v. 6. This piece was recopied when Corselli resumed his production of Lessons in 1761, for good reason.[98]

The changes, by decree or design, are evident in three SS Lessons of the following years. The Prayer of 1750 (#159) for alto and orchestra is set out in five large movements, symmetrically around D minor (title and vv. 1–2 in the tonic; vv. 3–6 in B♭; a contrasting v. 7 back in the tonic; vv. 8–11 in A minor; and the refrain returning to the parallel major). Vv. 3–6 form a three-section *Kirchenaria,* but vv. 8–11 belie the affect of their text ("We are dominated servants . . . "), since the movement is a virtuoso duet for alto and cello. There is an instrumental cadenza in the opening ritornello before the voice has even entered, and the thematic material is shared equally between singer and instrument, with a moment of sobriety only for "Mulieres in Sion humilaverunt."[99] An eight-voice SS/L1 from 1751 (#161) groups its verses in threes, with an imitative "Heth. Misericordiae Domini" for tutti, followed by vocal solos with obbligato violin for the next two verses. But counterpoint was by no means banished: the final "Jerusalem" is an eight-voice fugato *a due soggetti*. Finally, a duet (ST) L2 from 1753 (#267), uses motivic unification. The orchestral material from its opening ritornello and its "Aleph," a dark thirty-two-bar Adagio non troppo in D minor, comes back in the final "Jerusalem," while the six Hebrew letters are grouped in pairs each sharing material. In addition to the symmetrical solos (vv. 3–4 in the middle), and tonal planning similar to #159, Corselli's v. 5b "amplexati sunt

EXAMPLE 7.8. Corselli, SS/L2 (1749), "Adhaesit lingua."

EXAMPLE 7.8. (*Continued*)

stercora" again shifts from D minor to Bb minor within three bars, as "Jerusalem embraced the dunghills," the same modulation as at "instabilis facta est" in #155 of 1740. Clearly the moves to such flat tonal areas were meant to be rhetorical summations of change and misery.

But after this group of Lamentations, a switch in the division of labor or royal taste is suggested by the commissions to Nebra in 1752/53 and 1758/59 and a halt in Corselli's Lessons. Normally having written two or three a year from the beginning of Ferdinand's reign to 1753, the chapelmaster produced only one in the entire 1754–1761 span. Despite Farinelli's reputed Romanizing efforts, the only sign of imported music in the chapel's holdings is a copy (#747) of Leo's C-minor Miserere, also dated 1757 as is Leo's Lenten music manuscript. There are no pieces from the leading Roman composers, even those with connections to the Spanish national churches (Bencini, Pitoni, Ciampi, Biordi, Jommelli).[100] Thus the net effect of Farinelli's efforts in Madrid is unclear, and whatever he did would have run up against the extreme conservatism of court ritual.[101] Whatever caused the break in Corselli's production, it was not stylistic monotony.

The Spanish court repertory of these years most obviously replaced the last bits of seventeenth-century tradition with thoroughly modern music, and this stands in some contrast to the devotional literature based on the past. It also seems to run against the increasing social difficulties of the ritual else-where. Beyond the more subtle switches among Corselli's Lessons, the on-going production for the Bourbons is a testimony to their aesthetic/devotional need for up-to-date Tenebrae, echoed by the efforts at "their" Roman church of S. Giacomo and by their cousins in Naples in the very same years.

The production of orchestral Lessons at mid-century had different paces in socially diverse institutions: a slowly coalescing and fixed civic repertory in Lucca; large cycles of great novelty in Rome; and a steady stream of some-what contested individual Lessons in Madrid. The spread of such pieces to nuns in even small centers (Massa), and sisters' performances in general, shows the continuing diffusion of Triduum music throughout society. Some parts of the Euro-American world held to such practice, even as the ritual continued to feel devotional pressure.

Chapter 8

⌒⚬✤✤✤⚬⌒

Endings and Continuities

Listening to Tenebrae in many parts of the Catholic world around 1760, a crisis of the ritual would not have been audible. New Lessons or Responsories were produced in any number of places, from Naples to Bergamo, among the Jeronymites of Guadalupe (Extremadura), in the central European monasteries, and not least in the cathedrals of Spain and New Spain.[1] But few had the immediate resonance of the Portuguese repertory.

LAMENTING IN LISBON

The ruin of cities was starkly evident to Enlightenment Europe in the wake of the 1755 Lisbon earthquake. The catastrophe thrust the idea of a destroyed city into collective imagination in ways not seen since the Thirty Years' War. Given the physical conditions, the literal meaning of Lamentations verses was evident in the city: the walls destroyed, hunger and disease spreading, no fixed structures. The efforts of church authorities, besides ministering to the survivors' social needs, also aimed at restoring ritual life, not least the exact observance of Holy Week in 1756.[2] Thus the three Lis produced by Davide Perez for the chapel of the Patriarchal in the following years, more than a decade after his Lessons for Rome, had special meaning. They survive in some four manuscripts in Portugal and also in I-Nc, the latter source evidently written in Lisbon and sent back to Naples.[3] Perez's own Patriarchal migrated among various churches after 1755, as its original home had been destroyed, in an eerie echo of Jeremiah's "Migravit Juda propter afflictionem."[4]

Predictably, the local regulars invoked the prophet to explain the disaster. The Capuchin preacher Illuminato di Borgo San Sepolcro used Lamentations in his Italian-language *Relazione* of the quake and its aftermath, while the mendicant Manuel da Epifania also employed the text in his *Re-*

flexoens sobre os terremotos (Lisbon, 1756).[5] But the impassioned citation and expansion of F5/L1 that opened the Jesuit Gabriel Malagrida's *Juizo da verdadera causa do terremoto* (Lisbon, 1756) would have the widest consequences. Malagrida pointed directly to Lisbon's sins as the cause of the catastrophe, and systematically expanded each verse in the Lesson to underscore the physical destruction surrounding him, and its origin in the city's crimes. The third paragraph of this thirty-one-page outburst starts by putting its denunciation in Jeremiah's own mouth, and ends with the city's overwhelming guilt in words taken from F5/L1.[6] Once again, the problem of applying prophetic blame to an absolutist Catholic city obtained: if the earthquake was punishment for Lisbon's offenses, the idea could easily merge into anti-royal or anti-clerical "subversion." Malagrida's polemics, including attacks on the court's extravagant spending on opera, led to drastic consequences; he was eventually accused of conspiracy against the de facto ruler, the Marquis de Pombal, then imprisoned and executed in an *auto-da-fe.*

Lamentations' ambiguity in this context might explain the trajectory of Perez's production.[7] In 1757, after the immediate damage, he set a Miserere plus SS/L1, the only Lesson that does not mention the city's sins but begins "It is the mercy of the Lord that we have not been consumed" and goes on to praise Divine goodness to those who wait for Him. The concern with producing a new Tenebrae repertory continued in his Responsory cycle of 1758 (there is another undated one). Perez' F6 and F5/L1s—whose words indeed dwell on the city's sins and misery—are slightly later, 1761 and 1763 respectively. Whoever ordered these pieces in the 1760s might have waited for social stability to be restored, and the polemical, anti-absolutist interpretations of Jeremiah to wane in light of Pombal's reconstruction efforts, before hearing new settings of the more guilt-laden texts.

Beyond their social meaning, Perez's Lessons are without exact models, although some of the fugal writing recalls his F6/L3 for S. Giacomo in Rome. They are four-voice *concertato* pieces with solo/tutti indications (including continuo, but no other instruments), and marked by sub-verses using imitation. Such contrapuntal structures range from loose motivic repetition through fugato (specifically so noted twice) to fairly strict fugue. Against these marks of tradition, Perez also set letters or verses as modern-style trios (F5 and 6), duets (F6), and solos (SS). Some moments mix scorings for dramatic effect, as in the choral interjections "Non est lex" in the three lower voices, which are run against the top part's "et non invenierunt visionem a Domino" (F6, 2:9c). All the Lessons are in *mollis* regions (C minor, G minor, F minor, respectively, for F5–6 and SS), with almost no verses in any sharp tonality.

The first piece in this series, the SS/L1 of 1757, opens "sul grave," piano in the voices and "organo chiuso" (with shutters closed), over two iterations of a descending tetrachord. "De lamentatione," a repeated-pitch gesture, is declaimed regularly every two beats over a series of diminished-7th chords, leading from F minor to B♭ minor. The first "Heth," for voices only, quotes the Tone-6 letter formula in the tenor (called "a canto fermo" in the scores, with a final AT voice-exchange or rhetorical *heterolepsis* to finish the citation; example 8.1), while the opening verse, "Misericordiae Domini," reworks the motives first enunciated in "Incipit lamentatio" in imitation, leading to the first *forte* at the literal reality, "quia non sumus consumpti." The court—and possibly the composer—had only been spared by their accidental absence from Lisbon the day of the catastrophe. Among the title's *gravitas,* the letter's invocation of chant tradition, and the verse's emphasis on survival, the Lesson immediately conveyed both ritual continuity and current meaning. The "Jerusalem" refrain repeats the "organo chiuso" of the beginning, but this time with "Jerusalem, convertere" articulated *forte* in the lower voices, a "moral" closing for a Lesson in the earthquake's aftermath.

The text of 1761's F6/L1 limns the city's destruction. After a fugato for the title, Perez interrupted the declamation of 2:8a between "Cogitavit Dominus" and "dissipare murum," emphasizing "dissolving the city wall" with a 76-bar fugue in E♭ that restates the whole sub-verse; its extended iteration of urban destruction must have hit home. After v.8b ("tetendit") for four solo voices, Perez again articulated local and immediate meaning inside a sub-verse (8c) by counterpoint, separating the "mourning of the bulwark" ("Luxitque antemurale") from the resulting destruction of the wall, "et murus pariter dissipatus est." The latter is another long fugato in the local tonic, with literal motives ("dis-[rest]-sipatus est," a case of rhetorical *tmesis*). V. 9 has two moments of dramatic tutti declamation, as the opening sub-verse's "Defixae sunt" is projected in the top voices against octave leaps in the tenor and bass for "in terra," setting the walls' "implosion" against "into the earth"; this is paralleled by the "Non est lex" passage in 9c. As in v. 8, the last sub-verse of v. 10, "abicierunt in terram" is underscored with a fifty-five-bar fugato *a 3,* as the "virgins of Jerusalem hung their heads to the ground." Hence every verse has a rhetorical, often contrapuntal, climax: fugal procedures twice underline the destruction of the wall, while the Lesson concludes with the women's dejection conveyed through *stile osservato.* The setting's meaning for Lisbon was clear.

Like 1757's opening "Heth," many letters in the F5 Lesson of 1763 are brief moments of Fuxian counterpoint, and the polyphonic gestures start with the long imitative exordium for 1:1a, "Quomodo sedet." Perez then repeated its declamation against the simultaneous enunciation of 1b, "facta est quasi vidua," a texture like F6/L1's "Non est lex." Once again, the important sub-verses in this Lesson are articulated at length, as 1:2b alone runs some seventy-eight bars, and 3c almost the same. The closing of verses is clear from their harmonic demarcation: 1c is set off by a dominant pedal, while

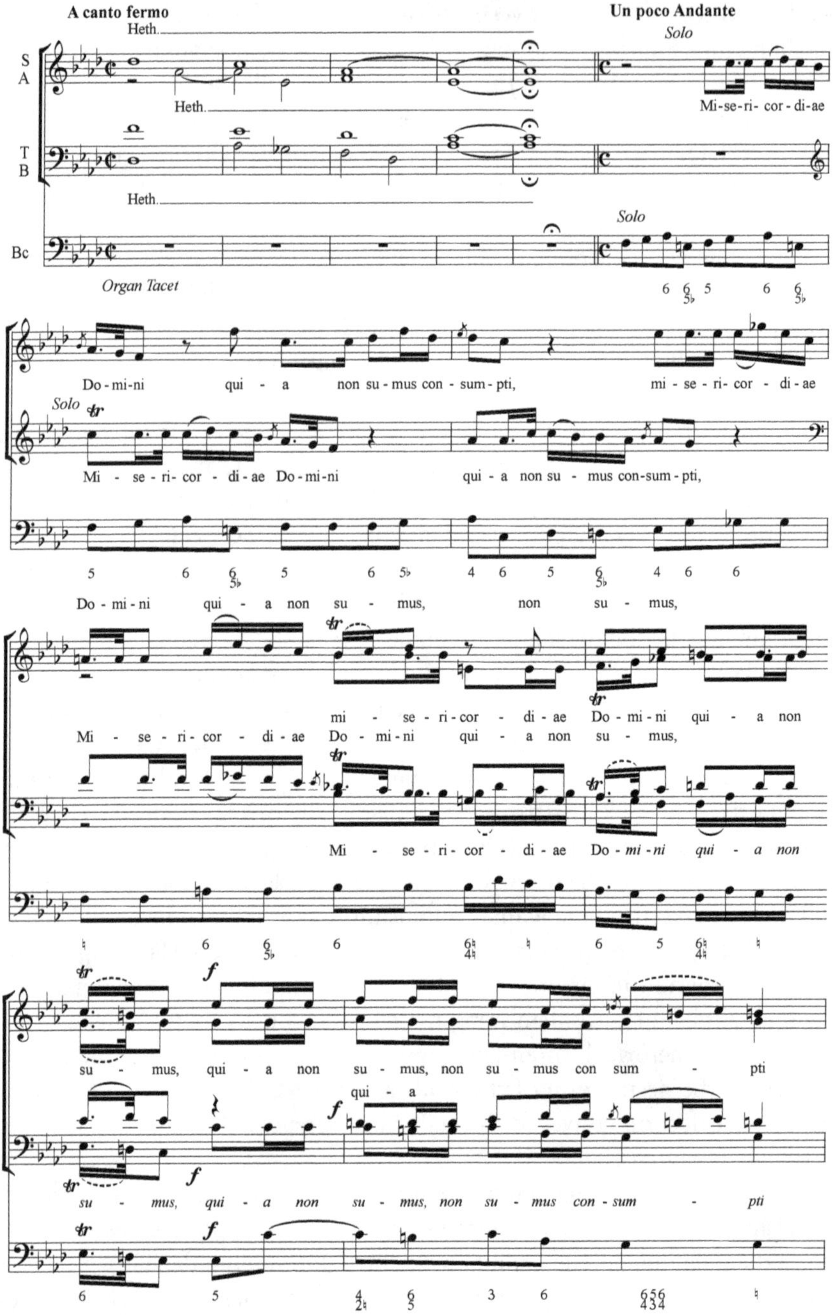

EXAMPLE 8.1. Perez, SS/L1 (1757), "Heth. Misericordiae Domini."

5c arrives at B♭ minor, a tonal marker of despair, before the surprise return of C minor for the "Jerusalem" refrain.

This music, meant for the highest levels of the clergy and perhaps the court, projected different meanings simultaneously. The reference to chant at the opening of SS/L1 connects to the overall use of fugue and fugato in passages referring to the city's destruction: gestures that conveyed tradition, given the social destruction all around. But the modern verses and letters also reaffirmed the court's commitment to contemporary sacred and operatic music. One point on which the Braganza dynasty, Pombal, the hierarchy, and even the unruly local regulars agreed was the need for penance, and here the striking gestures in whichever style—the flat sonorities overall, the highlighting of important sub-verses—underscore how Holy Week in post-quake Lisbon expressed social remorse. The new Lessons are one of the most striking musical reactions to catastrophe in the Enlightenment.

LESSONS IN THE HISPANIC WORLD

At the Spanish court, after Farinelli's departure and the accession of Charles III, the large-scale production of Lessons continued. In 1766, the Neapolitan Nicolò Conforto was commissioned to compose an entire cycle with orchestra, which also employed unusual instrumental effects (no violins in the F6 Lessons, and two viole d'amore used in SS/L1, evidently to set the affect of "Misericordiae Domini"). At a moment of decreased court spending on music, Corselli crafted an almost complete cycle in 1768, while Conforto wrote a twelve-voice, three-choir Miserere for the same year. Even as the chapelmaster aged, his production continued at a fast pace: six Lessons in 1772 and four in 1774.[8] His deputy and successor Antonio Ugena kept up the flow, with some seventy-three Lessons between 1770 and 1804.

In 1794, as Ugena in turn neared the end of his tenure, the court composer Gaetano Brunetti contributed three solo Lessons with orchestra, including an F5/L1 with obbligato bassoons and oboes that employs the same gesture for all its Hebrew letters. For the same Triduum, Brunetti's four-voice Miserere with only a double-bass continuo represented a different approach in *stile osservato*.[9] Brunetti provided primarily chamber music and symphonies to Madrid, and these Lessons feature complex orchestral writing in all the verses. Given his harmonic inventiveness, it is no surprise that v. 4ab of the F5/L1 descends by thirds (D minor-B minor-G major) for its setting of "Viae Sion lugent." Clearly the courts of Charles III and IV continued to hear innovative Lessons.

At the Escorial, the stylistic range went beyond court practice. From 1757 onward, the twenty-nine Lessons produced by Padre Antonio Soler run from eight-voice continuo-only pieces to modern solo settings with orchestra.[10] Still, any view of Spanish Lamentations is incomplete without the output of Antonio Ripa (1721–95), the famed chapelmaster of Seville, and that of F. J. García Fajer (1731–1809), both of whose Lessons found resonance outside Spain. Two of the former's settings are in Lima, while the only Lesson ever heard at the Parisian *Concert spirituel* seems to have been a French vernacular translation of a large-scale Lesson by the latter in 1760 (and hence Diderot must have known Jommelli's Lamentations from other venues). The Parisian piece may have been one of Fajer's eight-voice settings.[11]

Even on the empire's outskirts, new composition continued. At Santiago de Cuba's cathedral, Esteban Salas wrote Lamentations along with Passions and items for Palm Sunday and Holy Saturday in the years after his appointment in 1763. Before 1769 (the first surviving music inventory), he had already written Lessons for F5–6 (there survive only the F5 items).[12] As with Lisbon, the church was destroyed in an earthquake of June 1766; possibly Salas's settings date from after the catastrophe and were sung in the provisional chapel housed in a straw hut on the Plaza de Armas, although there are no musical markings of obvious sub-verses (e.g., F5/L1's "omnes portae eius destructae").[13]

In mid-century on the Jesuit *reducciones* of Chiquitos and Moxos in what is now lowland Bolivia, Triduum Office music attributed to Domenico Zipoli was preserved: Lessons (L1–3, the first two verses only of each) and simple four-voice Responsories for F5, the opening of F5/L1 citing the standard recitation tone pitched on G. Although much music was attributed to Zipoli after his death in 1726, a good deal of the repertory was actually written by later Jesuits (e.g., Martin Schmid). Whatever their authorship, the Triduum pieces were faithfully copied by Guaraní scribes in Moxos as late as 1922, and presumably performed up to that time and beyond, while newer Lessons were sent from Spain after the Jesuits' expulsion, in 1797.[14]

More central sites also combined importation with local production. In New Spain, older pieces, like the F5/L1 by Sebastián Durón preserved in Mexico City, were joined around 1760 by new Lessons by the cathedral musicians Mateo Tollis de la Roca and Ignacio Jerusalem. Around the same time, two of José Picañol's F6 Lessons were copied for Puebla, far from their origin in Spain.[15] The originals of these latter were more likely written to be performed by male musicians at the female house of the Encarnación in Madrid (after 1736) rather than during Picañol's time at Barcelona Cathedral (1726–36). There are also six anonymous Lessons in Puebla from before the tenure of Antonio Juanas at the end of the century.[16] Thus the cathedral repertory, like that of the capital, seems a mix of the local and the European. In other parts of New Spain, these years also saw new composition, such as the two L1s by Julián de Zúñiga for Durango.[17]

Mexico City Cathedral repertory around 1760 includes two L1s by Tollis de la Roca, and four large-scale pieces for voices and orchestra by Jerusalem (duplicate L1s for F5, an F6/L1, and an F6/L3). The latter's Lessons are linked by structural features: an insistence on the Hebrew letters, the demarcation of sub-verses by pauses or cadences, and an almost ubiquitous tremolo or repeated-note string accompaniment. But they must have been written for different sets of singers, as the F6/L3 (MEX-Mc Eb9) calls for two moderately florid soprano parts often declaiming simultaneously, while a large-scale F5/L1 (Eb7) uses only alto and bass solos, the *tiple* and tenor being reserved for homophonic tuttis or ripieno verses.

One of the few Lessons with trumpets and oboes, this F5/L1 is also alone in indexing features of the grand style, starting with its 58-bar *fuga a due soggetti* for the opening "Aleph" which ends with fourteen repetitions of the letter against the orchestral accompaniment. The emphasis is even more pronounced through the 15-fold declamation of the following "Beth." Long ritornelli frame the opening solo verses (vv. 1–2), cast as single movements, with clear demarcation of the sub-verses. The Lesson features two accompanied recitatives (vv. 3 and 5), of which the first changes the solos according to the sub-verses. The intervening v. 4 ("Viae Sion lugent") elaborates a surprising tonal plan leading from B♭ major to F major via V/D minor and an augmented sixth. The "Jerusalem" refrain (missing in the full score, but present in the parts) rounds off the piece with dramatic gestures.[18] The overall structure of the other F5/L1 (MEX-Mc Cc2) for alto and strings is similar, although on a smaller scale; it generally links the sub-verses while tacking the letters on to the end of the preceding verse.

Jerusalem's two F6 Lessons also balance the verse structure. The four-voice L1 (Cc8) sets v. 8a and c as solos turning into tuttis, while 8b is a solo, and the use of a single voice for the middle sub-verse also obtains in v. 9, while v. 11b goes the other way, from tutti to solo. The climax of the Lesson is a long iteration of the final words of v. 11c, "in plateis oppidi," declaimed six times in homophony against the orchestra, oscillating between F major and minor. The exegetical or social reason for this emphasis on "in the city's streets" is not clear, and again this seems a case of purely musical climax. The L3 for two sopranos takes this same tonal opposition as an emblem for its "Jerusalem, convertere," which starts in G minor and moves via B♭ towards the F major in which the piece would normally end, as it had begun. But the modulation is prepared by an augmented 6th (D♭-B♮), of which the flattened pitch simply remains and inflects the pitch content, bringing the Lesson to a somber close in F minor (example 8.2).

In some ways, Jerusalem's Lessons represent original solutions. But they might also be heard as responding to the pieces that had been imported from Rome: Ciampi's F5/L2 from his 1748 cycle for S. Giacomo (in its unexpected

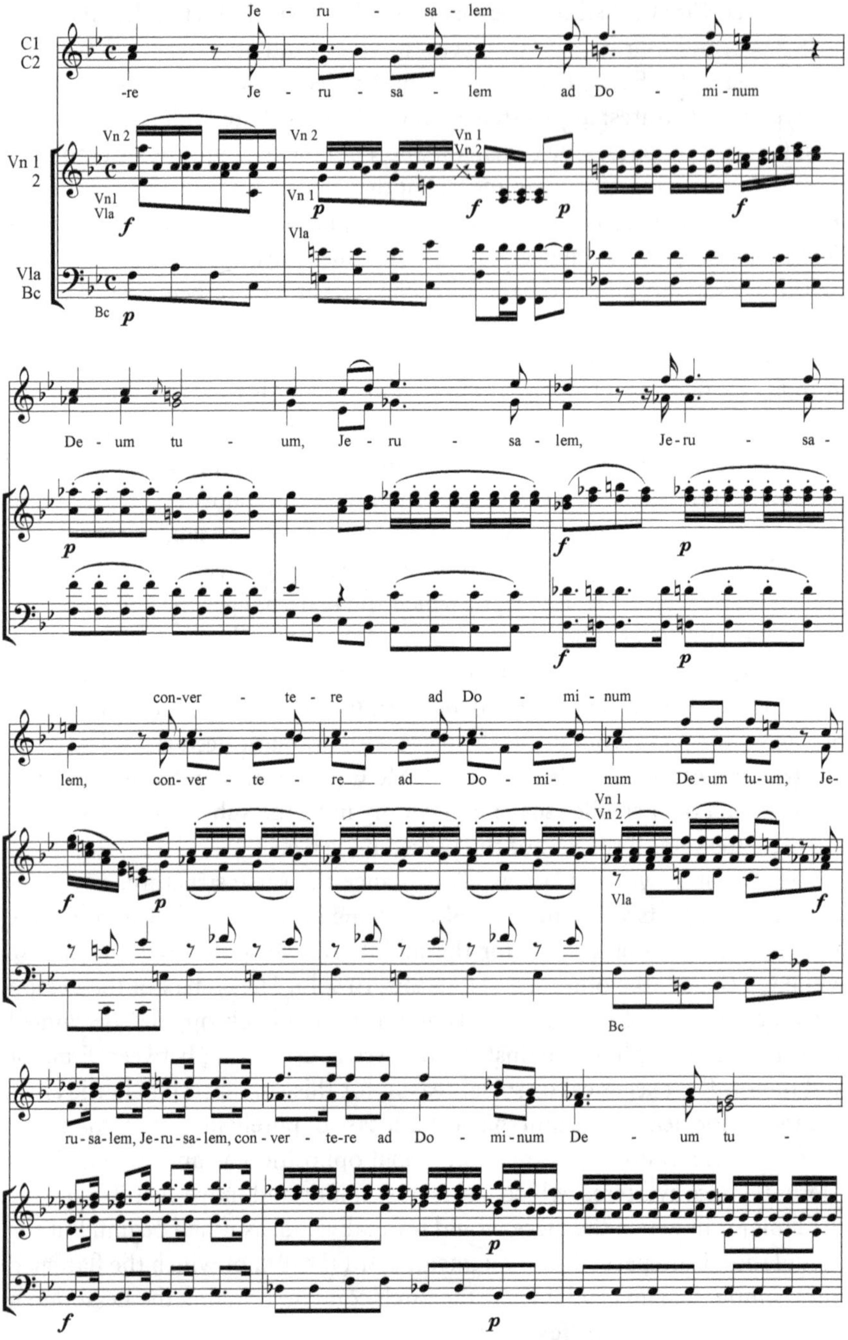

EXAMPLE 8.2. I. Jerusalem, F5/L2, "Jerusalem, convertere."

Finis Laus Deo

EXAMPLE 8.2. (*Continued*)

tonal goals), and the two L1s (for F5 and SS) by Aurisicchio from the 1752 set. Although Jerusalem's efforts in projecting the Hebrew letters would have delighted Feijóo (who might not have been as happy about the accompanied recitatives), their prominence also recalls Aurisicchio's emphasis via the ripieno sections. As copies of the Roman Lessons do not seem to survive in Spain, perhaps the New World cathedral chapter had some direct link with Spanish Rome. Jerusalem's extrovert gestures in the two F5/L1s, including the accompanied recitatives, seem to acknowledge pieces like S. Giacomo's repertory; distant parts of the Bourbons' world had surprisingly close connections in their Triduum music.

FROM EXEGESIS TO EMOTION

Despite this vitality of Triduum music across the Iberian world, the social difficulties of the ritual continued, and resulted in an affective move from penance to aesthetic melancholia. In 1766, Joaquín Castellot, the chaplain at the Encarnación in Madrid, published a translation of a French guide to the Week, which commented only on its "historical" meaning, hence the Passions and Mass readings, with no explication of the Tenebrae texts except for the allegory of the hearse.[19] Tomás de Iriarte's poem on the aesthetics and condition of the art, *La Música* (Madrid, 1779), treated sacred music in its third canto. After mentioning hymns, Masses, and motets and their various functions and affects, Iriarte gave his example of "sad" religious music:

> O lamentable, en fin, nos entristece, / Como en aquellos trenos del Profeta / Que de Sion la ruina compadece.[20]
> Or, lamenting, finally, [harmony] makes us sad, as in those laments of the Prophet who mourns the ruin of Zion.

Traditional strongholds also began to show the strains on Tenebrae. One prime example is the guide to Holy Week published in the century's last decades by the Cádiz canon Pedro Gómez Bueno, his *Semanero santo de seglares, en que se exponen los Oficios de Semana Santa.*[21] Although the cleric was based at the cathedral, his explanation seems to hold for Andalucian practice in general and is directed at clerics who needed to explain and manage the Holy Week ceremonies for a public evidently unfamiliar with the allegorical meanings of the rites. After a long explanation of the Seven Last Words ceremony held on Good Friday, Gómez drew attention only to the Miserere for his lay audience, and discounted any public understanding of the Lamentations and Psalms: "In the Days of Tenebrae, the psalm Miserere is sung at the end with much solemnity [there follows a vernacular translation for congregations to read during the polyphony] . . . and during Tenebrae, the faithful can read some pious meditations on the Passion of Christ, which will perhaps move them more than reading the psalms and Lamentations of the choir [i.e. canons and musicians], whose meaning they do not understand well."[22] Again, Gómez emphasized clearly penitential texts.

Still, Juan Domingo Vidal (1735–1808), chapelmaster at Cádiz Cathedral as the canon was writing, left some eleven Lessons in its archive, including a solo F6/L3 notable for its modulations inside verses.[23] And Gómez did allow for singing "una lamentación" or performing instrumental music in the Seven Words ceremony, after each Word, together with meditation.[24] Presumably his mention of "a lamentation" referred to settings of Office texts, with the audience left to place the prophet's words in relation to the Crucifixion. Although Haydn's *Seven Last Words of Christ* was commissioned by José Sáenz de Santamaria in 1786 for the Oratorio de la Santa Cueva chapel under the church of the Rosario in Cádiz, and not for the cathedral, still Gómez' comment suggests that such instrumental music was heard locally as substitutes for Lamentations.

The appeal of the purely affective traits of Jeremiah's text is evident in the free version (1772) of F5/L1 (no title nor Hebrew letters) by the most unlikely candidate in eighteenth-century Europe to write penitential music, Jean-Jacques Rousseau.[25] This was written in the latter phase of his activity as composer, as he looked back on his stage works and set French songs. Unsurprisingly, Rousseau's "Lesson" reacts immediately to individual words, as it switches from arioso to recitative in the middle of a phrase "et ipsa oppressa / amaritudine." Its seeming model is Leo's cycle, with an active bass line and unexpected shifts into recitative, along with soprano-bass octave passages ("facti sunt ei inimici") reminiscent of a similar passage in the SS/L2 of the Neapolitan pieces. The phrase also recalls Rousseau's own praise of the unison as the most harmonious interval.[26] But elsewhere, evidently unplanned parallel octaves ("Omnes amici eius") and fifths ("parvuli eius ducti sunt"), and uncertain handling of tonality (it starts on a first-inversion chord), mark it as an imitation of the Neapolitan repertory.

TONES AS ICONS AND ARTIFACTS

Given the diminishing presence of the Tone-6 recitation formula in composed polyphony after 1700, its revival around 1770 is all the more suggestive. In light of the sacrosanct nature of the tone in Germanic Catholicism, its structural use as a cantus firmus in the Adagio movement of Haydn's "Lamentation" symphony, no. 26 of 1767/68, has always been perceived as a kind of Passion symbolism, together with the Gospel reciting tone which had been heard in the secondary key/motivic area of the opening movement.[27] In the slow movement, Haydn placed both the letter and verse formulae in the second violins with counterpoint around them. The citation suggests a Lesson as an embedded text in the movement, one which not only symbolizes but also enacts both a ritual moment and Passion commemoration. But listening closely to the movement reveals, unsurprisingly, more ambiguity than simple reference. The projection of the tone emphasizes "letters" (table 8.1).

The most immediately audible feature of this movement for any 18th-century audience is that it starts with a "letter" gesture (*agfgf*) and *not* with an *fga* verse *initium*. It seems to be the only contemporary citation of the tone that begins thus. If we imagine it as a sign for a liturgical moment, this cannot be the opening Lesson of a Nocturne, because there is no musical signal for "Incipit" nor "De lamentatione." Furthermore, there are too many "letters" for the number of "verses": some fourteen if all the repeats are taken, as opposed to six or eight "verses." This numerical and hermeneutic surfeit of "letters" seems closer to a "Lesson" from ch. 3, with its repeated alphabet, and thus an indication of either F6/L3 (this is bolstered by the lack of a "title" in the movement) or SS/L1 (without its "De lamentatione" title). The symbolic centrality of the "letters" is audible at the beginning of the movement and at the theatrical moment at mm. 56–57, the only full *forte,* a seventh chord that presages the recapitulation inaugurated by a fuller scoring (the horn doubling of the cantus firmus in the violins).

The actual "verses" evoked depend on the parsing of the disjunction at m. 68, where the statement of the "verse" in the recapitulation that had begun at m. 61 is halted on the *mediatio aperta* pitch-class A. Harmonically, this coincides with a half-cadence on this pitch, again emphasizing the third relationship to the tonic. The tone begins again with a new *fga initium* back on F, in a structurally crucial echo of all the other third relationships in this symphony as a whole (and underscored by the *mezzo forte* dynamics).

TABLE 8.1.

Haydn, "Letters" (L) and "Verses" (V) in Symphony no. 26/ii

MM.	GESTURES	PITCH
1–16	L-V bipartite *mediatio/finalis*-L	F
17–23	interlude	to C
24–36	L-V bipartite *mediatio/finalis*	C :‖:
37–39	L	C
40–45	interlude	
46–48	L	B♭
50–52	L	F
53–57	interlude	to V/F, *forte* 7th chord
58–61	L	F, new counterpoint, tone + horn 1
61–67	V (?sub-verse [a]); *mediatio* half-cadence on A	F
68–80	V (?sub-verse [b] with new *initium*)	F :‖

To complicate the possible references, the eighteenth-century editions of the *Cantus ecclesiasticus* OHS chantbook circulating in German-speaking Catholicism usually do not employ a second *initium* for the single-phrase verses from ch. 3 or for the "Jerusalem" refrain. If m. 68, the last full statement of the chant tone, is meant to be a representation of the refrain, then the preceding fifth "verse" has been interrupted and telescoped into "Jerusalem, convertere." If the recapitulation starting at m. 61 is to symbolize a verse with two *initia*, then there is no refrain and hence not a complete "Lesson" in this movement. Since the second half of the Adagio was meant to be repeated, either we have a movement that represents three "verses" all repeated (the last interrupted) and a "Jerusalem" refrain, or a "Lesson" of four "verses" repeated, the last of which has two *initia*, and without a refrain. Neither of these possibilities line up, however, with the texts from ch. 3, both of which have nine verses.

One possible model here was the Lessons of Haydn's predecessor Georg Joseph Werner for the Esterhazy ensemble.[28] The cycle preserved in Budapest (anonymous copies from around 1790) uses the Tone-6 formula as a cantus firmus on different pitches, requiring a total of five singers with continuo, and obbligato instruments in some cases. Each SS Lesson is a solo piece with one of the lower voices (A, B, T), singing the recitation tone with instrumental counterpoint: respectively "viola amabile" (L1), two violins alternating pizzicato and bowing (L2), and the soprano lute known as the mandora (L3; alternatively a muted violin). The F5 and F6 Lessons use the tone in one voice with varied counterpoint in other vocal lines, normally without instruments. There are no added lines nor obbligato instruments in F5/L1 (the tone is sung by the alto), and so the chant formula's projection at the beginning of the Triduum was clear. An SAB group joins the tenor cantus firmus in the L2s of both Days, but only for the Hebrew letters and the "Jerusalem" refrain. The largest vocal scoring is in F5/L3, as two sopranos sing the entire text, one as a cantus firmus and one as counterpoint, with an ATB ensemble added in the letters and refrain. For F6/L1, the tone in one soprano is accompanied by SA and viola throughout the entire Lesson, and in F6/L3, two sopranos are used in the letters and refrain, with the complete text sung by the bass to the tone (example 8.3).

The princely vocal forces for church music were modest until mid-century, and two sopranos cannot be documented until 1754, joining an ATB ensemble.[29] The mandora player could have been a visitor from Vienna, but Werner used the "viola amabile" (possibly a viola d'amore) in Advent pieces from 1759, suggesting that this Lesson dates to around 1760.[30] It is possible that the pieces were not originally conceived as a cycle, but came about by accretion. Nonetheless, when the court's forces were divided in 1761 into church (Werner) and chamber (Haydn) groups, the Lessons could still have been performed by putting the two together.

Werner's set is an elaborate example in a wider tradition of concerted Lessons based on embellished tones, dating back to G. A. Bernabei's Munich cycle of 1716. But its relationship to Haydn's symphony is another matter: the instrumental counterpoint in violin I throughout the slow movement recalls the texture of the SS Lessons, not the F5–6 pieces, as the arpeggiated beginning of the mandora part in Werner's SS/L3 seems to anticipate the figuration of violin I in the symphony movement. If Haydn's work—probably composed in 1767–68—makes reference to these Lessons, it does so at a short temporal distance, perhaps a posthumous gesture after the older composer's death (3 March 1766).

In a wider sense, given the citation of the Passion tone in movement 1, the Tone-6 formula in Haydn's Adagio suggests a performance Day on which the Passion had been heard before the Lamentations, thus either Holy Wednesday or Good Friday. On purely devotional grounds, the latter seems more likely, and this correlates with the texture of cantus firmus vs. instruments in

EXAMPLE 8.3. Werner, F6/L3, "Aleph. Ego vir videns."

Werner's Lessons for SS. Ultimately, the neat heuristic identity between this Adagio and a given Lesson cannot be maintained; that is to say, the embedded text works as icon and not re-enactment. But the movement does set up the dramatic tension between "letters" and "verses," hinting at an ultimately cyclical process.

Citations of the tone later in the century are more straightforward; its use in the development section of Mozart's *Mauerische Trauermusik*, K. 477 (1785), seems simply to recall its function in noble funerals, as had been the case in Dresden in 1733. Beethoven's experiments in harmonizing it in Bonn before 1790, conveyed in the biographical anecdotes and notated in the "Kafka" sketchbook, go beyond the normal possibilities for accompanying a singer.[31] Here, the tone is given beginning on B♭ (it touches the leading-tone in the final cadence, and there is only one *initium*), with some ten complete harmonizations (eight for the letter gesture). As the formula recites inexorably on D, some of the chordal choices are remarkable (B minor, G major/minor, and even a C♭ sonority). In line with the eschewal of the organ in the Triduum, the sketchbook also refers to a knee pedal and thus a fortepiano as the accompanying instrument. Beethoven's exhaustive possibilities testify both to the ennui of church musicians having to accompany the fifty-seven iterations of the tone over the Triduum as well as to his own inventiveness.

Most devotionally and socially interesting is the citation of the chant formula at the opening of the second part of Carl Ditters von Dittersdorf's oratorio *Giob* (first performed in Vienna around Palm Sunday in 1786).[32] The suffering Job begins by singing a three-stanza song, eight lines each in *ottenari,* a loose paraphrase of his own book (7:3–7) in an appropriately nocturnal setting: "The day passes, and the dark [or "next"] night finds me still in suffering; and even if the night disperses the dark horrors, still the day finds me in pain" (example 8.4).[33] The chorus replies to each stanza of his song by asking his identity, learning it, and leaving him in his torments.[34] Job relates his degradation from human status by using the Lessons tone (at the same pitch as Beethoven) without the *initium,* reciting on D but harmonized in G minor. His complaint uses the *mediatio aperta* (here pitched on *cd*) for internal breaks, while lines four and eight of each stanza cadence vocally on B♭ harmonized on G minor. Dittersdorf thus combined the overall affect of a minor key with the Tone-6 formula conceived, in eighteenth-century terms, as being in major.

The oratorio as Passion music relies on the identification between the dolorous Old Testament figures (Job, Jeremiah) and Christ. Indeed, Job's closing recitative at the end of the piece prophecies the Savior's coming, discovering himself to be the "shadow of the future" and Christ a model of patience.[35] At the point of the tone's citation in the oratorio, though, Job is simply a suffering believer, and so the musical quotation evokes such first-person Lesson verses as F6/L3's "Ego vir videns." But the problems with allegory outside the Catholic world were evident at the Berlin performances of 1789 and 1791; a local, presumably Protestant, reviewer of the latter performance actually missed the citation of the tone, referring to Job's "heartwrenching" song as a "simple lamenting melody."[36]

RATIONAL TRIDUUM IN HABSBURG TUSCANY

Whatever the symbolism of the tones in central Europe, they also play a role in three extended Lessons "sopra lo stile corale" by G. G. Brunetti, Clari's successor after 1754 at Pisa Cathedral. Brunetti thus wrote his pieces in the changing devotional world of Austrian Tuscany. One source is dated 1786, although they might well stem from earlier.[37] Brunetti's Lessons (F5–6/L2 plus a Prayer) are for canto, canto/alto, and canto/alto/tenor with continuo plus two violas (and two flutes/recorders in the F5/L2); they seem to belong together and to eschew violins.[38] In the first two Lessons, the motivic use of the reciting tone involves only the *fga* initium (sometimes pitched on *c*) in the letters and at the beginning of verses, followed by florid vocal writing in modern style. Brunetti's Prayer employs a standard *Oratio* formula starting *fac* in the tenor ("parte fondamentale"), with counterpoint in the two upper

EXAMPLE 8.4. Dittersdorf, *Giob* (1786), "Passa il giorno."

voices and the instruments (example 8.5). This motive opens the title, vv. 1, 2, 4, 5, 6, 8, 9, and the refrain, while it closes vv. 3 and 10; thus its citation is partially symmetrical.

For all the gestures to chant, modernity is evident. V. 7, "Patres nostri peccaverunt," is set as an accompanied strophic recitative ("in stile recitativo, con variazione") without the tone, unmeasured ("senza obbligo di tempo"), as the lower voices echo, *sotto voce,* the affective declamation of the top line.

EXAMPLE 8.4. (*Continued*)

EXAMPLE 8.5. G. G. Brunetti, SS/L3, "Incipit oratio."

In the midst of ecclesiastical reform in Habsburg Tuscany, the signaling of the chant recalls the dynasty's interaction with the formulae dating back to Mahu's cycle in the 16th century. Thus the symbolic power of the tone was evident even in late Catholic absolutism. On a more "popular" level, three anonymous printed Lessons (F5/L1, F6-SS/L3) meant for use in Pistoia are simple harmonizations (SATB) of the formula, a far cry from the earlier Lessons of Clari.[39] These seem typical of the simplifications carried out in church life by the city's famed Quietist bishop Scipione de' Ricci, as they date (1786) to his tenure.

Carlo Antonio Campion's service to the Habsburg chapel of Florence ran from the early 1760s until his death in 1788. His Responsories were produced for this ensemble in the context of radical updatings of devotion and ecclesiastical practice in Tuscany.[40] The set for all three Days, along with *alternatim* Lauds items, was evidently originally written for an all-male scoring of TTTB plus continuo, perhaps in the late 1760s; this original sonority is preserved in the copies made for Vienna and held in Marie Therese of Austria's collection (now A-Wn), while the Lauds works are in I-Fc. In the Lents of 1781/82, Campion returned to his Responsories, rescoring them for a normal SATB ensemble and adding timings; these are transmitted in autograph (I-Fc, the basis for this discussion) as well as in other copies for the Viennese court chapel (A-Wn).[41] Given the diminishing profile of sacred music in Florence during the 1780s, it is not clear if the reworkings were actually used in Tuscany, and the rescoring may have been an effort to make them available to Vienna.

Campion's efforts were only part of a larger refashioning of Triduum repertory, which had begun even before Leopold's arrival in 1765. The first stage in this was the copying of Viennese court pieces into the holdings of Florence and Pisa Cathedrals, including a rapid reproduction of Georg Reutter Jr.'s

1753 Responsories (originally intended for Vienna as a replacement for Ingegneri's set) in Pisa in 1759.[42] In combination with Lessons like Brunetti's,
Holy Week music in the Grand Duchy was being renewed in line with enlightened piety; Campion also set Mass items for the Week, a Passion, and
pieces for the Easter Vigil in 1767.[43] Notably, he eschewed new Lessons, in
line with the traditional Austrian reluctance to have anything but chant or
Renaissance polyphony for Lamentations.

Whichever version of Campion's Responsories the Habsburgs in various places might have heard, the new approach of the composer is evident in
the opening declamation of F5/R1, set clearly in D major as a *forte* tutti: "In
monte, in monte Oliveti, oravit, oravit ad Patrem [*sotto voce* and then solo
voices:] oravit ad Patrem, oravit: [solo top line:] 'Pater, Pater, si fieri potest, si
fieri potest [*un poco forte*] transeat ad me calix iste' [tutti, *sotto voce:*] oravit, oravit ad Patrem, 'transeat . . . ,' oravit ad Patrem" (example 8.6). Campion's doubled *epizeuxis* (partial repetitions) and parallelisms override the
strict declamation of the liturgical text in the interest of setting up a dramatic
scena in Gethsemane. They first emphasize "praying" and then fade the scene
out, in an almost cinematographic way, via the *sotto voce* indication and the
reduction to soloists. The fade-out gives way to Christ's words, set for solo
voice and emphasizing "let this chalice pass from Me." In the first iteration of
the repetendum, the "infirmity" of "caro autem infirma" is represented by a
diatonic descent winding up on F♯ minor, and "fiat voluntas tua" closes this
section as a duet of the uppermost and lowest voices, probably symbolizing
the union of Christ's two natures in this final resignation to His Father's will.

The opening of the verse, "Vigilate et orate," begins as a solo, but then
its initial phrase of "watch and pray" migrates through individual voices, in
counterpoint to other parts declaiming the rest of the text, "ut non intretis
in tentationem." Like an emblem, the single word "Vigilate" actually concludes the declamation of the verse before the return to the repetendum. In
the repeat of the B section, Campion recomposed the original duet version
of "fiat voluntas tua" completely, setting it for four-voice tutti, and ending
the entire Responsory with yet another *sotto voce* statement of "oravit ad
Patrem." Thus the liturgical text was framed as Christ's prayer.

The cycle's weight is evident in this Responsory's length, as Campion
noted that the whole piece was to take six minutes. Among other contemporary sets, the versions of *In monte Oliveti* by Gennaro Manna (Naples,
1741) and Michael Haydn (Salzburg, 1778) both come in at under two minutes, and repeat no text, the approach also of Reutter's R1 copied in Pisa a
few years before.[44] Campion's textual freedom conveys the dramatic staging
of the scene and the imperatives of Christ's commands, addressed both to
the Apostles and, metaphorically, to the noble community of belief that was

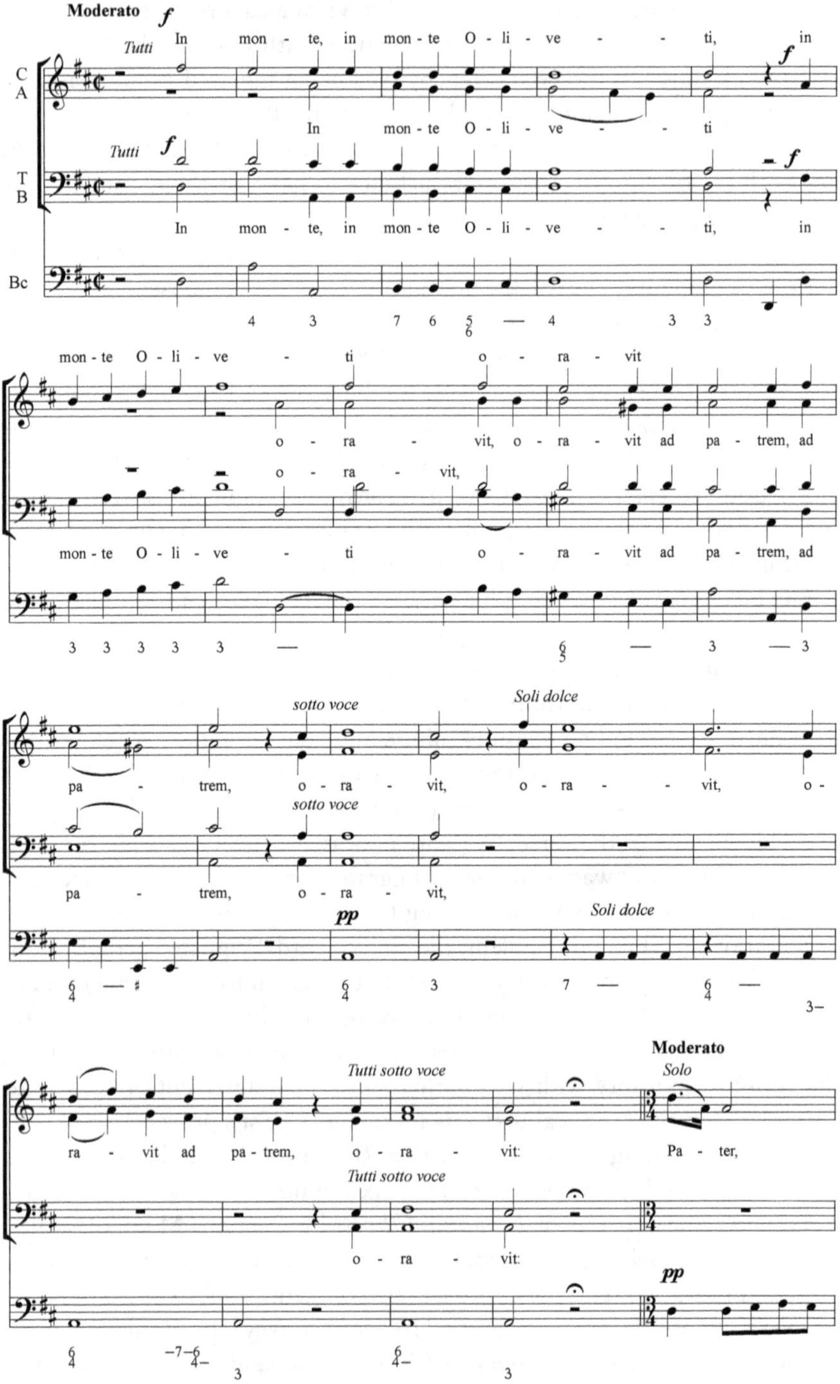

Example 8.6. Campion, F5/R1, "In monte Oliveti."

the primary audience of the settings in Tuscany and Vienna. He thus created imaginable Passion meditation for his court audience via polyphony.

The various travelers' accounts of Tenebrae in the Capella Sistina, from the 1770s onward, focus on the "ancient" repertory, increasingly the Misereres of Allegri and Tommaso Baj. But in some Italian cities new composition continued apace even after the social shocks of the 1790s and into the Restoration: the Lessons of J. S. Mayr for Bergamo, the Matins items of Saverio Mercadante for Novara in the early Ottocento, or those of later members of the Puccini family for Lucca. In mid-nineteenth-century Teramo, Matins were followed by the Good Friday funeral march of the city, using the same wooden clappers that had inaugurated the Office. As in many places, the *Stabat Mater* was sung in the procession.[45]

In north Italy, the last major example of new Triduum music is the five Lessons for Bergamo's S. Maria Maggiore by Amilcare Ponchielli (1885; op. 22–26, three for F5 and two for F6), completed just before his death for services that he never heard, at a time when new composition had dried up elsewhere.[46] In early nineteenth-century France and Austria, simple harmonizations of the Lamentations were issued for widespread use together with the other Office and Mass items, notably by Sigismond von Neukomm in Paris and Josef Preindl in Vienna.[47] In Habsburg lands, the ritual activity around the Office had had a hard time surviving the six thousand restrictions on Passion devotion issued by Joseph II in 1780–83.

But certainly in the Ibero-American world the traditions continued. Manuel Doyague Jimenez' Lessons with orchestra for Salamanca, written between 1804–33, made it all the way to Manila Cathedral. In a more popular vein, unspecified Lamentations were recited and sung in parts of Luzon during Lent.[48] Marcos Portugal wrote a Responsory cycle using the six organs of the monastery of Mafra (P-Mp) in 1807, while an 1839 copy of F5 Responsories with orchestra is attributed to José Mauricio Nunes Garcia, presumably for the court in Rio de Janeiro. Both composers wrote Triduum Misereres.[49]

An account reflecting the late nineteenth century in the Catalonian city of Tortosa records large numbers of townspeople crowding into the cathedral in order to hear Lamentations settings by the cathedral masters. Here, children of the town waited for the choir to sing the final words of the Miserere before beginning the loud *strepitus,* "els fassos."[50] According to local accounts, the candles represented the apostles and Mary, and the *strepitus* the earthquake at the Crucifixion, while in a modern vein, the single remaining candle was imagined as speaking in the voice of the Addolorata. It was for this community that the young Felip Pedrell in 1869 would compose three

Lessons, four decades before he would edit Victoria's OHS for modern use. Tortosa's practices were dying out by the 1920s; still, new Lessons were written for Valencia Cathedral into the 1940s by Eduardo Soler Pérez.

The evidently nineteenth-century reinterpretation of Tenebrae by the penitent confraternities of former northern Mexico as "las tinieblas" involved some traditional symbols and ritual action, for instance the hearse and the exaltation of the *strepitus* into multiple self-flagellations. Although the ethnographic work was necessarily fragmentary, the songs connected to the practice were in the vernacular and seem not to have paraphrased Lamentations or Responsories; their actual musical content is also unclear.[51]

In Italy, recordings of popular musical traditions in Triduum ritual have shown fragments of the Office transmitted in oral tradition, with the Miserere sung widely across the peninsula, along with occasional Responsories.[52] Lamentations verses in Latin, based on the Tone-6 formula in local tradition, were recorded by Giorgio Nataletti in the village of Bortigiadas (near Sassari) in 1950, sung by a soloist answered by a male vocal quintet, and similarly in Capoliveri on Elba as late as 1962. Other post-1950 field samples include a monophonic Lesson, also on the tone, from a singer in a small town in Istria, featuring a repetition of the "Jerusalem" refrain in Croatian. And a Lamentation with a soloist and harmonium from Sessa Aurunca (Caserta) mixes the chant *initium* at the beginning of verses with nineteenth-century operatic flourishes that close them, rather as if the twentieth-century singer was continuing an oral practice in which townspeople imitated the two kinds of music that they heard in the services as a whole.[53]

As in Sessa Aurunca today, Tenebrae practice is alive through communities' choice. Recent fieldwork in a number of towns in Corsica has testified to confraternity members' performance of an Office, still largely in Latin, with a hearse, psalms and Lamentations verses.[54] In Speloncato, a solo intonation is generally followed by three-part polyphony (*in paghjella*) for Lamentations verses, in which an ornamented chant tone is in the middle (*sigonda*) line; the singers emphasize their renewal of local traditions and even their study of a Benedictus recorded in previous fieldwork as their musical inspiration. In Calvi, solo singers of Lamentations verses use microtones, and report special affect in performing the Hebrew letters according to a polyphonic formula; in addition, the three local confraternities give special attention to singing the Benedictus at Lauds. Overall, as Ignazio Macchiarella puts it, "Rather than a series of pieces understood as 'discrete musical objects,' the Office is a mechanism to sing texts on the basis of recognizing a few musical schemas and the performance situation"—a description recalling both De Martino's lamenters and the traditions of improvised Tenebrae into the seventeenth century. Also recently in Brazil's Ouro Preto, Triduum Office traditions have been partially revived and partially reshaped by confraternity members.[55] Among other works, they perform late eighteenth-century pieces such as Manuel Dias de Oliviera's Miserere with orchestra.

Still, ethnography preserves more traditional Misereres than Lesson fragments. The preponderance of the psalm points to the situation that Gómez had identified in eighteenth-century Cádiz: the allegorical texts as more distant from a community that no longer understood the symbolism, and the emphasis on penance in Psalm 50 and the direct words of Christ from the Passion narration in the Responsories. Hence the musical forms followed the changes in piety.

RITUAL, DEVOTION, SIGNIFICATION

But in terms of social meaning, the trajectory of Tenebrae over two centuries marks a path more complex than a simple progression from "communities of belief" in Vergerio's time to "religious publics" in the eighteenth century. Clearly the "liminal" aspects of sixteenth-century ritual were tempered over the early modern era through the aristocratization of the complex music, as transcendent or demonic agency in the Hours gave way to affect and melancholy, just as improvisation was slowly replaced by fixed repertory. This trend also muted the obvious disjunction between the gruesome texts and the sheer beauty of the polyphony. But the words/music served for a very long time—indeed, for Iberian and Latin American elites, into the nineteenth century—as a vehicle for combining Passion and penitential sentiment, even when the classical exegeses of Jeremiah had been forgotten. In different situations, the Triduum expressed personal mourning, penance, and even exequies, and the Office music was a very specific part with its own cultural valence. It was a textually and ritually based social activity. Many of the norms that seemed absolute—e.g., the projection of the texts by only male singers—were actually variable or contested according to situation. That is, they retained their "illocutive" sense, and their enactment, if not entirely "performative," was a necessary part of the Week's action, symbolized by tears.

Similarly, the devotional literature shines only a partial, if important, light on the musical repertory. In certain moments—e.g., the mystical meaning of "shadows" in the seventeenth century—it provides a frame of reference for community understanding of what was sung. The proximity of Lessons to theater—in Calderón's plays, or the applause for nuns singing the Office, but also Ottoboni's oratorios and Jommelli's Lessons—was not entirely a sign of secularization, but rather the changing media for Passion devotion. The marginalization of the Benedictus, losing ground to the Miserere, is a further sign of allegory's decline.

Finally, if there were one ritual practice in Catholicism to which the music centrally mattered, Tenebrae had a good claim to that status. Even the chant—whichever liturgical genre it projected, east or west—carried enormous symbolic weight. Without music, the Hours would have retreated over the course of early modernity to the periphery of collective consciousness, but their sonic component—conservative or innovative—kept them as a central expressive moment. The tension between received tradition and aesthetically modern styles in the polyphony continued to give a charge to the ritual, and in that sense the flavors of Tenebrae after 1550 were most apparent in its music.

Appendix

TABLE I.
Roman Lamentation verse selection, 1568–1601; chapter numbers in Roman numerals are valid horizontally until changed; sub-verses given; "nl"=no Hebrew letter

	F5/L1	2	3	F6/1	2	3	SS/1	2	3
1568 Breviary	I:1–6	7–11	12–16	II:8–12	13–18	III:1–12	III:22–33	IV:1–7	V:1–16
1572 OHS	I:1–5	6–9	10–14	II:8–11	12–15	III:1–9	III:22–30	IV:1–5	V:1–11
Matelart	I:1–2	7–8	12–13	II:8–9	11–13	III:1–6	III:22–26	IV:1–4	V:1–5
Palestrina 1	I:1–2	6–7	10–12	II:8–9ab	12–13	III:1–4	III:22–25	IV:1–3	V:1–5
Palestrina 3	I:1–2	6–8	10–12	II:8–9	12–14	III:1–4	III:22–25	IV:1–3	V:1–8
Palestrina 4	I:1–2	6–8a	10–12	II:8–10	12–14	III:1–3	III:22–25	IV:1–3	V:1–5
Victoria CS186	I:1–2a	6,8a	10–11	II:8–9ab	12ab–13ab	III: 1–3	III:22, 25, 27	IV:1–2	V:1–5
Victoria 1585	I:1–2a	6	10–11	II:8	12ab–13ab	III:1–2	III:22, 27	IV:1–2	V:1–5
RomeSG58	I:1–2	6–7	10–12	II:8–10	12–14	III:1–6	III:22–27	IV:1–3	V:1–8
RomeBN77–88	I:1–2	6–8	10,12,14	II:8–9	12,13,15	III:1–6nl	III:22–25	IV: 1–3	V:1–7, 21
RomeSG87	I:1–2	6–7	10–12	II:8–10	12–15	III:1–5	III:22–26	IV: 1–3	V:1–4
RomeSG88	I:1–2	6–7	10–12	II:8–9	12–13	III:1–5	III:22–26	IV:1–3	V:1–6
Nanino (CapGiul)	I:1–2	6–7	10–11	II:8–9	12–13	III:1–2	III:22–23	IV:1–2	V:1–4
Giacobetti 1601	I:1	6	10	II:8	12	III:1–2	III:22–23	IV:1	V:1–3
Raval 1593	I:1–4	6–7b	10–12	II:8–11	12–13	III:1–9	III:22–27	IV:1–6	V:1–11
Cavalieri 1	I:1–3	6–8	10–12	II:8, 11	12–14	III:1–3, 6, 8	III: 22–24	IV:1–3	V:1–3

TABLE 2.
Modality in selected Lamentations cycles

	F5/L1	L2	L3	F6/L1	L2	L3	SS/L1	L2	L3
Carpentras 1532	6tr	6	3	6tr	2/1tr	2tr	4/3	1	2
Mahu/LaRue	6	6	6	6	6	6	6	6	4
Bivi 1546	2tr	2tr	2tr	1	1	1	6	9tr	9tr
I-PC3 cycle 1*	3	3	3	1tr	1tr	1tr	6	6	-
I-PC3 cycle 2*	6	6	6	1	1	1	4	4	4
Szamthuly 1553	6	6	6	2tr	6	6	6	6	4
Lattre 1554	6	6	6	6	6	6	6	6	6
Hollander	1	6/5	6	3	6/5	3	1tr	6	3
Nasco 1561	6	6/5	6/5	9tr	9tr	9tr	3	3	3
Contino 1561	2tr	2tr	2tr	4	4	4	2tr	2tr	6, 4
P. Ferrarese 1565 *a* 2	1	1	1	1	1	1	1	1	1
P. Ferrarese 1565 *a* 3	2	2	2	2	2	2	2	2	2
Jacquet 1567	5	5	5	5	5	5	5	5	6
Palestrina 1	6	6	6	6	4	1tr	4	3	6
Palestrina 3	5	1	12	2tr	3	1tr	9	7	5
Palestrina 4	6	3	4tr	6	1	3	8	12	6
Alcarotto 1570	2tr	2tr	2tr	10+	10+	10+	2tr	2tr	2tr
Isnardi 1572	2tr	2tr	2tr	3	3	3	6	6	2tr

MunBS 2747	6	6	6	3/4	3/4	1	1tr	1tr	1tr
Lasso 1585	3/4tr	3/4tr	3/4tr	3/4	3/4	3/4	7	8	5
Lasso *a 4*	6	6	6	4	1tr	4	2tr	8	7
Porta *a 5*	3	3	3	3	3	3	3	3	3
Falconio 1580	6	6	6	2tr	2tr	2tr	3	3	3
Asola 1584	6	6	6	4	4	4	2	2	2
Isnardi 1584	6	6	6	3	3	3	2tr	2tr	2/8tr
Victoria 1585	5	2tr	4	12	6	2	5	4	2
Varotto 1587	3/4	3/4	3/4	2tr	2tr	2tr	3/4	3/4	3/4
Handl 1587	5	5	3/4	5	4	5	2tr	11	4
Monte	1	1	1	2	2	2	3	3	4
Contino 1588	1tr	8	4tr	3	3	3	3	5	9tr,11tr
Guami 1588	10	10	10	2tr	2tr	2tr	5	5	2tr
Ingegneri 1588	2tr	2tr	2tr	4	4	4	2tr	2tr	1
Gubbio cycle 1	4tr	4tr	4tr	8	8	8	2tr	2tr	2tr
Gubbio cycle 2	5	5	5	4	4	4	4	4	4
RomeBN 77	6	4/3	6	6	1tr	3	3	6tr	7
RomeSG58	6	2	2tr	3	1tr	2	6	2tr	3
Nanino	11	11	11	2tr	2tr	2tr	11	3	8
RomeSG87	6	2	1tr	2tr	3	3	8	8	8
RomeSG88	6	2tr	3	4	2tr	2tr	2tr	8	2tr

Continued on the next page

	F5/L1	L2	L3	F6/L1	L2	L3	SS/L1	L2	L3
Matelart	6	2tr	6	3	3	8	1tr	1tr	1tr
Dentice 1593	1	1	1	2tr	2/1tr	2/1tr	3	3	3
Chiaula 1597	1	1	1	4	4	4	7	7	7
Magri 1597	6	2tr	2tr	3	3	3	6/5	5	6/5
Cavalieri cycle 1	2tr-10	10	10	2tr	2tr	8	8-2tr	2tr-10	4-10
Massaino 1599	1	1	1	2tr	2tr	2tr	3	3	3
BarcOC11a	6	6	6	6	3/4	10,1tr	6	3	6
Buonavita 1600	6	6	6	6	6	6	2tr	2tr	2tr
Giacobetti 1601	9tr	9tr	9tr	9tr	9tr	9tr	9tr	9tr	9tr
Montella 1602	2tr	2tr	2tr	1	1	1	2tr	2tr	2tr
Cantone 1603	1	1	1	2tr	2tr	2tr	4	4	4
Croce 1603	2tr	2tr	2tr	9	9	9	3/4	3/4	3/4
Luython 1604	1	1	1	2tr	2tr	2tr	3	3	3
Rimonte 1607	2tr	1tr	6	9(4)	8	10(3)	10(3)	8	2
Pujol BarcBC	4	9	5	4	9	1	4	5	-
Mogavero 1623	6	6	6	1tr	1tr	1tr	3	3	3

+ = frequent B♭s in Alcarotto suggest Mode 4tr without a notated flat; *Piacenza cycles incomplete

NB: Nasco = Spoleto 2; Dragoni/SGL 87 = Spoleto 1 (with attributions to Palestrina)

TABLE 3.
OHS contents, 1544–1603

	LESSONS	RESPONSORIES	BDDI/ANT	MISERERE	PASSION	PS	F5	F6
*Bivi 1544/46	9	27			1			
Contino 1561	10	9 (Noct III)	3	3	2			
Ferrarese 1565	19	27	3+2fb	3+2fb	4	3	14	7
FlorSL N/2	19	10	5					
MunBS2747	9	9(I)	1					
TrevBC38	7	27			2			
Alcarotto 1570	9	27	1+6fb/3	3+6fb				
Canale 1579	9	27	3/3	3fb	2			
*Falconio 1580	9	27	3	2	4			
*Asola 1583/4	9	27	1/3	1	4		1	4
Victoria 1585	9	18 (II/III)	1	1	2	1		2
*Ingegneri 1588	9	27	1	1				1
Contino 1588	11	9 (III)	3	3	2			
RomeBN77-88	9	18 (II/III)	4	7				
Cavalieri	15	9 (III)						
PistAC215	10	27	3†	5†	2	3		
Dentice 1593	9	18 (II/III)	2/3	3fb				

Continued on the next page

	LESSONS	RESPONSORIES	BDDI/ANT	MISERERE	PASSION	PS	F5	F6
Chiaula 1597	9	18 (II/III)	1	1				
*Massaino 1599/1609	9	27	3/3	3	2			
Giacobetti 1601	9	27			2			
*Montella 1602	9	27	1	1				4
Cantone 1603	9	18(II/III)	3	3	2		5	1

Lam = Lamentations; Resp = Responsories; BDDI = Benedictus Dominus Deus Israel; Ant = BDDI Antiphons; Mis = Miserere; Pass = Passions; PS = items for Palm Sunday; F5 = items for Holy Thursday; F6 = other items for Good Friday. Roman numerals in the Responsories column indicate the Nocturne(s) set. Multiple single prints are marked (*); Fb = settings in *falsobordone*.

TABLE 4.
Northern European Lesson texts and *breviaries*

	F5/L1	L2	L3	F6/L1	L2	L3	SS/L1	L2	L3
Mahu	P, I:1–3	I:4,6,5	I:11; IV:10; II:12	I:12, 15ab, 18bc	I:17; II:15; I:16	IV:11, 13; II:14	IV: 14, 15, 12	III: 41–42, 21–27	V:1–6
Szamtfuly 1553	P, I:1–3	I:4–6	I:8–11	III:1–9	III:10–18	III:25–36	IV:1–5	IV:7–11	V:1–10
Lattre 1554	I:1–3	I:4–5	[I:6–7]^	II:13–14	II:15–16	[II:17–18]^	III:64	IV:3,5,6	IV:7,9,10
MunBS 2747	I:1–2	I:10–12	I:20–21	II:8–9	II:15–18	III:1–2, 14, 11	III:21–22, 40	III:41, 46, 48	V:1–6
BrevR1568	I:1–6	I:7–11	I:12–16	II:8–12	II:13–18	III:1–12	III:22–33	IV:1–7	V:1–16
Lasso *a* 4	I:1–6	I:7–11	I:12–16	II:8–12	II:13–18	III:1–12	III:22–33	IV:1–7	V:1–16
Lasso *a* 5	I:1–3	I:7–9	I:12–14	II:8–10	II:13–15	III:1–2, 4–5, 7, 9	III:22–23, 25–30	IV:1–3	V:1–6
OHS1572	I:1–5	I:6–9	I:10–14	II:8–11	II:12–15	III:1–9	III:22–30	IV:1–6	V:1–11
Hollander	I:1–2	I:4–5, 6c	I:7–8a	I:6ab, 9,*	I:12–13	I:17–19*	III:1–2, 4	III:5, 3	IV:1, 3
Monte	I:1–3	I:6–8	I:10–12	II:8–9, 11	II:12–13, 15	III:1–6	III:22–30	IV:1–3	V:1–7
Handl1587	P, I:1–3	I:4–6	I:7–9	III:1–9~	III:10–11, 13–16, 18, 17, 19–21~	III:25–33~	IV:1–5	IV:12–16	V:1–8
PragueBrev1502	P, I:1–3	I:4–6	I:7–8	III:1–9~	III:10–21~	III:25–33*	IV:1–5	IV:12–15	V:1–12
Luython1603	I:1–2	I:4–5	I:11–12	III:40–42	III:49–51	III:55–57	IV:19–20	IV:21–22	V:1–5

P = Preface ("Et factum est . . .") included; ^ = 2 Lessons reversed; * = "wrong" letters; ~ = missing letters. There are no F6/SS titles in Hollander. This table is arranged so as to show possible textual sources, and not chronologically. The breviaries are: *Breviarium Romanum* (Rome, 1568 = Pian); *Officium hebdomadae sanctae* (Rome, 1572); and *Breviarium pragensis* (Nuremberg, 1502).

Notes

1. Symbolic Meanings, Sonic Penance

1. I thus omit long discussions of the following: Mass and processions on Palm Sunday; Thursday's commemoration of the Eucharist's institution (Mass, the Mandatum [Washing of Feet] and the Blessing of Oils); the Adoration of the Cross (including the Improperia, Christ's reproaches) on Friday; and the Easter Vigil. The Gospel Passions, sung at Mass on Sunday (Matthew), Tuesday (Mark), Wednesday (Luke), and Friday (John), are the best-known music not included here.

2. Matins/Lauds were returned to the middle of the appropriate night by Pius XII in 1955.

3. De Martino, *Morte e pianto rituale,* 64–65.

4. *Caeremoniale episcoporum* (1600), Bk. II, ch. 22, 222–26.

5. Most sixteenth-century settings, both of the canticle and of Psalm 50, alternate polyphonic verses with those chanted to a psalm-tone (*alternatim* practice); as a result, the polyphony for the Benedictus sometimes begins with the second half of the first verse "quia visitavit" and sets the odd-numbered verses. In other cases, the second verse "Et erexit" and the following even-numbered verses were polyphonic.

6. The standard study of practical and liturgical light in the Office is MacGregor, *Fire and Light,* 5–132.

7. E.g., one Italian breviary just before the major liturgical reforms specified "altius" for the repeat of the Miserere (*Breviarium romanum* [Venice: Giunta, 1562], fo. 154).

8. For Holy Week theatricality see Bernardi, *La drammaturgia,* 61–63.

9. Sehling, *Die evangelischen Kirchenordnungen,* vol. 17, pt. 2, 418.

10. Synodal restrictions on the *strepitus* are found in Corrain/Zampini, *Documenti etnografici,* 43, 88, 98, 153, 237, and 392.

11. *Den dienst van de Goede ende Paesch-Week* (1712), f. xx.

12. Artocchini, *Il folklore piacentino,* 52.

13. Ricci, "Sacre fonosfere."

14. The modern eds. are Davril/Thibodeau (eds.), *Guillelmi Dvranti Rationale Divinorum Officiorvm* and Douteil (ed.), *Johannis Beletii Summa.*

15. Timoteo, *In divinum officium, quaestiones* LX and LXIV, ff. 71v ff.

16. Pisa, Archivio Capitolare, Fondo Liturgico, C174–177, the anonymous "De antiquiis primatialis Ecclesiae Pisanae ritibus," takes up Durandus and Beleth in its discussion of the Triduum.

17. Durandus, *Rationale,* 335–345.

18. "Exequies" are found in Rupert of Deutz's *Liber de divinis officiis,* and Gavanti expressed it clearly: "In Horis Canonicis hujus tridui celebramus Exequias triduas mor-

tis Christi" (Part VI, ch. 13); I cite from an edition with Gaetano Merati's Settecento glosses: B. Gavanti, *Thesaurus sacrorum rituum* (1823), 234–235.

19. G. F. Haas's structurally aleatoric String Quartet no. 3 (Vienna, 2001), to be played memorized and in complete darkness, takes its subtitle from the liturgical rubric, "In iij Noct." of Carlo Gesualdo's setting of F5/R7, *Eram quasi agnus,* whose opening it cites as one of its sections; the title evidently comes from the rubric of the original print, *Responsoria et alia ad Officium Hebdomadae Sanctae spectantia* (1611) in the edition of Watkins, Gesualdo, *Sämtliche Werke,* vol. 7. Osvaldo Golijov's *Tenebrae* (2002) uses Couperin's F5/L3.

20. For the cultural and social meanings of early modern night, Koslofsky, *Evening's Empire.*

21. MacGregor's table (*Fire and Light,* 114) turned up only two medieval sources (from Poitiers and Gembloux) and two eighteenth-century testimonies (Angers and Auxerre) in which candles were extinguished in conjunction with the Lamentations Lessons—even in sites with more than fifteen candles.

22. I follow Snow, *A New-World Collection,* 45ff., in assuming that the Miserere was sung polyphonically only at its repeat at the end of Lauds, not at its first iteration at the beginning of the Hour.

23. Lasso's music for Lauds together with his Responsories for Nocturnes II and III, is in P. Bergquist (ed.), Lasso, *Sämtliche Werke, Neue Reihe* 24.

24. E.g., the Miserere (274 breves) compared to the first Benedictus *tertii toni* (190 breves).

25. Unsigned preface dated 1 May 1565 to Paolo Ferrarese, *Passiones, Lamentationes, Responsoria . . .* (Venice: Scotto, 1565). Since the anonymous writer refers to his having just published Isidoro Chiari's sermons, whose dedication Guidi had signed on 24 April, I have elsewhere identified him with the monk-poet ("Riflessioni sulla sorte"). Parts of this citation open the standard article on text selection and word-painting in Italian Lamentations, Bettley, "La composizione lacrimosa." The edition is also well-known since Agee's discovery of its privilege and its printing contract between Guidi and Scotto ("A Venetian Music Printing Contract"); see also Bernstein, *Music Printing,* 666–670.

26. From the annual letter of Alcaraz to the Jesuit college in Salamanca, written from Cochin on 31 Jan 1566, recounting the previous year's voyage in Wicki (ed.), *Documenta Indica VI,* 769.

27. Vergerio, *Operetta nuova,* pp. xxxii–xxxix.

28. Maggi, *Satan's Rhetoric,* esp. 35–37 (Prierio), 56–59 and 71–73 (de Moura). The latter was an inquisitor in Évora. Given the anti-Judaism of some Holy Week ritual (see below), the latter's attribution of evil *ensalmi* to Jews makes another sinister association with the "distortion" of Lamentations passages when heard in "bad" polyphony.

29. For all this, see the *Documenta Indica:* for music on ships, *DI* 3, p. 74; *DI* 5, p. 219; *DI* 9, p. 458. For Tenebrae on the South Asian missions and at Lahore as cited here, see *DI* 6, p. 113 (the first unambiguous reference to Holy Week polyphony in the Jesuit center of Goa, "Os oficios da semana santa forã qua mui celebrados, não faltando pera eles coro e cantores dos mais escolhidos que na terra se acherão"); *DI* 8, p. 291; *DI* 9, p. 547; *DI* 12, p. 154; *DI* 18, p. 543. By general consensus, in colonial situations, "canto de órgano/canto d'orgão" meant improvised polyphony like *falsobordone* (Woodfield, *English Musicians,* 227).

30. This can be inferred from the lack of music in the accounts of Holy Week in the 1550s and 1560s; see *Cartas que os Padres* (1598), pt. 1, f. 79v (1560) or f. 101v (1562).

31. Radole, "Musica e musicisti in Istria," at 189.

32. For this idea in Guidi's dedication, Bettley, "La composizione"; on Alcaraz's ship it seems unlikely that anyone was reading from written parts; and Vergerio's account, with its "folk" instruments joining in to the music, also seems to refer to improvisation.

33. *Officium hebdomadae sanctae* (1572), with F5 Matins at f. 24v.

34. Thus F5/L1 went from {1:1–6} to {1:1–5} so that that the verse 1:6 "Vau. Et egressus est . . ." was deleted from the first Lesson and moved back to begin L2, while F6/L2 was reduced from {2:13–18} to {2: 12–15}.

35. "Poi non posso più, forzato dal debito dell'Ufficio, et carica che ho da N. S. da Bibliothecario sarò escusato," letter to Vincenzo Navarra, I-Rvat, Vat. lat. 6946, f. 180v.

36. The 1572 breviary has the new readings at ff. 181v–187, whereas a deluxe 1570 folio ed. had retained the 1568 verse selection (I use the copies in I-Ma). Most later editions (e.g., *Breviarium romanum* [1574], f. 160v) give the new readings silently.

37. For concordances between north Italian Lessons and the liturgical prints, see Bettley, "La composizione lacrimosa."

38. The best explanation of the structure is Levin's entry, *Religion in Past and Present* 7, 311–12.

39. Stäblein, "Lamentatio," *MGG*, 8: col. 138.

40. For the formulae, see Stäblein, *ibid.*, and for their use in Lessons by Marc-Antoine Charpentier, Käser, *Die Leçons de Ténèbres*, 34–46.

41. Kubieniec, "Lamentacje Chorałowe."

42. Id., "Treny Jeremiasza," citing the *Agenda seu ritus ceremoniarium . . . regni Poloniae usum* (Cracow, 1591/2).

43. Hardie, *The Lamentations of Jeremiah*; ead., "Lamentations in Spanish sources."

44. Copies are found in E-Vac, Bbc and Zac.

45. Noone, *Music and Musicians*, 223–226, describes its contents, and Schwartz, "En busca de liberalidad," 577–578, notes changes to it.

46. Banchieri, *Direttorio*, p. 281.

47. For the dedication, the unofficial nature, and sometimes drastic changes from previous norms in Guidetti's books, see Molitor, *Die nachtridentinische Choralreform* vol. 2, 1–7.

48. For the use of the book at the Catholic court of Dresden until the 1860s, Fürstenau, *Geschichte der Musik*, 41.

49. The cataloguing of the printed sixteenth- and seventeenth-century repertory is owed to Cramer, "Music for the Holy Week Liturgy," and Kurtzman, "Italian Music for Holy Week." Recently Stanley Boorman announced the discovery of a new (incomplete) set of Lamentations by Philippe de Monte preserved in a Bohemian manuscript ("A New Source"). One comprehensive if occasionally uncritical Web site for Lamentations is www.lamentations.lesourd.eu, accessed 18 August 2011).

50. *Responsoria omnia* (1570–71). On Florentine Responsories and their musical context, the classic works are the essays now in D'Accone, *Music and Musicians and Music in Renaissance Florence*.

51. Reynaud, *La polyphonie tolédane,* 318–319 and Ramos López, *La música en la catedral de Granada,* 1:104.

52. On the Week's repertory as a whole in Mexico City, Marín López, *Los libros de polifonía,* 1: 62–69.

53. Rimonte's cycle has now been published from the almost complete choirbook (ed. Izquierdo/Margules, *Lamentationes Hieremiae Profetae sex vocum*). Pujol's two Lessons in OC 11altre are taken from the complete cycle in E-Bbc M.1623 (with two verses omitted in one setting).

54. The extract from Bonatti's letter of 14 April 1604 is in Veronelli, "Strategie politiche," at 399. For the "musique si douce et armonieuse qu'elle nous rauissoit tous" that Joly experienced in Valladolid, see Barrau-Dihigo, "Voyage de Barthélemy Joly," at 557.

55. My discussion is indebted to Nirenberg, *Communities of Violence,* 200–230. For the concept of Jewish music as "noise" and the meaning of Palestrina's *Improperia,* see HaCohen, *Vocal Fictions,* 34–39. None of the early modern commentators on the book seems to have noted the irony of Lamentations being used against the people of its origin.

56. Nirenberg, *Communities of Violence,* 207.

57. The "Discorso" is in I-Ma, B. 18 *sup.,* f. 1; "Tre sono le cause che mi hanno indotto a leggere . . . le Lamentationi di quel gran Profeta Jeremia in questi tempi. La prima è stata per sodisfare alcuni che di ciò mi hanno ricorso . . . La seconda causa è che essendo noi vicini alla Settimana Santa nella quale nelli nostri Divini Offitij recitiamo queste lamentationi et non da ogni persona si sa la causa perche noi diciamo Aleph, Bed, Gimel."

58. Still, modern performances of some Triduum texts should carry disclaimers. Insofar as some sixteenth-century Lamentations linked to the Austrian Habsburgs may conceal anti-Ottoman attacks (see chapter 4), similar considerations apply; this anti-Turkish interpretation is quite present in Peter Martyr Vermigli's Reformed commentary on the book.

59. Odenthal, *Die 'Ordinatio Cultus Divini et Caeremoniarium,'* 95–99 and 180–181.

60. *Lateinisches Gesang-Buch,* 72–88. The fragments of the 1564 *Kirchenordnung* also mention Tenebrae, given in Sehling, *Die Kirchenordnungen* (Leipzig, 1909), 3:379.

61. "Die Passion nebst den Lamentationen in der Finstermesse [*recte*: Finstermette] werden jetzt von den Primanern allein, ohne Zutuung eines Kollegen abgesungen," cited from C. Döhring's unpublished "Annales Gymnasii Zittaviensis" by Gärtner, *Quellenbuch zur Geschichte,* 1:117.

62. For some examples of Holy Week employment of musicians in Venice, see Quaranta, *Oltre San Marco,* 79–83.

63. The documents from Bergamo, Padua (at the Santo), and Parma are published in Baroncini, "L'ufficio delle Tenebre," while the phenomenon of florid Triduum music in such institutions and in Venice's S. Marco is well discussed in the wider aesthetic context of Holy Week by Padoan, "Ethos devozionale," 25–29.

64. Capello, *Lamentationi, Benedictus et Miserere,* op. 3 (1612) and Burlini, *Lamentationi per la settimana santa,* op. 7 (1614).

65. For Zaragoza, González Marín, "Aspectos de la practica musical."

66. *Lamentationes Hieremiae Prophetae,* (1553); on the chapel's forces and repertory, Czepiel, *Music at the Royal Court,* 134–135 and 168.

67. For nuns and the Triduum in Siena, see the model study of Reardon, *Holy Concord,* and for the familiar reports (*Mercure galant,* Lecerf de la Viéville) on Tenebrae in Parisian houses, see Gaudelus, *Les offices,* 109–113 and *passim.* There is no evidence that the "angelic" tone of Responsories led to settings for high voices only.

68. "Die 6 Aprillis 1569. Ordine da servarsi universalmente per le Monache di Bologna. Che alli offitij delli tre giorni della settimana santa non si canti cosa alcuna in canto figurato eccetto il Benedictus, et il Miserere qual si canti[no] in falso bordone in Choro, et non in altro locho." (AAB, Misc. V.808, fasc. 6); my thanks to Craig Monson for this citation.

69. Sas, *La música en la Catedral de Lima* pt. 1, 69.

70. In 1752, the Swiss composer Franz Josef Meyer von Schauensee wrote monophonic Lamentations for the church of St. Leongard in Lucerne which are rhythmicized versions of the chant formula ("Lamentationes 3 dierum," in CH-Lz). I-Bc Lit. 92 is a cycle of chant Lessons independent of the tone and in contemporary style written c. 1780 (the pitch centers of each Day's Lamentations are *c, f,* and *d* respectively).

71. On Irízar, Olarte Martínez, "Miguel de Irízar y Domenzain." The Lessons by Corselli are listed in *Catalogo del Archivo de Música del Palacio Real de Madrid;* I use the *catalogo* number as there is a newer system of *caja/legajo* not reflected in this work.

72. "In cena Domini finis est Quadragesime: initium paschalis observantiae, veteris legis conclusio; novi testamenti inchoatio"; this is found in the breviaries of Passau (1519) and Konstanz (1509). Cf. Beleth, *Summa,* 167, "quia novum testamentum nunc incipit et vetus terminatum fuit."

73. Timoteo, *In divinum officium,* f. 73.

74. Zacchia's *Il vitto quaresimale* gave detailed instructions on eating only once a day, at lunch, during all Lent.

75. *Lamentationes* (1553).

76. For such a conjuncture see Sherr, "Ceremonies for Holy Week."

77. The visitation to the Sistina's singers of 5 May 1630 (ASV, Congr. Visita Apostolica [Rome], vol. 4, f. 1139ff.) noted among their vacation periods "Dalla Domenica delle Palme sino al mercordì santo 2 [giorni]" (with a marginal note "per prepararsi per le lettioni / per le fatighe della 7.na Santa"), i.e. Monday and Tuesday off for rehearsals. In some years this was anticipated by a week (e.g., 1607; Rostirolla, "Il Diario Sistino del 1607," at 132–133). An overview of the practice is in Annibaldi's comprehensive history of the chapel, *La cappella musicale,* 9 and 250–254.

78. Cf. López Gay, *La liturgia en la misión del Japón,* 175.

79. See Bouchard's travel diary to Naples in 1632 (*Journal II*), and Antonio Canova's journal of his time in Rome (*Scritti,* 151).

80. Some pre-1600 breviaries and antiphoners cast this Responsory in Christ's first-person voice, "oravi" instead of the more familiar "oravit," while the early Cinquecento antiphoner for the Week in Florence's Duomo (I-Fd, G. 22, f. 45v) adds "Jesus" after "oravit."

81. The orders in Rome, Archivio Storico del Vicariato, *Editte e bandi* 1566–1609, f. 47ff., contain forty years' worth of evidently ineffectual restrictions on the Thurs-

day processions, including an attempt in 1590 to ban polyphony sponsored by confraternities. For Rome, see O'Regan, "Processions and Their Music"; on nocturnal processions on Thursday with polyphony in late Cinquecento Milan, including curial orders for the mode in which pieces were to be sung, see Kendrick, _The Sounds of Milan, 1585–1650,_ 146–50, and Salis, "Drammatizzazioni devozionali."

2. Textual Understandings, Musical Expressions

1. On torture and corporal pain in Passion literature, Bestul, _Texts of the Passion,_ 145–164.

2. Ingegneri, _Lamentationes Hieremiae,_ preface, in Rosa Barezzani, "I testimoni."

3. Ingegneri, _Responsoria Hebdomadae Sanctae_ (1588), dedication, also in Rosa Barezzani, "I testimoni"; these Responsories (attributed to Palestrina) would be sung at the Viennese court from the early seventeenth well into the eighteenth century; cf. Riedel, _Kirchenmusik am Hofe,_ 79–84 and 253–254.

4. On the fresco cycle and its division between _ecclesia_ and _synagoga,_ see Cohen, _The Art of Giovanni Antonio da Pordenone,_ 1: 69–221.

5. Campbell, "The Conflicted Representation of Judaism."

6. _Bibliorum sacrorum glossa ordinaria_ (1589; rpt. Venice, 1603).

7. Melion, "Parabolic Analogy and Spiritual Discernment."

8. Andrée, _Gilbertus Universalis: Glossa Ordinaria in Lamentationes._

9. A summary of the rhetorical use of _conquestio_ and _indignatio,_ starting with Cicero's _De inventione,_ can be found in Lausberg, _Handbook of Literary Rhetoric,_ 207–208.

10. I use the numeration of M. Ham, "Morales: The Canon," in Rees/Nelson (eds.), _Cristóbal de Morales,_ 272–277. In the _Glossa,_ "Caph. Vocavi amicos meos" (Ham 157a) is an example of _indignatio,_ as is "Zain. Candidiores Nazarei" (Ham 158a), while "Nun. Vigilavit" (Ham 159a;) embodies _conquestio_ (see Andrée, _Gilbertus . . . Glossa,_ 268, 170, and 240).

11. The edition of Quevedo's work by E. M. Wilson and J. M. Blecua (Madrid, 1953), pp. 13–15 and _passim,_ covers these issues excellently.

12. Cristo's pieces are discussed in Rees, _Polyphony in Portugal._

13. de Andrade, _Commentarii in Threnos_ (1609), 25ff.

14. Lapide ignored the verse, but commentators from Agelli (_In Lamentationes,_ 197) to Castro (_Commentarii,_ 479) gave the literal explication of rape; only del Río (_Commentarius,_ 237) referred to Jerome.

15. I list here those features of Lamentations cited by multiple exegetes, or, in the case of Figueiro's dissent on the Hebrew letters, those interpretations that problematize one or another aspect of the text.

16. E.g., "Sed differunt a nostris [carminibus] varia pedum qualitate, situ, et ordine: siquidem alios pedes recipiunt, et alio subordine ob linguae proprietatem, non quidem earundem syllabarum cum nostris, sed eorundem temporum. Interponunt etiam Hebraei contra nostrorum poetarum consuetudinem, in suis carminibus rithmos quosdam, quos simplex Lector . . . intelligere non potest," Castro, _Commentarii_ (1609), 845. For Jerome's comments on the acrostics, alphabet, and meter of the book, see _Epistula XXX,_ 3.

17. Muratori, _Della perfetta poesia italiana,_ bk. 1, ch. 13 (in the 1706 Modena ed., at 145).

18. Lapide, *Commentarius*, 826.

19. "Jeremias fuit Christi Domini typus, nomine, vita, morte, sanctificato in utero," del Río, *Commentarius*, 10.

20. "Come pure hora ho dato fine di mettere in musica i Responsi, et le lamentationi. . . . La qual mia musica, per quello ne giudicano quelli che sino ad hora l'hanno udita, non è priua di quello affetto, nel quale lamentandosi, horando il Profeta Hyeremia, cercaua indurre gli ascoltatori," letter of 13 March 1582/3 in Bertolotti, *Artisti in relazione coi Gonzaga*, 196. Bardi's 1634 letter to G. B. Doni is given by Solerti, *Le origini del melodramma*, 145; Galilei set "parte delle lamentationi e responsi della Settimana Santa, cantate, nella stessa materia, in devota compagnia." Vicentino's example is in *L'antica musica ridotta alla moderna prattica* (1555) f. 70v–71.

21. Del Río, *Commentarius*, 19.

22. "Notanda in his Threnis artificiosa malorum gradatio et ascensus ad maiora, vel saltem cohaerentium analysis. In hoc quidem versu gradatio talis est: (1) flere noctu largiter, nec dari spacium lacrymis abstergendis; (2) non esse quemquam qui lugentem allocutione consoletur; (3) ab amicis, quorum se fidei crediderat, sperni, affligi, impugnari, quid acerbius!," *ibid.*, 27.

23. The letter from Grazzini (il Lasca) to G.B. della Fonte of 29 March 1543 is in Bramanti, "Il Lasca," at 32.

24. Ed. D'Accone, *Music of the Florentine Renaissance*, vol. 11, Corteccia, *Music for the Triduum Sacrum*.

25. Vidal's *Lamentación en romance* is in E-Bbc, M. 770–778; the text (but not the music) is given and discussed in Barreiro, "Las lamentaciones en romance" (I have corrected the incipit according to the score).

26. Gómez's work is in E-V, 70/3; López-Calo, *La música*, 2: 16.

27. Vargas Ugarte (ed.), *Diario de Lima de Juan Antonio Suardo (1629–1639)*, 1: 106.

28. For the medieval tradition, Andrée (ed.), *Glossa ordinaria*, 78.

29. Bucchio, *Esposizione sopra l'orazione di Gieremia profeta* (1573), 11, 19.

30. There are earlier Portuguese examples in Manuel Cardoso's 1648 OHS, and the three L9s in Estevão Lopes Morago's choirbook anthology for Visau from before 1630. Veneziano's Lessons are in I-Nf; for Morago's and Cardoso's pieces, see the modern eds. in *Portugaliae Musica*, vols. 4 and 13 (Lisbon, 1961 and 1968). One F5/L8 by Sebastian Aguilera de Heredia from around 1610 is in E-Zac, with a now-lost one by Cosmo de Ferreira (*Primeira parte do index da livraria e de musica do . . . João o IV* [1649], 467).

31. "Exacuerunt tamquam gladium linguas suas. Non dicant Judaei: 'Non occidimus Christum' . . . et vos, o Judaei, occidistis. Unde occidistis? Gladio linguae: acuistis enim linguas vestras. Et quando percussistis, nisi quando clamastis: 'Crucifige, crucifige'?" Settings of this text are best not performed.

32. "Prima conexio est 'doctrina domus plenitudo tabularum ista,' quo videlicet doctrina ecclesiae, quae domus Dei est, in librorum repperiatur plenitudine divinorum"; Jerome, *Epistulae*, pt. 1, 245–247.

33. Ricciardi, *Commentaria symbolica* (1591).

34. "Eam ob causam hae lamentationes sunt quatuor, et quadruplici alphabeto distinctae, quia in illis Jeremias non solum Judaeorum, sed etiam totius mundi, qui est in quatuor praecipuas partes divisus, Ortum et Occasum, Setptentrionem et Meridiem, scelera deplorat, et omnes ad deplorandum invitat," Pinto, *In Danielem*, f. 204r.

35. Bisello, "Nel segno di Raziel."

36. Bradshaw (ed.), *Emilio de' Cavalieri, The Lamentations and Responsories,* and Kirkendale, *Emilio de' Cavalieri* 213–232; for the alternate letters, Bradshaw's ed., 195–197.

37. For the early French source and its link to female monastic music, see Bennett, *Sacred Repertories in Paris,* 156–160.

38. Genette, *Seuils.*

39. Del Río: "Initio versus iterum interloquitur propheta, & gravem totius populi describit famem; et postea in fine ponitur oratio populi atque ita sunt duae partes versiculi unius, et personarum mutatio, quae in sequentibus quoque versibus aliquoties occurret," *Commentarius litteralis,* 48.

40. "*Quaerens panem:* Loquitur de fame quae fuit in Jerusalem tempore obsidionis . . . *Dederunt praetiosa quaeque pro cibo:* Sic peccator pro pane, imo mica una consolationis, puta pro exiguis deliciis, pro modica gula, fastu, et ambitu, puncto honoris, dat omnia sua desiderabilia, quin et vires suas omnes, ipsamque animam impendit et daemoni vendit . . . *Facta sum vilis:* omni vilitate, quam hucusque recensui et planxi . . . hoc est quasi vilis serva, qua omnes ad libidinem abutuntur," Lapide, *Commentarius in Threnos,* 840.

41. "*Allegorice* multi haec adaptent Christo peccata urbis et orbis luenti, matrique ei compatienti, utriusque enim dolori nullus fuit similis," *ibid.*

42. This L3 of Palestrina's so-called "Libro terzo"(I–Rvatgiulia XV.21, with an abridged copy in I–Rsg 58) is edited in *(faute de mieux)* Casimiri (ed.), *Le opere complete,* vol. 13, xii and 120–127. Conjectural identifications of this source with Lessons copied by Giuseppe Antonelli for the Giulia in 1600, and these latter as a copy of Lamentations written by Johannes Parvus in 1575 (see Llorens, *Le opere musicali,* 87 and Rostirolla, *Il Codice 59,* 49) have led to a dating in the latter year, but there is no firm evidence for this. My thanks to Mitchell Brauner for his insights on the Giulia.

43. This presumes that Casimiri's ficta flat at m. 64 (Altus) is not needed and indeed wrong.

44. Ironically, in the abridged version found in the Lateran source, someone added a *si placet* cantus part to the low voices of "Omnis populus," and thus undermined the contrast; Rostirolla, *L'Archivio musicale della Basilica di San Giovanni in Laterano,* vol. 2, pp. 932–934.

45. Bergquist (ed.), Lasso, *Sämtliche Werke,* vol. 22, vi–xii; the verse is on 144–146.

46. Bradshaw (ed.), Cavalieri, *The Lamentations and Responsories,* 22–30.

47. Zarlino, *Istitutioni harmoniche* (1558), pt. 3, 247.

48. The "oravi"/"oravit" difference marks a change of speaker (in the case of "oravit," from impersonal narration to Christ's voice) and is found among earlier antiphoners and breviaries.

49. The first source without the phrase is Urban's *Breviarium romanum* (1632), p. 392, picked up by at least some northern European breviary prints immediately.

50. Graziani, *Responsoria hebdomadae sanctae* (1663); Berardi's piece is listed in Simi Bonini, *Catalogo del Fondo Musicale di Santa Maria in Trastevere* as 635,5a; while Calegari's score (I-Bc) can now be viewed at http://badigit.comune.bologna.it /cmbm/images/ripro/gaspari/DD230/DD230_001.asp (accessed 15 October 2011).

51. Cafaro, Sala, and Campion's settings are all in I-Nc, while Manna's are in I-Nf.

52. Limido's pieces are in E-E, 172–1, with partial copies in Libros de Parti-

tura, 12; Haydn's Responsories, MH 276–278, have been ed. by A. Kircher (Stuttgart, 2007).

53. E.g., the *Breviarium monasticum . . . pars verna* (1743), 245; the Dominicans also retained it.

54. Bartoli's setting is in I-Nf and GB-Lbm; Almeida's in P-Vv; Albazeda's in E-Bbc, M 1623 (f. 40v, a later addition to Pujol's Lessons); Perez' in I-Nc and P-Lf, and Durante's in I-Fc and other Italian sources.

55. Blount, *The Office of the Holy Week* (1687), 33–36.

56. Andrée (ed.), Gilbertus, *Glossa,* 252, 238, and 232: *conquestio* is found in 1:13 and *indignatio* in the others.

57. "In cantico isto Zacharias gratias refert Deo super variis beneficis ejus, potissimum de Verbi Incarnatione et Passione, generisque humani potentissimum Israelitici salvatione . . . Christi equidem incarnatio inchoatio fuit nostrae redemptionis atque salutis, quae per Christi Passionem completae sunt. Non enim per solam suam incarnationem nos salutare decrevit, sed salvationem nostram per suam Passionem consummare instituit . . . Postremo canticum istud sententiosum ac dulce devotissime concinamus, grata affectuosa mente," Denys, *In quatuor Evangelistas expositiones* (1538), ff. 122v–125v.

58. Agelli, *Commentarius in Psalmos, et in Divini Officii cantica* (1606; I cite from the 1611 Paris ed., 813ff.).

59. "Il flebile concerto di queste mie Compositioni Musicali deve havere per Uditori li seguaci compassionevoli di Christo patiente . . . ," Cazzati's dedication to his *Benedictus, Miserere, e Tantum ergo,* op. 45 (1668), addressed to the Cassinese abbot Angelo Bertuzzi (c.1605–72).

60. Fabris, *Da Napoli a Parma,* explains the sources for his Miserere and Lamentations.

61. Macey, *Bonfire Songs,* 153–307.

62. Bellarmine, *Explicatio in Psalmos* (I cite from the 1642 Paris ed., 376), on v. 20: "Effectus justificationis sunt opera justitiae, quae placent Deo, ut vera sacrificia spiritualia."

63. Eustachio, *Salutari discorsi,* f. 28v.

64. I cite from the 1605 Venice ed. of Calderari's discourses, 16–17.

65. *Ibid.,* 91.

66. Bettley, "La composizione," 170–175, which gives the north Italian verse selection up to 1600, makes this point clear. For Spain, see Snow, *A New-World Collection.*

67. On f. 48v of the 1572 book, "nostris" is abbreviated, but then appears in almost all later liturgical editions. Among Italian settings to 1600, it is found in the cycles of Ferrarese (1565), Asola (1584), Guami (1588), and Magri (1597); its only appearance in the Palestrina sources is in the seventeenth-century I-Rvat Ottob. Lat. 3387 (Casimiri's "Book IV").

68. De Martino, *Morte e pianto rituale,* 125.

69. Figueiro, *Commentarii,* 414.

70. Lapide, *Commentarius in Threnos,* 832. The first forty years of his life in the Low Countries (until the truce of 1609) would have been marked by the Spanish-Dutch war around him.

71. Andrade, *Commentarii,* 57, linking the scene to Jewish weeping over the ruined Jerusalem.

72. On the Seville repertory as a whole, see Ruíz Jiménez, *La librería de canto de órgano,* esp. 134–36 for Lobo's Lessons, and Súarez Martos, "El Archivo Musical de la Catedral de Sevilla en 1725" and "La música en la Catedral de Sevilla durante el s. XVII."

73. *Concerto degli Stromenti . . . in accompagnamento de' Responsi della Settimana Santa,* op. 3 (Florence, 1706). Casini's vocal *Responsi* volume was his op. 2.

74. The title of the part-books that contain settings of Responsories (MEX-Pc, ms. 30) reads "Motetes de quaresma."

75. "El 1 R. es de canto llano" is the note on the E-Sc source, which, like the copy of Alonso Lobo's SS/L1, was written by Juan de Ossorio in 1772.

76. de Jong, "Liturgical action from a language perspective" takes some issue with Habermas's classic formulations as applied to liturgy.

3. Devotion, Models, Circulation, 1550–1600

1. "Piovonmi amare lagrime dal viso / Con un vento angoscioso di sospiri / Quando a la croce avien che gli occhi giri / Ov'è di vita il Creator diviso / . . . Così dietro ai lamenti vengon poi / Amorosi concetti, atti soavi / Tal, ch'ascender mi fan quasi alle stelle," Malipiero, *Il Petrarca spirituale,* sonnet #15 (I cite from the 1587 Venice ed., f. 4v).

2. "Cuius livore sanati sumus" as opposed to Isaiah's "De eius livore."

3. My touchstone for chant Responsories in Italy is the early Cinquecento Holy Week antiphoner from Florence Cathedral, I-Fd, G. 22, ff. 55v, 79r, 111v ff.

4. "Il compositore dee hauere consideratione di trouare un Tuono, che naturalmente sia mesto, come il Secondo, il Quarto, & il Sesto. Vero è, ch'il prattico compositore farà mesta, & allegra la sua compositione per ogni Tuono, che gli piacerà; & questo averrà per gli moti veloci, & tardi, che faranno le parti"; Ponzio, *Ragionamento* [quarto], 159.

5. "Con Figuras de Longa, de Breve, de Semibreve, y de Minima, y a vezes en una parte sola con algunas pocas semiminas de grado," Cerone, *El Melopeo y Maestro* (1613), 691.

6. "Lo stile, che si tiene nel comporre le lettioni della settimana Santa, è tale, che communemente [le parti] vanno insieme, come va il Gloria del Magnificat, & come va l'Incarnatus est; & in simili occasioni il compositore deve servirsi delle dissonantie, acciò facciano lacrimosa la compositione . . . ma con figure gravi, come di Semibrevi in principio di misura poste, & ancora in elevatione," Ponzio, *Ragionamento,* 158–159.

7. Thus a request from Sforza Almeni (a court official writing from Livorno) to Pier Francesco Riccio (the dynasty's *maggiordomo* and a cathedral canon) of 25 March 1550 (Tuesday of Passion Week), I-Fas, Archivio Mediceo del Principato 1176, pt. 9, f. 41.

8. The contents, including the canticles, of the *Responsoria omnia* are in D'Accone (ed.), Corteccia, *Collected Sacred Works* ("Music of the Florentine Renaissance," 11).

9. On the theology and earlier musical reflections of this idea in earlier repertory, Anderson, "Symbols of Saints."

10. The rubric reads: "Qui natum est preibit ante me, et ego ante illum preibo parare vias eius," a reference to this canticle verse, which reads "praeibis enim ante faciem Domini parare vias eius."

11. "Tres sumus in Unum, sed Unus contra nos, et nos contra illum" is this rubric.

12. For Carpentras's Lesson (not the Prayer "secundum cantum Romanum"), see Seay (ed.), *Opera omnia* 2, 82–96; none of the manuscript sources have the same verse selection as the print. For Phinot, Höfler (ed.), *Opera omnia,* vol. 4, 172–189. In v. 5 Phinot omits the Vulgate's "nostris" as had Carpentras, a further indication of his textual source.

13. For the dedication of G. B. Corvo's 1556 Responsories to him and the duke's attempts to obtain now-lost settings of the same texts from Paolo Animuccia, see Piperno, *L'immagine del duca,* 123.

14. Cf. *Di Adriano et di Iachet i salmi appartinenti alli Vesperi* (Venice: Gardano, 1550), in Willaert, *Opera omnia,* vol. 8, *Psalmi vesperales;* Phinot himself contributed psalms to the 1550 collection.

15. Although the range of T1 is wide, the adumbration of the plagal octave at "Pupilli facti sumus" and the c_3-c_4 ambitus of T2 suggest that Phinot's *Oratio* is in Mode 6.

16. On Contino's series as a whole, see Bernstein, *Music Printing,* 199–200.

17. Agee, "The Privilege and Venetian Music Printing," 246–247, 250–251, 256–257.

18. The description reads "di [carte] cento cinquanta nove principia in Monte Oliveti, et finise Deus s*ecundu*m magnam misericordiam suam"; Bivi's print has 159 folios, beginning with an F5/R1 and ending with a Miserere [mei Deus secundum . . .].

19. Kerle's Lamentations *a 5* that appear in the 1628 Bergamo inventory (in Padoan, "La musica in S. Maria Maggiore," 202) may or may not have been the same as the four-voice volume of the printing privilege. Ursprung, *Jakobus de Kerle,* xii, and Leitner, *Jakobus de Kerle (1531/32–1591),* esp. 123–134 emphasize quite well the composer's overall publishing campaign across the major liturgical genres but are not aware of the Triduum volumes.

20. On Andrea and Tommaso, see Casati, "Nuove notizie intorno a Tomaso de Marini," at 597 and 601. The information is summarized and details added in P. Colussi's entry on the Palazzo, http://www.storiadimilano.it/citta/Porta_Orientale/palazzo_marino.htm, accessed 10 February 2010, which also gives the coats of arms of father and son.

21. "Tu piis, sanctissimisque parentum tuorum praeceptis a teneris annis eruditum, ita ad eorum consuetudinem moremque deductus es," not exactly a description of Andrea's character.

22. On the church, see Torre, *Il ritratto di Milano,* 194; for the inscription detailing Tommaso's bequests, Forcella, *Iscrizioni delle chiese,* 3: 59.

23. The standard article is Zeri, "Bernardino Campi: Una *Crocifissione.*"

24. Lama, *Discorso . . . intorno alla scultura et pittura . . .* (1584), 51; my thanks to Bob Miller for help on the issues around this painting.

25. The basic study of the technique is still Carey, "Composition for Equal Voices in the Sixteenth Century"; Cerone also recommended "vozes baxas y muy graves, (y mas, enterueniendo solamente voces varoniles)" for Lamentations.

26. A similar cleffing is found in Corvo's F6/R1–3 (F4/F4/F4/F5) of 1556.

27. The documents are given in Reardon, *Agostino Agazzari,* 48 (for the choir size), 60, 63 and 72 (for the purchases).

28. The 1585 print is discussed in the editions of Victoria's OHS by S. Rubio (Cuenca, 1977) and E. Cramer (Henryville, 1982).

29. SPd 9 opens with five-voice Lessons attributed to G. A. Dragoni in I-Rsg 87, even though the Spoleto volume gives three of them to Palestrina (discussed below).

The incipits of the Spoleto sources are in Innocenzi, *Il fondo musicale del Duomo di Spoleto,* 416–423, and "Il Codice 9," who notes Nasco's authorship of the second cycle, the possible ascription to Dragoni (although without the other concordances given here) and records an extra *Oratio* by the mysterious mid-century Roman composer Lerma.

30. Sub-verses (e.g., "Omnes amici eius") are demarcated by bars in all of Nasco's F5 Lessons and F6/L1–2.

31. d'Alessi, *La cappella musicale,* 182.

32. In TrevBC20, Nasco's F5 Lessons (f. 31v ff.) were dated 7 April 1557 (in Passion Week, copied possibly for use that year), and followed Jhan's, separated by two canticles. Although the dedication by Nasco's widow to his print calls the Lessons "queste ultime [compositioni], che egli fece poco prima, che morisse," some of these pieces must thus be backdated a few years.

33. For the purchase of Bivi's Lessons in Spoleto, see Fausti, *La cappella musicale,* 45; for Fermo, L. Virgili, "La cappella musicale della Chiesa metropolitana di Fermo" at 23 ff.

34. Padoan, "La musica in S. Maria Maggiore a Bergamo," 205.

35. Czepiel, *Music at the Royal Court,* 356 and 367; for the longevity of Szamotuł's Lessons, see Kubieniec, "Treny Jeremiasza."

36. The description of the Lamentations volume in Clementi, *La cappella musicale del Duomo di Gubbio* conflates various Lessons and misses the duplicate cycles.

37. These include Doni's *Christ Falling under the Cross* (1564), his *Pietà,* and Nucci's *Kiss of Judas* (1575).

38. Pacini, *La chiesa pistoiese,* vol. 3, 73, 91, 109, 124, 143; for the payment, *ibid.,* vol. 4, 23 and 28.

39. Banchieri, *Direttorio,* 281; on Alessandro's unhappiness in monastic life, *ibid.,* 277; for the "new" letters, Bovio, *Cantorino olivetano* (1661), 117.

40. On their copyist Pietro Martire Balzani CRSS, see Mischiati, *La prassi musicale presso i Canonici Regolari,* 63 and 115.

41. Bona's Lamentations are preserved in Trent, together with other music from Franciscan houses there, see Carlini, "La musica sacra nel Principato Vescovile di Trento"; his lost Lessons are noted in the 1591 Gardano catalogue and others in the 1604 Giunta catalogue, while eight-voice Responsories were in the 1655 Fugger library. The printed Lessons of his fellow friars Ludovico Balbi and Bartolomeo Ratti are not extant.

42. Franciscan tradition paused in the Seicento, as the large 1674 inventory of music belonging to the Santo's longtime chapelmaster Antonio dalla Tavola contained no Triduum music by the Franciscan or others (Sartori, *Documenti,* 46–50). It resumed with the two major Settecento representatives of the order: F. A. Vallotti with his solo-voice cycle of Lessons for Padua (I-Pca), and G. B. Martini, with twelve Lessons and two Responsory cycles (these latter for Dominicans; Wiechens, *Die Kompositionstheorie,* app. 2: 8–9).

43. Mischiati, *La prassi,* 129 gives the capitular orders from the early Cinquecento.

44. ASB, Demaniale, 175/2622, f. 187 (1551), lists him at S. Stefano in Mantua; for his later presence in Venice, f. 219v. He is given at various CRSS houses in this annual register of the congregation's members from 1551 into the 1570s, although there is no record of his other musical activity.

45. ASB, Demaniale, 175/2622, f. 208v.

46. Cf. Culley, *Jesuits and Music,* 80, 298, 302 and Crook, "'A Certain Indulgence,'" at 467.

47. Lauretano's note of "li mottetti malincolici, et il più delle lamentationi di Hieremia, che a ogni hora, et più spesso, si cantavano sopra l'organo con doi, o 3 voci sole" on 16 January 1583 (Second Sunday after Epiphany), is in Culley, *Jesuits and Music,* 297. For "cantare sull'organo" as solo improvisation, see Morelli, "'Cantare sull'organo.'"

48. Lamentations cycles by Lasso (1585), Lattre (1554), and the *Novus . . . thesaurus* Habsburg motet anthology with its Lessons by Mahu/LaRue (1568) are all listed in what must be post-1590 Jesuit instructions for "acceptable" music given and discussed by Crook, "A Sixteenth-Century Catalog," at 58–59.

49. For Lamentations sung by professional musicians in late seventeenth-century Paraguay, see Xarque, *Insignes missioneros,* 354.

50. *Lamentationi di Fabricio Dentice a cinque voci* (1593), ed. in Fabris, *Da Napoli a Parma.*

51. The general chapter's orders of that year noted that "Fu ordinato che in S. Maria Segreta di Milano si canti canto figurato solamente in quelle occasioni dove è obligo espresso in scritto et all'hora senza tumulto," Pellegrini (ed.), *Fonti per la storia dei Somaschi,* vol. 24, p. 96.

52. Cattin, "I benedettini e la musica," and "Tradizione e tendenze innovatrici."

53. The copy in US-Cn of the 1535 *Cantus monastici formula* bears the ownership note: "P uso di M.a Giacinta donatoli dalla Mre. D.a Anna Ifigenia"; given the title of the latter ("Madre Donna") these must be Benedictine nuns in a house following Cassinese Use.

54. Zucchino's print can be inferred from the German book-fair catalogues and its listing at Bergamo: Göhler, *Verzeichnis,* no. 1731; this also lists Paolo Ferrarese's OHS as being on sale in Germany as early as autumn 1565, and Padoan, *La musica,* 202.

55. Giustiniano was abbot of S. Pietro of Modena in 1606–08; see Spinelli, "Per una cronotassi"; Calzolai [Ricordati], *Historia monastica* (1575), ff. 465–67v, mentions him ("di Zordanilli") among Paolo Ferrarese and other musicians of the Congregation.

56. The standard article on Guidi and the cultural politics of the Cassinese in these years is Cooper, "Un modo per 'la Riforma Cattolica'?." Paolo's print is now online at http://badigit.comune.bologna.it/cmbm/images/ripro/gaspari/_U031/U031_001.asp.

57. For the Passions by Paolo, Falconio, and Cantone, see Botta Caselli, "Musiche per la Passione nei monasteri benedettini."

58. For the Pope's visit to S. Benedetto Po on 20 April 1543 (besides the Passion, Paolo's print includes an *Adoramus te* rubricated for it), see Luchino, *Cronaca della vera origine . . .* (1592), 168.

59. For the dating, see Blackburn, "Josquin's Chansons."

60. For other parts of the cultural program, see Zaggia, *La congregazione benedettina,* 615–616.

61. Ginzburg/Prosperi, *Giochi di pazienza,* 166ff. and Prosperi, *L'eresia del Libro Grande,* 273–274.

62. This led to Pampuro's trial and disgrace in 1568; see Prosperi, *L'eresia,* 285–288 and Zaggia, *La congregazione benedettina,* 628–640.

63. Macchiarella, *Il falsobordone,* 133 and 191–192, who sees the inclusion of

the technique as connected to the issues of intelligibility in Guidi's dedication; transcriptions of both an unmeasured and measured Miserere are in *ibid.*, 200.

64. E.g., F6/L2's "Repulit Dominus" and SS/L1's "Adhaesit lingua."

65. The practice continued elsewhere: the anonymous, probably Catalan, Responsories in E-Bbc 608 (c. 1600) likewise repeat phrases and lines from item to item.

66. For her ownership of the part-books now in GB-Lbl, see Bernstein, *Music Printing*, 670. Although she is unknown, the surname suggests South Germany, Switzerland, Austria, or Bohemia.

67. Paolo's Responsories were copied as late as 1592 by a Canon of S. Giorgio in Alga (I-Bc, U.32).

68. "Recordare pauperitatis, et transgressionis meae . . . et tabescet in me anima mea . . . et dixi [sic]: periit finis meus . . . sed [et] cum clamavero et rogavero, exclusit orationem meam."

69. It was later used by the Milanese chapelmaster Giulio Cesare Gabussi in his funeral motet for his employer Carlo Borromeo, appearing in Gabussi's *Magnificat X* (Milan: 1589).

70. For other internal monastic references in Cantone's 1596 motets, see Kendrick, "Riflessioni," 451–454.

71. The F6 letters "Aleph, Lamech, Sade, Gimel, Daleth, Beth" would equal "doctrina, disciplinae/cordis, justitiae, plenitudo, tabularum, domus," perhaps "The teaching of [?monastic] discipline [or "of the heart"] is the fullness of justice and the house of Scripture."

72. In Fabris' ed., p. 117, mm. 63ff.

73. Noe, *Die Präsenz*, 1: 60; Dufourcq, "Un inventaire," at 47.

74. Ducrot, "Histoire de la Cappella Giulia au XVIe siècle" (pt. 2) 517.

75. E.g., the classic—if unpublished at the time—*Roma sancta* (1581) of G. Martin, 89–92, mentions the Thursday processions and the *sepolcri* in various churches with no hint of Office music, even in the colleges.

76. "Per tutto questo, e ogn'altra cosa, che all'hora di Matutino patisti, quando (permetendolo tu) s'impadronirono le tenebre di te, che sei vera luce; . . . ti priego humilmente che con tua gratia illumini l'oscurità dell'anima mia, acciò . . . ti ami perfettamente," Loarte, *Trattato*, 17.

77. The exception is F6/L2, which uses the unusual {2: 11–13}.

78. On his time at the basilica, see Della Libera, "L'attività musicale nella basilica di S. Lorenzo in Damaso."

79. "Et" is also present in Rn 77–88, as well as the prints of Ferrarese, Alcarotto, Isnardi (1572 and 1584), and Alessandro Romano (1582); it is missing in most breviaries and OHS texts after 1585, as well as in Varotto's and Vecchi's cycles of 1587 and Guidetti's chantbook of the same year. A Paris text-only OHS of 1591 (D-Mbs, Liturg. 975), p. 170, shows it literally erased from the Lesson.

80. On the institutional aspects, see Ducrot, "Histoire de la Cappella Giulia au XVIᵉ siècle," who also gives the 1575 copying payment on 14 April, two weeks after the Triduum (pt. 2, 524); the placement of both in Jubilee Years is noteworthy.

81. On the differences between Victoria's two version of Lessons, the literature is Rive, "Victoria's Lamentationes Geremiae"; Cramer, "Tomás Luis de Victoria's Second Thoughts"; and Marx-Weber, "Die Entwicklung," esp. 223–225.

82. Felice's music and the chapel are studied in Couchman, "Felice Anerio's music for the church."

83. Rostirolla, *Il codice 59.*

84. The only graphic anomaly is the F6/L1 (f. 34v), from the "first" layer.

85. This is not exactly the same as Casimiri's "Book II."

86. Vita Spagnuola, "Gli atti notarili dell'Archivio di Stato di Roma," at 57–58. Of the 1588 Roman edition of Palestrina's Lessons, only two copies survive, neither in Italy; the 1589 Venice reprint adds five more (three in Italy, and the only one in Rome that of the Sistina). Briccio also owned fifteen copies of another unspecified Lamentations print.

87. On issues in Barcelona, see Zauner, "Las Lamentaciones de Jeremías en Barcelona."

88. On the problems of the chapel at the basilica, and its ownership of Palestrina's Lessons, along with other Triduum music, as well as the 1611 copying by Costantino Castiglione of a Palestrina cycle (possibly I-Rsm 11), see Della Libera, "Repertori ed organici vocali-strumentali nella Basilica di Santa Maria Maggiore."

89. I add small modifications to the description of Rostirolla, *L'Archivio musicale,* 932–935.

90. Casimiri, *Il Codice 59,* claimed to have documents placing its copying in late 1576, when Stabile was chapelmaster at the Lateran, but there is nothing in his notes on basilica documents as edited by Callegari, "Cantori, maestri."

91. Rostirolla, *Il Codice 59,* 66, seems correct on this point.

92. Jeppesen, *Italia sacra musica;* Rostirolla's edition in Palestrina, *Le opere complete* (Rome, 2001), 35/1; Innocenzi, *Il fondo musicale* and "Il Codice 9."

93. For other motion by thirds, see Innocenzi, "Il Codice 9," whose tentative attribution to Dragoni of all the music I thus follow.

94. The 1580 payment is in Callegari's ed. "Cantori, maestri," at 103. The excellent catalogue by Rostirolla, *L'Archivio musicale,* 942, omits Dragoni's *Oratio* at f. 35v in the first (and thus complete) cycle.

95. Callegari/Casimiri, "Cantori," 251, and Witzenmann, *Die Lateran-Kapelle,* 1:126 and 2: 366–369; the latter records the extra payments for Holy Week 1600 to the cathedral singers.

96. The commonplace that Carpentras's Lamentations were used exclusively in the Sistina until replaced by Palestrina's in 1587 was questioned already by Köhler, *Die Cappella Sistina,* 109, and also challenged by Bölling, *Das Papstzeremoniell.*

97. Giacobetti, *Lamentationes cum omnibus Responsoriis* (Venice: Vincenti, 1601), published after he had returned home to Ripatransone in the Marches, where his musical activity is unclear.

98. O'Regan, "Music at the Roman Archconfraternity of San Rocco."

99. For these books, see O'Regan, *Institutional Patronage,* 31 and 68–71, and *Catalogo del fondo musicale della Biblioteca Nazionale Centrale Vittorio Emmanuele II di Roma,* 88–103.

100. Couchman, "Felice Anerio," 215.

101. For instance, at "dixit ad eos" in the verse of "Tamquam ad latronem" (f. 9v of the new foliation for the Responsories), or in the verse of "Sepulto Domino."

102. On Turin's holdings, see Demaria, *La regia cappella,* xxiii; the 1585 purchase of the book is in Marchi, "La cappella musicale del Duomo di Torino nel tardo Cinquecento." Juan Ruíz Jiménez is preparing a study of the circulation of Victoria's print in Spain.

103. The F5 selections are {1: 1–2ab}; {1: 4, Mem, 13c}; {1: Sade, 20ab, Zain,

12a}; F6 continues with {Heth, 2:11 in a corrupt and probably incorrectly memorized form}; {Aleph, 3:41, Lamed, 3:58}; and {3: 9, 6, 2}. Isorelli's work is somewhat primitive.

104. Bradshaw (ed.), *The Lamentations,* 11.

4. Dynastic Tenebrae

1. Schilling, "Die religiösen und kirchlichen Zustände."

2. *Ibid.,* 120ff.

3. The basic study of its printing is Jackson, "Berg and Neuber," 276–281.

4. *Breviarium frisingense* (1482), f. 197ff.

5. On his life, his various skills, and some of the musical editions linked to him, see Jenny, "Gaspar Brusch und die Schweiz," esp. 141–144 for his musical activity and contacts, and 105 for Brusch's 1540 recommendation of Bartolomaeus Amantius to Grünenstein. I am grateful to Dr. G. E. Kreuz for his ideas on Brusch.

6. On the date, Jenny, "Gaspar Brusch," 113.

7. "Ante fores cum sint lugubria tempora nostras, / Qua referunt Christi fata crucisque necem" and "Cantari quibus [nobis] Hieremiae lamenta prophetae / In sacris templis hic et ubique solent, / Ut Christi fera mors et crux et passio acerba / Nos peccati odiis repleat atque mali."

8. "Et nostrae aetatis Crequilon certissimus Orpheus, / Saepe movens animum, Carole Quinte, tuum."

9. On the liturgical and musical vicissitudes of the Interim in Nuremberg, see Butler, "Liturgical Music in Sixteenth-Century Nürnberg," 263–273; on the arrangement and compromises for the (re-)introduction of Matins, 281–282.

10. Friedensburg, *Nuntiaturberiche,* vol. 11 (Berlin, 1910), 442.

11. Davison (ed.), La Rue, *Opera omnia,* 8.

12. On Mary as musician, see Király, "Königin Maria von Habsburg und die Musik."

13. Velius, *Querela Austriae,* sig. A3v. Another motet certainly by Mahu sets the verses of Psalm 125 on God's redemption of captives: *In convertendo Dominus captivitatem Sion/Converte, Domine, captivitatem nostram,* is in BerlGS 7, copied around 1540.

14. For the *fac* and *ega* formulae in Hungary see the 13th-century notated breviary of Esztergom (Szendrei [ed.], *Breviarium notatum Strigoniense*), and a later antiphoner (*ead., The Istanbul Antiphonal*).

15. *Glossa ordinaria* (1603), col. 893: for 2:13, "octavus locus indignationis."

16. Robledo Estaire, "La música en la casa del Rey," at 158; *id.,* "Vihuelas de arco y violones"; and Nelson, "Ritual and Ceremony in the Spanish Royal Chapel," at 145–148.

17. A-Wn Mus. ms. 11884; Lindell, "Music and patronage at the court of Rudolf II," at 257.

18. Senn, *Musik und Theater am Hof zu Innsbruck,* 113–114 and Tschmuck, *Die höfische Musikpflege,* 165–167.

19. For Echamer in Innsbruck, Tschmuck, *ibid.,* 360.

20. van der Straeten, *La musique aux Pays-Bas,* 2: 54–56.

21. For Hall's order of 1588, see Tschmuck, *Die höfische Musikpflege,* 80–81 ("und fünhemlich inn der heiligen carwochen, als auch zue ostern, inn der octaf cor-

poris Christi, unnd weichennechten, die metten, unnd da mangel ann geistlichen personen erschiene, die lectiones, propheceien, und lamentationes singen . . . nach dem Römischen Brevier unnd nit annderst").

22. *Pace* Schmid, *Musik an den schwäbischen Zollenhöfen,* at 560 (the chapel also had a copy of Lasso's 1585 Lessons) the Hechingen record is clearly of a manuscript set ("geschrieben") and not Utendal's 1570 printed Penitential Psalms.

23. On the visit, see the letter from Dresden in Zimmermann, *Evangelisch-katholische Fürstenfreundschaft,* 140ff.

24. Bruning, "Die kursächsiche Reichspolitik," at 84–85, and Fichtner, *Emperor Maximilian II.*

25. "The seeds of that art known as song have been installed in the human mind from on high. Thus the first people, moved by the power of their own intellect, discovered it, when the earth was [newly] put together. And thus our fathers sang these divine prophecies of the holy prophet, miracles of the great God. Since these divine seeds of the mind reside in men, who are pleased by the harmonic sound of sacred music, who can deny that it has heavenly virtue? Thus hail to the leader of the Austrian people, great in honor, Rudolf, patron of singers. Merciful Caesar, receive these gifts in music. Ferdinand, your [grand]father and ancestor, and your father, also Caesar, cultivated all such things with a pious spirit. So also follow these past examples of your elders, these songs, the sweet and high music of the Muses."

26. Letter of 6 April 1577 from Delfino in Prague, in Koller (ed.), *Nuntiaturberichte aus Deutschland,* sect. 3, vol. 9, 101.

27. E.g., in F6/L2, "in die irae furoris *Domini*" (for "sui") or "De *coelo* misit ignem" (for "excelso"), and "confectam maerore" instead of the reverse.

28. On the transition in 1564, see Fichtner, *Emperor Maximilian II,* esp. 129–131 on the anti-Ottoman wars.

29. Holeton, "Fynes Moryson's *Itinerary.*"

30. *Breviarium horarum canonicorum . . . pragensis* (Nuremberg, 1502), f. 164v ff.

31. Niemöller, "Lamentationen von Carl Luython."

32. Jacoby, *Hans von Aachen 1552–1615,* 183–204.

33. Schmid, *Musik,* 578, and Göhler, *Verzeichnis, passim.*

34. In Freiberg, however, there is no record of Triduum Office music, at least, in the 1537/8 visitations given by Sehling, *Die Kirchenordnungen,* 1: 459–470.

35. Federhofer, *Musikpflege und Musiker am Grazer Habsburgerhof,* 196, 287, 289.

36. Riedel, *Kirchenmusik,* 79–85.

37. Waldner, "Zwei Inventarien," 137–138 and 145.

38. Robledo, "La música en la casa del Rey," and Knighton, "Los libros de música de Felipe II," esp. 59ff. on the fate of the music copied after 1580.

39. The *Primeira parte do index da livraria,* 355 and 434, gives some five Lessons by Díaz (two of which involve instruments) along with 11 Responsories (also with instruments) and a Miserere; there are three surviving clearly attributable Lessons by Comes in E-VAc and VAcp (my thanks to Greta Olson for help with these pieces). Some 14 Lessons by Dentice are listed in *ibid.,* 396. For Dentice's printed Lessons left behind by Ghersem, see Bourligueux, "Géry de Ghersem, sous-maître de la chapelle royale d'Espagne," at 175.

40. Robledo, "Musica en la corte," 159.

41. "Los cantores cantarán la primera lamentación y las mas conforme estuvieren

encomendadas. Los responsorios de ellas algunos se cantan de canto de órgano y las más de canto llano nel libro [la pri*mera* Lamentacion cantan al doneil donde esta el Rey]. Las leciones cantan los capellanos de banco nel modo ya referido arriba. Quando nel choro se empecará el cantico *Benedictus,* se llevantan dos y las candelas del Altar se empeçarán apagar al verso *Ut sine timore,* enpeçando de la ultima de la parte de la ep*istol*a," Rivero, "Breve descripción de la Real Capilla de Madrid y de las ceremonias que en ella se exequien para el curso del anno," dated 1640, AGP, Real Capilla, 72/5.

42. "Quando los cantores que ovierten de cantar las lamentaciones llegaren al facistol, harán primero cortesia al Rey si entran por la puerta de la capilla, despues nuflexan al Altar, luego al Prelado," *ibid.*

43. For the earlier rule and for Manuel de Santa María's 1746 ordinal, see Hernández, *Música y culto divino* pt. 2, 132–133 and *id., Música en el monasterio,* 142ff. and *passim.*

44. These are now available in Lyman, "Peter Philips at the Court of Albert and Isabella," 68 and 72.

45. Russell, "Pedro Rimonte in Brussels."

46. "Nec immerito stupebit, cum vel ipsos sacros Vates dulcisono modulamine ad futura edicendium incitatos, vel miseros quidem rugientis adversarii saevitia oppressos, eadem Musicae energia liberari, ac lenius habere conspexerit [a reference to sung prophecies as consolation] . . . ipse nimirum salutis author [Christ], qui antequam se cruci immolandum traderet, Hymno dicto, velut sacri justa funeris decantavit [i.e., music before the Passion]," Rimonte, undated dedication to *Cantiones sacrae . . . ac Hieremiae prophetae lamentationes* (1607).

47. Duerloo, "Archducal Piety and Habsburg Power," at 267–270. There is no meaningful mention of Tenebrae in Chiflet's guide, *Aula sacra principum Belgii* (Antwerp, 1650).

48. The chapel list of 1612's first *tercío* allows for doubled adult voices; cf. Russell, "Pedro Rimonte," 188.

49. The text underlay at "de quibus praeceperis ne intrarent" is not logical, and some pitch readings are wrong (e.g., the augmented unison at m. 19 in Ruimonte, *Lamentationes* [2007]).

50. The entry by R. Baroncini in *DBI* gives the most complete information on his Italian (but not Spanish) years; cf. also the introduction by L. Ruggiero to Mogavero, *Vita e opera,* esp. 23–24. My thanks to Jonathan Glixon for checking on Venetian sources.

51. *Pace* the *DBI* entry, there is no evidence of his work at the Patriarca seminary in Valencia or his actual employment at the Madrid court; I am grateful to Greta Olson for her ideas on Mogavero and her notes on the chapel membership in 1623.

52. Ramos López, *La música en la catedral de Granada,* 1: 180–181; the chapter's decision to reimburse Mogavero came just after Easter 1625, and so presumably he had sent the books in time for the Triduum that year. The part-books surviving in Barcelona (E-Bbc) and Segovia (the sources for the text underlay here) may also stem from such shipments.

53. Cf. Bergquist's edition of the texts, *Neue Reihe,* vol. 22, xxii–xxxvi with the rpt. of the Pian breviary, ed. Sodi/Triacca, *Breviarium romanum: Editio princeps (1568),* 376ff. The essential discussion of local liturgy is Crook, *Orlando di Lasso's Imitation Magnificats,* 33–49.

54. The F5 readings in the 1516 Freising breviary, repeated in the 1571 OHS, are {1: 1–2}; {1:3–5}; and {1: 6–7}.

55. Although there is a copy of the 1572 Roman OHS with its abbreviated Lessons now in Munich (D-Bsb), its ex-libris suggests it was owned by a seventeenth-century count from the Veneto, Massimiliano de' Porcia, and thus not known at court.

56. Leuchtmann, *Orlando di Lasso,* 1: 175. The only discussion of Lasso's Triduum music, besides Bergquist's edition, is that of Boetticher, *Orlando di Lasso und seine Zeit,* 1: 654–660.

57. All these eds. are in D-Mbs; the 1571 Munich OHS (Liturg. 970a); the 1572 Roman OHS (Liturg. 971); the "rogue" 1579 Roman OHS (Liturg. 972); and the Munich 1581 book (Liturg. 973), and are all available online at http://www.digitale -sammlungen.de/index.html ?c=digitale_sammlungen&l=de (accessed 21 October 2011).

58. For the precise dating, Zagar, "Post-Tridentine liturgical change."

59. The original text of the much later account is given best by Culley, *Jesuits and Music,* 90 and 287–289, and thoroughly discussed by Crook, *Orlando di Lasso's Imitation Magnificats,* who also wisely cautions against attributing too much liturgical agency to the Jesuit efforts of 1581–2 in Munich.

60. I read the report of Tumler's request to Rome for "toni psalmorum responsorium et pio sacratiore hebdomada historiae Christi patientis, quibus ad Divum Apollinarem uti" (Culley, *Jesuits and Music,* 289) as referring to formulae for psalm-tones, Mass responses (not Matins Responsories), and Passions.

61. On the Lamentations, see Bergquist, *Neue Reihe,* vol. 22, and for the attribution/dating of the Responsories and Lauds items, id., *Neue Reihe,* vol. 24 (1993), x–xii.

62. In Bergquist's edition, mm. 22–23.

63. On these cultural choices in the Magnificat repertory, see Crook, *Orlando di Lasso's Imitation Magnificats.*

64. Palestrina's piece, which has no surviving source other than F. X. Haberl's edition from a now-missing Altemps manuscript, is reprinted in Palestrina, *Le opere complete* (Rome, 1981), 33: 130. Bergquist shows that the five-voice *alternatim* setting in Mbs 2747 cannot be by Lasso.

65. The exceptions are in the Tone-3 version, vv. 2 and 10, and in Tone-4, v. 6.

66. *Glossa ordinaria* (1603), col. 701.

67. Fiamma, *Rime spirituali* (1570), 348.

5. Static Rites, Dramatic Music

1. "Threni ex urgenti & compressionis affectu a Jeremia scripti sunt, unde pleni sunt affectum . . . ita Jeremias hic iisdem affectibus & dolori suo, sine ordine aut ordinato discursu indulget, atque sententias quasi tumultarie congerit, prout eas dolor effundit," Lapide, *Commentarius,* 829.

2. Exceptionally, the Dominicans retained their Lesson verses and Responsories, quite different from the Roman selection, and some music written for nuns in Naples and Lucca highlights this. The standard Dominican Lessons post-1600 were: F5 {1:1–3}, {4–6}, {7–9}; F6 {2:1–3}, {4–6}, {7–9}; SS {4:1–4}, {5–8}, {9–12}, with the *Oratio* sung in its twenty-two-verse entirety at the end of SS/Nocturne III as a tenth Lesson before the ninth Responsory; see *Breviarium . . . praedicatorum* (1719), 268ff.

3. "Hunc in modum totam Christi Passionem invenire est apud Hieremiam Prophetam; vel in solis quatuor capitibus Threnorum ejus; . . . verbis historicae Evangeliae Hieremias dat admirabilem interpretationem atque lucem, vicissimque eandem ab Historia Evangelica recipit," *Tractatus de variis passionem Domini nostri Jesu Christi meditandi modis,* 284–94.

4. Sommervogel, *Bibliothèque,* 3: 213.

5. Besides the citation of 3:1ff. ("Ego vir videns") in John of the Cross's *Dark Night of the Soul,* bk. 2, ch. 7, similar use of 3:2 to express the searching and unsatisfied *Anima* was made by the Franciscan Alonso Pastor ("el estar un alma intimamente ansiosa por su Dios . . . y no gozarlo . . . sino que se halla en lo contrario de lo que desea entre angustias de tristes tinieblas: *Me minavit, et adduxit in tenebras . . .*"), *Soledades del amor divino* (Valencia, 1655), 23, dedicated to Maria Luisa de Borja, a nun in Gandia.

6. Koslofsky, *Evening's Empire,* 111–112.

7. On M. A. Grancini's *O quam vilis* (1631), which uses both Lamentations and the Song of Songs, probably written as the 1630 plague raged in Milan, see Kendrick, *The Sounds of Milan,* 160.

8. M. A. Mattei, "Ceremoniale Sacrosanctae Basilicae Principis Apostolorum de Urbe," ACSP 9/2.9, 70–73: "cantores qui cantare debent lamentationes, veniunt ante legile in vestibuo positum, et facta genuflexione ante altare, et canonicis reverentia in eodem loco, cantant integre Lamentationes, et postquam fuerit cantatum, faciunt iterum genuflexionem altari, et reverentiam canonicis."

9. "Le Lamentationi, responsorij Bened. et Miserere si cantano dalli Musici solennemente," ACSP 9/2.7, unpaginated.

10. E.g., on 15 April (Wednesday) 1615: "le 2. prime lettione dalle lamentazioni furono cantate in canto fermo, una da un soprano, e l'altra da un Contralto, l'uno e l'altro sacerdoti, la 3.a fu cantata in musica da tutti li cantori" (ACSP, 9/2.3, p. 144); in 1616, "la prima lectione in canto fermo un soprano, la 2. un contralto et la 3.a s'è cantata in musica. Li Responsori la maggior parte sono stati cantati in musica nuova del Suriano nostro Maestro di Cappella" (*ibid.,* 320).

11. S. Maria Maggiore's orders from 1606 mandated only a single boy to chant the Lessons; "Lamentationes Hieremiae prophetae . . . non a toto cantantium choro, sed unica pueri[s] voce recitandas," cited in Burke, "Musicians of S. Maria Maggiore," at 93.

12. E.g., the diary of G. P. Mucenzio for Gregory XIII's reign, 1573–82, (I-Rvat, Vat. Lat. 12286, ff. 50, 99, 160v, or 210, all of which record the same routine in the Chapel), the Holy Year of 1625; see Rostirolla, "Celebrazioni ed eventi musicale durante l'Anno Santo 1625," at 186–187. For the Sistine repertory, including the singing of both Allegri's and Felice Anerio's Miserere, and the preponderance of years with Allegri's Lessons, see Couchman, "Felice Anerio's Music," 306ff. and now Annibaldi's definitive history, *La cappella musicale pontificia,* 27, 178, and 250–254, who notes the normal practice for L1 in polyphony and gives repertory plus solo singers for 1616 and 1641.

13. Annibaldi, *ibid.,* 184–185.

14. For 1647 ("si cantano in musica le lamentationi, il Benedictus, e l'ultimo Miserere"), see the outstanding ed. and commentary of Keller/Catalano, *Die Diarien und Tagzettel des Kardinals Ernst Adalbert von Harrach,* 3: 28. On the problems of

the cathedral's music, see Kostílková in *Ecclesia Metropolitana Pragensis Catalogus*, 83–87, and Štefan, "Hudba v katedrále v obdobi baroka."

15. *Die Diarien*, 3: 115; Harrach had just finished repairing his past tense relations with the court and hence was hypersensitive to Imperial desires, causing him to remain in Prague Castle and miss Tenebrae.

16. *Ibid.*, 3: 274–276, "i zoccolanti, che a cantare le lamentationi, massime l'oratione di Gieremia profeta, e le lettioni del 2.o notturno, hanno certi buoni straordinarii bizzarri"; cf. the excellent studies of C. Ruini, "Fonti settecentesche di polifonia semplice a Trento: un modello di trasmissione" and A. Lovato, "Polifonie semplici in fonti e trattati italiani dei secoli XVII–XIX," in Cattin/Gallo (eds.), *Un millennio di polifonia liturgica*, 187–199 and 291–309.

17. E.g., in St. Vitus in 1651 (*Die Diarien* 3: 491), when the fall of a footstool provoked the choirboys' premature outburst of the *strepitus* while the Miserere was still being sung.

18. "Dias en que ay canto de organo o Mussica en esta Santa Yglesia Patriarchal y Metropolitana de Seville . . . y estilo y costumbre immemorial de esta Sancta Yglesia observados por el Lic.do D.n Adrián de Elossu Presbitero Maestro de Ceremonias de d.ha Sanc.ta Yglesia Año de 1687," E-Sc, Archivo Capitular, III/70, f. 443ff. On the Triduum over two centuries in Seville, see Ruiz Jiménez, *La librería de canto de órgano*, 268–272 (for Elossu, *ibid.*, 231 and *passim*), along with Súarez Martos, "Música barocca." For the 1663 rules from León (which had owned one choirbook of Lamentations back in 1602), see Álvarez Pérez, "La polifonía sagrada y sus maestros en la Catedral de León," at 148 and 159.

19. The 1618 inventory given by Súarez Martos, "El archivo," 51, records a "Responssos viejos de Semana Santa de diferentes autores." The lists up to 1724 mention three L1s by Lobo, of which only the SS piece survives in Seville.

20. Santiago's Responsories (E-Sc, Mus. 90–1–1) for F5 are for two choirs, sometimes antiphonal; those for F6, for three voices and three *bajones* or *bajoncillos*.

21. Joaõ IV's lost library held Santiago's F5/L1 *a 8* and an L3 for voice and three instruments, along with an F6/L1 *a 6* and an L3 *a 12* in three choirs, two of which used instruments, *Livreria*, 419 and 437. The congruence of L1's scoring on both Days with Santiago's surviving Responsories is evident. Súarez Martos, "El archivo" and "La música," correctly points out the lack of Santiago's Lessons in the inventories and thus distances them from the cathedral, but it is also true that Salazar's F5-F6/L1s (E-Sc, Mus. 88–1–5), were copied in 1717 and do not appear in the 1724 inventory; hence the cathedral's collection of Lessons in *papeles* might have been larger than what was recorded.

22. L. B. Jalón's (in office in Seville 1643–59) incomplete F5/L1 *a 14* is in E-Zac, while of the three Lessons by Alonso Xuares (there 1675–84) in E-CU, an F5/L1 and an SS/L1 for eight voices are possible candidates, though an F6/L1 with violins seems less related to Sevillan practice, given that two violins were employed by Cuenca cathedral (where Xuares worked before and after Seville; see Martínez Millán, *Historia musical de la catedral de Cuenca*, 165).

23. Untitled ceremonial, Bologna, Biblioteca dell'Archiginnasio, B 3368, "Mercordì sera . . . a Matutino," f. 13ff.; e.g., "Le tre Lamentazioni ogni sera si cantano dalli Musichi."

24. The standard work is Vanscheeuwijck, *The Cappella Musicale of San Petro-*

nio, esp. 114–132 on the liturgical year; for Colonna's works, 249–250, 313–318. For the printed orders of 1658, see Padoan, "Ethos devozionale," 27.

25. Cicognini, *Lagrime di Gieremia profeta* (1627). On *Amor pudico,* Hill, *Roman Monody,* vol. 1, 279–297; on his later sacred plays, see Harness, *Echoes of Women's Voices,* 69–79 and 295–312.

26. "Piangi, Gerusalemme, e col tuo pianto / L'anima lava, e rinovella il core; / Torna, Gerusalemme, torna al Signore."

27. Tinghi's three-volume chronicle was first summarized by Solerti, *Musica, ballo e drammatica;* the first two volumes are in I-Fn, Ms. G. Capponi 261 and the last in I-Fas, Misc. Medicee 11. I have taken any music on Holy Wednesday as referring to Tenebrae, and "l'offizio" on other Days as the same.

28. On the role of these services in Caccini's career, see Cusick, *Francesca Caccini at the Medici Court,* 72–74, who also gives a list of the performances in which she participated. The descriptions of the 1602 and 1603 Weeks are in Tinghi's vol. 1, ff. 26 and 56.

29. In 1609 only men came from Florence, while the preceding year there were no imported musicians and hence music for only one choir (*ibid.,* ff. 253v and 207).

30. Paliaga/Renzoni, *Le chiese di Pisa,* 99.

31. Tinghi, vol. 1, f. 384, 1612: "Musica eccelente a tre cori con due giù in ciesa cantata da musici di S.A. et uno la su alto nella Cappella . . . le figlie di Giulio Romano et dalla Vitoria Archilei et altri musici e durò il Matutino persino ala una ora di notte, era la ciesa colentisima di gente."

32. On both these sides of Caccini's persona, Cusick, *Francesca Caccini,* 72–73 and 85, is essential; in a letter of March 1619 she mentioned two weeks of training for the Triduum.

33. Tinghi, vol. 2, f. 485v, 1622: "Nella ciesa di San Nicola et stettero l'ufittio del mercoledi santo et loro A.S. avevano fatto venire la Sig. Franc.ca Cigniorelli con la musica et fu musica [dalle] sue fanciulle et il fratello Picino et Mutio Frema [= Effrem] con la arpa e il pretino Caselato suo discepulo e tutti li altri musici di S.A. . . . le donne in sul medesimo corridore et i musici in coro in Ciesa et avendo fatto li due soliti palchi."

34. Tinghi, vol. 3, f. 120v, 1625: "la musica a tre cori due in ciesa et uno in sul Coridore dove erano loro A.ze fatta dalla Francesca Caccini Musica di S.A.S. et dalle sue fanciulle."

35. Tinghi, vol. 2, f. 341v, 1621: "l'uffitio et le musiche a tre Cori, due in ciesa de' musici di S.A. et l'altro su nel coridore di donne con la Fran.ca Caccini con le due sue fanciulle et l'Arciangiola con Mutio Frema."

36. Tinghi, vol. 3, f. 291, 1633: "S.A. sentì il Mattutino in casa cioè nella chiesa di San Nicola, havendo fatto venire di Firenza la Musica, e la sera fu composizione del S. Frescobaldi . . . Giovedì Santo il mattutino sul corridore in S. Nicola e fu composizione d'Agniolini . . . Venerdì Santo Mattutino su S. Nicola, composizione di Giovanb. da Gagliano."

37. The entries for these Florence years are in Tinghi, vol. 2, f. 133, 194, and 243 respectively.

38. This presages the cultural turn of the Regency chronicled in Harness, *Echoes of Women's Voices,* 40–208.

39. Carter, *Jacobo Peri 1561–1633,* 1: 84, both notes his leading the ensemble and downplays the compositions for the Week.

40. The omission is also in Alessandro Scarlatti's six Lessons (I-Baf).

41. E.g., the chromaticism in *Aspice, Domine* (the motet derived from 1:1), or at "piae lachrymae" in *O Jesu mi dulcissime,* both in *Liber secundus sacrarum modulationum* (Rome, 1627).

42. On Bertacchi, see T. Asiari's entry in *DBI* 9 (1967).

43. The standard work on Pecci is Buch, "Seconda prattica and the Aesthetic of Meraviglia," which mentions the Responsories and the composer's membership in the confraternity of S. Caterina in Fontebranda.

44. The reiteration of the word is missing in the Tuscan Responsories of Bivi (1544 and 1564) and Bartei (1607), Pomponio Nenna's two sets *a 4* or *a 5* (1607/22) from Naples, Asola's and Victoria's OHS editions (1584 and 1585), Massaino's *Quaerimoniae* (1609), and the Roman Responsories of Zoilo (Rn 77–88), G. F. Anerio (Rn 152), lngegneri, and Felice Anerio.

45. Sarzana, Archivio Diocesano, Confraternita S. Croce, *Libro di cassa* 10 (1610–66), f. 95, for 1623: "a di 25 [April] pagatto al R. musicho lire sette p il Giouedi santo e tre giorni di Pasqua L. 7."

46. For the payment, Sarzana, Archivio Storico del Comune, Opera S. Maria dell'Ospedale, *Libri di scrittura, Libri di cassa* 21 (1620–38), 17 October 1623; Milleville's normal salary was paid until his departure was negotiated with his Olivetan superiors on 26 March 1626 (ibid., *Libro de deliberazioni e strumenti* 1610–39, f. 86v).

47. *Pompe funebri nel mortorio di Christo, Responsori delli Matutini . . . quali possono anche servire da Motetti in occasione di quaranta hore . . .* op. 14 (Venice: Vincenti, 1624).

48. "Fit enim tunc temporis [Tenebrae Days] . . . nonnulli, ex rusticis praesertim, ipsius Sathanae fallacia non satis internoscentes, eo audaciae procedant, ut valido fuste percutientes, sedilia valvas, scamna, altarium ipsorum scabella, aliaque permulta frangant; Tibiarum, fistularum, ac sibilorum sonum emittant; vomeres, ligones, ac ferramenta idgenus multa pulsent; igneas corruscationes, tum ex silice scintillas excutiendo, tum super accensas candelas contritam resinam . . . et cornuum sonitu domum Dei terrere praesumant; strepitu concitato, petulanti fragore, effrenique audacia omnia perturbantes . . . alia quaecunque instrumenta districtius prohibentes, ligneas virgas tantummodo permittimus, quae minorem digitum crassitudine non excedant," *Constitutiones synodi secundae [Sarzanae],* 18; a letter of 30 July 1621 to the cathedral chapter conveyed Salvago's order for the canons to recite the Office better (Archivio Diocesano di Sarzana, C. 152).

49. Reardon, *Holy Concord,* 154–168, provides an excellent study of the 1650 edition.

50. The *Threni Jeremiae Prophetae super voces gregorianas* (2nd ed. Venice: Magni, 1628) by the Somascan cleric Rossi features the same opening to F5/L1 that had appeared as an example in the composer's treatise *Organo de' cantori* (Venice: Magni, 1618), a work that Rossi stated had been finished in 1585; hence its use of ornamented solo *falsobordone* reflects the Cinquecento. Outside his musical activity, the Somascan also updated Durandus (*Novum Rationale Divinorum Officiorum*; Venice, 1625) without mentioning Tenebrae and wrote *Meditationi sopra la Passione* (Venice, 1621) which cite Jeremiah only once and stand in the worst tradition of Italian urban regulars' anti-Judaism.

51. Strozzi, *Parafrasi delle Lamentationi di Ieremia,* "Ho ridotto in Parafrasi (Eminentissimo Principe) le Lamentationi di Ieremia, che dalla Chiesa ne' giorni santi con

flebil voce si cantano, hauendovi una Canzone come per ornamento congiunta," dedication, p. i. This Antonio (1569–1646) was the Capuchin brother of Urban VIII.

52. "Christo nella passione fu condotto dal Padre nelle tenebre de' dolori, senza
luce di conforto."

53. "La misericordia di Dio, quasi lume mattutino stenebra la notte delle nostre
calamità . . . Per le tenebre del peccato s'oscura l'oro della giustitia."

54. Keller/Catalano, *Die Diarien,* 4: 74–76.

55. For its tortured history and the abuses against students committed by one of
its members before 1640, see Liebreich, *Fallen Order.*

56. "Prophetae Ieremiae Lamentationes, a R. D. Petro Caesio Romano, de nostra
familia Religiosa optime merito, Musicis modis egregie inclusas, & in nostro Templo
cum omnium admiratione decantatas, typis edidimus." Given the order's financial
condition, probably Cesi himself paid for the printing.

57. "[Cesi] insegnava . . . ad alcuni figlioli poverelli per amor di Dio come se fusse
stato un nostro Padre," in Caputi, "Le notizie storiche," at 48ff.

58. AGSP, Domus Generalitiae 50, will of Cesi opened on 18 March 1703, notary
G. C. Lamparini.

59. Cf. Calasanz' letters of 31 May and 7 June 1642, nos. 3999 and 4003 in Picanyol (ed.), *Epistolario di S. Giuseppe Calasanzio,* vol. 8.

60. "Vesperae cantabunt, ubi non est diversa consuetudo, tono alto, et plano,
devoto, suavi, ac simplici . . . Eodom tono officium quod tenebrarum diei solet cum
suis caeremoniis hebdomada sancta fiat," "Regulae et Ritus CC.RR.PP. Matris Dei
Scholarum Piarum [1665/1659]," AGSP, Regesta Generalitatis 89, points 2 and 3.

61. I follow Morelli, *Il nobilissimo oratorio della Chiesa Nuova,* 14, in taking
the "Carlo del Viol*ino*" of Q. 43 as Carlo Caprioli. Carlo Mannelli, the other candidate for this identification, is never called "*del* Violino," as is Caprioli in the Roman
documents listed on Jean Lionnet's classic site for Roman musical life, "Les musiciens
à Rome (1570–1750)" (philidor.cmbv.fr/catalogue/, accessed 4 November 2011).

62. Ruffatti, "Curiosi e bramosi," whose "Santo A" watermark of I-Bc Q. 44–47
is found in Q. 43 at ff. 20–21, 26, 30, 37, 40, 48, and 51, while the "IHS+cross" mark
occurs at ff. 46, 55, 72–73, and 103–104 (this last in the section of vernacular pieces).

63. The best summary of Marcorelli's career is the entry by A. Morelli, *DBI* 70
(2007).

64. The score of the former is in A-Wn, Mus. Hs. 18705, while that of the latter
is lost (libretto in A-Wn).

65. "Già resterò sin che benigno il Cielo / Mi conceda momenti / A sparger pi-
anti, a radoppiar lamenti."

66. Steffan, "L'oratorio veneziano," 432 and 450, identifies the Ferrara work with
an item in Giuseppe Uliasse's shipment of a score with music by Legrenzi entitled *Pensieri funebri* whose incipit was "Lamenti profetici." However, the incipit of the 1676
Lamenti profetici is actually "Pensieri funesti / Che il duolo accoglieti"; even with a
switch of title and incipit, the two are not necessarily the same.

67. "Dabit percutienti se maxillam" becomes "Le sue gote offre a la mano, / Che
spietata i colpi appresta."

68. "Mortal, se da tuoi falli è Christo avinto / I mal nati pensieri a stilla a stilla /
In accorato pianto homai distilla," followed by "Lava colpa infinita / Stemprata da i
sospiri onda contrita."

69. Lines 1056–1064 and 1129–1137 in the excellent edition by M. C. Pinillos

("Autos Sacramentales Completos," 10; Kassel/Pamplona, 1996), which catches the citations to the book (although not to the actual Lessons), gives the penitential meaning of the passage, and notes both the importance of music in the play as a whole as well as the lines that would have been sung (*ibid.*, 46–47, 72–76, 79–80, and 258–263 for the text). The contract with Navas for the music is in Pérez Pastor, *Documentos para la biografía*, 371.

70. "Voces de los cielos son. / Qué justamente, qué bien / suena agora Jeremías, / llorando a Jerusalén!."

71. "[Damas cantan:] ¡Oh! Cómo yace postrada, / sin consuelo y sin placer, / la emperatriz de las gentes, diciendo cuantos la ven: ¡Jerusalén, Jerusalén! / [Música dentro]: Pues no hay dolor que iguale a tu dolor, conviértete a tu Dios y tu Señor, / que es el último bien," ll. 1056–1063.

72. "Doris, ¿qué triste canción / es esa? Una que leí / en un libro tuyo. Di, / ¿que libro? *Lamentación* / se llama, de Jeremías," ll. 1065–1069.

73. "[Damas:] ¡Oh! Cómo sola y viuda, / sin quien la alivie ni quien / la consuele, llora y gime," ll. 1129–1131.

74. On the company, see Pinillos' edition, 12–18.

75. On this piece, see Stein's comments in *Libro de Música de la Cofradía de Nuestra Señora de la Novena*, 60–62, who tellingly draws the parallels between it and chains of laments in Calderón's *Fortunas de Perseo y Andrómeda; ead., Songs of Mortals*, 368; Caballero, "*Arded, corazon, arded*," 45 and 163, and Barreiro, "Las lamentaciones en romance," an analysis of the text and its variants noted below.

76. "En una gruta Jeremías de Anciano Hebreo; y en el otro lado Jerusalem en el trage Turquesco, con cadenas, y los dos cantan, sonando las sordinas. . . . [con] sordinas y caxa ronca," Bances Candamo, *Poesías cómicas* (Madrid, 1722), 2: 101.

77. For Serqueira's piece in Valladolid, see Caballero, "*Arded, corazón, arded*," 45–46, 91, 163–166 (who also suggests some kind of Holy Week performance in Valladolid Cathedral), Barreiro, "Las lamentaciones" (pinpointing differences in the texts), and López-Calo, *La música en la cathedral de Valladolid*, 5: 272; the last strophe is "Lloren [i.e. "Viae Sion lugent"] y lloremos todos . . . que la culpa / reina es del humano ser."

78. I cite from his *Rime* (1731), 3: 125–141. Menzini's was not the only paraphrase, as the large-scale poem by the Observant Franciscan Agostino da Vicenza (Nicola Tessari; c.1660–1716), *Gerusalemme compianta* (Venice, 1705) is also based on the book.

79. "Un bellissimo oratorio in musica dedicato a San Filippo Neri et era la composizione li Treni di Geremia, tradotti in volgare da S. Eminenza, cantati da' migliori musici con l'accompagnamento di più istromenti, fra quali sei trombe sordine," Valesio, *Diario di Roma* 3: 577. On the pieces of 1704–06, see Franchi, *Drammaturgia romana* 2: 23, 38, and 42, and Matitti, "Il cardinale Pietro Ottoboni," docs. 253–254. The basics of the 1706 performance were provided by Poensgen, "Zu Alessandro Scarlattis Oratorium per la Passione," 82.

80. The original libretto's title page reads: "La Passione / Di Nostro Signore / Gesu' Cristo / Oratorio / *A tre voci* / Dedicato all'amante del Crocifisso / San Filippo Neri / [Ottoboni shield flanked by figures] / In Roma, MDCCVI." Thus the piece is clearly from 1706, and in later editions "Per" was added to the title. A table of the sections based on the Lessons, and some discussion of the verse forms, are in Wald, "Verführung zur Konversion," a different approach from that presented here.

81. Valesio, *Diario di Roma*, 3: 577; for the attendance, the *Avvisi* of 3 April, BAV Ottob.lat. 2733, f. 167v, cited in Matitti, "Il cardinale Pietro Ottoboni," 210, and for the decoration, *ibid.*, docs. 253–254. A forthcoming edition by R. Alessandrini has been announced by the Istituto Italiano per la Storia della Musica.

82. "L'em.mo Ottoboni fece martedì nel suo palazzo magnificamente apparato cantare da più esquisiti musici le lamentationi, ove oltre diversi cardinali intervenne la regina di Polonia, e molti forestieri . . ." [this must be a reference to Queen Maria Kazimiera Sobieska, then resident in Rome] "Avvisi di Roma al cardinale Marescotti," 10 April 1700, in Staffieri, *Colligit Fragmenta*, 143.

83. Griffin, "The Late Baroque Serenata," 500 and 503. The non-Neapolitan origin of Scarlatti's Latin Lessons is suggested by their scoring for two violins only, not the full string band used in Caresana and Veneziano's contemporary works in Naples (chapter 6).

84. Franchi, *Drammaturgia romana* 2: 48 and 50.

85. Żórawska-Witkowska, "Federico Cristiano in Italia," 304.

86. Franchi, *Drammaturgia romana*, 2: 67. The Tuscan Norcia might have been aware of a 1691 Florentine oratorio (by the *Compagnia dell'Arcangelo Raffaele*), *Gerusalemme distrutta da Tito*.

87. Franchi, "Il principe Livio Odescalchi e l'oratorio 'politico,'" at 252, who also posits the 1705/06 *Sedecia* in an opposite, anti-Austrian sense (i.e. the Jewish king as a not-so-hidden symbol for the Emperor, actually Leopold I at the time of the first Urbino performance of the work in Lent 1705).

88. After 1709, Ottoboni was associated with a revival of Scarlatti's *Cain* in 1710, and then sanctoral oratorios in 1711–13 before seemingly turning away from the genre later.

89. "Fosco orrore il tutto ingombra: / Ecco il Sol cangiato in ombra. . . ."

90. Aria: "Io vorrei, che in me discesa / Una fiamma di Santo Amore / Distrugesse il gel del core."

91. "Vidde Sion rapirsi / Dalla nemica destra i suoi tesori, / E le Sacrate Soglie esposte all'onte / Di sacrilego piè, che nulla teme / Il gran divieto, e'l giusto onor del Tempio, / tutto il Popolo suo languido chiede / Qualche alimento, e preziosi doni / Offre per poco cibo; Ah quanto io sono / Fatta vile, mio Dio, dal mio fallire!" Ottoboni's text is more faithful to the Vulgate than the equivalent passage in Menzini's *Trenodia 3*.

92. Guilt: "Se tra ceppi giace avvinta" and Penance: "Lasci il fallo."

93. "Gerusalem pentita," the reworking of a "Jersualem, convertere" refrain, is in the more normal *settenari*. Norcia's metrical choices for arias deriving from Lamentations in the 1709 *Trionfo* are similar: "Dissipar le eccelse mura" (2:8) in *ottenari*; "Io lagrimai cotanto" (2:11) in the *settenari/quinari* combination; the chorus "Madre, il cibo" in *ottenari*; or "Ahi, che per me" (3:6) in *quinari*.

94. "Il presente Sagro Componimento altro non è, che un preludio al gran Mistero della nostra Redenzione, che dovra in breve fra queste stesse pareti rappresentarsi."

95. These include a *Three Marys at the Cross* (private collection) and a *Deposition* (Wellesley); on these, see Olszewski, *The Inventory of Paintings*, 21–22, who relates the former picture to a *Dead Christ Mourned by Angels* (Stanford), also by Trevisani for the cardinal. Earlier paintings by Trevisani for other patrons feature

both a conscious (Messina, Museo Regionale) and a swooned (Rome, S. Silvestro in Capite) Madonna; thus Ottoboni's preference for the latter seems evident here.

96. Angel: "Si franga al Tempio il velo; / Disseratevi o Tombe, / Scotetevi o macigni; / Le tenebre piu' folte / Si raddoppino in Cielo . . . Or che del Padre Eterno appaga l'ira / Il Figlio in Olocausto, e Gesù spira," a combination of F6/R2 *Velum templi* and R5 *Tenebrae factae sunt.*

97. [Mary in recitative, with a marginal note of "Threni 1"]: "Come sola rimane / L'infelice Sion non d'altro piena, / Che di Popolo infido, empio, e crudele . . ." [Maddalena]: "Maria, queste querele / Non convengono a te, che sei innocente. / Dell'ingrata Sion pianger le colpe / Altri dovrà, e s'udiran ben presto / Con rimbombo funesto / Le fatidiche note oggi svelate. . . .."

98. "Mira in Cielo i decreti; / Ma se il guardo ti manca, odi i Profeti. [aria and gloss of 2:8:] Dissipar l'eccelse mura / Di Sionne Iddio pensò. . . ."

99. "Ah, se volgendo solo / Nel presago pensier l'ingiurie, e l'onte. . . ."

100. "O chiara di Sionne inclita figlia, / Il mio loquace di dolor pennello / A chi ti paragona, o ti somiglia?"

101. Priest: "O da stolti Profeti / Ingannata Sionne!" (equivalent to 2:14, "Prophetae tui viderunt tibi") and Mother: "Or passa intorno all'atterrate mura / Il Peregrin, battendo palma a palma (parallel to 2:15, "Plausuerunt super te").

102. "Io di sdegno immortal verga feroce," equivalent to "Ego vir videns" of 3:1.

103. "Con fiero braccio irato" and "Ahi, che per me / In Ciel non è / Raggio di Sol."

104. The aria begins "D'ognintorno veder parmi / Riquadrati alteri marmi, / Che la via serrino a me," a paraphrase of "Conclusit vias meas."

105. "Segui, o Colpa, il lamento / Di colei, che si rese / Per tua cagion tanto infelice, e mesta." [Guilt:] "La figlia di Sion non ha più in volta. . . ."

106. The Mother prefaces the first paraphrase by "confessing" that "Tito, l'eccidio Ebreo / negli eterni consigli era già scritto," and then in Part II assigns historical blame in a free recitative: "Venne Colui, che a te dovea mandarsi, / Per tua salvezza farsi, / E lo schernisti, e lo ponesti in Croce. / Lascia dunque, ch'io cangi e cuore, e voce, / Per goder del tuo scempio, / E per chiamarti di fierezza esempio."

107. The exhaustive work of La Via, "Il cardinale Ottoboni e la musica," notes the lack of documents after 1706, but records the payments for the 1725 revival at 435 and 481. Presumably the muted trumpets at the 1706 premiere played improvised preludes and interludes.

108. On the acquisition of the Dresden score, see Bacciagaluppi, *Rom, Prag, Dresden,* 163 and 170.

109. Over a D in the continuo, "segui, o Colpa" has an $F_4\sharp$ in WD and a G_4 in Dslb.

110. The "senza cembalo" indication is repeated in both sources at "Passeggia per sentir sordido."

111. In Dslb, the entire passage is signed with only one flat (and thus the vocal citation begins $E_4\natural$-F_4-G_4), but given the many cadences (including the final one) with a penultimate B♭ chord, the flat must be understood for the pitch-class E throughout.

112. The autograph is A-Wgm, III-16148, with the passage at pp. 90–94; the copies include A-Wn, Mus. Hs. 17069, ff. 99–106v and 17105, ff. 68–71. The work is catalogued in Kirkendale, *Antonio Caldara,* 180 and 182, and the 17105 copy can be seen online at data.onb.ac.at/rec/AL00221242 (accessed 4 August 2012).

113. Zeno, *Poesie sacre drammatiche* (I use the Venice, 1742 ed., 322–323). The aria is briefly discussed by Schickhaus, *Das Hackbrett,* 33–35; a (necessarily speculative, given the lack of surviving eighteenth-century *salteri,* but convincing) recording is on Caldara, *Cantate, Sonate ed Arie* (Ramée CD 0405, 2005). Zeno cited Lapide's commentaries in marginal notes of oratorio libretti based on Scripture.

114. The aria is marked "senza cembalo" in all sources, and Caldara's autograph shows rewriting in the continuo line at mm. 19–22 to include markings of "cembali soli" followed by "senza cembali" as the *salterio* re-enters.

6. European Tenebrae c. 1680

1. "Si canteranno da' Musici . . . anche le Lamentazioni della Settimana Santa, & il Passio nella Domenica delle Palme, e Venerdì Santo," *Rituale della venerabile archiconfraternita delle Sagre Stimmate del Padre S. Francesco di Roma* (1711), 85.

2. The payment record is in Franchi/Sartori, "Attività musicale nella chiesa nazionale di Sant'Antonio dei Portoghesi," 1: 224.

3. Graziani, *Responsoria Hebdomadae Sanctae* (Rome, 1663).

4. Falusi, *Responsoria Hebdomadis Sanctae* (Rome, 1684).

5. The pieces are listed in Simi Bonini, *Catalogo del Fondo Musicale,* 41–62.

6. There is discussion in Gianturco, *Stradella: uomo di gran grido,* 235–236, and Garavaglia, *Alessandro Stradella,* 59–60, who notes the lack of a doxology, and hence the Triduum destination, of the canticle; it is preserved only in non-Italian sources, while there are two manuscripts containing the Lesson in I-MOe.

7. Here and elsewhere I take timings from the excellent recorded performances: for Stradella, Virgin Classics 7243-5-61588-2 (1995/99), and for Q. 43, Harmonia Mundi HMC 901952 (2007).

8. *Pace* the Stradella literature, there is no indication that either source for this piece is lacking the setting of "Zain," as the sonority continues from "subsequentis" to "Recordata," and MoE F.1125 has *custodes* indicating the exact surviving pitches at the end of the preceding line.

9. M. Barrio Gonzalo, "Las iglesias nacionales de España en Roma en el siglo XVII" and R. Vázquez Santos, "La iglesia de San Giacomo degli Spagnoli a la luz del manuscrito 15449 del Archivio Storico Capitolino y otras fuentes del siglo XVII," both in Hernando Sánchez (ed.), *Roma y España,* 641–678.

10. Luisi, "San Giacomo degli Spagnoli" for the ample evidence of festivities and music at Easter in the Seicento and Lionnet, "La musique" for the chapel.

11. Martin, *Roma sancta,* 91.

12. Valesio, *Diario di Roma,* 9 April 1705 (3: 341): "una nuova machina per il Sepolcro, havendo tolto via l'antica che rappresentava gli 72 seniori dell'Apocalisse . . . un tempio rotondo ornato di colonne e pilastri . . . con il Venerabile" and Holy Week 1709 (4: 253) "non fu sepolcro positivamente nella cappella della Resurrezione per evitare le spese."

13. The dates are taken from Lionnet's database of Roman musicians, 1570–1750, at philidor.cmbv.fr (accessed 28 November 2011) and his entry in *DBI* 39 (1991).

14. The F5 Lessons are split between I-Rcns, carp. 8/22 (1697) and carp. 10/30, 33–36; the F6 pieces are all in carp. 12/44(1–2), 45(1–3), 46, and the SS items in carp. 14/56–61.

15. The first F5/L1, given to de Sanctis is on D/*durus,* and the latter (anonymous) on G/*mollis* in carp. 10/33 and 34, respectively; similarly for the SS/L3s, carp. 14/60 and 61.

16. Carp. 10/30 and 36; the two are given to "G. S." and anonymous. Possibly relying on memory, de Sanctis set "quomodo facta sum vilis" and not "quoniam."

17. There is no full score in carp. 14/58 and I have used D-MÜs 3806, a concordant source.

18. Lapide, *Commentarius . . . in Threnos,* 880–881.

19. Comes's setting is in E-VAcp; García's piece in E-SE (41/36; see also L. A. González Marín's entry in *Diccionario de la Música Española y Hispanoamericana,* vol. 5, 499–500); Romeo's in E-Zac; and Vargas's in E-VAc.

20. E-E 1870.

21. J. Pavia i Simó, "Calendari músico-litúrgic de la Catedral de Barcelona," at 119, where Compline started at 4 P.M. and merged into Matins/Lauds; Albazeda's Responsories in Bbc M. 1123 had evidently not stayed in the repertory.

22. Barter's pieces, in the Arxiu Comarcal de la Segarra, are dated 1687 and are described by Salisi i Clos, *La música de l'arxiu parochial de Santa Maria de Verdú,* 227, along with other Triduum items from Verdú in E-Bbc M.1168 and M. 1638, listed in *ibid.,* 93–94 and 209.

23. On Girona, see Civil, "La música en la Catedral de Gerona"; the repertory mentioned is all in E-Bbc M. 770.

24. For Tenebrae in the 1699 Valencia cathedral customary, Teodosio Herrera's "Consuetas" are helpful (E-VAc, legajo 652/70, pt. 1), while the 1739 "Constituciones" of the Patriarca are in Ferrer Ballester, *Antonio T. Ortells,* 315–316; these latter allow for simple polyphony in verses of the Lauds items.

25. In the small but important cathedral of Sigüenza, F5/L1 and the Miserere were to be sung in polyphony, with an option also for F6/L2 and SS/L1, thus spacing the complex music evenly throughout the Triduum; see Suárez-Pajares, *La música en la catedral de Sigüenza,* 1: 130, 225–246.

26. The *cuadernillo* E-SE 18/33 containing eight Lessons (written in the blank spaces of the composer's letters) was discussed in Olarte's 1992 dissertation, 286–329. García Camargo's F5/L2 is in E-V, 18/13 and the same Lesson by Martínez del Arce, 781/42. On Irízar's pieces as a whole, see Olarte, "Miguel de Irízar," 198–329.

27. "De la memoria que rezibi del cabildo mi señor han estas dos lamentaziones que por ser el tiempo tan ocupado no e podido sacarmelas," autograph note on his F6/L1, E-SE, 56/39, with a later copy in 42/1, while his SS/L1 is in *ibid.* 56/38, copied in 56/45. He also promised to return other pieces to the chapter.

28. Rios' piece is in E-VAcp, R6/5, and Durango's is in Santo Domingo de la Calzada, although not necessarily written there. Súarez Martos, "El archivo," notes Salazar's Lessons replacing Lobo's.

29. "Ad altro non servano questi Canti, e suoni, che per havere occasione di menare una vita à suo modo tutto l'anno senza osservanza alcuna delle sue Regole ma in particolare poi nelli matutini della Settimana Santa ne' quali si cantano Lettioni, Responsorij, Miserere, Benedictus, ed altre Compositioni con ogni sorte d'Instrumenti solo per farsi sentire Cantatrici bizarie dalli giovani loro Amanti, che à tale effetto si invitano alle Chiese, e le Monache, per mantenersi lasciva la voce, si fanno lecito di mangiar tutta la Quaresima la carne ancora," note of 5 April 1675 from Parma, ASV, VR, sez. monache, 1675 (apr). I am grateful to Craig Monson for the VR documents.

30. ASV, VR, Reg. Episcoporum 24 (1592–93), fol. 125r, 24 March 1593, and *ibid.* 1599, lettere N-P, respectively.

31. "Né voglio lasciare di far mentione dell'eccesso seguito nel Monast.o della Madalena nella settimana santa cinque anni sono, nel Cantare i Passij, et Officij con finire di notte, con invito non ordinario, con eccesso di Plausi nel cantare le lettioni," note of 19 February 1678, ASV, VR, monache, 1678 (gen-apr).

32. "Et anco le lamentationi della settimana S.ta si cantano talm.te sopra cembali, e conviti de secolari, che più tosto svegliono la dissolutezza, che la divotione," *ibid.*

33. Veneziano's include the Dominican pieces, recognizable by their incipits (e.g., F6/L1's "Aleph. Quomodo obtexit," L2's "Daleth. Tetendit arcum suum" [two different settings], or L3's "Zain. Repulit Dominus altare suum"), for Maria Giuseppa, Chiara, and an unnamed "Sotto Priora," dating from 1693 and 1700; his F5/L2 and Miserere verse for the women in Santo Spirito; and an SS/L7 for Suor Colomba, whose text selection from Hebrews ("Christus assistens Pontifex") points to a house using the normal Roman breviary. The entries are under Veneziano's name at http://www.urfm.braidense.it/cataloghi/msselenco.php, with the SS/L7 listed wrongly under "Spiritus meus," with the pieces for Maria Giuseppa and Chiara viewable at www.internetculturale.it. Christmas Matins Lessons for women in Santo Sprito by Veneziano are extant in I-Nf; for an overview of music in the house, see Magaudda/Costantini, *Musica e spettacolo*, 382.

34. The excellent study of Aguirre Rincón, *Un manuscrito para un convento*, provides a transcription of the pieces and discussion of performance practice.

35. Schleifer, "The Mexican Choirbooks," 243–264, who discusses the use of Iberian tones in the polyphony.

36. Pérez Puente *et al.* (eds.), *Autos de las visitas del arzobispo*, 33, 41, 72; these are the only female houses specifically recorded as doing Holy Week music.

37. On Holy Week in Lima in the period 1630–38, see Vargas Ugarte (ed.), *Diario de Lima*, including Wednesday at the female Augustinian house in each of the nine years 1630–38, see 1: 66, 156, 218, 267; 2: 20, 74, 122, 166, 182, while Tenebrae on other Days at La Concepción were recorded in 1634 and 1637 (2: 21 and 167).

38. The work of Patricia Ranum on chronology and destination of these Lessons is available online at http://ranumspanat.com/charpentier_pre-intro.htm (accessed 2 January 2012); for individual works, see below. The first, and still standard, analytic discussion of relationships between the Guise and Abbaye-aux-Bois works is due to Käser, *Die Leçons de Ténèbres*; see also Cessac, *Marc-Antoine Charpentier*, 193–200 on the Triduum music of the 1670s/1680s.

39. On the house, see Biver, *Abbayes, monastères, couvents de femmes*, 402–16, esp. 404–407 for its ties with the archbishop and for later music. Even in the eighteenth century, the nuns sang a Miserere by Lalande for a clothing ceremony, and their complex also included a theater which hosted ballet and other spectacle. For the Parisian breviary assignments, see Gaudelus, *Les offices de Ténèbres*, 59–69; Charpentier's selection in H. 111–119 thus runs against the normal Roman Responsories used by the order and found in e.g., the *Breviarium cisterciense, pars hyemalis* (Paris, 1752), 330–331.

40. The history, and the 18th-century descriptions of the house, are in Lambeau, "L'Abbaye-aux-Boix de Paris (1638–1906)," 238–313, who also reports on the altarpiece. The other possibility for identifying the artist would be his son (?), Jean Cani.

41. The preface notes "La ruine de Jerusalem par ses ennemis de Babylone a esté

la figure des malheurs d'une ame captive sous la tyrannie des pechez . . ." and the paraphrase begins: "Faut-il que cette Ville, en peuples si seconde / Soit comme Veuve & sans secours?," Charpy, *Les saintes tenebres,* 22–23.

42. For one theological debate over Tenebrae music, see Favier, "Les Leçons de Ténèbres mises en musiques."

43. On Lambert's two cycles and Miserere, see Massip, *Michel Lambert,* 215–239.

44. The court Lessons of Jean de Cambefort from 1661 and those of Jean Veillot for Montmartre (more nuns' music) in 1660 seem lost.

45. Käser, *Die Leçons de Ténèbres,* 27–50, with discussion of (sub-)verse structure and "phases" at 41–46.

46. On the Hebrew letters, *ibid.,* 46–50; on the Lessons beyond H. 96–110, see 105–117; and on the changes in the generation of Lalande and Couperin, 141–151.

47. The Lessons on G with no sharp are H. 92, 93, 97, 98, 102, 103, 104, and 106; G with a sharp H. 94, 95, 123–125; on F (always with a flat) H. 96, 105, 120–122, and 141–143; on C (no signature) H. 91 and 138–140; on C (two flats) H. 135–137.

48. Here and elsewhere, Charpentier does not employ the normative da capo (ABCBAB) for the final Responsory of a Nocturne.

49. Gaudelus, *Les offices,* 74.

50. Ranum has amassed circumstantial evidence for the Tenebrae music in Charpentier's *cahier* 6 as being for the Guise, though hard documentation for when he entered the noble household has not yet been found (my thanks to John Powell for his ideas); her arguments for linking the funeral music in *cahiers* 3–5, as well as these Tenebrae pieces, to Guise mourning are at ranumspanat.com/htmlpages/french _cahiers.html, and Marg_Magd_cah6.htm, accessed 11 February 2012.

51. Vv. 10 ("Averte faciem") and 17 ("Quoniam si voluisses") cadence on D, while other verses are elided by half cadences. H. 157 and H. 95 are accessible in the facsimile of the *Meslanges autographes,* vol. 1, 97–112; I take the performance times from good recordings (Opus 111 10-003 and Virgin 7-592952, respectively).

52. The instrumental parts in the Miserere are "flutes," while the lower of the two obbligato lines in the Prayer does not descend below G_4 and thus also suggests alto recorder.

53. The piece is discussed in in Cessac, *Marc-Antoine Charpentier,* 318–320 and Psychoyou, "The Historical Implications."

54. Charpy noted on the Latin that "Le pecheur pour remplir la faim qu'il a de sa beatitude, donne tout ce qu'il a, & tout e qu'il est, aux creatures lesquelles il espere de la trouver, mais en vain . . . [on "O vos omnes"] On applique cette plainte à Jesus-Christ," *Les saintes ténèbres,* 30–31.

55. As in much of the French literature, the lack of anti-Jewish explanation here is notable.

56. "Captivitate & vinculis quae fuit facta nocte a cohort & tribunis . . . [v. 3] conclavatione pedum & confessione," Carrière, *Commentarius,* 463.

57. Charpy, *Les saintes ténèbres,* 29–31and 145.

58. Schneider, "Observations on Charpentier's Compositional Process," together with C. Cessac, "Copie et composition: l'enseignement des ratures," in *ead.* (ed.), *Les manuscrits autographes de Marc-Antoine Charpentier* (Wavre, 2007), 55–65.

59. On the later works as a whole, see Cessac, *Marc-Antoine Charpentier,* 286–289.

60. Cf. Gaudelus' list in *Les offices,* 62–63.

61. On royal practice, see Maral, *La Chapelle Royale de Versailles,* 140–41.

62. The two Lully settings are recorded as being sung for Tenebrae (see Sawkins *et al., ibid.*), while it is harder to establish the exact occasions for which Charpentier wrote. The similarity of the ensemble is noted in Psychoyou, "The Historical Implications."

63. Gemelli Carreri, *Viaggio per Europa,* vol. 1, 212, letter of 11 April 1686. Carapella (1654–1736) was an important if private composer for the Neapolitan nobility with no surviving Triduum music (cf. the entry of F. Degrada in *DBI* 19 [1976]).

64. "Nel primo Alephbeto sotto chiascheduna lettera sono conchiusi tre versi di dodici sillabe. Nel secondo parimente sotto ciascheduna lettera tre versi, il primo de' quali è di sedici sillabe, gli altri di dodici . . . simbolicamente con questi quattro Alephbeti si dinota, che Geremia deplora i peccati non solo de' Giudei, ma delle quattro parti del mondo, cioè dell'Universo, e l'universo ancor invita a piangergli," Sarnelli, *Lettere ecclesiastiche* 4: 6–9.

65. Sarnelli, *Lezioni scritturali alla mente, e al cuore . . . e sopra i Threni del S. Profeta Geremia;* the lessons on Lamentations occupy pp. 278–328.

66. "Misticamente: Gerusalemme compianta significa l'Anima, che consentendo al peccato mortale . . . strage assai maggiore di qualsivoglia città . . . Simbolicamente: Geremia . . . ci fa vedere Christo Signor nostro in Croce . . . onde la S. Madre Chiesa usa leggere queste lamentationi . . . nelle Tenebre di Mercoledì, Giovedì, e Venerdì Santo, e le canta in tuono flebile per rappresentarci Christo paziente," *ibid.,* 280.

67. The pieces are preserved in I-Nf.

68. The saint disliked "darkness" as a spiritual method; for some resonances in seventeenth-century devotional literature, see Ossola, "Augustinus sine tempore traditus"; my thanks to Wilhelmine Otten for her ideas on Augustine.

69. I use the 27 Lessons, split between the two, currently available on www .internetculturale.it (accessed 2 January 2012); given the lack of consistent digitalization of the modern call numbers, I refer to pieces by the old inventory mark on the last page of the scores.

70. There is an excellent recording of Caresana's Lesson (Glossa GCD 922602, 2011).

71. Sarnelli, *Lezioni,* 303, Lesson X: "Allegoricamente parla della Passione di Christo Signor Nostro."

72. *Ibid.,* 304, "Alude al fabbro, che va voltando e rivoltando percuotendo, e ripercuotendo col martello il ferro."

73. *Confessions,* bk. VII, ch. 10.

7. *Ad honorem Passionis*

1. Another Lesson in this source closes with "ad laudem Passionis D. N. J. C.," an expression dating to Augustine.

2. I cite from the 1735 Rome edition and its preface, "Ragioni dell'opera," 1–4.

3. *Ibid.* 6–10.

4. *Ibid.,* 94–95, 124.

5. *Elucidatio literalis moralis ac anagogica in Threnos Jeremiae.*

6. Menochio, *Commentarii totius Scripturae,* 1: 474–479, rephrases Lapide. I cite from the Venice, 1799 edition of Scaramelli's work, Treatise V, ch. 17, 405.

7. Picart, *Cérémonies,* vol. 2, 17–18.

8. Liguori, *Opere spirituali,* pt. 2 (1768), 8–148.

9. Liguori, *Traduzione de' salmi e de' cantici, che si contengono nell'Officio Divino.*

10. Koslofsky, *Evening's Empire,* 110–117.

11. Morales, *L'artiste de cour dans l'Espagne du XVIIIe siècle,* 124.

12. The Jesuit *Diarium* excerpts are in Reich/Seifert, "Excerpte aus dem Diarium Missionis" and Stockigt, *Jan Dismas Zelenka,* 86–88, 113–118.

13. Reich, "Excerpte," 318, 330–331, 335.

14. Hernández, *Música y culto,* pt. 2, 389–390.

15. ASV, Fondo Finy, vol. 12, at f. 253v.

16. For issues of ritual in this repertory, Feldman, *Opera and Sovereignty,* 11–22.

17. The essential work on the Italian/South German Miserere is Marx-Weber, *Liturgie und Andacht,* 1–118.

18. The title of Jeremiah's book was appropriated by Manuel de la Virgen for his *Threnos, o lamentos virginales* (Salamanca, 1742), discourses on the Seven Sorrows.

19. Aresi (ed.), Porpora, *Sei duetti latini.*

20. The Venetian pieces are discussed in Tanenbaum, "The partbook collection of the Ospedale della Pietà," 224ff. and 389–391, in a manuscript with about 40 Lessons from the Pietà (I-Vc B. 52/119) also includes items for F5 (L7 [*recte,* not 1]), F6 (L8), and SS (L6), some with names of female singers; for Puccini's Lessons, cf. below.

21. For the Ouro Preto repertory, see Castagna *et al.* (eds.),*Quinta-Feira Santa; Sexta-Feira Santa;* and *Sabato Santo.*

22. Feijóo, *Teatro critico universal* (I cite from the Madrid, 1765, edition), 1: 348–350; cf. Martín Moreno, *El padre Feijóo,* 126–127.

23. *Sanctissimi Domini Nostri Benedicti Papae XIV Bullarium,* vol. 3, 7–19, with remarks on the Triduum at 17–18 (English translation in Hayward, *Papal Legislation,* 92–108).

24. The text is in Bacciagaluppi, "E viva Benedetto XIV," 251–252.

25. *Delle feste* (I cite from the Venice, 1767 ed.), 51–54; Benedict also quoted Mazzinelli on the proper understanding of the Week.

26. The pieces, part of the Oratorians' larger archive in I-Bof, are listed at opac .sbn.it (accessed 24 May 2011; I use the archive's call numbers). Musical life at the church is discussed in Vitali, "L'oratorio alla Madonna di Galliera."

27. Fontana, *Vita di Benedetto Marcello,* 93, and cf. Selfridge-Field, *The Music of Benedetto and Alessandro Marcello,* B674; the Lessons are now in D-Hs as "Lectioni / Del Mercoledì, Giovedì, e Venerdì Santo / Del H.H.Z. Benetto Marcello."

28. For Porpora's activity and the liturgical calendar, see Over, *Per la Gloria di Dio,* 47ff., esp. 56, and 84; and Gillio, *L'attività negli ospedali di Venezia,* 290–300, 284 (Pollarolo) and docs. dd5 and dd20. Żórawska-Witkowska, "Federico Cristiano," notes the prince's visit to the Derelitti, also including Tenebrae at the Pietà on Wednesday. For Porpora's works, see Sutton, "The Solo Vocal Works of Nicola Porpora." The 1745 pieces are in GB-Lbm Add. ms. 14131 (*ibid.* 288–293, as #401–06); there is a further copy of #404 in US-NH, Misc. ms. 587, no. 1.

29. For the women who sang these Lessons, and for the lists of Porpora's production in 1744–5, see Gillio, *L'attività musicale,* 295–98. In addition to Sutton's #407–409 in I-Nf, Porpora's solo Lessons with continuo include an F6/L2 in I-Bof (#69B), an F5/L2 which is no. 2 in the New Haven source, and an SS/L1 in HR-Sk.

30. The pieces with strings are in GB-Lbm Add. 14130; in Sutton's catalogue, the

group is #410–414, with parallels between #413 (with strings) and 405 (with continuo), and between 414 and 402, while Sutton's 411 is like no. 2 in New Haven.

31. Florimo, *La scuola musicale di Napoli* 1: 316. There is no mention of these performances in the *Gazzetta*'s reports.

32. The Royal Chapel's Office was recorded in the *Gazzetta* in these years; Magaudda/Costantini, *Musica e spettacolo,* appendix, 52, 159, 307, 457, and main text, 302.

33. For the *Gazzetta di Napoli* reports of 1744, *ibid.,* 39 and appendix (CD), 643.

34. The manuscript is in US-Wc, ML96.L465; there are at least five other sources for the Lessons, but this one, with its dating of individual items, seems to have a close relationship to Leo's activity. The basic study of Leo's sacred output is Krause, *Die Kirchenmusik von Leonardo Leo,* 82–97 and 202–219; these Lessons (as presented in the D-MÜs copy) and those of Feo (I-Nf) are outlined by H. Marx-Weber in "Lamentationskompositionen des 18. Jahrhunderts," with Leo's treated differently by Blankenburg, "De lamentatione," 232–239.

35. The flyleaf reads: "Carlo Broschi Farineli pone ai Piedi de V. Maestà questi componimenti di musica, originali del fù Leonardo Leo Maestro di Musica Napolitano. F[atto] a dì 1 Marzo 1757 Buon Ritiro," the first Tuesday in Lent.

36. Sacchi, *Vita del cavaliere Don Carlo Broschi detto il Farinello,* 45–46.

37. Carroccia, "Fenaroli e le composizioni liturgiche per la Settimana Santa."

38. I-Nc, available at www.internetculturale.it.

39. The Responsories are in two manuscripts, both in I-Nc, Casa Reale 77.1.4; one set of Nocturnes II–III for all three Days is complemented by Nocturne I items and duplicates of the Third Nocturne in another codex.

40. Rossi Melocchi, "Memorie antiche di Pistoia," f. 45v, 18 April 1726: "Vi sono state cantate le Lamentazioni in musica composizione del Sig.re Gio: Carlo Maria Clari Maestro di Cappella di Pisa e vi anno fatto far venire il Padre Flavio Torelli di Siena Agostiniano . . . così s'è udita in tutte le tre sere delli detti tre giorni della detta Settimana Santa con applauso . . . Mons.re Vescovo vi è stato due sere a sentire le dette Lamentazioni ma dopo che sono state cantate le Lamentationi se ne andavano tutti." These passages were first noted by Fanelli, *The Oratorios of Giovanni Maria Clari.*

41. Rossi, "Memorie antiche," f. 240v.

42. The two SS Lessons are in I-Ls, B. 11.

43. The first essays were Lazzareschi, "La famiglia Puccini e il diario musicale di Giacomo Puccini sen."; Guidotti, "Musiche annue ed avventizie nelle chiese lucchesi"; and Comastri, "I Puccini e la musica per i Benedettini." For his non-Tenebrae pieces for the nuns of S. Giovanetto, see Guidotti /Comastri, "'Il ridotto di quelle che maritar non puonsi.'" The pieces are in the "Fondo Puccini" in I-Lim.

44. Guidotti, *"Musiche annue ed avventizie"* (2012) gives an authoritative account of the Republic's entire sacred music in its ritual calendar; for the Triduum, see esp. 218–221 and 551–554, although there are many references to Holy Week music.

45. The surviving three books of Puccini's "Libro delle Musiche Annue ed Avventizie fatto da me Giacomo Puccini . . ." are in I-Las, Deposito Istituto Pacini 1–3, vols. B, C, and D (A is missing). Guidotti, *"Musiche annue,"* and Comastri, "I Puccini," 176–177, describe Puccini's service at S. Ponziano on Thursday and Friday, also documenting Nocturnes in the Cappella di Palazzo, to which the Palatina went after the Olivetans' Tenebrae.

46. Nerici, *Storia della musica in Lucca,* 212.

47. Montuoli's 1715 Lauds are in I-Lim, Fondo Puccini, A. 23g.

48. Giacomo's Lessons are in *ibid.*, G. 41p-z, with the 1741 BDDI as G. 10b and a Lesson for nuns as G. 41g. Of these ten, G. 41y is a copy of G. 41r, and thus there are eight pieces for the Palatina (a Lesson in I-Ls is a copy of G. 41v).

49. "A dì 23 e 24 Marzo, Giovedì e Venerdì Santo. Musica a S. Ponziano. Per gli ofizii della Settimana Santa ove si cantano le 3 lezzioni del Primo Notturno a solo e VV. ed i Responsori del sopradetto Notturno a 4, poi Miserere con le VV. intero, e Benedictus spezzato. Il Giovedì si canta prima il Benedictus del Miserere, cantandosi l'ultimo Miserere, ed il venerdì il Miserere delle Laudi, nel qual tempo il coro [of Olivetans] satisfà al rimanente de' salmi, quale terminato da' musici si canta dal coro l'antifona al Benedictus che si canta poi questo de i musici spezzatamente e dal coro [i.e. *alternatim*]," Puccini, "Libro delle musiche," vol. B, *sub* 1758, f. 121r, first published by Comastri, "I Puccini"; on *alternatim* in Lucca, see Guidotti, "*Musiche annue,*" 552.

50. I-Lim, Fondo Puccini, G. 41p (F5/L1), u (SS/L2), and r (F6/L1) respectively.

51. For the "medium" level of the city's musical forces at the services in S. Girolamo and S. Ponziano, Guidotti, *ibid.* 194 and 395 along with the ritual calendar, 730 and 736.

52. "Libro delle Musiche," vol. D, *sub* 1775: "Il giovedì si fece il mio Miserere del [17]40 in A *la mi re* = Benedictus [17]41 = e quantunque in detto giorno non venisse Mons. Arciv.o a prendere il perdono per non trovarsi in città bensì a Roma, si cantò al solito l'ultimo Miserere dopo essersi cantato il Benedictus . . . Se in avvenire si potranno metter i corni alla composizione, si potranno provedere, desiderando ciò il Padre Abate di Governo Compagni . . . Il venerdì avendo fatto una lezione nuova Antonio figlio, la prima cioè in Soprano con violoncello e viola obbligate, suonò il violonetto obbligato il Baldotti e la viola il Franceschi, non essendosi preso uno suonatore di violoncello (come si volea prendere di più dal solito non poteasi capire con comodo, né ha da succedere ciò negli anni avvenire a quando si faranno meglio i mantici sotto l'organo e levati di sulla cantoria)" [I have reversed the order in the diary so as to give a successive progression through the Days]. No SS/L1 by Antonio seems to have survived.

53. Baldotti's diary is "Musiche, paghe del Prencipe, ed altro," I-Lim, O.IV.5.

54. Richter's cycle is in F-Ssc; see Reutter, *Studien zur Kirchenmusik Franz Xaver Richters*, 2: 371–376; for Ricci, Picchi, *Archivio Musicale del Duomo di Como*, 118.

55. The bassoon part is relatively difficult; it is in I-PAc, Sanvitale C. 225.

56. These pieces are G. 41p (F5/L1, for soprano with violins) and 41v (SS/L3, soprano with violins and viola) in I-Lim, Fondo Puccini. The former reads "1739/ Lezione Prima del Mercdrì Santo / In Soprano / Con strumenti / di / Giac.o Puccini . . . A di 4 marzo 1752 datane altra copia per la figlia monaca in Massa della S.a Cat.a Monzoni, copiata dal Partini," with a similar inscription in the latter. The score of 41v notes "anche in Contralto" (a transposition not preserved), and thus the two Lessons were possibly for different singers. In the "Libro di fondazione del monastero del Corpo di Cristo ora detto Santa Chiara" (Massa, Archivio Storico Diocesano, D 8/19), the list of nuns professing in 1749 includes two sisters from Lucca, Lavinia and Maria Maddalena Monzoni, who would take the religious names of Caterina Celeste and Maria Cecilia (possibly the latter was the musical one, given her choice of name). I am grateful to Prof. Franca Leverotti for this information. On earlier music in S. Chiara, see Radicchi, "La musica nel monastero delle principesse Cybo."

57. I-Lim, Fondo Puccini, G.41g: "Orazione di Geremia intera secondo il rito domenic.o & [cross-out: "francesc.no"] a 2 Canti con Org.o per accomp.to o Cemb.o fatta per alcune monache di S. Micheletto" along with 41q, "Lezione P.ma del 3ro Notturno di Giovedì Santo fatta per ordine avutone dal R.mo P.dre Ab.te D. Giuseppe Nicolao Micheli Lateranense essendone egli stato di ciò richiesto dal suo amico di Genova." The stipulation of the latter piece was that it fit inside a tessitura of B$_3$♭-G$_5$; although no nun is specifically named, the similarities with other Third Nocturne Lessons for sisters suggest female monastic performance.

58. Raw genealogical information is from www.genmarenostrum.com/pagine -lettere/letteread/d'andrea.htm, accessed 19 September 2011. Pescopagano is between Naples and Potenza, but the family seems to have been rooted in Naples. My thanks to Alessandro d'Andrea di Pescopagano for other family history.

59. The dates of profession are from ASDN, Vicario delle monache, S. M. Regina Celi, 329-A-221, 330-A-238, and 330-A-221, respectively; I am very grateful to Prof. Elisa Novi Chavarria for this information.

60. There were no other women from the family who professed in the house, and thus the names given in the musical dedications imply that one or the other Isabella became "Anna."

61. For the battle over one Carnival "infraction" won by the nuns, see Weber, *Bischöfe, Generalvikare und Erzpriester*, 99–100; for the choir architecture, Hills, *Invisible City*, 153 and fig. 33.

62. Magaudda/Costantini, *Musica e spettacolo*, 381 and appendix, 643.

63. The piece is #408 in Sutton's catalogue, and 69A in I-Bof.

64. The Lesson is catalogued in Murphy, "The Sacred Music of Gian Francesco di Majo," 343–344, without identification of the singer.

65. For the musical connections of Antonio, see Tufano, "La musica nei periodici scientifico-letterari napolitani," at 133–136; the duke also provided texts for Paisiello.

66. Agnese's musicality is noted in G. B. Paziani's "Elogio storico," a preface to Antonio di Gennaro, duca del Belforte, *Poesie* (Naples, 1796), vol. 1, cited in *Efemeridi letterarie di Roma* 25 (1796), at 357. This volume also contains the pieces for clothing ceremonies.

67. This was catalogued by Melucci/Morgese, *Il fondo musicale del Monastero delle Benedettine*, with other essays in Bonsante/Pasquandrea (eds.), *Celesti Sirene*, 141–188. Much of this archive is listed at sbn.opac.it.

68. Museo di Roma, Palazzo Braschi, Rome, reproduced by Olszewski, *Cardinal Pietro Ottoboni (1667–1740)*, 30.

69. Żórawska-Witkowska, "Federico Cristiano in Italia," 304; he had been brought by Cardinal Troiano Acquaviva, the pro-Bourbon former legate in Spain resident in Rome.

70. Moli, "Compositores e interpretes," 28–34, covers Terradellas' service at the church and the regular corps of 12 singers.

71. In 1740 Costanzi, who had been in the service of Ottoboni, passed to that of Acquaviva, the Spanish ambassador at the Papal court and the protector of S. Giacomo as part of the Spanish "nation" in Rome (M. Lopriore, *DBI* 30 [1984]), who could have arranged for Costanzi to write pieces for the church. Costanzi's F6/L1 from 1742 (A-Wn, Mus. Hs. 18723) for alto with horns and strings features the choral interjections at "Non est lex" and "Cum defecerunt"; in addition, there is an F6/L3 from 1744 (or 1743) in F-Pn, Rés. 1709, for soprano, flutes and strings. Both these sources are from the collection of Alois Fuchs (1799–1853).

72. For the fourteen singers and twenty-three instrumentalists involved in the 1746 music, conducted by the famed castrato Francesco Finaja, Moli, "Compositores e interpretes," 40–43. Burney's account of these Lessons has thrown even the best scholarship off track, leading to their speculative placement for the Cappella Giulia or elsewhere in Rome in the years from 1749 to 1753, but the dated autographs of Perez and the payment records show the original destination at S. Giacomo in 1746.

73. Gillio, *L'attività musicale,* 352; the opera premiered on 6 February.

74. The Lessons are in I-Rcns, carp. 9/27–29 (Jommelli), 12/47–49 (Perez), and 13/50–52 (Durante), as of summer 2011.

75. Burney, *A General History of Music,* 4: 538: "I am in possession of a Miserere and a Mass, by this master, which are inferior to no productions of the kind that I have seen." The lesser payments (15 or 10 *scudi*) for the various Misereres are recorded in Moli, "Compositores," 42–43.

76. Moli, "Compositores," 122.

77. For a discussion of Durante's overall Lesson production, Blankenburg, "De lamentatione," 227–232.

78. My thanks to Geoff Burgess for ideas on Roman oboes; Perez and Durante's scores also call specifically for "flauti lunghi," i.e. recorders, in some movements.

79. "En chantant un lambeau des *Lamentations* de Jomelli, il [the Nephew] répétait avec une précision, une verité et une chaleur incroyable les plus beaux endroits de chaque morceau: ce beau recitatif obligé où le prophéte peint la désolation de Jérusalem . . . ," Diderot, *Le neveu de Rameau,* 111. On musically-induced automatic behavior in Diderot's undated work, see McClymonds/ Rex, "'Ce beau recitatif obligé.'" It should be noted that the Nephew seems to perform multiple sections of multiple Lamentations, not just "Viae Sion," all the more remarkable for his being a baritone (*basse-taille*).

80. The four added *zecchini* were for what the deputies called the "particular gusto, que con ellas [Durante] ha dado"; Moli, "Compositores," 122.

81. *A General History of Music* (1789), 4: 563: "The productions of Jomelli and Perez are in an elegant and expressive oratorio style; and that of Durante more in the ancient style of church Music: more learned in modulation, more abounding in fugue, and more elaborate in the texture of the parts, as might be expected from his maturer age, and the solemnity of the day on which his Music was to be performed"; cf. also Dottori, "The church music," 46–47.

82. Ciampi's F6 pieces are in I-Rcns, carp. 11/41 (L1) and 12/42–43 (L2–3), while the SS works are all in carp. 13.

83. I-Rcns, carp. 8/21, "Lectio Prima in P.ma Die a Canto solo / con violini viole obligate, / e Corni da Caccia e Flauti / 1748 / Del Sig.re Francesco Ciampi." For the organization of Tenebrae in 1748–49, see Moli, "Compositores," 70–82.

84. MEX-Mc D c 20.

85. I-Rcns, carp. 10/31, "Lectio 3a in P.ma Die a 3 Canto alto e Basso / con Violini Viole obligate / e Corni da Caccia / 1748 / del Sig.re Francesco Ciampi."

86. Moli, "Compositores," 70 and 91.

87. These pieces are in carp. 10/32 (F5), 11/40 (F6), and 13/53 (SS).

88. Carp. 8/24–26, 11/37–39, and 14/62–64; on the 14 singers, 13 strings and organ for the 1752 cycle, see Moli, "Compositores," 91–92. Aurisicchio's two L1s are in MEX-Mc, leg. I, letra A.

89. De Conti, *Viaggio d'Italia,* 138–139.

90. "Quaderni di viaggio (1779–1780)," now in Canova, *Scritti* (2007), 151:

"Dopo il pranso andiedi a San Giacomo de' Spagnoli, e sentij a cantare tre lementazioni in musica ma molto bene . . . La sera poi andiedi alla Congregazione e sentij a cantare le lamentazioni, una da Davide tenore bergamasco, e la cantò per eccellenza." This singer (1750–1830) was the father of Rossini's tenor Giacomo David.

91. These are preserved in the Santini collection, D-MÜs Hs. 1087 and 1088.

92. "De los Maytines del Jueves Santo," 65–74.

93. *Ibid.,* 80–96, e.g., "Jeremìas Profeta lloró con grandes gemidas . . . la Santa Iglesia con lastimosas palabras llora amargamente la muerte de Christo Su Esposo."

94. *Versión parafraseada de las Lamentaciones de Jeremias* (Madrid, 1772; Barcelona, 1778; Mexico City, 1782); the editions testify to the poems' success and their relevance to the Novohispanic repertory.

95. This is painstakingly chronicled in Morales, *L'artiste de cour,* 95–124. The standard discussion of Corselli's career and sacred output is in Torrente's excellent edition, *Fiesta de Navidad en la Capilla Real de Felipe V,* esp. 17–24. Strohm, "Francesco Corselli's *drammi per musica* for Madrid," stresses the composer's "tendency towards chromaticism, phrase interruptions and surprise harmonies."

96. For the location and the chapel's 1739 makeup, Morales, *Las voces de Palacio,* 53 and 59; winds were available in 1735 and 1745 but evidently not in 1739. By the 1760s services had moved to the chapel in the newly-completed Palacio Real.

97. E-Mp, #1111 (Torres) and #154 (Corselli).

98. An excellent recording is available, Glossa GCD 920307 (2002).

99. Corselli's scribe even had to add a paste-in so as to accommodate the final cello ritornello.

100. Leo's Miserere is #757 in E-Mp.

101. A note of 25 March 1726 from the Marquis Grimaldi to Cardinal Carlos de Borja, Patriarch of the Indies, reads "El Rey me manda decir a S. Em.a desea D. Phelipe Falconis [Filippo Falconio, co-chapelmaster at this point, who left no Tenebrae music] de una de las tres noches de tinieblas de la próxima semana santa, como se hizo el año pasado, y que en todo lo demás que entra a este sugeto, y función que ay que hacer se observa lo mismo en todo lo que se essecutò el citado año próximo pasado," E-Mp, Real Capilla, caja 112, exp. 2.

8. Endings and Continuities

1. For the Lesson cycle and Miserere by Giuseppe Giordani ("Giordaniello") for Fermo, see his *Opera omnia,* ser. I/vol. 3.

2. Marques, "A acção da igreja no terramoto de Lisboa," gives an exhaustive view of ecclesiastical efforts to repair the damage and re-institute liturgical life, also noting the moralizing commentaries.

3. Dottori, "The church music," 361–366, listed the autographs in P-Lf, with other copies in P-La (two), P-VV (the organ book in these parts is heavily figured), and I-Nc; the rubrics in this last source are largely in Portuguese.

4. Dottori, "The church music," 95–97 and C. Fernandes, "O Terramoto de 1755 e as suas implicações," both of whom remark the split in the court's musical forces between the royal residence at the Ajuda and the Patriarchal.

5. Francisco Antonio de S. José's *Canto funebre, ou Lamentaçaõ harmonica* (Lisbon, 1756) eschews Jeremiah's words.

6. "Porém eu naõ vejo mais que a montes inconsolaveis ruinas, á vista dos

quaes, naõ podia deixar de lançar rios de lagrimas hum Jeremias, e fazer como pro-prias deste lastimoso estrago as lamentaçoens, que já fez sobre a sua amada Jerusalem: *Quomodo [. . .] gentium.* Todos os seus moradores a desempararaõ, submergindo-se no seu pranto: *Plorans [. . .] charis ejus;* porque a dor, e o estrago immenso, naõ admitte consolaçaõ: *Viae Sion [. . .] solemnitatem,* e como haõ de acodir passageiros ás festas, e solemnidades, se naõ ha, nem ruas, nem casas, nem Templos, nem Altares, nem Sacramentos? *Omnes portae [. . .] squalidae;* quebradas as suas clausuras sa-hem dos seus Conventos as Esposas do Senhor, fazendo de huma Cidade taõ pia, e taõ Catholica huma Babilonia de inconsolavel confuszaõ: *et ipsa [. . .] amaritudine.* E donde procederaõ tantas ruinas? *Propter inquitatem ejus,*" Malagrida, *Juizo,* 3–4.

   7. The dates and sources of Perez' pieces are in Dottori, "The church music"; in 1761, he finished his F6/L1 on Passion Saturday (14 March), five days before the first performance.

   8. The only item missing from Corselli's 1768 group is F6/L1, and the compos-er's eight-voice Lesson for this slot from 1766 might complete this new cycle. Con-forto's pieces are #1395–1403 in E-Mp. It is not clear why the upturn in production happened in 1766–68, at a politically stable moment both in Charles III's reign and in the tenure of the Patriarch of the West Indies, Cardinal Buenaventura de Córdoba Espínola.

   9. E-Mp, #99–102.

   10. Rubio, *Catálogo del Archivo de Música,* 1: 478–483.

   11. On Fajer's Lesson, a "motet française nouvelle," see Pierre, *Histoire du Con-cert Spirituel,* 278. The seven Lessons (all L1/3s) by him in E-H include pieces with large orchestra (de Mur Bernad, *Catalogo del Archivo de Música,* 119), with Lessons also in E-E, E-VAcp, and E-SC. Marín (ed.), *La ópera en el templo,* provides new evi-dence for the reception of his works plus a list of sources for Lessons.

   12. These are discussed and transcribed in Escudero (ed.), *Esteban Salas y la Ca-pilla de Música de la Catedral de Santiago de Cuba,* vol. 4, 15–25 and 141–204, and vol. 8 (2011), 184–186, who also gives a local ordinal of 1867 suggesting that SS Lessons were not sung in Santiago.

   13. On the seismicity of the quake, see Cotilla Rodríguez, "The Santiago de Cuba earthquake of 11 June 1766"; for a contemporary record, Bacardí, *Crónicas de San-tiago de Cuba,* 1: 176.

   14. In the Moxos archives, #676 and Concepción #373–81, Nawrot (ed.), *Mis-iones de Moxos, Catálogo,* 2: 729–731; the Chiquitos Responsories are listed in the forthcoming catalogue of this archive by L. Waisman and B. Illari (my thanks to Gustavo Leone for checking the Chiquitos materials). For the 1797 shipment, total-ing 21 Lessons, to El Carmen de Guarayos, see Gembero-Ustárroz, "Enlightened re-formism versus Jesuit utopia," at 277–279.

   15. I use the numeration system in Stanford, *Catálogo de los acervos musicales;* these pieces are preserved in the respective cathedral archives, MX-Mex and MX-Pc.

   16. Picañol's pieces are in MX-Pc 7 and 66, an F6/L2 for solo alto and an eight-voice F6/L1.

   17. On Zuñiga's pieces for Durango, see Davies, "The Italianized frontier," 315–320.

   18. In v. 4b, "destructae" is also missing.

   19. Castellot, *Semana santa Christiana,* 216ff.

   20. Iriarte, *La música: Poema* (1779), 63.

   21. (Écija, n.d.); the author published other works from 1784 to 1806.

22. "En los días que se tienen las tinieblas se canta con mucha solemnidad al fin el Salmo del Miserere . . . y mientras las tinieblas de estos días podrán los fieles estar leyendo algunas piadosas consideraciones sobre la Pasión de Jesucristo, que quizá les moverán mas que la lectura sola de los Salmos y Lamentaciones del Coro, cuyo sentido no entienden bien," Gómez Bueno, *Semanero santo,* 43.

23. Pajares Barón, *Archivo de Música,* 552–556, and for an edition of Vidal's Lesson, Díez Martínez, *Música sacra en Cádiz,* 26–28 and 307–341.

24. Gómez Bueno, *Semanero santo,* 132, 139, 145, 150, 155, 160, 165, 171.

25. F-Pn Vm^7 667.

26. Rousseau, *La nouvelle Héloïse,* part V, letter 7 (e.g., in *Oeuvres complétes* [Paris, 1959], vol. 2: 610).

27. The most accurate view of the piece's sources and origins is in the critical edition by Friesenhagen/Heitmann, *Joseph Haydn Werke* I/5a, x–xi; the pioneering article was Deak, "Haydn's Lamentation Symphony."

28. H-Bn, Manuscripta Mus. III. 266–268; Deak, "Haydn's Lamentation Symphony," was the first to point to the importance of the *mediatio* pitch and the third relationships in the recapitulation; he also viewed the movement as Haydn's synthesis of all Werner's Lessons.

29. Pratl, *Acta Forchtensteiniana,* 42ff. and 51. In 1761 female singers from outside the normal forces were brought in for Holy Week (15–21 March), a possible occasion for Werner's pieces; Haydn may have started his employment just after this.

30. For instance, the reports on music in Vienna in 1766 mention "Molli" and "Winter" as virtuosi on the instrument, cited after Heartz, *Haydn, Mozart, and the Viennese School 1740–1780,* 726. Werner's two Advent pieces with "viola amabile" are in H-Bn, Manuscripta mus. III. 307–308, both dated 1759.

31. J. Schmidt-Görg, "Ein neuer Fund," and Kerman, *The Kafka Sketchbook,* 1: f. 96r and 2: 131, 287. The dating is based on the service of the singers Simonetti and Delombre mentioned on the leaf.

32. The autograph is in A-Wgm, Q-732, with the scene complex in vol. 2, pp. 1–69; this source has only cues for the orchestration of successive stanzas, and also indications for cuts, evidently from a later performance. The source in D-Bspk, KHM 783, pt. 2, ff. 1–27, seems to relate to the 1789 Berlin performance. I am grateful to my colleague Thomas Christensen and to the staff of both libraries for tracking down the sources. The piece is #319 in Krebs, *Dittersdorfiana,* 128–137.

33. "Passa il giorno, e me ritrova / L'atra [in A-Wgm: "altra"] notte fra i dolori, / E se sgombra i foschi orrori, / Me fra il duol ritrova il dì. . . ." The librettist is unknown.

34. "Quale mai voce dolente . . . Questo è Giob . . . Ah, si lasci nel dolore. . . ."

35. "Ombra son del futuro. Oh nuovo Giobbe! Quale di tolleranza, essempio mostrerai!."

36. "ist das leise Klageton des Hiob, das eine einfache, heimliche Melodie hat, sehr herzangreifend . . . ," *Musicalische Wochenblatt* (1791), after Krebs, *Dittersdorfiana,* 136.

37. I-Vl, C.F. B. 12, of unclear provenance.

38. The scoring, with two violas and winds, is reminiscent of F. X. Richter's 1773 solo Lessons for Strasbourg, which also use the chant *initium* and the letter formula as points of departure for a florid vocal line.

39. I-PSac, B 21.5.

40. On him and the Tuscan chapels, see Floros, "Carlo Antonio Campioni als Instrumentalkomponist," and Rice, "Music in the Duomo during the Reign of Pietro Leopoldo I (1765–1790)."

41. The I-Fc manuscripts (i.e. the new, mixed-voice version of the Responsories and the originals of the Lauds pieces) are available at www.internetculturale.it (accessed 19 September 2011); the original scoring is in A-Wn, Mus. Hs. 15927. On the Empress's collection, see *id., Empress Marie Therese and Music,* 264, 301. The Austrian court chapel copies are in A-Wn, HK. 505–507, and transmit the SATB version of the Responsories with some vocal and continuo rescorings.

42. Reutter's Responsories are in A-Wn, HK. 1653; the copy in I-PId has added strings, dated 1759. The first attempt at replacing Ingegneri's pieces seems to have been that of Matteo Palleotta in 1746.

43. "Musica per servizio di chiesa," preserved in I-Rrostirolla, #352.

44. Timings from two recent Hungaroton recordings of Manna (HCD 32652, 2010) and Haydn (HCD 32596, 2008).

45. R. d'Ortensio, *La processione del Venerdì Santo in Teramo nel 1854* (Teramo, 1854), cited in D. di Virgilio, "I suoni delle processioni." Possibly the Lessons were by the local chapelmaster Camillo Bruschelli.

46. Sirch, *Catalogo tematico delle musiche di Amilcare Ponchielli,* 305–313.

47. Preindl, *Lamentationes, welche in der heiligen Charwoche . . . gesungen werden* (Vienna, n.d.), or Neukomm, *Semaine sainte* (Paris, c. 1840).

48. Irvine, *Colonial Counterpoint,* 152; for the diffusion of nineteenth-century Spanish Lessons in the Philippines, see *id.,* "The Lamentations of Manuel José Doyagüe."

49. I am grateful to Prof. David Cranmer for information on Portugal's works; Garcia's set is #214 in de Mattos, *Cátalogo tematico das obras do Padre José Mauricio Nunes Garcia.*

50. Moreira, *Del folklore tortosí,* 559–562, who mentions Lamentations by the late 19th-century Catalan composers J. A. Nin Serra and M. Baixauli (along with earlier music) as performed in the Seu. The waiting for the end of the Miserere and the ensuing *strepitus*/symbolic "killing of Jews" is described as "I allà va la briva a «matâ judiets» . . . [the city's boys] estàn alèco, per a quan al chor canten allò del «super altarem tuum vitulos,"" and cf. Nirenberg, *Communities,* 202. This is one of the linkages between Tenebrae and the actual enactment of anti-Jewish sentiment. For Lamentations and Misereres still in the cathedral archives (as far back as 1723), see Pavia i Simó, "Archivo de Música de la Catedral de Tortosa (Tarragona)"; for a summary of eighteenth-century musical activity, see Rosa Montagut, "Una aproximación a la capilla de música de la catedral de Tortosa (Tarragona)."

51. Carroll, *The Penitente Brotherhoods,* 24, mentions popular Tenebrae in and around Durango from 1762 to 1852 as the background to the practice, while Lozano, *Cantemos al alba,* 664, discusses the noise-makers used in the *tinieblas;* cf. also Weigle/White, *The Lore of New Mexico,* 16.

52. For a sample of Misereres in Triduum rituals across Italy, see Arcangeli *et al., Canti liturgici di tradizione orale;* for their practice in the Cilento district, see Agamennone, "*Varco le soglie,*" 121–138; for Sicily (with fewer instances of the Miserere) and Sardinia, Macchiarella, *Il falsobordone,* 34–97, and *id.* "I canti della Settimana Santa in Sicilia," along with Lortat-Jacob, *Canti di passione.*

53. For the Lamentations verses from Sessa Aurunca and Istria, see Arcangeli,

Canti liturgici, 83 and 115, while the recordings by Nataletti are now online in the Ethnomusicology Archives of the Accademia di Santa Cecilia (bibliomediateca .santacecilia.it, accessed 11 April 2012), collections 10 and 14.

54. The excellent essays in Macchiarella (ed.), *Tre voci per pensare il mondo,* include the editor's work in Speloncato (33–43) and the views of local singers (J. D. Poli, "Il canto e la sua pratica nella confraternita di Speloncato," *ibid.,* 188–205), along with studies of Tenebrae in Calvi by J. Ayats *et al.,* "Delle Tenebre a Calvi," *ibid.,* 68–89 and the sentiments of singers there (P. Bertoni, "Il canto nell'attualità della confraternita di Sant'Antonio a Calvi," *ibid.,* 209–217).

55. Reily, "Remembering the Baroque Era."

Bibliography

Abbreviations

AAB   Archivio Arcivescovile, Bologna
ACSP Archivio Capitolare di San Pietro, Rome
AGP   Archivo General de Palacio, Madrid
AGSP Archivio Generale Storico delle Scuole Pie, Rome
ASB   Archivio di Stato, Bologna
ASDN Archivio Storico Diocesano, Naples
ASV   Archivio Segreto Vaticano; VR Congregazione dei Vescovi e Regolari
BA   Biblioteca Ambrosiana, Milan
BAV   Biblioteca Apostolica Vaticana
DBI   *Dizionario biografico degli italiani* (online at www.treccani.it)
MGG   *Die Musik in Geschichte und Gegenwart*

A. Major Sources, Print and Manuscript, of Music Discussed (short-title; includes theory treatises)

Alcarotto, Giovanni Francesco. *Lamentationes Ieremiae*. Milan, 1570. (Chapter 3)
Argilliano, Ruggiero. *Responsoria hebdomadae sanctae*. Venice, 1612. (5)
Banchieri, Adriano. *Direttorio monastico*. Bologna, 1615. (2)
de' Bivi (Aretino), Paolo. *Sacra responsoria*. Venice, 1544. (3)
———. *Pie ac devotissime Lamentationes Hyeremie prophete*. Venice, 1546. (3)
———. *Responsoria hebdomadae sanctae* (combined ed.). Venice, 1564. (3)
Bologna Oratorian=I-Bof, 50 Lessons by various composers, probably 1700–1750. (7)
Bona, Valerio. *Lamentationi della Settimana Santa*. Venice, 1616. (3)
Bovio, Alfonso. *Cantorino olivetano*. Venice, 1661. (3)
Brunetti, Gaetano. 3 Lessons (1794), in E-Mp. (8)
Brunetti, Giovanni Gualberto. Lessons (ms. 1786), I-Vlevi. (8)
Burlini, Antonio. *Lamentationi per la settimana santa,* op. 7. Venice, 1614. (5)
Caldara, Antonio. *Sedecia* (Vienna, 1732), mss. in A-Wgm, A-Wn. (5)
Campion, Carlo Antonio. Responsories (final version 1781/2), in I-Fc, A-Wn. (8)
Canale, Floriano. *Harmonica officia in triduo*. Venice, 1579. (3)
Cantone, Serafino. *Officium Hebdomadae Sanctae*. Milan, 1602. (3)
Cantus monastici formula. Venice, 1535. (3)
Capello, Giovanni Francesco. *Lamentationi, Benedictus et Miserere,* op. 3. Verona, 1612. (5)
Caresana, Cristoforo. 23 Lessons (c. 1685–1700), mss. in I-Nf. (6)

Carpentras, Eleazar (Genet). *Liber lamentationum Jeremiae Prophetae* (Avignon, 1532); mod. ed. in *Opera omnia,* vol. 2, (n.p., 1972). (3)

Casini, Gianmaria. *Concerto degli Stromenti . . . in accompagnamento de' Responsi della Settimana Santa,* op. 3. Florence, 1706. (2)

Cavalieri, Emilio de.' Lessons and Responsories, ms. in I-Rv; mod. ed. M. C. Bradshaw, *Emilio de' Cavalieri, The Lamentations and Responsories of 1599 and 1600* (Neuhausen-Stuttgart, 1990). (3)

Cazzati, Maurizio. *Benedictus, Miserere, e Tantum ergo,* op. 45. Bologna, 1668. (2, 5)

Cerone, Pietro. *El Melopeo y Maestro.* Naples, 1613; facs. ed. Bologna, 1969. (3),

Cesi, Pietro. *Lamentationes Jeremiae Prophetae.* Rome, 1653. (5)

Charpentier, Marc-Antoine. 28 Lessons, 19 Responsories, 4 Misereres, Benedictus, mss. in F-Pn; facs. ed. in *Mélanges autographes,* Geneva, 1990–2004. (6)

Chiaula, Mauro (Palermitano). *Lamentationes ac Responsoria.* Venice, 1597. (3)

Contino, Giovanni. *Threni Jeremiae.* Venice, 1561. (3)

Corselli, Francesco. 67 Lessons, 1739–1777, mss. in E-Mp. (7)

Corteccia, Francesco. *Responsoria omnia.* Florence, 1570–71; mod. ed. F. d'Accone in *Music of the Florentine Renaissance,* vol. 11, (n.p., 1985). (3)

Della Ciaia, Alessandro. *Lamentationi sacre e motetti.* Venice, 1650. (5)

Dentice, Fabrizio. *Lamentazioni di Fabrizio Dentice.* Milan, 1593. (3)

De Sanctis, Giuseppe. 18 Lessons (c. 1690), mss. in I-Rcns. (6)

Dittersdorf, Carl Ditters von. *Giob* (1786), mss. in A-Wgm, D-Bspk. (8)

Dragoni, Giovanni Antonio. Lesson cycle(s) (c. 1580), mss. in I-Rsg (held in I-Rvic). (3)

Durante, Francesco. 3 Lessons (1746), mss. in I-Rcns and elsewhere. (7)

Falusi, Michelangelo. *Responsoria Hebdomadis Sanctae.* Rome. 1684. (6)

Gesualdo, Carlo. *Responsoria sancta.* Gesualdo, 1611; mod. ed. G. Watkins, *Sämtliche Werke,* vol. 7 (Hamburg, 1959). (5)

Giacobetti, Pietro Amico. *Lamentationes cum omnibus Responsoriis.* Venice, 1601. (3)

Giordani, Giuseppe. Lamentations and Miserere, I-FERd, ed. U. Gironacci/I. Vescovo, *Opera Omnia,* ser. I, vol. 3 (Lucca: Libreria Musicale Italiana, 2009).

Graziani, Bonifazio. *Responsoria Hebdomadae Sanctae.* Rome, 1663. (6)

Gregori, Annibale. *Cantiones ac sacrae lamentationes.* Siena, 1620. (5)

Guidetti, Giuseppe. *Cantus ecclesiasticus officii majoris hebdomadae.* Rome, 1587. (2)

Handl (Gallus), Jakob. 9 Lessons in *Opus Musicum,* vol. 2 (Prague, 1588); mod. ed. E. Becezny (Vienna, 1905). (4)

Hasse, Johann Adolf. 4 Lessons (c. 1725), mss. in I-Nf. (7)

Haydn, Franz Joseph. Symphony no. 26, "Lamentatione" (c. 1767–68). (8)

Hollander, Christiaan. 9 Lessons (? c. 1565), ms. in A-Wn. (4)

Ingegneri, Marcantonio. *Lamentationes Hieremiae* and *Responsoria Hebdomadae Sanctae.* Venice, 1588. (2)

Jacquet of Mantua, *Orationes complures ad Officium Hebdomadae Sanctae pertinentes.* Venice,1567. (3)

Jerusalem, Ignacio. 5 Lessons (c. 1760), mss. in MEX-Mc. (8)

Jommelli, Niccolo. 3 Lessons, (1746), mss. in I-Rcns and elsewhere. (7)

Lamentationes Jeremiae Prophetae. Nuremberg, 1549. (4)

Lasso, Orlando di. 2 Lesson cycles, Responsories, Lauds items, mss. in D-Mbs and print (Munich, 1585); mod. ed. by P. Bergquist, *Sämtliche Werke,* vols. 22 and 24 (Kassel, 1992–93). (4)

Leo, Leonardo. 9 Lessons for Naples, 1744, mss. in US-Wc and elsewhere. (7)

Lully, Jean-Baptiste. Psalms LWV 67 and 77/17, ed. L. Sawkins/C. B. Schmidt, *The Collected Works*, ser. IV, vol. 5 (New York: The Broude Trust, 1996).

Luython, Carl. *Opus musicum*. Prague, 1604. (4)

Mahu, Stephan. 9 Lessons, in P. Giovanelli, *Novus Thesaurus Musicus* (Venice, 1568); mod. ed. N.S.J. Davison, in Pierre de La Rue, *Opera omnia*, vol. 8 (Neuhausen, 1998). (4)

Marcello, Benedetto. 7 Lessons, ms. in D-Hs. (7)

Matelart, Johannes. 8 Lessons (post-1568), in ms. I-Rsld. (3)

Milleville, Barnaba. *Pompe funebri . . . Responsori delli Matutini*, op. 14. Venice, 1624. (5)

Mogavero, Antonio. *Lamentationes Jeremiae Prophetae*. Venice, 1623. (4)

Nasco, Jan. *Lamentationi a voce* [sic] *pari*. Venice, 1561. (3)

Palestrina, Giovanni Pierluigi da. ~40 Lessons, mss. in I-Rvat, Rsg, and elsewhere; also *Lamentationum Jeremiae Prophetae Liber Primus* (Rome, 1588); most ed. R. Casimiri, *Opere complete*, vol. 13 (Rome, 1941). (3)

Paolo Ferrarese. *Passiones, Lamentationes, Responsoria*. Venice, 1565. (1, 3)

Pecci, Tommaso. *Musici modi in Responsoria Divini Officii*. Venice, 1603. (5)

Perez, Davide. 3 Lessons, 1746, mss. in I-Rcns and elsewhere; 3 Lessons, 1757–1763, mss. in P-Lf and I-Nc. (7, 8)

Pérez Roldán, Juan. 2 Lessons (c. 1670), mss. in E-SEG. (6)

Phinot, Domenique. 1 Lesson (1548); mod. ed. J. Höfler, *Opera omnia*, vol. 4 (Neuhausen, 1982). (3)

Ponzio, Pietro. *Ragionamento di musica*. Parma, 1588; facs. ed. Kassel, 1959. (3)

Porpora, Nicola. ~20 Lessons, mss. in I-Nf, I-Bof, GB-Lbm, US-NH. (7)

Porta, Costanzo. 9 Lessons, ms. in I-Bc; mod. ed. S. Cisilino/G. M. Luisetto, *Opera omnia*, vol. 7. Padua, 1971. (3)

Puccini *sen.*, Giacomo. 11 Lessons, Benedictus, Miserere (1739–80), mss. in I-Lim. (7)

Q. 43, ms. in I-Bc, [Lamentations and oratorios by Roman figures, copied c. 1650]. (5)

Rimonte, Pedro. *Cantiones sacrae . . . ac Hieremiae prophetae lamentationes*. Antwerp, 1607; mod ed. J. Izquierdo/A. Margules, *Polifonia Aragonesa*, 14 (Zaragoza, 2006). (4)

Rousseau, Jean-Jacques. Lesson (c. 1770), ms. in F-Pn. (8)

Rossi, G. B. *Threni Jeremiae Prophetae*. Venice, 1628. (3, 5)

Sánchez [de] Azpeleta, Juan. *Opus harmonicum in historia passionis Christi*. Zaragoza, 1612. (1)

Scarlatti, Alessandro. *Per la Passione* (Rome, 1706), mss. in D-WD, Dslb (Dslb score viewable at http://digital.slub-dresden.de/werkansicht/dlf/22678/1/0/cache.off). (5)

Szamtouł, Wacław z. *Lamentationes Hieremiae Prophetae*. Kraków, 1553. (3)

Torres, José de. 3 Lessons (1720–26), mss. in E-Mp. (7)

Veneziano, Gaetano. 25 Lessons (c. 1685–1710), mss. in I-Nf and Nc. (6)

Victoria, Tomás Luis de. *Officium Hebdomadae Sanctae*. Rome, 1585; various modern eds. (3)

B. Printed and Manuscript Literature before 1800 (includes oratorio libretti)

Acosta, Gabriel. *Commentaria quinque in totidem libros veteris testamenti* Lyon: Gabriel Boissat and L. Anisson, 1641.

Agelli, Antonio. *Commentarii in Psalmos, et in Divini Officii cantica.* Rome: Typographia Vaticana, 1606; Paris: Chevalier, 1611.

———. *In Lamentationes Jeremiae Commentarium.* Rome: F. Zanetti, 1589.

Andrade, Sebastiao da Costa de. *Commentarii in Threnos et Orationem Jeremiae Prophetae.* Lyon: Horace Cardon, 1609.

Bances Candamo, Francisco Antonio. *Poesias cómicas póstumas.* Madrid: Blas de Villa-Nueva, 1722.

Belforte, Antonio di Gennaro, duca del. *Poesie.* Naples: V. Orsino, 1796.

Bellarmine, Robert. *Explanatio in Psalmos.* Cologne: Bernardus Gualterus, 1611.

Benedict XIV, "Annus qui" (1749), in *Sanctissimi Domini Nostri Benedicti Papae XIV Bullarium*, vol. 3. Venice: F. Pitteri, 1768; trans. Robert Hayburn, *Papal Legislation on Sacred Music, 95 A.D. to 1977 A.D.* Collegeville: Liturgical Press, 1979.

Blount, Walter K. *The Compleat Office of the Holy Week.* London: Matthew Turner, 1687.

Breviarium cisterciense . . . pars hyemalis. Paris: M.-A. David, 1752.

Breviarium horarum canonicorum . . . pragensis. Nuremberg: Georg Stuchs, 1502.

Breviarium monasticum . . . pars verna. Einsiedeln: Typis Principalis Monasterii, 1743.

Breviarium . . . praedicatorum. Rome: Francesco Gonzaga, 1719.

Breviarium romanum. Venice: Giunta, 1562.

Breviarium romanum. Rome: Typis Vaticanis, 1632.

Bucchio, Geremia. *Esposizione sopra l'orazione di Gieremia profeta, et sopra il Cantico di Zaccheria.* Florence: Bernardo Sermartelli, 1573.

Burney, Charles. *A General History of Music from the Earliest Ages to the Present Period.* London: For the Author, 1789.

Caeremoniale episcoporum (Rome, 1600). Facs. ed. Vatican City: Libreria Editrice Vaticana, 2000.

Calderari, Cesare. *Concetti scritturali intorno al Miserere.* Naples: H. Salviani/ C. Cesari, 1584.

Calzolai [Ricordati] Pietro. *Historia monastica.* Rome: V. Accolti, 1575.

Carrière, Francois. *Commentarius in universam Scripturam.* Lyon: Horace Boissat/ G. Remee, 1643.

Cartas que os Padres e Irmaõs da Companhia de Jeus escreverão dos Reynos de Iapão. Évora: M. de Lyra, 1598.

Castellot, Joaquin (trans.). *Semana santa Cristiana.* Madrid: J. Ibarra, 1766.

Castro, Cristóbal de. *Commentariorum in Ieremiae Prophetias, Lamentationes, et Baruch Libri Sex.* Paris: Michael Sonnius, 1609.

Charpy de Sainte-Croix, Louis. *Les saintes tenebres en vers français.* Paris: Guillaume Desprez, 1670.

Chiflet, Jules. *Aula sacra principum Belgii.* Antwerp: Plantin, 1650.

Cicognini, Jacobo. *Lagrime di Gieremia profeta.* Florence: Zanobi Pignoni, 1627.

Constitutiones synodi secundae [Sarzanae] per Illustrissimum ac Reverendiss. d. Ioan. Baptistam Salvagum. Lucca: Ottavio Guidobono/B. de Giudici, 1618.

del Río, Martin. *Commentarius litteralis in Threnos.* Lyon: Horace Cardon, 1608.

Denys the Carthusian. *In quatuor Evangelistas enarrationes.* Cologne: I. Gennepeum, 1538.

Den dienst van de Goede ende Paesch-Week . . . vertaelt in 't nederduyts. Brussels: Serstevens, 1712.

Druzbicki, Gaspar. *Tractatus de variis passionem Domini nostri Jesu Christi meditandi modis.* Lublin: G. Forster, 1652.

Epifania, Manuel da. *Novas, e curiosas reflexoens sobre os terremotos.* Lisbon: M. Rodrigues, 1756.

Eustachio, Giovanni Paolo. *Salutari discorsi.* Naples: G. B. Cappelli, 1582.

———. "Discorso di Giovanni Paolo Eustachio sopra le Lamentationi di Geremia," BA, B. 18 *sup.*

Feijóo, Benito. "La música de los Templos" (1726), in *Teatro critico universal.* Madrid: Imprenta Real de la Gaceta, 1765.

Fiamma, Gabriele. *Rime spirituali.* Venice: Francesco de' Franceschi, 1570.

Figueiro, Pedro de. *Commentarii in Lamentationes Hieremiae Prophetae.* Lyon: Giunta,1596.

Fontana, Francesco Luigi. *Vita di Benedetto Marcello.* Venice: A Zatta and sons, 1788.

Gemelli Carreri, Giovanni Francesco. *Viaggi per Europa,* vol. 1. Naples: Giuseppe Roselli, 1708.

Glossa ordinaria: publ. as *Bibliorum sacrorum glossa ordinaria* (Lyon, 1589); rpt. Venice: Giunta, 1603.

Gómez Bueno, Pedro. *Semanero santo de seglares.* Écija: B. Daza, 1780.

Iriarte, Tomas de. *La música: Poema.* Madrid: Imprenta Real de la Gazeta, 1779.

Lami, Alessandro. *Discorso . . . intorno alla scultura et pittura.* Cremona: C. Draconi, 1584.

Lambertini, Prospero. *Delle feste di Gesù Cristo signor nostro* (Bologna, 1740). Venice: Francesco Pitteri, 1767.

Le lamentazioni di Gieremia da Cantarsi nell'Oratorio de' RR.PP. della Congregazione dell'Oratorio di Roma. Rome: F. B. Komarek, 1766.

Lamenti profetici da cantarsi nella Passione di Cristo. Bologna: G. Monti, 1676.

Lapide, Cornelius a. *Commentaria in Jeremiam Prophetam, Threnos et Baruch.* Antwerp: Martin Nutius, 1621.

Liguori, Alfonso Maria de. *Operette spirituali,* pt. 2. Naples: Gianfrancesco Paci, 1768.

Loarte, Gaspar de. *Trattato della continua memoria, che si debbe havere della sacra Passione di Christo redentor nostro.* Venice: G.G. de' Ferrari, 1575.

Luchino, Benedetto. *Cronaca della vera origine . . .* Mantua: F. Osanna, 1592.

Malagrida, Gabriel. *Juizo, da verdadera causa do terremoto, que padeceo a corte de Lisboa.* Lisbon: M. Soares, 1756.

Malipiero, Girolamo. *Il Petrarca spirituale* (1536). Venice: Heirs of A. Griffio, 1587.

Mazzinelli, Alessandro. *Uffizio della Settimana Santa.* Rome, 1704; Rome: Rocco Bernabo, 1735.

Menocchio, Giovanni Stefano. *Commentarii totius Sacrae Scripturae.* Paris: G. Cavelier, 1719.

Menzini, Benedetto. *Lamentazioni del santo profeta Geremia* (Rome, 1704); in *Rime,* vol. 3. Florence: Michele Nesteno, 1731.

Modestus a S. Joanne Evangelista. *Elucidatio literalis moralis ac anagogica in Threnos Jeremiae.* Prague: Helm, 1715–1719.

Muratori, Ludovico Antonio. *Della perfetta poesia italiana.* Modena: Bartolomeo Soliani, 1706.

Norcia, Antonio Domenico. *Il trionfo di Tito per la distruzione di Gerusalemme,*

espressa nelle lamentazioni del profeta Geremia. Rome: Antonio de' Rossi,
    1708.

Officium hebdomadae sanctae. Munich, 1571.

Officium hebdomadae sanctae. Rome: "In aedibus Populi Romani," 1572.

Officium hebdomadae sanctae. Rome, 1579.

Officium hebdomadae sanctae. Munich, 1581.

[Ottoboni, Pietro]. *Per la Passione di Nostro Signor Giesù Cristo Oratorio.* Rome:
    Antonio de' Rossi, 1706 (1708 libretto viewable at http://bsb-mdz12-spiegel
    .bsb.lrz.de/~db/0004/bsb00049887/images/)

——. *Introduzione all'oratorio della Passione.* Rome, 1707 (viewable at http://
    bsb-mdz12-spiegel.bsb.lrz.de/~db/0004/bsb00049794/images/)

Pastor, Alonso. *Soledades del amor divino.* Valencia: Heirs of Crysostomo Garriz,
    1655.

Picart, Bernard. *Cérémonies et coutumes religieuses de tous les peuples du monde.*
    Amsterdam: J. F. Bernard, 1723.

Pinto, Heitor. *In Danielem, Lamentationes . . . Commentarii.* Cologne: Birckmann,
    1582.

Primeira parte do index da livraria e de musica do . . . João o IV. Lisbon, 1649/rpt.
    Lisbon, 1874.

Puccini, Giacomo (sen.). "Libro delle Musiche Annue ed Avventizie fatto da me
    Giacomo Puccini." I-Las, Deposito Istituto Pacini 1–3.

Ricciardi, Antonio. *Commentaria symbolica in duos tomos distributa.* Venice:
    Francesco de' Franceschi, 1591.

*Rituale della venerabile archiconfraternita delle Sagre Stimmate del Padre S. Francesco
    di Roma.* Rome: Bernabò, 1711.

Rivero, Manuel. "Breve descripción de la Real Capilla de Madrid y de las ceremonias
    que en ella se exequien para el curso del anno" (1640), AGP, Real Capilla, 72/5.

Sacchi, Giovenale. *Vita del cavaliere Don Carlo Broschi detto il Farinello.* Venice,
    1784; rpt. Naples: Pagano, 1994.

Salas, Francisco Gregorio de. *Las nueve lamentaciones de la Semana Santa, dispu-
    estas en verso castellano.* Madrid: A. Ramirez, 1773; later as *Versión parafra-
    seada de las Lamentaciones de Jeremias.* Barcelona, 1778; Mexico City, 1782.

Sanchez, Gaspar. *In Jeremiam Prophetam Commentarii cum Paraphrasi.* Lyon:
    Horace Cardon, 1618.

San José, Francisco Antonio de. *Canto funebre, ou Lamentaçaõ harmonica na in-
    feliz destruicao de famosa Cidade de Lisboa.* Lisbon: M. Rodrigues, 1756.

Sarnelli, Pompeo. *Lettere ecclesiastiche.* Venice: Antonio Bortoli, 1716.

——. *Lezioni scritturali alla mente, e al cuore sopra il sagro libro del profeta
    Giob . . . e sopra i Threni del s. profeta Geremia.* Naples: Antonio Gramig-
    nani,1707.

Scaramelli, Giovanni Battista. *Il Direttorio mistico, indirizzato a' direttori.* Venice:
    S. Occhi, 1754.

Strozzi, Nicolo. *Parafrasi delle Lamentationi di Ieremia.* Rome: Lodovico Grignani,
    1635.

Timoteo, Michele. *In divinum officium trecentum quaestiones.* Venice: Francesco
    Ziletto, 1581.

Tinghi, Cesare, ["Diario, vols. 1–3"]. I-Fn, Ms. Gino Capponi 261; I-Fas, Miscel-
    lanea Medicea, 5.

Tirinus, Jacobus. *Commentarius in Vetus et Novum Testamentum.* Antwerp: Petrus
    Bellerus, 1632.
Torre, Carlo. *Il ritratto di Milano.* Milan: Agnelli, 1714.
Velius, Caspar. *Querela Austriae sive epistola ad reliquam Germaniam.* Augsburg:
    A. Weyssenhorn, 1532.
Vergerio, Pietro Paolo. *Operetta nuova . . . nella qual si dimostrono le vere ragioni,
    che hanno mosso i Romani Pontifici ad instituir le belle ceremonie della Setti-
    mana Santa.* Zurich: Gesner, 1552.
Xarque, Francisco de. *Insignes missioneros de la Compañia de Jesus del Paraguay.*
    Pamplona: J. Micón,1687.
Zacchia, Paolo. *Il vitto quaresimale.* Rome: Pietro Antonio Facciotti, 1637.
Zeno, Apostolo. *Poesie sacre drammatiche.* Venice: Giuseppe Bettinelli, 1742.

C. Literature after 1800

Agamennone, Maurizio. "*Varco le soglie e veglio"*: *Canto e devozioni confraternali nel
    Cilento antico,* Rome: Squlibri, 2008.
Agee, Richard J. "The Privilege and Venetian Music Printing in the Sixteenth Cen-
    tury," Ph.D. diss., Princeton University, 1982.
———. "A Venetian Music Printing Contract in the Sixteenth Century," *Studi musi-
    cali* 15 (1986): 59–65.
Aguirre Rincón, Soterraña. *Un manuscrito para un convento: el Libro de Música
    dedicado a Sor Luisa en 1633, Convento de Santa Clara de Carrión de los
    Condes.* Valladolid: Las Edades del Hombre, 1998.
Álvarez Pérez, José Maria. "La polifonía sagrada y sus maestros en la Catedral de
    León durante el siglo XVII," *Anuario musical* 15 (1960): 141–63.
Anderson, Michael A. "Symbols of Saints: Theology, Ritual, and Kinship in Music
    for John the Baptist and St. Anne, 1175–1563." Ph.D. diss., University of Chi-
    cago, 2008.
Andrée, Alexander (ed.). *Gilbertus Universalis: Glossa Ordinaria in Lamentationes
    Ieremie Prophete, Prothemata et Liber I.* Stockholm: Almquist & Wiksell, 2005.
Annibaldi, Claudio. *La cappella musicale pontificia nel Seicento,* vol.1. Palestrina:
    Fondazione G. P. da Palestrina, 2011.
Arcangeli, Pietro G. *et al. Canti liturgici di tradizione orale.* Udine: Nota, 2011.
Aresi, Stefano (ed.). Nicola Porpora, *Sei duetti latini sulla Passione di Nostro Sig-
    nore Gesù Cristo.* Pisa: Edizioni ETS, 2004.
Artocchini, Carmen. *Il folklore piacentino.* Piacenza: UTEP, 1971.
Augustine. *Confessions* trans. H. Chadwick. Oxford: Oxford University Press, 1998.
Bacardí y Moreau, Emilio. *Crónicas de Santiago de Cuba.* Madrid: Graf Preogran,
    1972.
Bacciagaluppi, Claudio. *Rom, Prag, Dresden: Pergolesi und die neapolitanische
    Messe in Europa.* Kassel: Bärenreiter, 2010.
———. "'E viva Benedetto XIV': L'enciclica 'Annus qui" (1749) nel contesto dei
    rapporti musicali tra Roma e Bologna," in *Papsttum und Kirchenmusik vom
    Mittelalter bis zu Benedikt XVI,* ed. K. Pietschmann (Analecta Musicologica,
    47), 222–62. Kassel: Bärenreiter, 2012.
Baroncini, Rodolfo. "L'ufficio delle Tenebre: pratiche sonore della Settimana Santa
    nell'Italia settentrionale tra Cinque e Seicento," *Recercare* 17 (2005): 71–133.

Barrau-Dihigo, Louis. "Voyage de Barthélemy Joly en Espagne (1603–1604)," *Revue hispanique* 20 (1909): 459–618.

Barreiro, Emma J. "Las lamentaciones en romance en *El Austria en Jerusalén* de Francisco de Bances Candamo: un caso de lírica tradicional," in *Lyra minima: del cancionero medieval al cancionero tradicional moderno,* ed. A. González *et al.,* 201–18. Mexico City: UNAM, 2010.

Beleth, Johannes. *Johannis Beletii Summa de Ecclesiasticis Officiis,* ed. H. Doutheil, ("Corpus Christianorum Continuatio Mediaevalis," XLI). Turnhout: Brepols, 1976.

Bennett, Peter. *Sacred Repertories in Paris under Louis XIII: Paris, Bibliothèque nationale de France, MS Vma rés. 571.* Farnham: Ashgate, 2009.

Bernardi, Claudio. *La drammaturgia della Settimana Santa in Italia.* Milan: Vita e Pensiero, 1991.

Bernstein, Jane. *Music Printing in Renaissance Venice: The Scotto Press, 1539–1572.* New York: Oxford University Press, 1998.

Bertolotti, Antonino. *Artisti in relazione coi Gonzaga Duchi di Mantova nei secoli XVI e XVII.* Modena: Vincenzi, 1885.

Bestul, Thomas H. *Texts of the Passion: Latin Devotional Literature and Medieval Society.* Philadelphia: University of Pennsylvania Press, 1996.

Bettley, John. "«La composizione lacrimosa»: Musical Style and Text Selection in North-Italian Lamentation Settings in the Second Half of the Sixteenth Century," *Proceedings of the Royal Musical Association* 118 (1993): 167–202.

Bisello, Linda. "Nel segno di Raziel: Esegesi e simboli in età tridentina," *Rivista di storia e letteratura religiosa* 40 (2004): 475–514. Biver, Paul and Marie-Louise Biver. *Abbayes, monastères, couvents de femmes à Paris.* Paris: PUF, 1975.

Blackburn, Bonnie J. "Josquin's Chansons: Ignored and Lost Sources," *JAMS* 29 (1976): 30–76.

Blankenburg, Heidi. "De lamentatione Jeremiae Prophetae: Aspekte zur Entwicklung und Verbreitung der Lamentation im 18. Jahrhundert." Ph.D. diss., Universität der Künste Berlin, 2008.

Boetticher, Wilfried. *Orlando di Lasso und seine Zeit, 1532–1594.* Kassel, 1958; rpt. Wilhelmshaven: F. Noetzel, 1998.

Bölling, Jörg. *Das Papstzeremoniell der Renaissance: Texte, Musik, Performance.* Frankfurt a.M.: Lang, 2006.

Bonsante, Annalisa and R. M. Pasquandrea (eds.). *Celesti Sirene: Musica e monachesimo dal Medioevo all'Ottocento.* Foggia: C. Grenzi, 2010.

Boorman, Stanley. "A New Source, and New Compositions, for Philippe de Monte," in *«Recevez ce mien petit labeur»: Studies in Renaissance Music in Honour of Ignace Bossuyt,* ed. M. Delaere/P. Bergé, 35–48. Leuven: Leuven University Press, 2008.

Botta Caselli, Ada. "Musiche per la Passione nei monasteri benedettini agli inizi dell'età moderna," in *Laeta dies: Musiche per San Benedetto e attività nei centri benedettini in età moderna,* ed. S. Franchi/B. Brumana, 121–152. Rome: IBIMUS, 2004.

Bouchard, Jean-Jacques. *Journal II: Voyage dans le Royaume de Naples (1632).* Turin: G. Giappichelli 1977.

Bourligueux, Guy. "Géry de Ghersem, sous-maître de la chapelle royale d'Espagne (Documents inédits)," *Melanges de la Casa de Velazquez* 2 (1966): 163–78.

Bramanti, Vanni. "Il Lasca e la famiglia della Fonte (da alcune lettere inedite)," *Schede umanistiche* 10 (2004): 19–40.

Bruning, Jens. "Die kursächsiche Reichspolitik zwischen Augburger Religionsfrieden und Dreißigjährigem Krieg—nur reichspatriotisch und kaisertreu?" in *Die sächsichen Kurfürsten während des Religionsfriedens von 1555 bis 1618,* ed. H. Junghans, 81–94. Leipzig: Sächsiche Akademie der Wissenschaften, 2007.

Buch, Laura J. "Seconda prattica and the Aesthetic of Meraviglia: The Canzonettas and Madrigals of Tomaso Pecci (1576–1604)." Ph. D. diss., University of Rochester, 1993.

Burke, John. "Musicians of S. Maria Maggiore Rome, 1600–1700," *Note d'archivio per la storia musicale* n.s. 2 (1984), suppl.

Butler, Bartlett Russell. "Liturgical Music in Sixteenth-Century Nürnberg: A Socio-Musical Study." Ph.D. diss., University of Illinois, 1970.

Caballero Fernández-Rufete, Carmelo. "*Arded, corazón, arded*": Tonos humanos del Barrocco en la Península Ibérica. Valladolid: Las Edades del Hombre, 1997.

Calderón de la Barca, Pedro. *El cordero de Isaías,* ed. M. C. Pinillos ("Autos Sacramentales Completos," 10). Kassel/Pamplona: Reichenberger, 1996.

Callegari, Laura (ed.). "Cantori, maestri, organisti della Cappella Lateranense negli Atti Capitolari (sec. XV–XVII)" [by R. Casimiri], *Quadrivium* 25/2 (1984).

Campbell, Stephen J. "The Conflicted Representation of Judaism in Italian Renaissance Images of Christ's Life and Passion," in *The Passion Story: From Visual Representation to Social Drama,* ed. M. Kupfer, 67–90. University Park, PA: Penn State University Press, 2008.

Canova, Antonio. *Scritti,* ed. H. Honour/P. Mariuz. Rome: Salerno Editrice, 2007.

Caputi, Giancarlo. "Le notizie storiche del P. Giancarlo Caputi di S. Barbara," *Archivum Scolarum Piarum* 65 (2009): 3–142.

Carey, Frank. "Composition for Equal Voices in the Sixteenth Century," *Journal of Musicology* 9 (1991): 300–342.

Carlini, Antonio. "La musica sacra nel Principato Vescovile di Trento e a Villa Lagarina nel XVII secolo," in *La policoralità in Europa al tempo di Paris Lodron,* 15–30. Trent: Provincia Autonoma di Trento, 2006.

Carroccia, Antonio. "Fenaroli e le composizioni liturgiche per la Settimana Santa e l'Ufficio dei Defunti," in *Fedele Fenaroli: Il didatta e il compositore,* ed. G. Miscia, 225–47. Lucca: LIM, 2011.

Carroll, Michael. *The Penitente Brotherhoods.* Baltimore: Johns Hopkins University Press, 2002.

Carter, Tim. *Jacobo Peri 1561–1633: His Life and Works.* New York: Garland, 1989.

Casati, Carlo. "Nuove notizie intorno a Tomaso de Marini," *Archivio Storico Lombardo* (1886): 584–640.

Catalogo del Archivo de Música del Palacio Real de Madrid. Madrid: Editorial Patrimonio Nacional, 1993.

Casimiri, Raffaele. *Il 'codice 59' dell'Archivio musicale lateranense.* Rome: Tipografia poliglotta vaticana, 1919.

Cattin, Giulio. "I benedettini e la musica. Il contributo dei monaci italiani alla polifonia," *Schede medievali* 5 (1983): 383–401.

———. "Tradizione e tendenze innovatrici nella normativa e nella pratica liturgico-musicale della congregazione di S. Giustina," *Benedictina* 17 (1970): 270–287.

———. and F. A. Gallo (eds.). *Un millennio di polifonia liturgica tra oralità e scrittura.* Bologna: Il Mulino, 2002.

Cessac, Catherine. *Marc-Antoine Charpentier.* Paris: Fayard, 2004.

———. "Copie et composition: l'enseignement des ratures," in *Les manuscrits autographes de Marc-Antoine Charpentier,* ed. ead., 55–65. Wavre: Mardaga, 2007.

Civil, Francisco. "La música en la Catedral de Gerona durante el siglo XVII," *Anuario musical* 15 (1960): 219–246.

Clementi, Maria C. *La cappella musicale del Duomo di Gubbio nel '500.* Perugia: Centro di studi musicali in Umbria, 1994.

Cohen, Charles E. *The Art of Giovanni Antonio da Pordenone: Between Dialect and Language.* Cambridge: Cambridge University Press, 1996.

Cooper, Tracy E. "Un modo per 'la Riforma Cattolica'? La scelta di Paolo Veronese per il refettorio di San Giorgio Maggiore," in *Crisi e rinnovamenti nell'autunno del Rinascimento a Venezia,* ed. V. Branca/C. Ossola, 271–292. Florence: Olschki, 1991.

Corrain, Cleto and P. Zampini. *Documenti etnografici e folkloristici nei sinodi diocesani italiani.* Bologna: Forni 1970.

Cotilla Rodríguez, M. O. "The Santiago de Cuba earthquake of 11 June 1766: some new insights," *Geofísica Internacional* 42/4 (2003): 589–602.

Couchman, Jonathan. "Felice Anerio's music for the church and for the Altemps Chapel," Ph. D. diss., UCLA, 1989.

Cramer, Eugene C. "Tomás Luis de Victoria's Second Thoughts: A Reappraisal," *Canadian University Music Review* 6 (1985): 256–83.

———. "Music for the Holy Week Liturgy in the Sixteenth Century: A Study of the Single-Composer Prints," in *Encomium musicae: Essays in Memory of Robert J. Snow,* ed. D. Crawford/G.G. Wagstaff, 395–407. Hillsdale: Pendragon Press, 2002.

Crook, David. "'A Certain Indulgence': Music at the Jesuit College in Paris, 1575–1590," in *The Jesuits II: Cultures, Sciences and the Arts 1540–1773,* ed. J. W. O'Malley *et al.,* 454–78. Toronto: University of Toronto Press, 2006.

———. "A Sixteenth-Century Catalog of Prohibited Music," *JAMS* 62 (2009): 1–78.

———. *Orlando di Lasso's Imitation Magnificats for Counter-Reformation Munich* Princeton: Princeton University Press, 1994.

Culley, Thomas D. *Jesuits and Music: A Study of the Musicians Connected with the German College in Rome during the 17th Century and of their Activities in Northern Europe.* Rome: Jesuit Historical Institute, 1970.

Cusick, Suzanne G. *Francesca Caccini at the Medici Court: Music and the Circulation of Power.* Chicago: University of Chicago Press, 2009.

Czepiel, Tomasz M. M. *Music at the Royal Court and Chapel of Poland, c.1543–1600.* New York: Garland 1996.

D'Accone, Frank A. *Music and Musicians in 16th-Century Florence.* Aldershot: Ashgate, 2007.

———. *Music in Renaissance Florence: Studies and Documents.* Aldershot: Ashgate, 2006.

d'Alessi, Giovanni. *La cappella musicale del Duomo di Treviso.* Vedelago: Ars et Religio, 1954.

Davies, Drew E. "The Italianized frontier: music at Durango Cathedral, Español culture, and the aesthetics of devotion in eighteenth-century New Spain." Ph.D. diss., University of Chicago, 2006.

Deak, James. "Haydn's Lamentation Symphony and Werner's Lamentations," *Haydn Society of Great Britain Newsletter* 2 (1980): 5–10.

de Conti, Giuseppe. *Viaggio d'Italia: Un manoscritto del Settecento,* ed. B. Corino. Novara: Interlinea, 2007.

de Jong, Aad. "Liturgical action from a language perspective: about performance and performatives in liturgy," in *Discourse in Ritual Studies,* ed. H. Schilderman, 111–145. Leiden: Brill, 2007.

Della Libera, Luca. "L'attività musicale nella basilica di S. Lorenzo in Damaso nel '500," *Rivista italiana di musicologia* 32 (1997): 25–59.

———. "Repertori ed organici vocali-strumentali nella Basilica di Santa Maria Maggiore a Roma: 1557–1624," *Studi musicali* 29/1 (2000): 3–57.

Demaria, Enrico. *Il fondo musicale della regia cappella Sabauda.* Lucca: LIM, 2000.

De Martino, Ernesto. *Morte e pianto rituale nel mondo antico: Dal lamento funebre antico al pianto di Maria.* Orig. ed. 1958; rpt. Turin: Bollati Boringhieri, 2008.

de Mattos, Cleofe Person de. *Catálogo temático das obras do Padre José Mauricio Nunes Garcia.* Rio de Janeiro: Ministerio da Educaçao e Cultura, 1970.

de Mur Bernad, J. J. *Catalogo del Archivo de Música de la Catedral de Huesca.* Huesca: Ayuntamiento de Huesca, 1993.

Diderot, Denis. *Oeuvres complètes,* v, 12 *Le neveu de Rameau.* Paris: Hermann, 1983.

Díez Martínez, Marcelino. *Música sacra en Cádiz en tiempos de la Ilustración.* Cádiz: Universidad de Cádiz, 2006.

Di Virgilio, Domenico. "I suoni delle processioni e il paesaggio intorno ad essi," in A. Gasparroni, *La Settimana Santa a Teramo,* 42–53. Teramo: Cooperative Arké, 2005.

Dottori, Mauricio. "The church music of of Davide Perez and Niccolo Jommelli, with especial emphasis on their funeral music." Ph.D diss., University of Wales Cardiff, 1997.

Ducrot, Ariane. "Histoire de la Cappella Giulia au XVIe siècle," *École Française de Rome: Mélanges d'Archéologie et d'Histoire* 75 (1963): 179–240 and 467–559.

Duerloo, Luc. "Archducal Piety and Habsburg Power," in *Albert & Isabella 1598–1621: Essays,* ed. id./W. Thomas, 267–83. Turnhout: Brepols, 1998.

Dufourcq, Norbert. "Un inventaire de la musique religieuse de la Collégiale Notre-Dame d'Annecy 1661," *Revue de musicologie* 41 (1958): 38–59.

Durandus, Guglielmus. *Rationale divinum officiorum* in *Guillelmi Dvranti Rationale Divinorum Officiorvm V–VI,* ed. A. Davril/T.M. Thibodeau ("Corpus Christianorum, Continuatio Medieualis, CXL A"). Turnhout: Brepols, 1998.

Fabris, Dinko. *Da Napoli a Parma: itinerari di un musicista aristocratico: opere vocali di Fabrizio Dentice (1530 ca.–1581).* Rome: Accademia Nazionale di Santa Cecilia, 1998.

Fanelli, Jean G. *The Oratorios of Giovanni Maria Clari.* Bologna: Pendragon, 1992.

Fausti, Luigi. *La cappella musicale del Duomo di Spoleto.* Perugia: Unione tipografica cooperativa, 1916.

Favier, Thierry. "Les Leçons de Ténèbres mises en musiques: Les enjeux d'une querelle théologique," *Revue de l'histoire des religions* 217 (2000): 415–27.

Federhofer, Helmut. *Musikpflege und Musiker am Grazer Habsburgerhof der Er-*

zhöge Karl und Ferdinand von Innerösterreich (1564–1619). Mainz: B. Schott, 1967.

Feldman, Martha. *Opera and Sovereignty: Transforming Myths in Eighteenth-Century Italy*. Chicago: University of Chicago Press, 2007.

Fernandes, Cristina. "O Terramoto de 1755 e as suas implicações na organização da prática musical na Capela Real e na Patriarchal," in *1755: Catástrofe, Memória e Arte,* ed. H. C. Buesca, 219–28. Lisbon: Colibri, 2006.

Ferrer Ballester, Maria-Teresa. *Antonio T. Ortells y su legado en la música barroca española*. Valencia: Institut Valencià de la Música, 2007.

Fichtner, Paula S. *Emperor Maximilian II*. New Haven: Yale University Press, 2001.

Florimo, Francesco. *La scuola musicale di Napoli e i suoi conservatori*. Naples: V. Morano, 1880.

Floros, Constantin. "Carlo Antonio Campioni als Instrumentalkomponist." Ph.D. diss., University of Vienna, 1955.

Forcella, Vincenzo. *Iscrizioni delle chiese e degli altri edifici di Milano*. Milan: G. Prato, 1890.

Franchi, Giacomo and M. Lallai. *Da Luni a Massa-Carrara: il divenire di una diocesi fra Toscana e Liguria dal IV al XXI secolo*. Modena: Aedes Muratoriana, 2000.

Franchi, Saverio. *Drammaturgia romana,* vol. 2 *1701–1750*. Rome: Edizioni di Storia e Letteratura, 1988.

———. "Il principe Livio Odescalchi e l'oratorio 'politico,'" in *L'oratorio musicale italiano e i suoi contesti (secc. XVII–XVIII),* ed. P. Besutti, 141–258. Florence: Olschki, 2002).

Franchi, Saverio and O. Sartori. "Attività musicale nella chiesa nazionale di Sant'Antonio dei Portoghesi," in *Musica se extendit ad omnia: studi in onore di Alberto Basso in occasione del suo 750 compleanno,* ed. R. Moffa/S. Saccomani, 1: 211–79. Lucca: LIM, 2007.

Friedensburg, Walter (ed.). *Nuntiaturberiche aus Deutschland 1533–1559,* vol. 11, *Nuntiatur des Bischofs Pietro Bertano von Fano 1548–1549*. Tübingen: Niemeyer, 1910.

Friesenhagen, Andreas and C. Heitmann (eds.). *Joseph Haydn Werke,* ser. I, vol. 5a, *Sinfonien um 1766–1769*. Munich: Henle, 2008.

Fürstenau, Moritz von. *Geschichte der Musik und des Theaters am Hofe zu Dresden*. Dresden, 1861–2/rpt. Leipzig: Edition Peters, 1971.

Garavaglia, Andrea. *Alessandro Stradella*. Palermo: L'epos, 2006.

Gärtner, Theodor. *Quellenbuch zur Geschichte des Gymnasiums in Zittau*. Leipzig: G. G. Teubner, 1905.

Gaudelus, Sebastian. *Les offices de Ténèbres*. Paris: CNRS Editions, 2005.

Gavanti, Bartolomeo. *Thesaurus sacrorum rituum . . . cum novis observationibus . . . R. P. D. Cajetani-Mariae Merati*. Venice: Balleoniana, 1823.

Gembero Ustárroz, María. "Enlightened reformism versus Jesuit utopia: Music in the foundation of El Carmen de Guarayos (Moxos, Bolivia), 1793–1801" in *Music and Urban Society in Colonial Latin America,* ed. G. Baker/T. Knighton. Cambridge: Cambridge University Press, 2011.

Genette, Gerard. *Seuils*. Paris: Editions du Seuil, 1987.

Gianturco, Carolyn. *Stradella: uomo di gran grido*. Pisa: Edizioni ETS, 2007.

Gillio, Pier Giorgio. *L'attività negli ospedali di Venezia nel Settecento: Quadro storico e materiali documentari*. Florence: Olschki, 2006.

Ginzburg, Carlo and A. Prosperi. *Giochi di pazienza: Un seminario sul "Beneficio di Cristo."* Turin: Einaudi, 1975.

Göhler, Albert. *Verzeichnis der in den Frankfurter und Leipziger Messkatalogen der Jahre 1564 bis 1769 angezeigten Musikalien.* Leipzig, 1902/rpt. Hilversum: Knuf, 1965.

González Marín, Luis Antonio. "Aspectos de la practica musical española en el siglo XVII: voces y ejecución vocal," *Anuario Musical* 56 (2001): 83–95.

Griffin, Thomas. "The Late Baroque Serenata in Rome and Naples: A Documentary Study with Emphasis on Alessandro Scarlatti." Ph. D. diss., UCLA, 1983.

Guidotti, Fabrizio. "Musiche annue ed avventizie nelle chiese lucchesi," in *La famiglia Puccini: una tradizione, Lucca, la musica,* 97–109. Milan: Museo Teatrale alla Scala, 1992.

———. *"Musiche annue ed avventizie" in una città d'antico regime: Lucca al tempo dei primi Puccini.* Lucca: Accademia Lucchese di Scienze, Lettere e Arti, 2012.

Guidotti, Fabrizio and C. Comastri. "'Il ridotto di quelle che maritar non puonsi': Documenti lucchesi per una storia della musica nei monasteri femminili," pts. 1–2, in *Florilegium Musicae: Studi in onore di Carolyn Gianturco,* ed. P. Radicchi/M. Burden, 1: 67–136. Pisa: Edizioni ETS, 2004.

Habermas, Jürgen. *Theorie des kommunikativen Handelns.* Frankfurt a. M.: Suhrkamp, 1981.

HaCohen, Ruth. *Vocal Fictions of Noise and Harmony: The Music Libel against the Jews.* New Haven: Yale University Press, 2011.

Ham, Martin. "Morales: The Canon," in *Cristóbal de Morales: Sources, Influences, Reception,* ed. O. Rees/B. Nelson, 263–393. Woodbridge/Rochester: Boydell, 2007.

Hardie, Jane M. "Lamentations in Spanish sources before 1568; notes towards a geography," *Revista de Musicología* 16 (1993): 912–42.

Harness, Kelley. *Echoes of Women's Voices: Music, Art and Female Patronage in Early Modern Florence.* Chicago: University of Chicago Press, 2006.

Heartz, Daniel. *Haydn, Mozart, and the Viennese School 1740–1780.* New York: W.W. Norton, 1995.

Hernández, Luis. *Música y culto divino en el real monasterio de El Escorial (1563–1837).* San Lorenzo del Escorial: Ediciones Escurialenses, 1993.

———. "Música y culto divino en el Monasterio de El Escorial durante la estancia en él de la Orden de S. Jerónimo," *La Música en el monasterio del Escorial: Actas del Simposium,* 75–122. San Lorenzo del Escorial: Ediciones Escurialenses, 1992.

Hernando Sánchez, Carlos José (ed.). *Roma y España: un crisol de la cultura europea en la Edad Moderna.* Madrid: Sociedad estatal para la acción cultural exterior, 2007.

Hill, John W. *Roman Monody, Cantata, and Opera from the Circles around Cardinal Montalto.* Oxford: Oxford University Press, 1997.

Hills, Helen. *Invisible City: The Architecture of Devotion in Seventeenth-Century Neapolitan Convents.* Oxford: Oxford University Press, 2004.

Holeton, David. "Fynes Moryson's *Itinerary:* A Sixteenth-Century English Traveller's Observations on Bohemia, its Reformation, and its Liturgy," in *The Bohemian Reformation and Religious Practice* 5/2 (2005): 379–410.

Innocenzi, Alceste. *Il fondo musicale del Duomo di Spoleto: sintesi cronologica e nuovi dati.* Spoleto: Archidiocesi di Spoleto-Norcia, 2007.

———. "Il Codice 9 del Duomo di Spoleto: problemi di attribuzione," *Rivista internazionale di musica sacra,* n.s. 31 (2010): 161–167.

Irvine, David R. M. *Colonial Counterpoint: Music in Early Modern Manila.* Oxford: Oxford University Press, 2009).

———. "The Lamentations of Manuel José Doyagüe: Recently Rediscovered Manuscript Sources from Manila," in *Music Research: New Directions for a New Century,* ed. M. Ewans, 242–52. London: Cambridge Scholars Press, 2004.

Jackson, Susan. "Berg and Neuber: Music Printers in 16th-Century Nuremberg." Ph. D. diss., CUNY, 1998.

Jacoby, Jörg. *Hans von Aachen 1552–1615.* Munich: Deutscher Kunstverlag, 2000.

Jenny, Beat R. "Der Historiker-Poet Kaspar Brusch (1518–1557) und seine Beziehungen zur Schweiz," in *Aus dem Werkstatt der Amerbach-Edition,* ed. *id./U. Dill,* 93–307. Basel: Schwabe, 2000.

Jerome. *Epistulae,* pt. 1 ("Corpus Scriptorum Ecclesiasticorum Latinorum" 54). Vienna: Verlag der Österreichischen Akademie der Wissenschaften, 1996.

Käser, Theodor. *Die Leçons de Ténèbres im 17. und 18. Jahrhundert unter besonderer Berücksichtigung der einschlägigen Werke von Marc-Antoine Charpentier.* Bern: Haupt, 1966.

Keller, Katrin and A. Catalano (eds.). *Die Diarien und Tagzettel des Kardinals Ernst Adalbert von Harrach (1598–1667).* Vienna: Böhlau, 2011.

Kendrick, Robert L. *The Sounds of Milan, 1585–1650.* New York: Oxford University Press, 2002.

———. "Riflessione sulla sorte della musica nella Congregazione Cassinese," in A. Colzani *et al.* [eds], *Barocco Padano* 4 [Como: AMIS, 2006], 433–74.

Kerman, Joseph (ed). *Autograph Miscellany from circa 1786 to 1799: British Museum Additional Manuscript 29801, ff. 39–162 "The Kafka Sketchbook"* (London: British Museum, 1970),

Király, Peter. "Königin Maria von Habsburg und die Musik," in M. Fuchs/O. Réthely (eds.), *Maria von Ungarn (1505–1558): Eine Renaissancefürstin* (Münster: Aschendorff, 2007), 363–79.

Kirkendale, Ursula. *Antonio Caldara: Life and Venetian-Roman Oratorios.* Florence: Olschki, 2007.

Kirkendale, Warren. *Emilio de' Cavalieri 'gentiluomo romano': His Life and Letters, his Role as Superintendent of All the Arts at the Medici Court, and His Musical Compositions.* Florence: Olschki, 2001.

Knighton, Tess. "Los libros de música de Felipe II: la formación de una colección real," in J. Griffiths/J. Suárez-Pajeres (eds.), *Políticas y prácticas musicales en el mundo de Felipe II* (Madrid: Instituto Complutense de Ciencias Musicales, 2004), 47–67.

Köhler, Rafael. *Die Cappella Sistina unter den Medici-Päpsten.* Kiel: Ludwig, 2001.

Koller, Alexander (ed.). *Nuntiaturberichte aus Deutschland,* sect. 3, vol. 9, *Nuntiaturen des Giovanni Delfino und des Bartolomeo Portia (1577–1578).* Tübingen: Niemeyer, 2003.

Koslofsky, Craig. *Evening's Empire: A History of the Night in Early Modern Europe.* Cambridge: Cambridge University Press, 2011.

Kostílková, Marie. *Ecclesia Metropolitana Pragensis Catalogus.* Prague: Supraphon, 1983.

Krause, Rolf. *Die Kirchenmusik von Leonardo Leo (1694–1744): ein Beitrag zur Musikgeschichte Neapels im 18. Jahrhundert.* Regensburg: Gustav Bosse Verlag, 1987.

Krebs, Carl. *Dittersdorfiana.* Berlin: Gebr. Paetel, 1900.

Kubieniec, Jakob. "Lamentacje Chorałowe w krakowskich rękopisach liturgicznych od XII do XVIII wieku." *Muzyka* 44 (1999): 7–42.

———. "Treny Jeremiasza w potrydenckiej liturgii polskiej," *Muzyka jest zawsze wspólczena: Studia dedykowane Alicji Jarzebskiej,* ed. M. Wozna-Stankiewicz/ A. Sitarz, 268–284. Krakow, 2011.

Kurtzman, Jeffrey G. "Italian Music for Holy Week," in *Barocco padano 6,* ed. M. Padoan *et al.,* 347–408. Como: AMIS, 2009.

Lambeau, Lucien. "L'Abbaye-aux-Boix de Paris (1638–1906)," *Commission Municipale du vieux Paris,* Année 1905, *Procès-Verbaux* (Paris, 1906) 238–313.

Lausberg, Heinrich. *Handbook of Literary Rhetoric: A Foundation for Literary Study.* Leiden: Brill, 1998.

La Via, Stefano. "Il cardinale Ottoboni e la musica: Nuovi documenti (1700–1740), nuove letture e ipotesi," in *Intorno a Locatelli,* ed. A. Dunning, 1: 319–526. Lucca: LIM, 1995.

Lazzareschi, Eugenio. "La famiglia Puccini e il diario musicale di Giacomo Puccini sen.," *Atti dell'Accademia Lucchese di Scienze, Lettere, ed Arti* 10 (1959): 21–57.

Leitner, Christian T. *Jakobus de Kerle (1531/32–1591): Komponieren im Spannungsfeld von Kirche und Kunst.* Turnhout: Brepols, 2009.

Leopold, Silke. *Stefano Landi: Beiträge zur Biographie, Untersuchungen zur weltlichen und geistlichen Vokalmusik.* Hamburg: K. D. Wagner, 1976.

Leuchtmann, Horst. *Orlando di Lasso.* Wiesbaden: Breitkopf & Hartel, 1976.

Liebreich, Karen. *Fallen Order: A History.* London: Atlantic, 2004.

Liguori, Alfonso Maria de. *Traduzione de' salmi e de' cantici, che si contengono nell'Officio Divino.* Bassano: Remondiana, 1805.

Lindell, Robert. "Music and patronage at the court of Rudolf II," in *Music in the German Renaissance: Sources, Styles and Contexts,* ed. J. Kmetz, 254–71. Cambridge: Cambridge University Press, 1994.

Llorens, Jose-Maria. *Le opere musicali della Capella Giulia.* Rome: Biblioteca Apostolica Vaticana, 1971.

López-Calo, Jose. *La música en la cathedral de Valladolid.* Valladolid: Ayuntamiento de Valladolid, 2008.

López Gay, Jesus. *La liturgia en la misión del Japón del siglo XVI.* Rome: Università Gregoriana, 1970.

Lortat-Jacob, Bernard. *Canti di passione.* Lucca: LIM, 1996.

Lozano, Tomas. *Cantemos al alba: Origins of Songs, Sounds and Liturgical Drama of Hispanic New Mexico.* Albuquerque: University of New Mexico Press, 2007.

Luisi, Francesco. "San Giacomo degli Spagnoli e la festa della Resurrezione in Piazza Navona," in *La cappella musicale nell'Italia della Controriforma,* ed. O. Mischiati/P. Russo, 75–103. Florence: Olschki, 1993.

Lunelli, Renato. "Di alcuni inventori delle musiche già possedute dal coro della parocchiale di Merano," *Studien zur Musikwissenschaft* 25 (1962): 347–362.

Lyman, Anne E. "Peter Philips at the Court of Albert and Isabella in Early Seventeenth-Century Brussels," Ph. D. diss., University of Iowa, 2008.

Macchiarella, Ignazio. *Il falsobordone,* Lucca: LIM, 1995.

————. "I canti della Settimana Santa in Sicilia," in *Echos: l'indagine etnomusico-logica,* ed. G. Garofalo, 108–27. Palermo: Istituto di Scienze Antropologiche e Geografiche, 1989.

————. (ed.), *Tre voci per pensare il mondo: Pratiche polifoniche confraternali in Corsica.* Udine: Nota, 2011.

Macey, Patrick. *Bonfire Songs: Savonarola's Musical Legacy.* Oxford: Oxford University Press, 1998.

MacGregor, Alastair J. *Fire and Light in the Western Triduum: Their Use at Tenebrae and at the Paschal Vigil* ("Alcuin Club Collections," 71). Collegeville: Liturgical Press, 1992.

Magaudda, Ausilia and D. Costantini, *Musica e spettacolo nel Regno di Napoli attraverso lo spoglio della "Gazzetta" (1675–1768).* Rome: Ismez, 2011.

Maggi, Armando. *Satan's Rhetoric: A Study of Renaissance Demonology.* Chicago: University of Chicago Press, 2002.

Maral, Alexandre. *La Chapelle Royale de Versailles sous Louis XIV: cérémonial, liturgie et musique.* Wavre: Mardaga, 2010.

Marchi, Lucia. "La cappella musicale del Duomo di Torino nel tardo Cinquecento e la reggenza di Simon Boyleau," in *Barocco padano 2,* ed. A. Colzani *et al.,* 385–407. Como: AMIS, 2002.

Marín, Miguel Angel (ed.). *La ópera en el templo: Estudios sobre el compositor Francisco Javier García Fajer.* Logroño: Instituto de Estudios Riojanos, 2010.

Marín López, Javier. *Los libros de polifonía de la Catedral de México: Estudio y catálogo crítico.* Jaén: Universidad de Jaén, 2012.

Marques, Joaõ Francisco. "A acção da igreja no terramoto de Lisboa de 1755: Ministério espiritual e pregação," *Lusitania sacra* ser. 2/18 (2006): 219–329.

Martin, Gregory. *Roma sancta* (1581), ed. G. B. Parks. Rome: Edizioni di Storia e Letteratura, 1969.

Martínez Millán, Miguel. *Historia musical de la catedral de Cuenca.* Cuenca: Diputación Provincial de Cuenca, 1988.

Martín Moreno, Antonio. *El padre Feijóo y las ideologías musicales del XVIII en España.* Orense: Instituto de Estudios Orensanos Padre Feijóo, 1976.

Marx-Weber, Helga. *Liturgie und Andacht.* Paderborn: Schönigh, 1999.

————. "Lamentationskompositionen des 18. Jahrhunderts: Leonardo Leo und Francesco Feo," in *"Critica musica": Studien zum 17. und 18. Jahrhundert; Festschrift Hans Joachim Marx zum 65. Geburtstag,* ed. N. Ristow *et al.,* 185–200. Stuttgart: J.B. Metzler, 2001.

Massip, Catherine. *L'art de bien chanter: Michel Lambert 1610–1696.* Paris: Société française de musicologie, 1999.

Matitti, Flavia. "Il cardinale Pietro Ottoboni mecenate delle arti: Cronache e documenti (1689–1740)," *Storia dell'arte* 84 (1995): 156–243.

McClymonds, Marita P. and W.E. Rex. "'Ce beau recitatif obligé': 'Le Neveu de Rameau' and Jommelli," *Diderot Studies* 22 (1986): 63–77.

Melion, Walter S. "Parabolic Analogy and Spiritual Discernment in Jéronimo Nadal's *Adnotationes et meditationes in Evangelia* of 1595," in *The Turn of the Soul: Representations of Religious Conversion in Early Modern Art and Literature,* ed. L. Stelling *et al.,* 299–338. Leiden: Brill, 2012.

Mele, Donato. *L'Accademia dello Spirito Santo: Un'istituzione musicale ferrarese del sec. XVII.* Ferrara: Liberty House, 1990.

Melucci, Maria Grazia and A. Morgese, *Il fondo musicale del Monastero delle Benedettine di San Severo*. San Severo: Gerni Editori, 1993.

Mischiati, Oscar. *La prassi musicale presso i Canonici Regolari del Ss. Salvatore nei secoli XVI e XVII*. Rome: Torre d'Orfeo, 1985.

Moli Frigola, Monserrat. "Compositores e interpretes españoles en Italia en el siglo XVIII," Eusko Ikaskuntza/Sociedad de Estudios Vascos, *Cuadernos de Sección: Música 7* (1994): 9–125.

Molitor, Raphael. *Die nachtridentinische Choralreform zu Rom*. Leipzig: F.E.C. Leuckart, 1901–2.

Morales, Nicolas. *Las voces de Palacio: El Real Colegio de Niños de Madrid*. Madrid: Ayuntamento de Madrid, 2005.

———. *L'artiste de cour dans l'Espagne du XVIIIe siècle: étude de la communauté des musiciens au service de Philippe V (1700–1746)*. Madrid: Casa de Velázquez, 2007.

Moreira, Joan. *Del folklore tortosí*. Tortosa: Querol, 1934.

Morelli, Arnaldo. *Il nobilissimo oratorio della Chiesa Nuova: Musiche per l'Oratorio di Santa Maria in Vallicella*. Rome: Accademia Nazionale di Santa Cecilia, 2001.

———. "'Cantare sull'organo': *an unrecognised practice*," *Recercare 10 (1998): 183–208.*

———. (intro.). *Catalogo del fondo musicale della Biblioteca Nazionale Centrale Vittorio Emmanuele II di Roma*. Rome: Consorzio IRIS per la valorizzazione dei beni librari, 1989.

Murphy, Sharon. "The Sacred Music of Gian Francesco di Majo (1732–1770)." Ph. D. diss., University of Texas/Austin, 1996.

Nawrot, Piotr (ed.), *Misiones de Moxos, Catálogo*. Santa Cruz de la Sierra: Fondo Editorial APAC, 2011.

Nelson, Bernadette. "Ritual and Ceremony in the Spanish Royal Chapel, c. 1559–c.1561," *Early Music History* 19 (2000): 105–200.

Nerici, Luigi. *Storia della musica in Lucca*. Rpt. Bologna: Forni, 1969.

Niemöller, Klaus Wolfgang. "Studien zu Carl Luythons Lamentationen" in *Kirchenmusik in Geschichte und Gegenwart: Festschrift Hans Schmidt zum 65. Geburtstag*, ed. H. Klein and *id.*, 185–96. Cologne: C. Dohr, 1998.

Nirenberg, David. *Communities of Violence: Persecution of Minorities in the Middle Ages*. Princeton: Princeton University Press, 1996.

Noe, Alfred. *Die Präsenz der romanischen Literatur in der 1655 nach Wien verkauften Fuggerbibliothek*. Amsterdam: Rodopi, 1994.

Noone, Michael. *Music and Musicians in the Escorial Liturgy under the Habsburgs, 1563–1700*. Rochester: Boydell & Brewster, 1998.

Odenthal, Andreas. *Die 'Ordinatio Cultus Divini et Caeremoniarium' des Halberstädter Domes von 1591*. Münster: Aschendorff, 2005.

Olarte Martínez, Matilde. "Miguel de Irízar y Domenzain (1635–?1684): Biografía, epistolario, y estudio de sus Lamentaciones." Ph.D. diss, University of Valladolid, 1992.

Olszewski, Edward J. *Cardinal Pietro Ottoboni (1667–1740) and the Vatican Tomb of Pope Alexander VIII*. Philadelphia: American Philosophical Society, 2004.

———. *The Inventory of Paintings of Cardinal Pietro Ottoboni (1667–1740)*. New York: Peter Lang, 2004.

O'Regan, Noel. "Orlando di Lasso and Rome: Personal Contacts and Musical Influences," in *Orlando di Lasso Studies,* ed. P. Bergquist, 132–157. Cambridge: Cambridge University Press, 1999.

———. "Music at the Roman Archconfraternity of San Rocco in the Late Sixteenth Century," in in *La musica a Roma attraverso le fonti d'archivio,* ed. B. M. Antolini, 521–552. Lucca: LIM, 1994.

———. *Institutional Patronage in post-Tridentine Rome: Music at Santissima Trinità dei Pellegrini, 1550–1650.* London: Royal Musical Association, 1995.

———. "Processions in post-Tridentine Rome" *Recercare* 4 (1992): 45–80.

Ossola, Carlo. "Augustinus sine tempore traditus," in *Augustin au XVIIe siècle,* ed. L. Devillairs, 263–87. Florence: Olschki, 2007.

Over, Berthold. *Per la Gloria di Dio: solistische Kirchenmusik an den venezianischen Ospedali im 18. Jahrhundert.* Bonn: Orpheus-Verlag, 1998.

Pacini, Alfredo. *La chiesa pistoiese e la sua cattedrale nel tempo: Repertorio di documenti,* vol. 3. Pistoia: Editrice CRT, 1994.

Padoan, Maurizio. "La musica in S. Maria Maggiore a Bergamo nel periodo di Giovanni Cavaccio (1598–1626)," *Studi sul primo Seicento,* 1–220. Como: AMIS, 1983.

———. "Ethos devozionale e spettacolarità nella musica sacra. Quaresima e Settimana Santa nel Nord Italia nel primo Barocco," in S. Martinotti (ed.), *La musica a Milano, in Lombardia, e oltre,* Milan: Vita e Pensiero, 2000, vol. 2, 13–64.

Pajares Barón, Máximo. *Archivo de Música de la Catedral de Cádiz.* Granada: Centro de Documentación Musical de Andalucía, 1993.

Paliaga, Franco, and S. Renzoni. *Le chiese di Pisa: Guida alla conoscenza del patrimonio artistico.* Pisa, 1991.

Pavia i Simó, Josep. "Calendari músico-litúrgic de la Catedral de Barcelona, finals del s. XVII–inicis del s. XVIII." *Anuario musical* 55 (2000), 99–153.

———. "Archivo de Música de la Catedral de Tortosa (Tarragona)." *Anuario Musical* 51 (1996): 270–99.

Pellegrini, Carlo (ed.). *Fonti per la storia dei Somaschi,* vol. 24, *Atti dei capitoli generali* pt. 2, *1581–1591.* Rome: Curia Generalizia dei Padri Somaschi, 1997.

Pérez Pastor, Cristóbal. *Documentos para la biografía de D. Pedro Calderón de la Barca.* Madrid: Fortanet, 1905.

Pérez Puente, Leticia *et al.* (eds.). *Autos de las visitas del arzobispo fray Payo Enríquez a los conventos de monjas de la ciudad de México (1672–1675).* Mexico City: UNAM, 2005.

Picanyol, Leodegario (ed.). *Epistolario di S. Giuseppe Calasanzio,* vol. 8. Rome: Edizioni di Storia e Letteratura, 1956.

Picchi, Alessandro. *Archivio Musicale del Duomo di Como: Catalogo delle opere a stampa e manoscritte dei secoli XVI–XVIII.* Como, 1990.

Pierre, Constant. *Histoire du Concert Spirituel.* Paris, Société Française de Musicologie, 1975.

Piperno, Franco. *L'immagine del duca: Musica e spettacolo alla corte di Guidobaldo II duca d'Urbino.* Florence: Olschki, 2001.

Poensgen, Benedikt. "Zu Alessandro Scarlattis Oratorium per la Passione," in *Händels Italianità: Göttinger Händel-Festspiele 1997.* Göttingen: Gottinger Handel-Gesellschaft, 1997.

Pratl, Josef. *Acta Forchtensteiniana: die Musik-Dokumente im Esterhazy-Archiv auf Burg Forchtenstein.* Tutzing: Hans Schneider, 2009.

Prosperi, Adriano. *L'eresia del Libro Grande: Storia di Giorgio Siculo e della sua setta.* Milan: Feltrinelli, 2000.

Psychoyou, Theodora. "The Historical Importance of a Distinctive Scoring: Charpentier's Six-Voice Motets for Mademoiselle de Guise," in *New Perspectives on Marc-Antoine Charpentier,* ed. S. Thompson, 207–28. Farnham: Ashgate, 2010.

Quaranta, Elena. *Oltre San Marco: Organizzazione e prassi della musica sacra nelle chiese di Venezia nel Rinascimento.* Florence: Olschki, 1998.

Quevedo, Francisco de. *Lágrimas de Hieremías Castellanas,* ed. E. M. Wilson/J.M. Blecua. Madrid: CSIC, Insituto "Miguel de Cervantes," 1953.

Radicchi, Patrizia, "La musica nel monastero delle principesse Cybo," in F. Leverotti (ed.), *I tesori di Santa Chiara* (Pisa: Edizioni ETS, 2012), 45–73.

Radole, Giuseppe. "Musica e musicisti in Istria," *Atti e memorie della Società Istriana di Archeologia e Storia Patria* n.s. 65 (1965): 147–214.

Ramos López, Pilar. *La música en la catedral de Granada en la primera mitad del siglo XVII: Diego de Pontac.* Granada: Centro de Documentación Musical de Andalucía, 1994.

Reardon, Colleen. *Agostino Agazzari and Music at Siena Cathedral 1597–1641.* Oxford: Oxford University Press, 1993.

———. *Holy Concord Within Sacred Walls: Nuns and Music in Siena, 1575–1700.* New York: Oxford University Press, 2002.

Rees, Owen. *Polyphony in Portugal, c. 1530–c.1620: Sources from the Monastery of Santa Cruz, Coimbra.* New York: Garland, 1995.

Reich, Wolfgang and S. Seifert, "Excerpte aus dem Diarium Missionis S.J. Dresdae," in *Zelenka-Studien II,* ed. W. Reich, 315–79. Sankt Augustin: Academia-Verlag 1997.

Reily, Suzel. "Remembering the Baroque Era: Historical Consciousness, Local Identity, and the Holy Week Ceremonies in a Former Mining Town in Brazil," *Ethnomusicology Forum* 15 (2006): 39–62.

Religion in Past and Present. Leiden: Brill, 2011

Reutter, Jochen. *Studien zur Kirchenmusik Franz Xaver Richters (1709–1789).* Frankfurt a. M.: Peter Lang, 1993.

Reynaud, François. *La polyphonie tolédane et son milieu des premiers témoignages aux environs de 1600.* Paris: CNRS Editions, 1996.

Rice, John A. "Music in the Duomo during the Reign of Pietro Leopoldo I (1765–1790)," in *"Cantate Domino": Musica nei secoli per il Duomo di Firenze,* ed. P. Gargiuolo/G. Giacomelli, 259–71. Florence: Edifir, 2001.

———. *Empress Marie Therese and Music at the Viennese Court, 1792–1807.* Cambridge: Cambridge University Press, 2003.

Ricci, Antonello. "Sacre fonosfere: Paesaggi sonori della Settimana Santa calabrese," in *Le forme della festa: La Settimana Santa in Calabria: studi e materiali,* ed. id./F. Faeta. Rome: Squilibri, 2007.

Riedel, Friedrich W. *Kirchenmusik am Hofe Karls VI. (1711–1740).* Munich/Salzburg: Musikverlag E. Katzbichler, 1978.

Rive, Thomas. "Victoria's Lamentationes Geremiae: A comparison of Cappella Sistina MS 186 with the corresponding portions of *Officium Hebdomadae Sanctae* (Rome, 1585)," *Anuario Musical* 20 (1965): 179–208.

Robledo Estaire, Luis. "La música en la casa del Rey," in *Aspectos de la cultura musical en la corte de Felipe II,* ed. *id. et al,* 99–194. Madrid: Editorial Alpuerto, 2000.

———. "Vihuelas de arco y violones en la corte de Felipe III," in *España en la música de Occidente,* ed. E. Casares Rodicio et al., 2: 63–76. Madrid: Instituto Nacional de las Artes Escenicas y de la Música, 1987.

Rosa Barezzani, Maria Teresa. "I testimoni a stampa e le edizioni moderne di Marc'Antonio Ingegneri" in *Marc'Antonio Ingegneri e la musica a Cremona nel secondo Cinquecento,* ed. *ead./*A. Delfino, 269–356. Lucca: LIM, 1995.

Rosa Montagut, Marian. "Una aproximación a la capilla de música de la catedral de Tortosa (Tarragona): 1700–1750." *Anuario musical* 61 (2006): 155–166.

Rostirolla, Giancarlo. "La Cappella Giulia in San Pietro negli anni del magistero di Giovanni Pierluigi da Palestrina," in F. Luisi (ed.), *Atti del Convegno di studi palestriniani,* ed. F. Luisi, 99–283. Palestrina: n.p., 1975.

———. "Il Diario Sistino del 1607, autografo di Ruggiero Giovannelli," in *Ruggiero Giovannelli "musicista eccellentissimo e forse il primo del suo tempo,"* ed. *id.* and C. Bongiovanni, 115–56. Palestrina: Fondazione G. P. da Palestrina, 1998.

———. *Il codice 59 dell'Archivio musicale della Basilica di San Giovanni in Laterano: autografo di Giovanni Pierluigi da Palestrina.* Palestrina: Fondazione G. P. da Palestrina, 1996.

———. (ed.) Palestrina, *Le opere complete,* vol. 35, pt. 1. Rome, 2001.

———. "Celebrazioni ed eventi musicale durante l'Anno Santo 1625: Dal Diario redatto dal compositore e cantore Francesco Severi perugino, con l'edizione integrale d'esso," in *"Vanitatis fuga, aeternitatis amor": Wolfgang Witzenmann zum 65. Geburtstag,* ed. S. Ehrmann-Herfort/M. Engelhardt (Analecta Musicologica, 36), 151–226. Laaber: Laaber-Verlag, 2005.

———. *L'Archivio musicale della Basilica di San Giovanni in Laterano: catalogo dei manoscritti e delle edizioni (secc. XVI–XX).* Rome: Istituto Poligrafico e Zecca dello Stato, 2002.

Rubio, Samuel. *Catálogo del Archivo de Música del Monastero de San Lorenzo de El Escorial.* Cuenca: Instituto de Música Religiosa, 1976.

Ruffatti, Alessio. "«Curiosi e bramosi l'oltramontani cercano con grande diligenza in tutti i luoghi»: La cantata romana del Seicento in Europa," *Journal of Seventeenth-Century Music* 13 (2008), online at sscm-jscm.press.illinois.edu /v13/no1/ruffatti.html.

Ruggiero, Lorenzo. *Vita e opera: Antonio Mogavero.* Brindisi: Amici della "A. de Leo," 1993.

Ruíz Jiménez, Juan. *La librería de canto de órgano.* Granada: Centro de Documentación Musical de Andalucía, 2007.

Russell, Eleanor. "Pedro Rimonte in Brussels (c. 1600–1614)," *Anuario musical* 28/29 (1973–74): 181–94.

Salis, Giovanni. "Drammatizzazioni devozionali del Venerdì Santo," tesi di dottorato, University of Bologna, 2012.

Salisi i Clos, Josep Maria. *La música de l'arxiu parochial de Santa Maria de Verdú (segles XVII i XVIII).* Lleida: Institut d'Estudis Llerdencs, 2010.

Sartori, Antonio. *Documenti per la storia della musica al Santo e nel Veneto.* Vicenza: N. Pozza, 1977.

Sas, Andrés. *La música en la Catedral de Lima durante el Virreinato*. Lima: Universidad Nacional Mayor de San Marcos, 1971.

Schickhaus, Karl-Heinz. *Das Hackbrett: Geschichte & Geschichten*, Folge 1. St. Oswald: Tympanon, 2001.

Schilling, Andreas. "Die religiösen und kirchlichen Zustände der ehemaligen Reichsstadt Biberach unmittelbar vor Einführung der Reformation," *Freiburger Diöcesan-Archiv* 19 (1887): 1–191.

Schleifer, Eliahu. "The Mexican Choirbooks at the Newberry Library (Case MS VM 2147 C 36)." Ph. D. diss., University of Chicago, 1979.

Schmid, Ernst F. *Musik an den schwäbischen Zollenhöfen der Renaissance*. Kassel: Bärenreiter, 1962.

Schmidt-Görg, Joseph. "Ein neuer Fund in den Skizzenbüchern Beethovens: die Lamentationen des Propheten Jeremias," *Beethoven-Jahrbuch* 3 (1959): 107–110.

Schneider, Herbert. "Observations on Charpentier's Compositional Process: Corrections in the *Mélanges*" in *New Perspectives on Marc-Antoine Charpentier*, ed. S. Thompson, 229–50. Farnham: Ashgate, 2010.

Schwartz, Roberta F. "En busca de liberalidad: Music and musicians in the courts of the Spanish nobility, 1470–1640." Ph. D. diss., University of Illinois Urbana-Champaign, 2001.

Sehling Emil. *et al., Die evangelischen Kirchenordnungen des XVI. Jahrhunderts*, vol. 17, pt. 2. Tübingen: Mohr 2009.

———. *Die Kirchenordnungen des XVI. Jahrhunderts*. Leipzig: Reisland, 1909, vol. 3.

Selfridge-Field, Eleanor. *The Music of Benedetto and Alessandro Marcello: A Thematic Catalogue*. Oxford: Oxford University Press, 1990.

Senn, Walter. *Musik und Theater am Hof zu Innsbruck*. Innsbruck: Osterreichische Verlagsanstalt, 1954.

Sherr, Richard. "Ceremonies for Holy Week, Papal Commissions, and Madness (?) in Early Sixteenth-Century Rome," in *Music in Cities and Courts: Studies in Honor of Lewis Lockwood*, ed. J. A. Owens/A. M. Cummings, 391–403. Detroit: Harmonie Park Press, 1996.

Simi Bonini, Eleonora. *Catalogo del Fondo Musicale di Santa Maria in Trastevere nell'Archivio Storico del Vicariato di Roma*. Rome: IBIMUS, 2000.

Sirch, Licia. *Catalogo tematico delle musiche di Amilcare Ponchielli*. Cremona: Fondazione Claudio Monteverdi, 1989.

Snow, Robert J. *A New-World Collection of Polyphony for Holy Week and the Salve Service: Guatemala City, Cathedral Archive, Music MS 4* ("Monuments of Renaissance Music," 9). Chicago: University of Chicago Press, 1996.

Sodi, Manlio and A.M. Triacca (eds.), *Breviarium romanum: Editio princeps (1568)*. Vatican City: Libreria Editoriale Vaticana, 1999.

Solerti, Angelo. *Musica, ballo e drammatica alla corte medicea*. Florence, 1905/rpt. Bologna: Forni, 1989.

———. *Le origini del melodramma*. Florence, 1903/rpt. Bologna: Forni, 1969.

Sommervogel, Carlos. *Bibliothèque de la Compagnie de Jésus*. Rpt. Louvain: Editions de la Bibliothèque S. J.,1960.

Spinelli, Giovanni. "Per una cronotassi degli abati cassinesi di S. Pietro di Modena e dei SS. Pietro e Prospero di Reggio Emilia (secc. XV–XVIII)" in *Il millenario di S. Pietro di Modena*, 2: 31–49. Modena: Aedes Muratoriana, 1985.

Stäblein, Bruno. "Lamentatio," *MGG* (Kassel, 1960), vol. 8: col. 138.

Staffieri, Gloria. *Colligit Fragmenta: La vita musicale romana negli 'Avvisi Marescotti' (1683–1707)*. Lucca: LIM, 1990.

Stanford, E. Thomas. *Catálogo de los acervos musicales de las catedrales metropolitanas de México y Puebla*. Mexico City: Instituto Nacional de Antropologia e Historia, 2002.

Štefan, J. "Hudba v katedrále v obdobi baroka," in *Pražske arcibiskupství 1344–1994*, ed. Z. Hledikova/J.V. Polc. Prague: Zvon, 1994.

Steffan, Carlida. "L'oratorio veneziano tra Sei e Settecento: Fisionomia e contesti," in *L'oratorio musicale italiano e i suoi contesti (secc. XVII–XVIII)*, ed. P. Besutti, 423–452. Florence: Olschki, 2002.

———. "Oratori senza sepolcri e sepolcri senza oratori: Su alcune consuetudini paraliturgiche della Settimana Santa nel Seicento italiano," in *'Quel novo Cario, quel divin Orfeo': Antonio Draghi da Rimini a Vienna,* ed. E. Sala/D. Daolmi, 321–340. Lucca: LIM, 2000.

Stein, Louise K. "El manuscrito de música teatral de la Congregación de Nuestra Señora de la Novena. Su música, su carácter y su entorno cultural," in *Libro de Música de la Cofradía de Nuestra Señora de la Novena*, ed. A. Álvarez Cañibano/J. I. Cano Martín, 53–101. Madrid: Instituto Nacional de Artes Escenicas y de la Música, 2010.

———. *Songs of Mortals, Dialogues of the Gods: Music and Theatre in Seventeenth-Century Spain*. Oxford: Oxford University Press, 1993.

Stockigt, Janice B. *Jan Dismas Zelenka: A Bohemian Musician at the Court of Dresden*. Oxford: Oxford University Press 2000.

Strohm, Reinhard. "Francesco Corselli's *drammi per musica* for Madrid," now in *Dramma per musica: Italian Opera Seria of the Eighteenth Century,* 97–120. New Haven: Yale University Press, 1997.

Súarez Martos, Juan Maria. "El Archivo Musical de la Catedral de Sevilla en 1725: Génesis y pervivencia de libros manuales y de facistol," *Musicalia* (Córdoba) 5 (2007): 41–124.

———. "La música en la Catedral de Sevilla durante el s. XVII: apogeo y crisis económicas," *Anuario de historia de la iglesia andaluza* 1 (2008): 349–62.

Suárez-Pajares, Javier. *La música en la catedral de Sigüenza, 1600–1750*. Madrid: ICCMU, 1998.

Sutton, Everett L. "The Solo Vocal Works of Nicola Porpora: An Annotated Thematic Catalogue." Ph. D. diss., University of Minnesota, 1974.

Szendrei, Janka. (ed.), *Breviarium notatum Strigoniense*. Budapest: Magyar Tudományos Akadémia Zenetudományi Intézet, 1998.

———. [ed.], *The Istanbul Antiphonal*. Budapest: Akadémiai Kiadó, 2002.

Tanenbaum, Faun. "The partbook collection of the Ospedale della Pietà and the sacred music of Giovanni Porta." Ph. D. diss., New York University, 1993.

Torrente, Álvaro, *Fiesta de Navidad en la Capilla Real de Felipe V: Villancicos de Francisco Corselli, 1743*. Madrid: Ediciones Alpuerta, 2002.

Tschmuck, Peter. *Die höfische Musikpflege in Tirol im 16. und 17. Jahrhundert*. Lucca: LIM, 2001.

Tufano, Lucio. "La musica nei periodici scientifico-letterari napolitani," *Studi musicali* 30 (2001): 129–80.

Ursprung, Otto. *Jakobus de Kerle (1531/32–1591). Ausgewählte Werke,* pt. 1. Augsburg: Breitkopf & Hartel, 1926.

Valesio, Francesco. *Diario di Roma,* ed. G. Scano. Milan: Longanesi, 1977–79.

van der Straeten, Edward. *La musique aux Pays-Bas avant le XIXe siècle.* Brussels, 1867/rpt. New York: Dover, 1969.

Vanscheeuwijck, Marc. *The Cappella Musicale of San Petronio in Bologna under Giovanni Paolo Colonna (1674–1695).* Brussels: Institut Historique Belge de Rome, 2003.

Vargas Ugarte, Ruben. (ed.), *Diario de Lima de Juan Antonio Suardo (1629–1639).* Lima: Universidad Católica del Peru, 1936.

Veronelli, Sara. "Strategie politiche di un piccolo stato a fine Cinquecento: il Ducato di Mantova tra Impero e monarchia cattolica," in (eds.), *La Lombardia spagnola: Nuovi indirizzi di ricerca,* ed. E. Brambilla/G. Muto, 389–404. Milan: Edizioni Unicopli, 1997.

Virgili, Lavinio. "La cappella musicale della Chiesa metropolitana di Fermo dalle origini al 1670," *Note d'archivio per la storia musicale* 7 (1930): 1–86.

Vitali, Carlo. "L'oratorio alla Madonna di Galliera: aspetti storico-istituzionali," in *'Magnficat Dominum musica nostra': Atti della giornata di studio sulla musica sacra nella Bologna d'un tempo dedicate alla memoria di Oscar Mischiati (1936–2004),* ed. P. Mioli, 43–52. Bologna: Patrón, 2007.

Vita Spagnuola, Vera. "Gli atti notarili dell'Archivio di Stato di Roma. Saggio di spoglio sistematico: l'anno 1590," in *La musica a Roma attraverso le fonti d'archivio,* ed. B. M. Antolini, 19–65.

Wald, Melanie. "Verführung zur Konversion: Scarlatti, Händel, und das italienische Oratorium um 1700," *Jahrbuch des Staatlichen Instituts für Musikforschung Preußischer Kulturbesitz* 2010: 99–122.

Waldner, Franz. "Zwei Inventarien aus dem XVI. u. XVII. Jahrhundert über hinterlassene Musikinstrumente und Musikalien am Innsbrucker Hof," *Studien zur Musikwissenschaft* 4 (1915–16): 128–147.

Weber, Christoph. *Bischöfe, Generalvikare und Erzpriester: Ein Beitrag zur Geschichte der kirchlichen Leitungsämter im Königreich Neapel in der frühen Neuzeit.* Frankfurt a. M.: Peter Lang, 2000.

Weigle, Marta and Peter White, *The Lore of New Mexico.* Albuquerque: University of New Mexico Press, 1988.

Wicki, Joseph (ed.), *Documenta Indica* ("Monumenta Historica Societatis Iesu"); Rome: Apud "Monumenta Historica Soc. Iesu," 1948.

Wiechens, Bernhard. *Die Kompositionstheorie und das kirchenmusikalische Schaffen Padre Martinis.* Regensburg: Gustav Bosse, 1968.

Witzenmann, Wolfgang. *Die Lateran-Kapelle von 1599 bis 1650* (Analecta Musicologica, 40). Laaber: Laaber-Verlag, 2008.

Woodfield, Ian. *English Musicians in the Age of Exploration.* Stuyvesant, NY: Pendragon Press, 1995.

Zagar, Daniel. "Post-Tridentine liturgical change and functional music: Lasso's cycle of polyphonic Latin hymns," in *Orlando di Lasso Studies,* ed. P. Bergquist, 41–63. Cambridge: Cambridge University Press, 1999.

Zaggia, Massimo, *Tra Mantova e la Sicilia nel Cinquecento,* vol. 2, *La congregazione benedettina cassinese nel Cinquecento.* Florence: Olschki, 2003.

Zauner, Sergio. "Las Lamentaciones de Jeremías en Barcelona," *Nassarre* 26 (2010).

Zeri, Federico. "Bernardino Campi: Una *Crocifissione,*" *Paragone,* iv/27 (1953): 36–41.

Zimmermann, Reiner. *Evangelisch-katholische Fürstenfreundschaft: Korrespondenzen zwischen den Fürsten von Sachsen und den Herzögen von Bayern von 1513–1586.* Frankfurt a.M./New York: Lang, 2004.

Żórawska-Witkowska, Alina. "Federico Cristiano in Italia: esperienze musicali di un principe reale polacco," *Musica e storia* 4 (1996): 277–323.

Index

Page numbers in *italics* refer to musical examples and to items in the Appendix's Tables 1–4.

ROBERT L. KENDRICK is Professor of Music at the University of Chicago, where he served as Chair of the Department of Music in 2004–2008 and 2009–2010. His previous books include *Celestial Sirens* (1996) and *The Sounds of Milan, 1585–1650* (2002), and his articles treat early modern sacred music, historical anthropology, and music/ritual connections.